Date Due

Oc 17 '30	Mar 10'42		
Fe 11 '31	Feb 22 43		
Fe 9 '32	Mar 15 43		
Mr 13 '32	NOV 11		
Oc 27 '33	NOV 18		
Fe 5 '34	Mar. 9, 54		
Fe 4 '35	apr 18		
Mr 14 '35	MAR 15 2005		
Feb 3 '36	OCT 16 2005		
Mar 2 '36	MAR 05 2007		
Feb 8 '37	MAR 11 2009		
Feb 11 '37	MAR 23 2009		
Feb 23 '37	4/22/09		
Mar 11 '37	MAY 11 2009		
Feb 7 '38	DEC 04 2010		
Feb 21 '38	DEC 20 2010		
Feb 6 '39			
Oct 4 '39			
May 10 '40			
Feb 10 '41			
Feb 20 '42			

No. 293 DEMCO-MADISON-WIS

Leudner pinx. 581. Ausführung u. Stich d. Manz' Kunst-Verlag.

THE LIFE AND LABOURS

OF

SAINT THOMAS OF AQUIN.

BY

ARCHBISHOP VAUGHAN, O.S.B.

Abridged and Edited with Preface

BY

DOM JEROME VAUGHAN

(Monk of the Cassinese Congregation of the Pristine Observance.)

SECOND EDITION.

LONDON: BURNS AND OATES, LD.

NEW YORK: CATHOLIC PUBLICATION SOCIETY COMPANY.

1890.

BURNS AND OATES, LD., PRINTERS, LONDON, W.

TO THE
RIGHT REVEREND JOHN BUTT
FOURTH BISHOP OF SOUTHWARK
WHO IN THE EVENING OF A LONG
AND LABORIOUS PRIESTHOOD
ACCEPTED THE CARES OF THE EPISCOPATE
WHOSE GOVERNMENT HAS BEEN CONSPICUOUS
FOR A SINGULAR SELFLESSNESS
IN WHOM THE CLERGY OF HIS DIOCESE
HAVE RECOGNISED A FATHER
AND THE POOR HAVE CONFESSED TO CHRIST
WHO HAS STRENUOUSLY UPHELD
THE SACRED CAUSE OF EDUCATION
ECCLESIASTICAL AND SECULAR
WHO HAS BEFRIENDED THE REGULAR ORDERS
AND HAS ASSISTED THEM
TO TEACH THE WORLD
THE IDEALS OF CHRISTIAN PERFECTION
THIS NEW EDITION OF THE LIFE
OF THE ANGELICAL DOCTOR
WRITTEN BY ONE WHO
BURDENED ALSO WITH THE EPISCOPATE
FULFILLED HIS MISSION IN AN ALIEN LAND
IS AFFECTIONATELY DEDICATED BY THE AUTHOR'S BROTHER
JEROME VAUGHAN, O.S.B.

EDITOR'S PREFACE TO SECOND EDITION.

It was a happy inspiration which moved the lamented Archbishop Vaughan, now more than twenty years ago, to undertake the herculean work of writing a colossal *Life of St. Thomas of Aquin.* What the pious Touron had done for France, the learned Werner for Germany, and the eloquent Frigerio for Italy, that the late Archbishop of Sydney achieved for England. He might have contented himself with a humbler task, producing merely a translation of one of the works of these standard authors. A volume, even of this description, would have been welcomed in a language which hitherto could boast of no exhaustive *Life* of the Angelical. But the ambition, the genius and the devotion of Archbishop Vaughan aimed at something loftier and more worthy of his illustrious Saint. A translation, even at its best, is but a work of second rate rank. Languages, like nations, have each their own ingrained caste and character. As soon might one hope to transform the rugged German into a polished Frenchman, the diplomatic Italian into a straightforward Englishman, as to reproduce the beauties and musical cadence of one tongue in the foreign idioms and rhythm of another. Dante, presented in an English dress, even by such a master-hand as Cary, pales, and Shakespeare 'done' into French reads like a burlesque. Archbishop Vaughan was fully alive to this, and preferred to devote his facile and fervid pen to an original work, thus giving to the world that vivid portraiture of the life, times, character, genius, and influence of the 'Prince of Theologians,' of which the present volume is an abridgment. To grapple with his vast theme he prepared himself by many years of incessant study, eagerly devouring every book which seemed likely in any way to throw light upon the subject which engrossed his mind. Frequently he remained in his cell for whole months together engaged with the 'Angelical,' and the rising sun often found him at his desk pen in hand where on setting it had left him the previous evening. Whilst walking in the woods of his monastery, or along the green banks of the river Wye, he would sometimes suddenly stop short and break out into a rhapsody touching some trait he had recently come across in the life of his Saint. On more than one occasion he was so overcome as to be unable to proceed any further; and leaning upon the shoulder of his companion, and bowing his head, he wept with emotion. What touched our author most in the life of S. Thomas was its closing scene and the low opinion the Saint at length came to entertain of his sublime writings. The story is soon told and can never be too often repeated. 'After his last great ecstasy the Angelical became so absorbed in heavenly things that even the 'Summa' itself failed to interest him, and the tractate he had begun remained unfinished. Reginald, his constant companion, was amazed at the extraordinary turn things had taken, and began to fear that overwork had affected his master's brain. Perplexed and distressed he inquired the cause: 'My Father, why hast thou put on one side so great a work which thou didst begin for the glory of God and the illumination of the world?" All the reply the Saint made was, '*non possum.*' 'I cannot write more.' Again and again on different occasions Reginald implored the Saint to continue writing, but always met with the same answer—"*non possum.*" At length Reginald began one day to urge the Saint with greater vehemence than ever to complete his work, or at least to divulge why it was he persisted in refusing to put his pen again to paper. Constrained by his entreaties, S. Thomas at length exclaimed: 'I adjure thee by the living and omnipotent God, by thy holy vows, and by the charity which binds thee now, not to reveal during my lifetime what I am about to say!' and then he added: 'All I have written appears to me to be so much rubbish—*rubbish*—compared with what I have seen and what has been revealed to me!'" What a lesson, what a reproach are these sublime words to the arrogance and pride of the nineteenth century! How thoroughly should they knock the intellectual conceit out of modern scientists and inspire with some mistrust of self those oracular writers who place implicit confidence in their own rationalistic philosophy and pose as safer and more enlightened guides than the Church herself!

Impregnated with a tender love of the 'Angel of the Schools,' smitten by the simplicity and grandeur of his mind, and ravished with delight at the sight of his keen intellect severing with clean cuts as with a double-edged sword truth from error, Archbishop Vaughan foresaw with the clearness of an intuition that fresh honours were in store for St. Thomas, and hesitated not to assert that the time was not far distant when his hero would be reinstated in his position of preeminence in the schools, and his transcendent genius would receive anew the universal homage of Christendom. The Sovereign Pontiffs, to whose care is committed the supreme charge of feeding and guarding the entire flock, were in former days lavish in their eulogiums on S. Thomas as one of the ablest exponents of the Church's mind, and one of the most successful champions who had taken up arms in her defence. But if Benedict XI. was in the habit of calling him 'My Master' and 'My Doctor'; if John XXII., when some persons referring to the canonisation of the Saint, ventured to suggest that his life had not been illustrated by numerous miracles, exclaimed, 'Tot fecit miracula quot scripsit articulos'—that he had wrought as many miracles as he had written chapters; if other learned writers had referred to him as a 'sun illuminating the universal Church,' a 'mighty sword dividing heresies,' a 'master and guide in Christian doctrine,' the utterances and action of Leo XIII. have not been less ardent and weighty. Perhaps no Pontiff throughout the Church's history has made such strenuous efforts as the reigning Vicar of Christ to restore and enforce the supremacy of the teaching of St. Thomas in the schools, or has so eagerly seized every opportunity of encouraging the learned faithful to take him as their model, master, and intellectual guide. These circumstances render the publication of a second edition of the present volume seasonable and opportune. The clients and students of S. Thomas are yearly increasing in number, and those who have made a serious study of his works will be glad to have within reach the picture of his Life.

One word more in conclusion. There will be, perhaps, some readers who may feel inclined to smile at the prominence given in this volume to the part Benedictine influences played in shaping the mind and character of St. Thomas. But to the thoughtful student who looks beneath the surface and considers the deep impressions which early associations and the tender affections of boyhood leave upon the heart, especially when these are brought to bear upon a noble and sensitive nature, the philosophical reason for emphasising these Benedictine influences becomes not only patent, but the most natural thing in the world. They are referred to, as our Author remarks in the Preface of his first volume, in no narrow or jealous spirit; but simply because effects cannot be explained without their causes, and because the specialities of the Angelical's character could not be fully understood without reference to the patristic spirit of the Benedictine Order. It could not be shown how the excellence of the old method of *quies* was synthesised in him with the more modern method of activity, unless by describing how he became impregnated with the one as well as how he became a master of the other. Yes! S. Thomas had been taught from his earliest dawn of reason to revere the *Holy Rule* of S. Benedict, and its sweet, peaceful, and prayerful spirit must have chimed in harmoniously with his contemplative and angelic nature. His ancestral estates marched with the broad possessions of Monte Cassino, and one of the first objects pointed out to him as a child must have been the lordly Abbey standing on the distant mountain top. His family had been intimately bound up with the traditions of the Order. His uncle was a Benedictine Abbot, and it was the hope and ambition of his parents to see their son one day raised to the Abbatial dignity of Monte Cassino. Such a position was in those days one of the most important in the Church. The Rule of S. Benedict, though on the eve of being partially superseded by the new societies constructed by the Church to confront the intellectual anarchies and social revolutions then threatening the world, was yet the dominant Order in Europe. The power wielded from the citadel of Benedictine glories was still mighty and far-reaching. Thither, therefore, his designing parents sent their boy to be taught by the monks and to have his plastic and expanding mind tinged and toned by the venerable traditions of that spot whose surroundings and very atmosphere were redolent of St. Benedict. In accordance with the custom of those times, touching children destined for the sanctuary, the boy Thomas was taken to the Basilica, and offered to God at the altar, most probably by the hands of his own parents, and then received into the Abbey as a monk. In so strict a sense was he regarded from that day as part and parcel of the monastic family that, had he remained at Monte Cassino all his life long, no further ceremony of profession would have been exacted. How often the Angelical stole away from his companions to pray, prostrate and alone, before the shrine of Blessed Benedict; how deeply he drank of the refreshing waters of the monastic spirit at its fountain-head; how copiously the graces of God thence inundated his soul; how in times of crises he there sought and found—as so many others had done before him, such countless numbers since—rest, courage, and strength for heart and head, who shall say? Certain it is that his mind was permeated with the *Holy Rule.* To be convinced of this, it is enough to note the frequency with which he quotes and refers to it in the pages of his golden writings. It was at his advice that his sister, when she was thinking of becoming a nun, entered the Benedictine Convent at Capua, later on becoming its Abbess. And when stricken with his last illness and escorted by Benedictine monks to Fossa Nuova, lo! as the procession wended its way beneath the great portals of the Abbey, and bore him along the silent, peaceful cloisters to the church, the glorious visions of his boyhood broke in upon him, and, turning to the monks who surrounded him, he exclaimed: 'This is the place where I shall find rest!.' And then prophetically to the faithful Reginald in the presence of all: 'This is my rest *for ever and for ever;* here will I dwell, for I have chosen it.'

It will not, therefore, be considered derogatory to the 'Prince of Theologians,' nor will it wound Dominican susceptibilities, if it be pointed out that to the dialectical skill and chivalrous activity of St. Dominic, St. Thomas added the Patriarchal calmness and Divine gentleness of S. Benedict. His lustre is to-day what it was five hundred years ago, spotless and undimmed. To the Friar Preacher he will be for all time to come the glory and the most perfect exemplar; whilst the Benedictine will never cease to invoke and revere him as the cherished child of the Metropolis of Western Monasticism.

DOM JEROME VAUGHAN, O.S.B.

BUCKFAST ABBEY,
DEVON,
September 8th, 1890.

EDITOR'S PREFACE.

THE *Life and Labours of S. Thomas of Aquin* was written by Archbishop Vaughan during the period he spent presiding as Cathedral-prior over the peaceful cloisters of S. Michael's Priory, Hereford. The first volume, consisting of 866 pages, was published in the year 1871, and was followed a year later by a second volume, containing 993 pages. The book, in spite of its inconvenient bulk and the many abstruse subjects of which it treats, received a cordial welcome by Catholics and Protestants alike, the first edition, with the exception of some sixty copies still in the hands of the publisher, Mr. Hull, Hereford, being now exhausted. The work, with its deep and broad foot-notes in every page, was the fruit of ten years of incessant reading, meditation, and thought, and was from beginning to end a labour of love. It was regarded, however, by the Author, merely as preparatory to a *Life of S. Benedict* which he had in contemplation when his literary labours were suddenly cut short by his elevation to the dignity of Archbishop of Nazianzum and Coadjutor to the venerable Archbishop Polding, O.S.B., of Sydney.

The *Life of S. Benedict* will doubtlessly fare ill amidst the cares and anxieties consequent upon the administration of a vast diocese and the arduous work of establishing a College of Higher Studies, to serve as the great centre of Catholic education in Australia; and its publication, it is feared, will now be indefinitely deferred.

In undertaking an abridged and popular edition of the *Life and Labours of S. Thomas of Aquin*, the Editor believes he is serving the cause of the Church and of souls, and has been urged on in his humble task in no slight degree by the desire of putting within the reach of the loyal and generous-hearted Catholics of New South Wales a *Life* which they will hail with grateful thanks, and, it is hoped, peruse with thoughtfulness and profit. There is no Saint whose character exhibits such a variety of features that meet the precise wants of the present generation, or whose life presents so perfect a model for the times in which we live.

as does that of S. Thomas of Aquin, the 'Prince of Theologians' and the 'Angel of the Schools.' Combining in a preëminent degree a marvellous power of intellect with a child-like obedience and submission to the Church, tenderest love and angelic purity, heroic self-abnegation and Christ-like humility, he stands forth in the pages of history as the brightest pattern of Christian sanctity, and furnishes us by the constraining beauty and loveliness of his wonderful career with an antidote against the rationalism, infidelity, licentiousness, softness, and lawlessness of the nineteenth century. This alone would be a sufficient excuse, if one were needed, for publishing the present volume. The two cardinal lessons which his life teaches as portrayed in this volume are loyal devotedness to the Church, and burning love towards the Divine Person of Jesus Christ. Thomas of Aquin was something more than a man of stupendous genius. He was an earnest, practical, every-day follower of his Blessed Redeemer—a glorious Saint; that is to say, a creature of heroic sanctity cleansed of all the dross of earth, and transformed by the charity of God into the sanctity of an angel; a man who would without one moment's hesitation have gladly sacrificed all his learning to gain one spark more of the love of God. The contemplation of abstract truths, the intricate reasonings of theologians and of philosophers, may entertain and gratify the mind, but they cannot satiate the heart. Man is created to love as well as to think; and therefore, when he has spent long years in deep thought, and has elaborated ingenious theories, and given to the world learned and profound tomes, there will still rise up from the innermost depth of his being a spontaneous cry calling for the possession of an infinite and personal God, whom he can fall down before and adore and worship and serve. Man's most exalted position is on bended knee with eyes lifted up to the Cross of the Crucified. It is the attitude in which art, ever true to nature, loves to represent the Angelical Doctor. He differed, in common with other Saints, from the ordinary Christian chiefly in this: that he trod the world completely under foot, and lived and laboured whilst on earth totally and solely for God, by whom his mind was illuminated and his heart ardently inflamed. The portraiture sketched in this volume of his outer life and interior spirit, of his characteristic virtues and stupendous gifts, of his intellectual labours and far-reaching influence, will, it is hoped, stir the Catholic reader to make fresh efforts in the path of holiness and justice, and be a source of light and refreshment to those also who are not of the true Fold, but whose refined natures and cultured tastes are instinctively drawn to appreciate and sympathise with whatever is grand and heroic and pure and lovely in the lives of great men.

In reducing the two volumes of the *Life and Labours of S. Thomas* to their present size the Editor has been guided by the principle of excluding all those chapters and portions of the work which only bear upon the life of S. Thomas indirectly, but of scrupulously retaining all that belongs to what may be called his Life proper. The book in its original form is what may be termed a veritable History, whilst this popular edition aspires to be nothing more than a Life. Learned disquisitions on S. Thomas's method, philosophical expositions of some of his more abstruse writings, and other such matters as will not interest the general reader, have been omitted. Thus, out of the first volume, the following chapters have been necessarily sacrificed: 'Teaching down to S. Anselm:' 'Rationalism and Irreverence—Abelard:' 'Authority and Reverence—S. Bernard:' 'Monastic Theology—S. Victor:' 'Eastern Influences—Arabians and Jews:' 'Commentary on the Sentences:' 'Monastic Principles defended:' 'Monastic Principles exalted.' From the second volume nearly three hundred pages, which were devoted to the Fathers of the Church, and introduced as exhibiting the fountains from which S. Thomas in great measure drew his inspirations and the models on which he formed his lofty character, have been left out. These chapters are entitled: 'S. Thomas and the Fathers (Part I.)—S. Anthony, S. Athanasius.' 'S. Thomas and the Fathers (Part II.)—S. Basil, S. Gregory *Theologus*, S. Jerome.' 'S. Thomas and the Fathers (Part III.)—S. Chrysostom, S. Ambrose, S. Augustine, S. Gregory the Great.' Care, however, has been taken to preserve the thread of the life throughout unbroken, and where the transitions from one paragraph to another appeared to be too sudden and abrupt, a few sentences have been supplied by the hand of the Editor. Thus the reader in perusing this volume will behold the picture of S. Thomas whole and unmutilated. The background, indeed, in its primitive richness is no longer to be seen, the distant hills have faded, and the noble figures that grouped around the Saint have disappeared, but yet the one grand prominent and central hero still remains the same as before. The devout reader may draw near and make of him a tender and loving friend, and look into the beauty of his face, and muse upon the unbounded generosity of his heart; and beholding how wonderful and glorious is God in His Saints, may ask himself, in the words of the Angelical Doctor, 'Quid sit Deus?'

CORPUS CHRISTI, 1875.
S. Michael's Pro-Cathedral Priory, Hereford.

CONTENTS.

SAINT THOMAS OF AQUIN.

CHAPTER I.

HIS PARENTS AND BIRTH.

'Questi, che m' è a destra più vicino,
Frate e maestro fummi; ed esso Alberto,
E di Cologna, ed io Tomas d'Aquino.'
DANTE, *Parad.* x. 97-99.

S. THOMAS OF AQUIN sprung from a noble and illustrious race. His mother, Theodora, was descended from the Caraccioli, a noble Norman family, and was Countess of Teano in her own right. Her ancestors had left the plains of Normandy two hundred years before, and having driven the Saracens and Greeks out of the plains of Southern Italy, established themselves at Naples and Messina; and having made prisoner the Roman Pontiff, received the crown from the trembling hands of that venerable man.

Landulf, Theodora's husband, of the house of Sommacoli—otherwise called Counts of Loreto, D'Acerra, and Belcastro—belonged to one of the most remarkable families of middle Italy. Doubtless, in youth, his ears had been accustomed to the din of arms, and his eyes had seen many a gorgeous pageant in the court of

Frederick Barbarossa. His father, Thomas, achieved so high a military reputation, that the Emperor nominated him Lieutenant-General of the Holy Roman Empire, and gave him his sister, Frances of Suabia, to wife. Landulf could call to mind, with pleasing recollection no doubt, that the blood of the turbulent Frangipani flowed in his veins, that he was connected with Gregory the Great, and that his ancestors had distinguished themselves years ago in the wars of Charlemagne. His name was not unknown before the destruction of the Lombard kingdom. Antenulf and Landulf were Dukes of Capua and Salerno in 879: and, after their inheritance had been wrested from them, they assumed the title of Aquino, and settled themselves between the Volturno and Garigliano. In the reign of Otto III., one of these rough warriors wrested Rocca Sicca from the Abbot of Monte Cassino, and levelled it with the ground (996). Another, equally successful in his enterprises, assumed the title of Count of Gaeta, stormed Minturna, beat the Normans, subjected the lords of Capua with the sword, and chased Guimar, lord of Salerno, out of his dominions.

Lando was not so fortunate. He lost Gaeta, and resumed the name of Aquino, while Rainald, son of Landulf, was glad to exchange Monte Libretto for San Giovanni—preferring the mastership of Adrian to the despotic and uncertain violence of Frederick (1157). But, if the Aquinos lost in one way, they gained in another. The panegyrists of the Saint, who always appear to appreciate most keenly nobility of ancestry, relate, with effusion, how, under the rough garb of the shaven friar, flowed the blood of kings: how the young Dominican was nephew of Frederick I. and Henry IV., and cousin of Frederick II., and how he could claim connection with the royal houses of Arragon, Sicily, and France.

Of the character of the Saint's father little is known; though it seems pretty certain that he combined a martial spirit with a large sentiment of faith; while his mother, with immense energy of character, and a somewhat haughty spirit, kept herself in control by severe fasts, frequent vigils, and constant prayers.

Theodora's home was quite in the mediæval style. The little town of Aquino occupies the centre of a vast and fertile plain, commonly called Campagna Felice, in the ancient Terra di Lavoro. This plain is nearly surrounded by bare and rugged mountains, one of which pushes further than the rest into the plain; and on its spur, which juts boldly out, and which was called significantly Rocca Sicca, was situated the ancient stronghold of the Aquinos. The remnants of this fortress, as seen at this day, seem so bound up with the living rock, that they appear more like the abrupt finish of the mountain than the ruins of a mediæval fortress. Yet they are sufficient to attest the ancient splendour and importance of the place; and the torrent of Melfi, which, tumbling out of the gorges of the Alps, runs round the castellated rock, marks it out as a fit habitation for the chival rous and adventurous lords of Aquino, Loreto, and Belcastro.

It was in a chamber of this castle that a rough hermit, who had gained a name for his godly life, suddenly, and to the amazement of Theodora, made his appearance. Like another Elias the Thesbite, with his flowing hair and coarse garment, he pointed to a picture of S. Dominic, which hung from an image of the Blessed Virgin round his neck, and exclaimed: 'Rejoice, O lady, for thou art with child, and thou shalt bring forth a son, whom thou shalt call Thomas; and thou and thy husband will think to make a monk of him in the Monastery of Monte Cassino, in which the body of blessed Benedict rests, hoping to obtain possession of the great income of that Monastery through his elevation. But God will provide otherwise, for he will become a brother of the Order of Preachers.' She replied, 'I am not worthy to bear such a son; may the will of God be done!'

The event foretold by Bonus the Solitary in due course came to pass. In the eleventh year of the Pontificate of Honorius, the ninth of the reign of Frederick, the same year that S. Louis became King and S. Francis of Assisi died, Theodora gave birth to the future Angel of the Schools. The date of the event, however, is contested. Most reliable authorities put it at the year 1227. Some say it took place at Rocca Sicca, some at Aquino, others at Belcastro.

Thomas was not Theodora's only child, she had three boys and three girls. The two eldest boys took to a military life—according to the custom of their ancestors—and for some time followed the varying fortunes of Frederick II. The youngest girl, when an infant, was killed by a stroke of lightning in one of those terrific storms which now and then burst from the mountain ranges over the plain of the Terra di Lavoro. The second girl married Count Sanseverino, and became a saintly woman of the world; and the eldest entered religion, became Abbess, and after a life of great perfection, died with the reputation of a saint.

Some curious legends are related of S. Thomas's early childhood; for instance, when at the baths of Naples a scroll of paper was miraculously placed in his hands. He made violent opposition when his mother took it from him; and she, finding to her astonishment the words 'Ave Maria' upon it, gave it back instantly to the child. He seized it eagerly, and swallowed it—some say in imitation of Ezechiel the Prophet. Then he would prefer books to any other playthings. If he cried, a book would pacify him at once. And from time to time, a crown of heavenly glory was seen to hover over his head. Again, on Sunday, the first of June 1230, the earth began to tremble violently; and for a whole month earthquake shocks were felt from Capua to Rome. Rocca Sicca did not escape. Thomas was sleeping with his nurse and his little sister, as the storm struck the castle, and a fork of lightning shot through the window and burnt the little girl to death, but left the boy gently sleeping in his nurse's arms.

Many will believe in these legends about as much as in the story of those bees which are said to have dropped honey on the lips of the infant fast asleep in the bower of myrtles on Mount Hymettus; or in the dream of Socrates, when he saw a young swan coming from an altar in the Grove of Academus, which, after nestling in his bosom, soared up the heavens, singing sweetly as it rose aloft. Still, if they do not reflect from the past upon the future, they do what tends, perhaps, still more to the Saint's renown, they are reflections of the future on the past.

When S. Thomas was five years old, his parents sent him to Monte Cassino, hoping, in spite of Bonus the Solitary, that he would eventually join the Order, and become master of those vast possessions which were under the dominion of its Abbots.

This mighty Abbey, placed upon the mountain side, and looking down on the teeming plain of Aquino, about six miles from Rocca Sicca, even in those days could be looked upon as an antiquity. Once a bushy grove, full of the impure worship of lascivious gods, in the sixth century S. Benedict laid the foundation of its history. When S. Thomas went there, it had already thrice been jolted to the ground by earthquakes, over and over it had been besieged by barbarians, it had been clean destroyed by the Lombards, and burnt to cinders by the Saracens; but it sprang up as often as cast down, and, in the early days of S. Thomas, was the most distinguished school of letters in the land.

Through that dark passage, along which the future Angel of the Schools was led by his nurse to marvel at dark-robed monks, vast corridors, and silent cloisters, the sons of kings—Carloman, Ratchis, Adelard, Gisulfe—leaving the din of life for the rest of God, had gone before him, and had slept in peace. Through that narrow passage, whose darkness received the young Aquino out of sight, the civilisation of modern Europe had flowed out. But Theodora and Landulf had more personal motives for loving the mighty Abbey. Thrice, in old times, their ancestors—students and protectors of the monastery—had risked their fortunes and their lives in its defence; whilst the same year the child was born, his uncle, Landulf Sinnebald, though a simple deacon, was chosen by the monks fifty-sixth in its glorious line of Abbots.

The times of S. Thomas cannot be adequately sketched without touching upon the relation of this mighty Abbey to the Empire and the Holy See.

For it was at this period that Gregory IX. and Frederick came to an open rupture. When Sinnebald was in Rome the following year (1228) for his ordination, he heard many rumours about the duplicity of the Emperor, and the deceit he had practised upon the Pope. The time specified by the Parliament of San Germano for commencing the Crusades had expired, and Frederick had embarked at Brindisi. But after three days he turned the ships about, and came to port, declaring that delicacy of health prevented him prosecuting the voyage.

The Pope was exceedingly angry, and after thundering an excommunication against him, sent two Cardinals and Abbot Sinnebald to wait upon him, and bring him to a knowledge of his duty. But Frederick, maddened by the excommunication, protested against its injustice, and would listen to no accommodation. He dismissed the Cardinals with scant courtesy, and after telling the Abbot that he altogether disapproved of his election, ordered him, in future, to provide him with a hundred armed men, and to pay one thousand two hundred ounces of gold for their support.

The Emperor at length set sail, and left Rainald of Spoleto his representative in Naples. But it was not the holy places, so much as his thirst to be king of Jerusalem on his marriage with Jolanda, that spurred him on in this undertaking. With the cross upon his breast, and the Papal anathema hanging over his head, Frederick set about a work which in the middle ages was essentially a religious undertaking. No wonder that the Patriarch of Jerusalem, the Templars, the Hospitallers, and all good men, were scandalised at a crusader fighting for Christ with the curse of Christ's Vicar upon him. They could not help regarding him, not so much as a champion of Christianity amongst the Pagans, as a declared enemy of Christ, publicly denounced by the successor of S. Peter.

To keep the Pope well occupied whilst he was in the East, Frederick succeeded in raising, by means of the turbulent Frangipani, a dangerous sedition at the foot of the Pontifical throne; and, furious at his bad reception in the East, which he attributed to the Pope, he ordered the Duke of Spoleto to ravage the Papal States. In vain Gregory excommunicated him; in vain the Lombard Guelfs tried to make a stand against him. Gregory, with a courage which he inherited from Innocent, raised an army, and sent it by the Ciprano road into the Terra di Lavoro. They went by the name of the 'Clavissignati,' and the Army of Christ, on account of the banner which they carried into battle, blazoned with the great keys of S. Peter. They were commanded by two rebel Counts, Fondi and Celano, while the general supervision was intrusted to Pandulf D'Alagna, Legate of the Holy See. These men soon set to work. Filled with religious enthusiasm, they forced themselves into the stronghold of Pontescelerato; and having terrified its defenders, captured without resistance the castles of San Giovanni in Carico and Pastena.

The Imperialists were stirred up like a nest of ants when they heard of these successes. Morra, the Grand Justiciary, raised a band of soldiers; and the Baron of Balzano, Landulf, and Ardenolf of Aquino, and many others, assembled in haste at San Germano, burning to rid the country of the invaders.

The Abbot was puzzled which side to take. As a churchman, he was with the Pope. But, on the other hand, his family were with the Emperor; and he himself, possibly, was not without some secret sympathy with the great Ghibeline party, which ever supported the nobles against the plebs. Besides, he did not forget the fury of the Imperial troops, nor the violence which the old Abbey had suffered at their hands. However that may be, he filled the Abbey with provisions, summoned his vassals to arms, and prepared the House of God to withstand an attack from the army of the Vicar of Christ. There was no less excitement down in San Germano. Morra forced the citizens to work at the fortifications, and build up the crumbling walls of Rocca Janula. The city was in arms, and sounds of war resounded throughout the property belonging to the Abbey. The Imperialists, too weak to act on the offensive, awaited the attack, the Clavissignati made a raid on Rocca d'Arce, but being ingloriously repulsed retired to Ceprano, from whence they sallied forth to devastate the surrounding neighbourhood, and plunder the wealthy church of S. Peter and S. Paul della Foresta.

On the third of March the Legate marched straight into the patrimony of S. Benedict. He took Piedimonte, belonging to the Abbey, by assault; and, drawing up in order of battle before San Germano, hoped to draw the enemy into an engagement. Finding his bravado ineffectual, he marched away, and ravaged Pignaturo, and coming upon S. Angelo, a strongly fortified place, received so ugly a reception from its defenders that he gladly passed it by, and marched into Termini, which was particularly loyal to the Emperor. Here, at first, he was very roughly handled by the valour and desperation of the inhabitants. But numbers finally prevailing, the Papal force obtained the mastery, and having plundered and sacked whatever they could lay their hands upon, set the whole country side on fire, and ravaged their way back into the Campagna Romana.

On the seventeenth they appeared once more in the patrimony of S. Benedict. They determined now to strike a decisive blow. At Piedimonte, they divided their force; one detachment had orders to keep the plain, and attack Morra in front; the other was to creep up round the mountain, by circuitous and solitary paths towards Monte Cassino, and, whilst their comrades were sharply attacking the Justiciary in the city, to threaten the Abbey, and from the eminence that commands the town to bring panic and confusion on the enemy. When Morra got to hear of this, he sent a handful of men to watch their movements; and, having strengthened his forces, held himself in readiness to render assistance as it might be required.

To the west of the mighty Abbey runs a chain of mountains, increasing in elevation up to Monte Cairo, which dominates the rest, and then branches out on one side towards Campagna Romana, on the other in a more westerly direction, till it joins the Aprutini. Now, two miles from the Abbey stands the Monastery of Albaneta, and farther on, a little to the west, close at hand, on a mountain crest, stood the Monastery of S. Matthew Servorum Dei. It was at this place that the soldiers of the Empire came upon the soldiers of the Church. Instantly they closed, and on a sudden those quiet rocks resounded with shouts of onset, and clang of arms. The Justiciary with young Ardenolf of Aquino led a reinforcement up the mountain side to the scene of action. Morra behaved like a lion. But the Papal troops had the advantage of the ground, and making a diversion through the gorges of the mountain, a party of them came out near the Albaneta, and cut off the Imperialists' retreat. Thus surrounded, Morra and his men thought to cut their way through the enemy with the sword. But they met with a terrible discomfiture. Of the few who survived, some, like Ardenolf and Morra, took refuge in the Abbey, whilst the rest rushed away down the mountain side towards San Germano, followed in hot pursuit by their opponents.

In the mean time Pandulf attacked the town. The citizens defended themselves stoutly, relying on the Abbey. The Legate, on perceiving this, went up the mountain, and under threat of deposition and extermination, commanded the Abbot to open the gates and deliver up the Justiciary. After considerable delay the Justiciary and the troops were set at liberty, and the Abbey was delivered to the Legate, who, in the morning, took triumphant possession of San Germano; and, having fortified and garrisoned the Abbey, hurried off to other conquests.

At this period the Franciscan Friars had circulated

a report that the Emperor had been carried off by plague in the Holy Land. When Sinnebald had heard of this, he at once declared himself in favour of the Pope. But Frederick had not died, for he suddenly appeared in full vigour of life at Brindisi, and being joined by Rainald, pushed on into the Terra di Lavoro. The miserable people of that devastated country were panic-stricken at his approach, and fled to the mountains to escape the Saracens and Turks, and the brutality of soldiers who had but just left the hallowed precincts of the Holy Sepulchre. Desolate indeed was the land of Villa S. Lucia, consumed by fire and sword, whilst the Monastery of S. Matthew Servorum Dei became a spectacle of rapine, and pollution of everything human and divine. Next, the mighty Abbey was attacked, but the Legate defended himself with such valour that the Emperor was compelled to retire to San Germano. Frederick then tried another plan. He threatened to confiscate all the property of the Cassinese. This produced the desired effect. The Abbot suddenly appeared humbly before him, and with many supplications besought him to recall his threat. The Emperor consented on one condition, that the Legate should leave the Abbey under a safe escort to be provided by himself, as far as the borders of the Papal States.

This is a specimen of the state of things in the neighbourhood of Rocca Sicca during the childhood of S. Thomas. Thus was the mighty Abbey on the mountain mixed up with the turmoils and struggles of the outer world, penetrating into silent cells and holy shrines. Thus did the Empire and the Church struggle for the mastery.

And in the midst of all these scenes, the self-possession of the monks, who were men, as well as solitaries of the mountain, did not forsake them. They still watched and prayed: still, in the silent night, their voices rose up, singing the *Deus in adjutorium meum intende*. Still did they with courage cry, *Ad te Levavi oculos meos qui habitas in Cœlis*, as they lifted their hearts and eyes to Him whose love is perfect peace. It is to be expected that men who could abandon a bright future to live in penance on the mountain, who could give up the society of tender friends out of affection for the Crucified, should be men of deep, large heart; of free, strong spirit; of lovely, pure lives—fit to regenerate a world.

Nor did the ascetic life interfere with the due cultivation of the mind. The first disciples of S. Benedict himself were poets and literary men. Faustus and Sebastian are names which are still familiar. Marcus, their companion, is praised by Paul the Deacon as an accomplished scholar and an elegant poet. In the palmy days of the Roman Empire, tradition says that Terence established a seat of learning on the mountain: anyhow, from the sixth to the thirteenth century, the education of Europe was Benedictine. During the period following the ravages of the north, monks, in their cells upon mountain sides, were composing homilies, writing lives of saints, penning chronicles and legends, framing treatises on grammar and theology, making miniatures and mosaics, and planting the mustard-seed of future European intellectual growth. Autpert and Theophanus, Hilderic and the heroic S. Bertarius, were men of letters. Whilst Paul the Deacon, having abandoned the highest post a king could bestow upon a subject, retired into solitude to pray and study;—a monk, a poet, an historian, a linguist, and a familiar friend of Charlemagne. He not only established a tradition of intellectual activity at Monte Cassino, but did much towards forming a purer and more cultivated taste; and gave a new impetus to letters in France.

In the ninth century the histories of Sozomen and Theodoret, and fine copies of S. Augustine, and of several other Fathers, were transcribed. Abbot Theobald, a great patron of poetry and painting, gave a fresh impulse to the work. But Desiderius did the most for learning. At the age of forty, he set to work to study letters and music; and then, to write books and compose chants. He erected a new library, in which could be found, besides other works, Virgil, Horace, Terence, Cicero, and the voluminous writings of Justinian. Then the poets, the chroniclers of history, and physical and medical science, were represented by famous men. It will suffice to mention such names as Constantine Africanus, Leo of Ostia, Amatus of Salerno, Guaiferio and Alfano, to recall many of equal celebrity to the mind.

It is only natural, when the moral scope of the Benedictine rule is considered, and the nobility of monastic life, and the tradition of letters which clung to the mighty Abbey, that Landulf and Theodora—having seen enough of strife and ignorance at Rocca Sicca—should give up their gentle boy to the care of his uncle Sinnebald.

To educate youth was one of the objects which S. Benedict had in view when he founded his order. He makes provision for this in the Holy Rule. For example, the twenty-third chapter, on correction, manifests his firmness and his prudence. The thirty-seventh speaks of the *pia consideratio* with which children should be treated, and the fifty-eighth and fifty-ninth lay down rules for their reception at the Abbey. These instructions are full of that wisdom which, without meddling with detail, sketches, with remarkable clearness and precision, the outline of that system of firmness and freedom, which is characteristically Benedictine.

The reception of a child in those days was almost as solemn as a profession in our own. His parents carried him to the church; and whilst they wrapped his hand, which held the petition, in the sacred linen of the altar, they promised, in the presence of God and of His saints, stability in his name. There is no hint that the sacrifice was not considered to have been irrevocably offered, after this oblation had been made to God.

The children's training was in keeping with the holiness of their consecration. They were confided to the care of a large-hearted and God-fearing man. The one object was, to fill their souls with God, to teach them the power of knowledge, and the force of love,—to educate the intellect, and to purify the heart.

Nor are there any adequate grounds for thinking that the case of S. Thomas was an exception to the general rule. He, naturally, would join the other little Benedictines, who were being trained for the monastic state. So he wore the holy habit, observed the Holy Rule, and attended the offices of the Church, according as the *pia consideratio* was interpreted by his superiors. His references to S. Benedict, whom he is never tired of citing as an example, and many of his references also to the rule, show a deep and minute acquaintance with the Benedictine spirit, and testify to vivid images impressed in early youth. To all intents and purposes S. Thomas of Aquin was a Benedictine monk. Had he continued in the habit till his death—without any further solemnity beyond the offering of his parents—he would have been reckoned as much a Benedictine as S. Gregory, S. Augustine, S. Anselm, or S. Bede.

CHAPTER II.

S. THOMAS AT MONTE CASSINO.

It would be difficult to imagine a child with the temperament of young Aquino, living five or six years under monastic influence, without receiving an indelible mark. There are many subtle influences which thrill to the inmost sanctuary of a sensitive spirit, which the less delicately strung have not the capacity to feel. The Saint's brothers, for instance, might, no doubt, have spent a great portion of their lives amidst the most impressive religious scenes, without being very much influenced. But Thomas was formed of quite another clay. The picture which his biographers draw of his early youth is singularly Benedictine. Those qualities, which most persons acquire as the fruit of a long and painful course of self-control, sat upon him gracefully from the first. For example, the rule enjoins silence: Thomas was a singularly silent, meditative boy. It condemns levity with great severity of language: Thomas never joined in the thoughtless merriment and childish amusements of his companions. It treats of fraternal charity and correction: Thomas observed this perfect theory by perfect practice, and was known to use his influence to draw to their duty some of his companions who had gone astray. The rule lays great stress on prayer: Thomas spent hours together, as a child, in meditation, so that all 'wondered at his power and his holiness.' It advocates devotion: Thomas was *oratione devotus*. It prescribes solitude: Thomas loved nothing better than to be alone. S. Benedict lays special stress on observance of rule: Thomas had an instinctive dread of breaking rule.

This suffices to show how the character of young

Aquino was in harmony with the highest theory of monastic life, and to what an unusual degree, in his earliest years, he possessed those habits of perfection, which the whole mechanism of the rule is constructed to foster in less gifted souls.

His companions tacitly acknowledge his superiority; and his force of character appears to have made itself felt from the very first. The combination of character and genius, in large proportions, tends to render a man supreme. But character is more powerful than ability. Many a man who had been dull at books as a boy has shot out a later growth of talent. But is there a single instance of a man, who as a boy had not sufficient character to control his companions at school, acquiring such a power after he had become a man?

The personal appearance of young Aquino indicated the presence of a governing spirit; not the command of brute force, but the command of intellect. He possessed that rare class of spiritual beauty which tells of gentleness, purity, and power. His massive head betokened strength. His broad tranquil brow, his placid meditative eyes, produced the impression, not so much of quickness and vivacity, as of breadth and of command. He seemed to live in a sort of spiritual light,—as the sunbeam striking upon a landscape naturally beautiful invests it with a kind of transfiguration. Though he seldom spoke,—when he did speak, he set hearts beating faster; and often, whilst thus conversing with his companions, the monks would approach the little gathering by stealth, to listen to the precocious wisdom of this extraordinary child.

Contrasts often suggest themselves, especially when associated with a likeness. No two men ever had more intellectual traits in common than S. Thomas and the Stagyrite; and yet no two men were ever more unlike each other in appearance. Aristotle had slender legs and little eyes; a feeble voice, and a hesitating utterance. He was a dandy, wore smart clothes, and several rings; while in morals, some say, he combined ingratitude and impiety, with the vices of the parasite and the glutton.

But, though S. Thomas had great influence over his companions at the Abbey, there was one thought that seemed to oppress his mind by reason of its mysterious greatness. He seems to have felt the thrilling touch of the finger of another world, which acts with galvanic power on the systems of the saints,—so highly wrought, so exquisitely strung. The boy was continually asking his masters, *quid esset Deus?*—what God was. This one question gives the key to his character, and to the whole history of his life. *Puer cœpit solicite quœrere à Magistro quid esset Deus?* But this will appear later in the volume.

Nor was mental culture neglected in the midst of these spiritual influences. Thomas was taught the first elements of knowledge by the monks. The fragmentary Latin Grammar of the period, Donatus, Priscian, or Didymus would, by frequent repetitions, be fixed upon the memory. Then the Psalter, and passages from the poets, were learnt by heart. Æsop's Fables, Theodulus, and the Sentences of Cato, led into the gallery of the ancient Classics. Ovid, Horace, and Persius were favourite authors ; while Seneca was treated with special reverence, as one of the most enlightened moralists of ancient times. Then Lucan, Statius, and Virgil, who were looked upon as seers in the midst of heathendom, on account of certain curiously prophetic passages in their writings, prepared the student for his course of rhetoric. Cicero, Quintilian, and the Stagyrite opened the door to the science of God, and of the saints. That S. Thomas passed through a course resembling this, to say the least, is eminently probable. The Dominican, Fra Tolomeo da Lucca, who was his confessor, declares that, besides grammar—which in those days included poetry—he studied his logic and his philosophy at the mighty Abbey.

These were tranquil days for the young Aquino, days of growth—just as nature rests in the first warm days of early spring, before it bursts into leaf and flower. To breathe at peace under the light of truth, far from the contention of tongues, and then to meditate and resolve in the presence of one Eternal Witness,—this has been the education of many a man of iron will, of soaring spirit, and of blameless life. It was thus that S. Gregory learnt how to rule the destinies of the Universal Church. It was in a little cell that S. Augustine was taught how to subjugate a pagan island to the

Cross. S. Boniface, whilst he appeared to waste away his life in solitude, was converting the German race. Lindisfarne, Ripon, Canterbury, Wearmouth, Jarrow, Fulda, Ferrières, Corby, Richenau, S. Gall, Croyland, Bec, and hundreds more, were springs of peace, where, instead of the imagination being disturbed by the sophisms of intellectual charlatans, the spirit could drink silently of the deep fountains of its Saviour. From the centre of stability, where rest alone is found, springs the activity of the thoughtful mind. The mind that was taught to have no stay but God partook of God's repose ; and exulted in that freedom which expands above the senses. Thus the monks thought much, but talked little ; thus the monastic system encouraged meditation, rather than intellectual tournaments ; reserve, rather than display ; deep humility, rather than dialectical skill. The Benedictines did not aim so much at unrestrained companionship of free discussion, as at self-control ; not so much at secular-minded fantasy, as at much prayer and sharp penance, till self was conquered, and the grace of God reigned, and giants walked the earth. Self-mastery, springing from the basis of a supernatural life, moulded the heart to sanctity, and imparted to the intellect an accuracy of vision, which is an act of nature directed and purified by grace. Theodore, Aldhelm, Bede, Boniface, Alcuin, Dunstan, Wilfrid, Stephen, Bernard, Anselm, these names are suggestive of this influence of the monastic system.

The traditions of the Benedictine spirit, springing

from the Abbey, permeated Europe, Christianised society, and still maintained at Monte Cassino when S. Thomas was a boy. But, no doubt, there were watchmen on that mountain, whose keen eyes could perceive the signs of a coming change. The conflicts of the Empire and the Church, of the Guelfs with the Ghibelines, and between the various cities and families in Italy, the impetus given by Frederick to freedom of discussion, and the license introduced by the Crusades, were sufficient to make men forecast the future with anxiety.

Though the monks did not go down the mountain side, and mix in the world below, they watched its movements, as they ever do, with intelligent concern. Whilst those who take part in the pageant see nothing of its general effect, monks, being at a distance from it, can view it as a whole, perceive its scope, and prophesy pretty shrewdly its ultimate destination. Paris, Bologna, Naples, the university life, and the din of the city, were to replace the system of the school of quiet. When the change, with many shocks and throes, was working itself into the stability of a new order of things, the monks cried bitterly in their silent cells. But the world stops for neither priest nor layman. The energy of a new principle had entered into society; and, in spite of all efforts to the contrary, that energy would work itself fairly out. The *primum mobile* of the old system was rest; the *primum mobile* of the new system was everlasting motion.

But there were other movements which gave an unexpected turn to the career of young Aquino, and which must briefly be indicated here.

They begin with a gleam of sunshine. The Emperor and the Pope, after the peace of San Germano, met at Anagni, sat at the same board, and made many civil speeches to each other during the meal. The patrimony of S. Benedict was restored to the Benedictines; and the Emperor sent the Duke of Austria to Monte Cassino, to assure the Abbot of the Imperial favour. Gregory, on the other hand, confirmed the Magna Charta of the monks by renewing the privileges and freedoms granted by Pope Zachary; and the Abbey, to all appearances, being established in the friendship of the Empire and the Church, seemed at length to have acquired a stability, which many a holy Abbot had aimed at acquiring by diplomacy, but which none had ever been able to attain.

But this gleam of light was speedily quenched. Frederick and Gregory were not merely energetic individuals, for they represented two master principles, which, during a long term of years, were struggling for the mastery. The principle of matter and of mind, of reason and faith, had not yet, under the changing conditions of society, wrought out a solution of the question—Who is to rule the world? The arrival of Imperial ministers at San Germano, the energy with which the troops were fortifying Rocca Janula, were harbingers of anything but security. Abbot Landulf's mind was ill at ease. He felt that the keenness of Gregory, and the duplicity of Frederick, were qualities little likely to cement a lasting peace. The political atmosphere looked dark and threatening. Rainald, who had repeatedly been excommunicated, on his submission to the Pope, created for himself an enemy in Frederick. Messina was in rebellion. The Lombard league was growing more formidable every day. And Errico, the Emperor's son, encouraged, it was imagined, by the Pope, had taken up arms against his father. These events filled the soul of Landulf Sinnebald with deep distress. And death (1236) saved him the bitterness of witnessing a catastrophe which would most probably have brought him to the grave.

Five months elapsed before the Emperor consented to the election of another Abbot. The community, impatient of delay, assembled of their own accord, declared Pandulf da Stephano (1237) their Abbot; and then solicited the confirmation of the Emperor and the Pope. After considerable intrigue, the monks obtained Frederick's confirmation. But Gregory would come to no decision, till further instructions had been issued by the Holy See. The monks then determined on a new election (1238). As they were unable to agree among themselves upon a candidate, they intrusted the case to the Archbishop of Messina, and declared that they would consider the Archbishop's nominee as canonically elected: so Stephen di Cervario was nominated, accepted by the monks, approved by the Emperor, ordained priest, blessed Abbot, and with splendid pomp installed in the Abbatial chair.

And now came the storm which had been threatening so long. Frederick was highly pleased by his successes against the Lombards and the Milanese. Gregory, on the contrary, was in deep distress at the rebellion of the Romans, and the ruin which was threatening the Guelfs. The Emperor was well aware of this. In vain did Gregory attempt to bring him to a reasonable accommodation with the Lombards; and the cup of his displeasure was filled to overflowing, when Frederick nominated one of his many bastards, Enzio, to be King of the Island of Sardinia, which was in reality a portion of the patrimony of the Holy See.

On Palm Sunday, the Holy Father, in full consistory, excommunicated Frederick, absolved his subjects from their allegiance, and branded with interdict every place on which he put his foot.

True to the policy of his predecessors, Stephen was shrewd enough to know, says Tosti, that excommunication would act upon the Emperor as medicine does upon a dying man—simply assisting corruption to do its work more speedily. And as it seemed to him that Gregory was on the losing side, he at once set about conciliating the good wishes of the Emperor. He took the trouble to travel from Monte Cassino into Lombardy, to take an oath of fealty. Frederick received him very graciously. But at the very time that the Emperor was conferring privileges on the Abbot, a band of soldiers, by that same Emperor's command, forced their way into Monte Cassino, laid violent hands upon the monks, drove some of them into the mountains ; and murdering the rest, in the name of their master, took possession of the Abbey. They began at once to fill it with provisions, and having laid heavy contributions on the inhabitants of the plains below, forced them to drag wood and stone up the mountain side, and to help in fortifying the Abbey against attack.

Eight of the monks, not without some trembling, and amidst the desecration of all they held most sacred, clung to the Monastery. Historians relate how that mighty Abbey, to which pilgrims resorted from all quarters of the world, and which had been the shrine of piety and letters, was turned into a nest of thieves. Its vast treasures, the accumulation of many years, princely gifts of massive gold and silver, gems, and splendid cups, the legacies of Emperors, Kings, and Knights, became the booty of the soldiery. The sanctuary was darkened on the mountain. Of the eight monks, some betook themselves to other Abbeys, some went to Naples, whilst others, like S. Thomas, took refuge with their families.

Such was the stormy termination of S. Thomas's career under the influence of Monte Cassino. Seven years of such an influence could not have been without effect. S. Thomas seems, indeed, to have combined, in a remarkable degree, the perfection of the old system of repose with the new system of activity. Whilst S. Thomas of Aquino was a perfect Dominican, he never, for one moment, ceased to be a thorough Benedictine.

CHAPTER III.

S. THOMAS AT NAPLES.

LORETO, a castle belonging to the Aquinos, was situated in the Abruzzi, not far from Aquino, and between Cività di Chieti and Cività della Penna. Here his parents were residing when S. Thomas left the Abbey. Some say that he was removed, and sent by his parents to the University of Naples, at the advice of his uncle, Abbot Sinnebald. But this can hardly be the case, first, because superiors always prefer to retain their choicest subject, and, then, because Abbot Sinnebald had been some time dead and buried when the Imperial soldiers took possession of the Monastery. Nor is it likely that his parents, who sent him to the Abbey with the settled purpose of his becoming some day Abbot, would willingly remove him from it, and cast him, at twelve years of age, into one of the most dissolute towns in Italy. The real cause of his departure has already been described; and, naturally enough, the boy resided with his parents till they could place him at another school.

The change must have been a violent one for the young Aquino. The noise and excitement of a great feudal castle must have offered a great contrast to the uneventful monotony of the cloister. Horses, and falcons, and the tramp of armed men, the free carousing, the singing of troubadours and minstrels, the shouts of mirth which accompanied the amusements of knights and esquires, must have been the occasion of many temptations to a boy of twelve. But Thomas, though but a boy, had a mind which was occupied with higher things than the mere transitory pastimes of his father's castle. It must be remembered that he had often poured out his heart by the tomb of blessed Benedict, and had joined the solemn throng of godly men in holy prayer. Under such influences, a new standard had been set up, and life had been tuned to another harmony.

An anecdote is related of him at this period, which shows how full his young heart was of charity. During his sojourn at Loreto a terrible famine decimated the inhabitants of the plains of Southern Italy. The people, at length, could only look for succour from the bounty of the rich. Crowds of starving peasants besieged the gate of the castle of Loreto. The hardest heart would move, to witness the strong man perishing for want of bread, and mother and child sinking gradually into a common grave. The Aquinos were charitable to the poor; and Thomas acted as his father's almoner. But not satisfied with this, sometimes he stole secretly into the kitchen, filled his cloak with whatever came to hand, and hurried triumphantly to the castle gate, to divide his spoils amongst the famishing people, who looked upon the boy as an angel sent to them from heaven. On one of these occasions, as he was carrying his cloak full of provisions, he suddenly perceived his father standing opposite him. With a voice full of displeasure Landulf asked the child what he was carrying. Disconcerted by the severity of his father's manner, he let fall his burden; but, in the place of bread and kitchen-stuff, a shower of roses covered the ground beneath his feet. Quite overcome by this sudden manifestation of the Divine will, the old man burst into tears, and embracing the child with transport, declared that, as long as he had an obolus in his pocket, or a piece of bread in his kitchen, his boy should not be prevented following the dictates of that charity which had guided him throughout.

To those who might be inclined to smile incredulously at this legend, it may be remarked, that it is the tendency of the Catholic mind to believe that great holiness will be accompanied by great favours. Yet, it is not the Catholic tendency to believe without reasonable grounds. In the case of S. Thomas, knowing that he led a life of singular purity and love, we feel no temptation to smile with incredulity at the miracle of the roses;—our tendency is in the opposite direction. It is a very beautiful legend, and there is no reason to believe it is not founded on fact; anyhow, it leaves upon the mind a pleasing and edifying impression. Scoffing and contempt, and even highly educated and courteous incredulity, is less reasonable than the Catholic tendency, and certainly has a lowering moral effect, and a vulgarising influence upon the mind.

It may possibly be objected that there could be no virtue in taking food, even for the poor, without permission. But the answer to this is simple. What is a sin in one man is not necessarily a sin in another man. S. Thomas was, I take for granted, divinely guided to carry out the action of a higher law. Did God command, it would have been a sin in Thomas to have neglected carrying the food from the kitchen to the poor. Both father and son are subject to the higher law: for the earth is the Lord's, and the fulness thereof, though He may, for a time, appoint Count Landulf of Aquino as His steward.

The story of the roses is the only event recorded of S. Thomas during his sojourn at Loreto. He did not remain there long. Theodora still clung with ardour to her first idea of seeing the boy one day Lord Abbot of Monte Cassino. His brothers, fierce young Ghibelines, were winning their spurs amidst the bloodshed that tracked the path of Frederick II. His father, and the Count D'Acerra, his uncle, were both men of strong Ghibeline tendencies. If Thomas could only be enthroned Abbot of the vast possessions of the Abbey, if Rocca Sicca were strongly fortified,—with Aquino in possession of the family, and Belcastro held by Count D'Acerra,—the Aquinos would be formidable even to the Emperor himself.

But how could this idea be realised now? For the boy to return to the Abbey was impossible. To secularise him would not do. There was only one combination which could meet the case,—to send him to study at Naples, under the shadow of S. Benedict; for, to send him to live amongst young men, notorious for their lascivious lives, at the University, would have been equivalent, not simply to destroying his vocation, but to throwing away his soul.

For the dangers at the University of Naples at that period were greater, most probably, than those at Oxford and Cambridge are at present. The ferment in the mind of society, the immorality of the place, the undisciplined condition of the schools, where each student shifted for himself as best he could, rendered such a position, for any young man, perilous in the extreme. The city itself, edging the double crescent of blue water, with perfect sky, sea, and air; then the luxuriant Campagna to the east, with its villas buried amongst branching pines and groves of orange blossom; then the stretch of the azure Mediterranean, dotted with gay barges of pleasure and dark galleys of war, tended to relax the virility of a religion which teaches that the road to heaven is the road of prayer, mortification, and self-restraint. All writers of this period unite in describing Naples, with its houses running up seven stories high, with its tortuous narrow streets and teeming population, as the most beautiful and the most wicked city in the world.

Then there was the dangerous influence of Frederick II., which is too important to be passed over altogether.

Naples fell into the possession of the house of

Suabia, after it had been conquered by the Normans. Henry, son of Frederick Barbarossa, married Constance, daughter of King William II. Frederick II. was the issue of this marriage. Innocent, Honorius, and Gregory, in turns, were his instructors. Had it not been for the genius of Innocent, to whom the young man behaved with marked ingratitude, instead of becoming the greatest Emperor of the middle ages, he would probably have died in exile, or have fallen a speedy victim to the treachery of his enemies. But his genius and address, his subtlety and learning, encouraged at the Court of Innocent III., together with the protection of so powerful a Pontiff, gave him an opening for the display of his unusual ability. Frederick was emphatically a representative man. He represented the brute force, intellectual license, and moral depravity of the thirteenth century. His versatility, learning, and political finesse; his love of pleasure, of novelty, of free speculation; his courage, his perfidy, his chivalry, his cruelty, his arrogance, his superstition—all combined in one man—were specimens of the various vices and excellences of the subjects over whom he ruled. He was a thorough Italian. He appears to stand superior to the movements of his day, and while a typical representative of them, he bends them to his pleasure. His ambition, not content with four crowns, carried him through forty years of continual and aggressive war. His influence was greatly strengthened by the extinction of many great feudal houses in Italy, Tuscany, and

Romagna ; but at last he fell—as Henry did opposing Gregory, as Barbarossa did opposing Alexander—when proudly endeavouring to break the power of the Holy See.

His enthusiasm for poetry and letters, for music and art, was quite as remarkable as his ambition, and his taste for war. He spoke Latin, Italian, German, French, Greek, and Arabic, when, in all probability, not one in four hundred of his knights knew how to sign his name. He occupied many of his leisure hours in his choice library, poring over rolls of Greek and Arabic manuscripts, which he had carefully collected in the East. Through his brilliant Chancellor delle Vigne he announced that translations were to be made of many scarce and important works. He gave a code of enlightened laws to Sicily, and published for the first time the code for Germany, in the national tongue. He opened the University of Naples, as will appear later on ;—and shrewdly perceiving how the study of jurisprudence was damaging his influence at Bologna, he took the direction of political education into his own hands ; and, closing the University, constrained its ten thousand students to leave the town. So great a sympathy did he entertain for struggling genius, that he supported two hundred students at the University out of his own private purse, that they might thus acquire a tincture of philosophy.

But Frederick was a thoroughly worldly man. Learning did not lead him to the practices of Christianity. If he ever did seriously hold its teaching, his life amongst the infidels of the East appears to have upset his faith, and to have delivered him over to the influences of political materialism. He publicly declared that he possessed the right to determine definitively every question, human and divine. Some say that, no longer believing in the reality of a future life, he abandoned himself to all the licenses of sensuality. A legislator, a tyrant; generous, dissolute, courteous; a barbarian king under his tents in Lombardy in the North;—when in the South he slept away his time, with all the voluptuous softness of a Sultan, in his harems of Puglia and Sicily. He founded colonies of Saracens at Nocera. His castle, Foggia, was built in the Moorish style, was furnished according to Moorish taste, and was surrounded by Mohammedan mosques, schools, and bazaars. At his splendid court were collected together from Germany, Italy, and the East, the highest that could be found at that day, of courage, eloquence, and learning, the flower of chivalry, the depth of science, kings and warriors, troubadours and minstrels, wits and beauties—all that was gayest and brightest, all that was gorgeous and magnificent. Here were nurtured the grandchildren of Averroës, the most celebrated of Arabian philosophers. Here were to be seen swarthy Saracens, with their strange costume, standing guard; graceful Mamelukes, attentive in their silent service to every want; astrologers from Bagdad, with their loose garments and flowing beards; and

Jews, learned and sedate, the interpreters of the wisdom that lay concealed in precious manuscripts brought over from Arabia. Here, shocking indeed in a Christian country, but manifesting all the more the morality of those days, was Frederick's harem filled with prostitutes, living in the courtly magnificence of Eastern luxurious repose, waited upon by meek and gentle eunuchs, and ministering to the sensuality of a man who once longed for the hand of S. Elizabeth of Hungary, and offered his heart to S. Agnes of Bohemia.

Frederick was never more at ease than when in the company of the subtle, polished natives of the East. When in Palestine, he lived among the Mussulmans, and sent as a present to the Sultan a learned solution of difficult problems in mathematics and philosophy. The Sultan sent him, in return, an artful and curious instrument for indicating the movement of the stars. Whatever seemed capable of offering enjoyment to his mind in science, or to his body in sensuality, that Frederick II. made no scruple of acquiring, and of using with all the elegance and prodigality of a sinful man of genius.

He naturally surrounded himself with minds in harmony with his own. Michael Scott and Pietro delle Vigne, who is fitly placed in hell by Dante to exclaim:

> 'I' son colui che tenni ambo le chiavi
> Del cor di Federigo,'

were noted for the brilliancy of their talents, and the pagan tendencies of their minds. Cardinal Ubaldini, the Emperor's familiar friend, professed open materialism, and was accustomed to declare that, if he did happen to possess a soul, he would willingly lose it for the Ghibelines. His words carry all the more weight, inasmuch as he was the mouthpiece of a large section of *litterati*, who preferred the teachings of Epicurus or Pythagoras to the religion of Jesus Christ. Dante points to two Florentines—Farina and Cavalcanti—as types of thousands. The Ghibelines were noted materialists, and scoffers at Christianity; and in Florence the infidels formed a wild unruly sect. A poem, called the 'Descent of Paul into Hell,' alludes to a secret society, which was formed with the express purpose of expunging Christianity, and introducing the exploded obscenities of Paganism in its place. Then the overweening admiration of classical antiquity, political schemes for reconstructing pagan Rome, the ferment produced by the newly-discovered philosophy of the Greeks, the slavish imitation of pagan poets, and the biting satires of buffoons and troubadours—such as Rutebœuf, Jehan, and Renard—helped to spread amongst nobles, scholars, and general society an infidelity and licentiousness, which was a foretaste of the more elegant and polished wickedness of the renaissance.

Naples, being a Greek city, possessed from the first a school of liberal letters. The capacious mind of Frederick fixed upon a plan for turning the obscure private schools of the beautiful city into one grand academy for the two kingdoms,—for establishing, in one word, an University. His reasons for so doing, drawn out by his brilliant and unhappy secretary Delle Vigne, are worthy of his reputation for shrewdness and enlightenment. He declared that, from the earliest period of its history, Naples had been the mother and home of letters. He alluded to the salubrity of the air; and said that the city, lying with the sea on one side, and a stretch of land teeming with the richest produce of nature on the other, would offer the student the riches of both earth and water for his support.

Then he did not shrink from making use of his despotic power for facilitating his designs. He compelled the students of Puglia and Sicily to come to Naples, whether they would or no. For no one was permitted to study medicine or surgery except at Naples or Salerno. No degree could be conferred in any other seat of learning. No professor dared lecture in any other chair. The Moderators of the Provinces were under strict command to see that no student presumed to study anywhere in or out of the kingdom, except at the privileged University. The Captains of Sicily were strictly enjoined to send all young Sicilians to Naples. And, in 1226, the swarm of students which filled the city of Bologna had orders to make choice between Naples and Salerno.

On the other hand, the Emperor gave every encouragement to students to fall in with the Imperial commands. The Naples University was provided with first-class lawyers, doctors, and theologians. The Emperor remunerated with royal munificence the professors of every faculty; and, just as Ptolemy called to his aid Apion of Oasis, Aristarchus of Samothrace, and Dionysius of Thrace, so Frederick procured the services of celebrated foreign doctors, at enormous cost, to give as much *éclat* as possible to the lectures in the schools—such men, for instance, as Pietro d'Ibernia and Roberto di Varano, whom the Emperor calls *civilis scientiæ Professores, magnæ scientiæ, notæ virtutis, et fidelis experientiæ.* Pignatello, a name conveying little meaning to the general reader, the greatest canonist of that day, left Brindisi for Naples, and astonished matured and learned men by his masterly lectures on canon law. Theology was represented by the Franciscans and Dominicans till the profound Erasmus was forced from the repose of Monte Cassino into the whirl of the gay city, to pour forth his accumulated learning in the University chair of Theology. Then the students had many personal privileges. They could select for themselves the best houses, and could borrow money. And they were provided, like the citizens themselves, with the necessaries, if not the luxuries of life. Then they were treated with exceptional respect, they were responsible only to the University, and were independent of all tribunals except their own.

The prosperity of the University had its effect upon the prosperity of the town. As the Emperor often resided here with his court, Naples became the fountain of fashion as well as the seat of wisdom. The establishment here of the Gran Corte—the highest tribunal of judicature in the two kingdoms—added to the general *éclat*. Here it was that Pietro delle Vigne, the brilliant orator, and Thaddeus of Sessa, who gained unenviable notoriety at the Council of Lyons, and Roffred Beneventum, celebrated for his Treatise on Legal Discipline, by their exceptional abilities, acquired a lasting fame.

By the time S. Thomas arrived at Naples, the University, which was hardly old enough to have a history, had undergone a revolution. This was brought about by the industry of the Franciscan friars. The Minorite professors, as has been said before, when Frederick was absent in the Holy Land, industriously circulated a report that he had been carried off by plague. This report gave occasion to the rising of the enemies of the Emperor in different parts of the kingdom. On the return of Frederick these Franciscan professors, together with the Dominicans and Cassinese, were turned out of their chairs, and driven from the kingdom. Naturally, other professors had to be found to supply their place; and this new staff was in activity when S. Thomas first became connected with the University. Three of them are known to have had relations with the Saint. There was Pietro Martini, Professor of Humanities and Rhetoric; Pietro d'Ibernia, the Chancellor of the University, who lectured in Philosophy; and the profound Erasmus, the Benedictine, under whom, if we may follow Tosti, S. Thomas commenced the study of Theology.

It is more probable that S. Thomas lived with the

Benedictine monks, than that he lived in lodgings, when he first went to Naples. It seems more probable that his parents should station him in a religious house, than that they should leave him, like another Daniel in Babylon, or another Tobias in Nineveh. It is a little curious that neither the ingenious Touron nor the modern Bareille throws out a hint at such a probability. Touron speaks strongly of the corruption of Naples, he touches beautifully on the piety of Theodora, and thinks well of Landulf, and of Abbot Sinnebald. And he must have been aware that S. Thomas was bound up, not only by relationship and old tradition, but by the ambition of his mother, with the Cassinese. And, finally, he could not have been ignorant that there were two Benedictine Monasteries in connection with Monte Cassino at Naples, viz. S. Severino and S. Demetrio, both of which would joyfully have welcomed the nephew of Abbot Sinnebald into their community. That Theodora would have thrown up the darling project of her heart, when she saw her way to realise it, by keeping her boy in connection with the Benedictines;—that his father would suffer him to be exposed to the contagion of vice in the city, when he could live in a religious house;—or that the Saint himself, with his quiet disposition and antecedents, would not have done his best to remain with the children of S. Benedict, to say the least of it, is scarcely probable. The supposition that he lived at S. Demetrio, or San Severino, tends to solve all difficulties; the supposition that he lived in lodgings tends to create objections which seem to offer no solution.

His biographers, unfortunately, give us hardly any information with regard to the Saint's life during this early and important portion of his career. But there are two statements of Malvenda that contain more information than many a long history. It was the custom for the students, after the professor had delivered his lecture, to present themselves at a stated time, and deliver what they had heard before their companions in the schools. By this means they exercised their memory, and had an opportunity of manifesting their ability. It could not be expected that the young students, in these repetitions, would reproduce the lectures they had heard with the same ability with which they were delivered; especially when they had been composed by such professors as lectured in the University of Naples.

It was young Aquino's duty, when the time came round, to reproduce the lectures of his professor. He not only reproduced them with the same perfection with which they were delivered—which would have been surprising enough—but he surpassed the original compositions, and repeated them with greater depth of thought and greater lucidity of method than the learned professor himself was enabled to command. The second statement follows as a necessary consequence from the first, viz. that the fame of this extraordinary boy spread amongst all the schools connected with the University, and throughout the city of Naples.

Whilst Naples was ringing with the praises of young Aquino, the gentle youth himself was occupied with more serious and important thoughts. Had he been a young man without much breadth or penetration, in all human probability he would have lived and died a Benedictine monk. But his mind was far too clear, and his judgment far too accurate to be swayed either by the prejudices of his parents or by the pressure of circumstances. A youth who was a more brilliant expositor of truth than its professors, who could enunciate it with greater lucidity than masters of philosophic method, would surely, during his stay in the gay centre of Southern Italy, have observed with interest the various phases of the period in which he lived. Men of ordinary understanding take little account of the huge levers that move the world, and experience little temptation to grapple with them as instruments of good, or to master them as powers of destruction. They are made for a work fitting their compass; and their hearts are not stirred, because their vision is narrowed within the range of their intellectual capacity. Such men are full of usefulness, and make up the staple of labouring humanity in the world and in the Church. But they are not the originators of great undertakings; nor the men to watch keenly the great movements of the world, to master them and guide them to great results.

But Thomas must have been sensible of his power; and when looking on the world's great energies for evil or for good fighting fiercely for the mastery, he must have asked his heart this question: 'Am I to gird myself to the struggle, or am I to live in solitude on the mountain?'

S. Thomas must have seen that an organised power alone could meet the world; and that the Church alone, out of the fulness of her own life, had created influences which had broken the enemy to pieces, and had left her more triumphant than ever, because the heroine of another marvellous success. In civilising the Northmen, who came from their forests into the fertile plains of the South, S. Benedict was the instrument made use of by the Almighty. Young Aquino saw what an immense power monasticism had been in the world which was passing away. He could trace the influence of men of solitude, who, when brought by accident amidst the conflicts of active life, proved to the world that they had not ventured a life of loneliness in vain. He could follow the track of silent men who had gone down the mountain-side, and had left at their deaths tokens of their labours worthy of their origin, in spite of Goth, Hun, Tartar, or Lombard—splendid cloisters, learned schools, precious libraries, stately churches, and a civilised and happy people, living in cultivated and fertile plains, where they had found wild morass and impenetrable forest, robbers, snakes, and wild beasts.

But he also saw that the world had changed. The efforts of the reformers of solitude and contemplation had not been able to direct its course. Citeaux and Clairvaux had done a work indeed, but it was not the work of directing the stream of human thought. They had not perceptibly affected the world. The old methods seemed to have dropped out of use. The principle of *quies* had done its work for a time. Monte Cassino and its glories were almost visions of the past. Men would no longer fly the world, and bury themselves in monastic retreats. They would not be content with the silent monotony of the cloister, and take wisdom from the lips of men whose principal conversation was with nature and nature's God. Some great flow had entered into the channels of human life. Discovery and travel and enterprise excited the imagination, and men loved activity better than silent thought. They congregated in towns, and the teaching of the monastery gave way to the excitement and uproar of university life. Meditation and singing psalms, and long vigils, were little suited to the nervous and almost fanatical temper of the growing world. What, then, Thomas would ask himself, is the instrument or the organism created to oppose the powers of the world?

The Order of S. Francis and the Order of S. Dominic were created by the Church for resisting the mighty pressure: the former, whose characteristics of poverty and love, the latter, whose specialties of eloquence and learning, were to manifest the perfection of Christianity in a world full of the pomp of riches, the fire of passion, the secret canker of misbelief, and the maddening influences of pantheistic mysticism. Fortunately for humanity, those passions which were most sensitive to the action of fanatics were no less responsive to the eloquence of men, who, despising the comforts of life, and abhorring the aberrations of philosophy, aimed at raising up humanity from the anarchy of passion, and the idolatry of pride.

These two Orders had chairs in the University of Naples when S. Thomas was surprising the students with his talents. The Order of S. Dominic seems to have been particularly flourishing. No doubt young Aquino was struck by the devotedness and ability of the Dominican professors. Besides counteracting the evils which were raging in society, the Order was charged with the heroism of an institution in its primitive fervour, whose founder had not long been taken to his reward. Thomas, no doubt, had heard this man's history, and had found in it much that fascinated a mind so noble and so gentle as his own. The special scope of the Order, its love for learning, its active ministrations to humanity while still retaining the self-restraint of solitaries and the humility of monks, must have struck a new chord, or an old chord in a new fashion, in the heart of the Saint. Anyhow, he soon became intimate with the fathers of the Order. Many an earnest talk he had, no doubt, with his dear familiar friend, John a Sancto Facundo; many a discussion on the merits of the old method of contemplation, and of these spiritual knight-errants who mixed in the dust and joined in the battle of active life.

The young man was often seen in the Church of S.

Dominic, after his companions had retired to their cells to rest, and when gay young men were wasting their energies away in the wicked city. The Dominicans, perceiving how deeply he was impressed, watched him with a lively interest, and prayed fervently that so much talent and so much promise might find the most favourable field for its display. Hundreds, famed for their genius, many of high lineage and alluring prospects, had been seduced by the heavenly influences that radiated from the great Order of S. Dominic. Why not Thomas of Aquin also? He was a Benedictine; but so was S. Dominic a Canon Regular of S. Augustine. Once, one brother, who had employed himself in watching the Saint, returned full of admiration to his brethren, declaring that he had seen the face of young Aquino, like that of another Stephen, darting forth, on all sides, rays of supernatural light, as he prayed before the great altar in S. Dominic's.

The issue was what might have been anticipated. S. Thomas expressed a wish to abandon the monks, and join the friars. To the stability, largeness, and self-control of the Benedictine he was going to add the learning, eloquence, and judicial steadiness of a Dominican. If the Dominicans were raised up to combat the special errors of those days, S. Thomas was providentially raised up amongst the Dominicans for reducing to practice the perfection of S. Dominic's spirit. It was by a special Providence that the Saint became a Benedictine, the Providence was no less special that turned him into a Dominican. He petitioned for the habit. His request was granted. Thomas of Aquino became a brother of the Friars Preachers.

CHAPTER IV.

S. FRANCIS AND S. DOMINIC.

In the middle ages, in spite of the power of her enemies, the Church had reached the topmost height of social eminence and worldly splendour. Never before, in the eyes of the world, had she appeared more full of vigour, and never before had she used that vigour with more triumphant success. But she had her human element. The vast riches which had been accumulated by the monastic bodies, the wealth of the secular clergy spread throughout Europe, became a source of envy to the laity, who began to long more after the temporal goods which she possessed than after her spiritual ministrations. Pride, and simony amongst the clergy, and other scandals, which godly men bewailed, held out to thousands of prying eyes, sharpened by hunger and fanaticism, arguments which were difficult to answer, when once they had been impressed upon the popular mind. The Popes had constantly directed their energies to upset abuses. From Gregory VII. downwards, they were ever striving to purify and elevate the mass of corruption which had encrusted itself about the sanctuary. Holy men saw, with eyes illuminated by the

Holy Ghost, the dangers which threatened the Church, and, with great effort, attempted to renew the early days of Pentecost. But the steady pressure of the tide seemed almost too heavy for Popes, councils, and reformers, till Dominic and Francis created two enormous instruments for elevating the Christian world out of its entanglements, into a more healthy and a freer atmosphere.

The Orders of S. Dominic and S. Francis were so intimately bound up with our Saint, that to omit touching upon them would render it very difficult fully to appreciate his life.

S. Francis was eminently a child of the religion of the thirteenth century. He was the son of a merchant of Assisi, and was brought up by his parents, according to Cellano, in carelessness and godlessness. Their neglect of his moral training was not long producing its fruits. He soon became famous amongst the dissipated men about town. If the young coxcombs of the period wanted a leader in their carousals, a comic singer in their boisterous meetings, or a rollicking boon-companion, who could spend with the best of them, and surpass them all in the daintiness of his attire, Francis was the man. Of all the dissipated young men of Assisi, Francis had the reputation of being the most dissipated. He gave himself up to this kind of life till five-and-twenty years of age. About this period he was struck down by a terrible sickness. He had to keep his bed, and could no longer indulge in his favourite sports and dissipations. During this sickness, a great change was wrought in his mind. When he got a little better, and was able, with the aid of a crutch, to totter to the door, he was excessively surprised to find that the beauties of nature, which formerly had had such a charm for him, seemed to have lost all their attractions. He not only felt contempt for worldly things, but he began to feel contempt for those who valued them. This was the beginning of his extraordinary conversion.

About this period he had a dream, in which he saw his father's house filled with innumerable shields, and swords and spears, and other engines of war. This imagination affected him so deeply that he retired into a crypt close by, and prayed to God for light. Here he remained some considerable time in great dejection and uncertainty. At length he was suddenly possessed by an extraordinary seizure of light and joy. He came forth from his hiding-place exulting, and was inebriated with so overwhelming an effusion of delight, that he could not prevent his feelings from pouring themselves out upon the first person he met. Being asked if he would marry, 'Marry!' he exclaimed, radiant with glee, 'yes, the most beautiful of women, and filled with purest wisdom.' For true religion, say his biographers, was to be his immaculate spouse. Then he rode off, sold his horse and clothes, and, hurrying to S. Damasus', offered the money to the priest for repairing the church. The priest refused the offer. Francis flung the money out of the window, and then buried himself in a dark pit, fearing the anger of his father. Here he lay a whole month. At the end of this period, so great a courage was wrought in him that he came forth, and offered himself, freely, to the insults and passionate reproaches of his persecutors. The people of the town, on seeing him so emaciated and changed, thought that his head was turned, and that he had gone mad. They hunted him with shouts and yells, and pelted him with mud and stones. But Francis, his heart brimming with that strange supernatural joy, gave thanks to God. Next, his father throttled him, and having flogged him unmercifully, cast him into a fetid dungeon. His mother set him free. And again the extraordinary young man presented himself before his father, and declared that he would bear with joy any ill-treatment he thought fit to inflict upon him. Finding that he could not move the youth, the father thought to secure his property; so he hurried him off to the Bishop, to make an act of formal resignation. Francis accompanied his father with the greatest delight. Before the Bishop could say a word, he had stripped himself stark naked, and in this condition stood before his judge, intoxicated with the idea of abandoning all he had for Christ. The Bishop here saw the finger of God, and throwing his cloak about the young man, embraced him tenderly.

The next thing that we hear of him is of his singing joyfully through the woods songs and hymns in praise of God. Whilst thus engaged he was set upon by thieves, who demanded brutally of him, 'Who are you?' 'I am the herald of the Mighty King,' he replied, singing out to them with transports of joy; upon which they took him, and beat him, and hurled him into a deep ditch, full of drifted snow, and shouted down at him, 'Lie there, then, thou rough herald of God!' When they had departed Francis got out, shook himself free, and set forth as before, singing away through the woods his cheerful melodies to God. Next he disguised himself, and did scullion's work in a monastery. Then he tended lepers, a class he once so greatly loathed, and kissed their miserable sores and wounds with loving transport. He repaired churches. He dressed like the hermits of S. Augustine. But hearing in church one day the Gospel which tells of the Apostles abandoning all things to follow Christ, he was set on fire with a new delight, and exclaimed, 'This is what I want, this is the very thing I seek! This I yearn after with all the intensity of my heart!' With incredible joy he cast away his shoes and his stick, and putting on a rough tunic, commenced a life of utter poverty and self-contempt.

Now he began preaching with intense vehemence, with wonderful simplicity. With all the fire of his beating heart, he spoke of God, of Christ, of peace, of poverty. He always began with the words *Dominus det vobis pacem*, for at this period the world was filled with factions and war. A poor idiot first joined him, then Ægidius and Philip, and four others. They often beheld him rapt in ecstasy. In one of those states he saw, like S. Paul, what no human language could express, was assured of pardon, and saw in vision the future spread of his mighty Order. He now sent his disciples two and two to preach penance, peace, and remission of sins. Eager multitudes pressed around them; many joined the Order. Villages and towns went forth to listen to him. He was regarded as a visitant from another world. Men were impressed by his deep earnestness, his intense self-immolation, and his vehement impetuosity of Divine affection. We are assured that the whole face of society was changed by the fiery simplicity of the extraordinary eloquence welling up from that large and loving heart.

He called his brethren *Fratres Minores*, to remind them that they were last of all. Their practice of poverty was most severe. They slept in caves and pits, and joyfully partook of the hospitality of lepers and outcasts. Their spirits overflowed with supernatural joy when, in imitation of Christ, they had an opportunity of suffering chains, and prisons, and smitings. They were ever meek, gentle, and filled with guileless charity. Their prayers were simple and earnest, their austerities terrific. In temptation they would cast themselves, in mid-winter, into ponds floating with broken ice. Their food was rarely cooked, often it was mixed with ashes. On one occasion Francis, being ill, indulged in a piece of chicken. Of this he afterwards bitterly repented. Putting a rope round his neck, he bade a brother lead him through the town, and obliged him like a town-crier to cry out: 'Look at this glutton, who has been caught eating chicken on the sly!' He commanded the brothers to call him names, and when they did so he was transported with delight. He would preach to the birds of the air, and remind them all what God had done for them, then he would dismiss them with the sign of the cross, and they would fly away obedient to his voice. He would command the swallows, who were building their nests, and twittering and circling round him, to stop and listen to his word. They remained motionless and attentive till he dismissed them with incredible joy. He loved nature with all the tenderness of a little child. His prayer sums up his whole character.

'O Most High Almighty, Good Lord God,' he says, 'to Thee belong praise, glory, honour, and all blessing. Praised be my Lord God, with all His creatures, and especially our brother the sun, who brings us the day, and who brings us the light: fair is he, and shining with a very great splendour. O Lord, he signifies to us Thee.

'Praised be my Lord for our sister the moon, and for the stars, the which He has set clear and lovely in the heavens.

'Praised be my Lord for our brother the wind, and for air and clouds, calm and all weather, by the which Thou upholdest in life all creatures.

'Praised be my Lord for our sister the water, who

is very serviceable unto us, and humble, and precious, and clean.

'Praised be my Lord for our brother the fire, through whom Thou givest us light in darkness; and he is bright and pleasant, and very mighty and strong.

'Praised be my Lord for our mother the earth, which doth sustain us and keep us, and bringeth forth divers fruits, and flowers of many colours, and grass.

'Praised be my Lord for all those who pardon one another for His love's sake, and who endure weakness and tribulation: blessed are they who peaceably shall endure: for Thou, O Most Highest, shalt give them a crown.

'Praised be my Lord for our sister the death of the body: from whom no man escapeth. Woe to him who dieth in mortal sin! Blessed are they who are found walking by Thy most holy will, for the second death shall have no power to do them harm.

'Praise ye and bless ye the Lord, and give thanks to Him, and serve Him with great humility.'

So inebriated was he with the love of Jesus that he could not steadily pronounce the Holy Name. Such was the passionate lover of poverty, the ardent disciple of the passion of Christ. A creature full of vehement, sovereign devotion to the folly of the Cross, and to the shame. His life was profound forgetfulness of self, and unquenchable charity, and unutterable heroism, beyond all words of mine to express. In his soul and in his body he bore the marks of the fruit of Christ's passion. He poured himself out to God, and he poured himself out on men, drawing them with the cords of Adam to peace, penance, and the love of Christ. No wonder that in a few years (1219) he collected round him five thousand brothers from all quarters of the world, whose heroic lives of penance, prayer, and gentleness, did a work which no other influence of the day could possibly have accomplished. Thirty-five years later there were eight hundred convents, and at least twenty thousand religious belonging to the Order; a century later there were one hundred and fifty thousand friars. Such men as these, filled with so great a fire, would, of the very stones, if possible, raise up children to Abraham. Poverty, prayer, and preaching, these were the instruments in the hands of detachment and of love for regenerating the world.

And what the Franciscans did principally amongst the people at large that S. Dominic did for the higher and more educated classes.

The founder of the Dominicans, whom Innocent III. beheld in a vision, supporting with his shoulders the tottering walls of the Lateran Basilica, had only been dead twenty years when S. Thomas joined the Order. His birth, like that of S. Thomas and S. Bernard, was preceded by influences of a supernatural character. His mother, Joanna d'Aza, dreamt that she carried in her womb a hound with a flaming brand between his teeth. So terrified was she by this dream that she often threw herself on the tomb of the Benedictine, S. Dominic of Silos, and implored him to protect her in her desolation.

In return for the comfort she experienced, she called her boy, after the holy Benedictine, Dominic. Sprung of the bluest blood of the Guzmans, Dominic summed up in his character the noblest and fairest traits for which the Spanish nobility are justly famed. His creative fantasy loved to explore the highest region of ideal chivalry, living in a world of poetry, and burning with high resolves of startling enterprises. With a heart gentle as a woman's, and elevated by the most careful education, his will was excessively tenacious, and of unalterable resolution. He seems to have embraced, within the wide circumference of his elevated character, all that is most perfect in the dispositions of either sex. When seven years old he was confided to his uncle, the Archpriest of Gumiel d'Izan. At fifteen he went to Palencia, the most celebrated university in Spain, and studied with great ardour and success literature, eloquence, philosophy, and theology. His heart overflowed with singular generosity. He created a sensation amongst his companions by selling his clothes, and even the books annotated with his own hand, to relieve the poor during a famine. He dried the tears of a woman, who came to lament to him that her brother had been dragged into captivity by the Moors, by offering at once to take his place. At five-and-twenty he was induced by the Bishop of Osma to join the Canons Regular. He threw himself into his new life with his characteristic earnestness. He passed his time in contemplation and penance, in preaching, in studying the Epistles of S. Paul, in turning over with delight the pages of Cassian, and in bringing about stricter discipline in the somewhat relaxed observance of the Convent.

But the energies of such a man were not destined to be confined within the compass of an obscure convent of Augustinians. Alfonsus VIII., of Castille, wished his son to marry a Danish Princess. Don Diego de Azevedo, the successor of Martin in the see of Osma, was intrusted with the delicate mission of arranging the preliminaries of the alliance, and took Dominic with him through the South of France. There he saw the fearful ulcer that was eating into the heart of the Church in the heresy of the Albigenses, which has been already touched upon. Dominic felt that a single man was but as a drop in the ocean in the midst of such a vast and organised corruption. Man may be met by man, but a system only can oppose a system. A religious institution, combining the poverty of the first disciples of Christ with eloquence and learning, alone would stand a chance of success in working a regeneration. The poor men of Lyons and the followers of Waldo, he was well aware, would simply mock at men who came preaching to them the poverty of Jesus, in the trappings of worldly wealth; and the starved ascetic, who in his fantastic studies had arrived at scientific heresy, could not be overthrown, he felt convinced, without a profounder knowledge of theology than was possessed by the majority of clergymen at that period. The pomp of the ecclesiastical nobility, which was a scandal enough to make earnest men turn sick, is illustrated forcibly by the conduct of the Cistercians and the Papal Legate. At the synod of Montpellier (1206), these men bitterly lamented the ill success of their perilous mission. S. Dominic, with that freedom with which Christ had made him free, told them out, that the number of their attendants, the splendour of their costumes, and the magnificence of their equipages and horses, would ever stand in the way of the simplicity of Gospel truth ;—that they ought to begin by practising what they preached, and that the heretics had been seen making a mockery of those Apostles, who came amongst them on the backs of gallant horses to preach Jesus Christ, who was poor, and who walked on foot. The monks and Legate dismissed their servants, got rid of their gay horses, and adopted a greater simplicity of life.

It is not necessary to remind the reader of the struggles which took place in France. That treachery and cruelty went hand in hand, is to be expected of men fighting in a cause which stirs up the keenest and most violent passions of mankind. The Saint, through all that time, conducted himself with that gentleness, charity, and courage, which became so well the noblest soul of the noblest of Saints. By his devotedness to the poverty of Christ, he manifested the true spirit of the Gospel to those acting a horrid parody upon it. By his high courage and large charity, he contrasted the true religion with the cruel fanaticism of men devoured with spiritual pride and ill-regulated piety. By his eloquence, his tender heart, his intense compassion for sorrow, and by the exquisite refinement of his cultivated nature, he converted into friends those whom he had not the good fortune to convert into Christians. Amidst all the fire and fanaticism of that time, it was always said of Dominic that his charity and compassion were never for a moment eclipsed by any less amiable influence in his nature. To say this of a man under these circumstances, is to say simply that he was a saint. Being asked what would be his conduct if threatened by the enemy with death, he replied with the boldness of inspired chivalry, 'I would beg them to kill me by degrees, that thus I might witness the more fully to the truth which I profess!'

In 1215 there were sixteen men in the little institute—eight Frenchmen, six Spaniards, one Portuguese, and an Englishman. In five years there were sixty convents of the Order spread throughout Western Europe.

The greatest wisdom was shown in the construction of the rule. The society was divided into three parts, two for men and women engaged in the convent, the third for men and women living in secular employments. The third order was of immense service to religion. By its means S. Dominic was enabled to touch and transform—what so much required touching and transforming—the souls of persons dwelling in the world. By joining them in holy union, not so severe as to interfere with their domestic duties, and yet sufficiently strict to remind them what they were, he elevated them, and strung them together in the interests of religion. Men and women of every class, from polished ladies of the first courts in Europe, to the ignorant and poor, were here bound together in a spiritual sodality, which seemed to partake of the sanctity of monastic life. S. Dominic's experiences at Osma, and the requirements of the new institute, induced him to found his rule on that of S. Augustine. Poverty was enforced with great severity. The brothers lived on alms. Like the children of S. Francis, they were mendicants. The principle of *quies*, which gave the monk a permanent habitation, and insured to him a resting place which he loved more tenderly than anything else after Christ, was not in keeping with the new principle of motion. That his children might be ready at a moment's notice, S. Dominic was excessively strict on the observance of holy poverty. If they had nothing to leave, they would have little to regret. On one occasion, a brother was sent on a journey without money. He complained to the Saint. Dominic flung himself on his knees before the brother, and with tears gathering in his eyes, implored him to go forth bravely, and trust in God. At times the community would sit down to an empty board. On one occasion, whilst they were meekly and silently sitting at the bare table, Dominic prayed over it. Instantly, two youths, whom none of those present had ever seen, walked up the refectory, and divided amongst the astonished friars wine and bread of such a quality, that they rose from table filled with a species of supernatural strength they had never experienced before.

They prayed, and studied, and fasted; their Church-services were simple; they lay on hard beds; and the very manner of their travelling manifested the tenor of their lives.

After its approval by Honorius, the Order spread abroad with great rapidity. Men of high birth, accustomed to living in the lap of luxury, men versed in many kinds of learning, listened with rapture to the eloquence of Dominic, and breaking up, and abandoning the traditions of their lives, bound themselves in the holy vows of religion. With an eye steadily fixed upon his object, Dominic selected the men of greatest promise amongst his followers, and sent them to the universities to take degrees, to mature their scholarship, and to conduct schools. His forecasting wisdom is evident in his fixing the three centres of his Order in the three most flourishing university towns. From Rome, the capital of authority; from Paris, the capital of theology; and from Bologna, the capital of jurisprudence, radiated the activity of scholars, saints, and confessors. The fame of the Friars Preachers soon spread, when men of mark who had left the world entered into it again—with their cords, and hoods, and shaven crowns, and full of spiritual knowledge, and of supernatural eloquence. Brother Reginald, on his return from the holy sepulchre, entranced the citizens of Bologna by his extraordinary gifts: 'I see the heavens open,' he exclaimed on one occasion, 'I see the heavens open—the doors are yawning wide to receive all who would gaze upon the majesty of its glory! The heavens, I tell you, stand open wide; why do you delay?' He then spoke with so great persuasiveness on the scope and object of his Order, that priests, students, and professors, and even lawyers, who are not often carried away, there and then abandoned their occupations, and entreated to be allowed to take the habit.

Some, however, who entered the society with eagerness, soon became as eager to depart as they had been to join it. Two men, for instance, remarkable for the breadth of their attainments, joined the little community. After a while, becoming wearied of restraint, they said that they could stay no longer. This was a heavy blow. B. Reginald called a Chapter, and announced the calamity to the assembled friars. His discourse was often interrupted by sobs and tears, as he stood in the midst with his eyes fixed on heaven, expressing his unshaken confidence in God. Then Brother Clarus, who had been a professor at Bologna, offered to speak a few consoling words. As he was beginning, to the surprise of all, Master Roland of Cremona, a famous professor of philosophy at Bologna, burst into the Chapter-room, threw himself at the feet of Reginald, and implored to be received. Reginald, being stunned at first, at length recovered himself, took off his own scapular, and, with joy almost too great for his control, clothed the professor in the garb of a Dominican; then the sacristan hurried off and began ringing a noisy peal on the church bells, the community broke forth with the *Veni Creator Spiritus*, and the church was quickly filled with an astonished crowd, who, when they had heard of this singular *grazia* or intervention, set the whole town in a violent commotion of joy and admiration. To crown all, the two professors who had cast aside the habit, with tears streaming from their eyes, and with hands stretched to heaven, begged on their knees in the Capitulum to be received once more amongst the brethren. This is but a specimen of the temper of those strange ages of emotion, so full of high aspirations, intense faith, and overwhelming passion.

John of Germany was General when S. Thomas entered the Order 1239-1254), and a constellation of famous men shone with a steady light from the *Corona Fratrum.* In Germany there was Albertus Magnus—a wonder to posterity, on account of the vast circumference of his knowledge, and the extraordinary versatility of his elastic mind. Hugh of S. Caro edified all France by his sanctity, and was consulted as a heavenly oracle; —and, whilst Peter of Verona pierced his enemies with the lance of controversy, John of Vicenza electrified Lombardy by the thrilling effects of his powers of speech. Men not only listened to him with delight, but consulted him in their most delicate affairs. In all matters of difference between individuals, families, and states, John was sure to be consulted, and was sure to set things right. At his word prisons were opened, and enmities, which for hundreds of years had been handed down as traditionary in families, melted by the heat of his charity into lasting friendships. Cities, Kings, and Popes sought his counsel, and were sure to find in it a solution of the difficulties they had not been able to solve before.

Many Dominicans became martyrs amongst the Albigenses. In Spain the Order flourished exceedingly. S. Hyacinth was an extraordinary missioner—Poland, Bohemia, both Russias, Livonia, Sweden, Denmark, the coasts of the Black Sea, the sea-board of Asia Minor, and the islands of the Grecian Archipelago, were studded with convents which marked the progress of his missionary enterprise. His strange supernatural power converted Mussulmans, drew barbarians round the Cross of Christ, and established schools and convents in Pomerania, and along the shores of the Baltic. Within twenty years after S. Dominic's death, the Gospel had been preached in almost every country. In the following century it spread still more widely. During the middle ages, the pulses of the mighty heart of the great Order were felt throughout the whole of the known world, from the north-west coast of Africa, to the great water-courses of Asia; from Fez and Morocco, as far as Greenland. A party of Dutch sailors were struck with astonishment, when, at the beginning of the seventeenth century, touching on the coast of Greenland, they found that men clothed in the white wool of S. Dominic had been preaching, praying, and studying in that inhospitable region for upwards of four hundred years. It was through Dominican influence at the Court of Spain that Columbus obtained the ships in which he made the discovery of the new world; and they were Dominicans who followed upon the footsteps of the enterprising subjugators of that vast continent, and planted the standard of the Cross wherever the others had been victorious with the sword. At the commencement of the sixteenth century, they colonised the East and West Indies. In 1550, in the Peninsula of Malacca and the adjacent islands the Dominicans had eighteen convents, and made sixty thousand converts. Then they penetrated into Siam, and were the first Christian missioners who set foot in China,—where they established schools, and built churches. They had already settled in S. Domingo, Mexico, and the Floridas. In 1526 they sent twelve brothers to New Spain, where they soon had a hundred houses and convents. In 1540, they possessed in New Granada sixty houses and churches. In Chili they had forty convents. The Philippine Isles, Mozambique, and the Eastern Coast of Africa, were under Dominican influence, while at Manilla and Lima they established universities for the education of the higher classes. Within a hundred years (1234 to 1334), the Order could number thirteen thousand three hundred and seventy martyrs.

To this marvellous activity corresponded an immense influence over the minds of men. The Dominicans played an important part in questions of science and religion; and ever aimed at purifying and making free the social positions of mankind. Bartholomew de las Casas was a Dominican. Four thousand writers of distinction were brothers of the Order. Antoninus wrote the first complete history of the world. The Golden Legend of Jacobus de Voragine has been translated into every language of the West. The church at Florence of Santa Maria Novella, where Michael Angelo daily prayed, and which for the severe purity of its style has received the name of Sposa, was built by Fra Sisto, Fra Ristoro, and Fra Giovanni, three Dominican brothers. Fra Angelico, who could never paint Christ and His Blessed Mother without tears gathering into his eyes, nor would consent to paint them in any other position than on his knees, was a Dominican. Michael Angelo declared that Giovanni da Fiesole's picture of the Annunciation must have been copied from a vision in the skies. Fra Bartolomeo and Benedetto, as well as Fra Angelico, were brothers of the Order; while S. Catherine of Sienna, and S. Rose of Lima, were under Dominican control.

To sum up: in six hundred years (by 1825), there had been seventy Cardinals, four hundred and sixty Bishops, four Presidents of General Councils, twenty-five Legates *a Latere*, eighty Apostolic Nuncios, four Popes, and a Prince-Elector of the Holy Roman Empire, belonging to the Order of S. Dominic. Such is a rapid sketch—these are the mere *cartoni*—of that religious system which, in its days of energy and expansion, captivated the mind and imagination of young Thomas of Aquino.

The historians of the Saint give a glowing description of his reception to the habit. The news of his clothing soon spread throughout the town. The Dominicans made the ceremony as public as possible. From a very early hour, the Church of S. Dominic was 'inundated by an enormous crowd, amongst which might be observed persons of the highest distinction in the city.' When the hour arrived, Thomas, in presence of a great multitude, advanced between two rows of friars—whose eyes must have beamed with delight as he passed before them—and received from the Superior, Fra Tomaso d'Agni di Lentino, the badges of penance and subjection.

The sentiments awakened in the breasts of the beholders were anything but harmonious. Whilst the friars were filled with joy at so signal a mark of Divine favour in their regard, more worldly-minded men did not shrink from saying that the reception of one so young, who had so brilliant a career before him, amounted almost to sharp practice. Some admired a spirit which could exchange the fascinations of life, and the hopes of the future, for the scanty fare and rough garments of a Mendicant friar. Others thought it a great pity that one so accomplished, so well connected, and so virtuous, should throw away his gifts in practising poverty and blind obedience. Many considered the step rash and inconsiderate. There were not wanting those who blamed the Prior, and were highly indignant at the diplomacy by which the cunning *frati* had entrapped the young fellow into the Order. Doubtless, the gossip of the world then was something like the gossip of the world now—very flowing, very flippant, and very contradictory.

CHAPTER V.

TRIALS OF VOCATION.

IT may be imagined that the family of S. Thomas felt little gratified when they heard of the clothing. The report of the ceremony was not long reaching Rocca Sicca. Theodora first heard of it from the lamentations of her vassals, who had seen the young Count dressed up like a Dominican friar, and at once returned home to bewail the disgrace which had fallen on the family. She forthwith hurried off to Naples, accompanied by a large retinue. Some say she was excessively angry with her son for joining the Mendicants; others, that she wished to encourage him in a vocation which she considered had come direct from heaven. The former opinion is the more probable one. Theodora had already made up her mind about the will of God in her son's regard. She had reasons in abundance, human and divine, for making him a Benedictine. And it is hardly to be supposed that she hurried to Naples *cum gaudio*, as Tocco has it, to confirm her boy in a state of life about which she had not been consulted; the first notion of which she received from the gossip of her servants; and which would simply be the death-blow to her cherished aspirations.

It is pretty clear what the Dominicans thought; for, no sooner did they hear that Theodora was on her way to Naples, than they hurried the boy off—some affirm, at his own request—by a different route, with several companions, to Rome. And so greatly did they fear his meeting the excited Countess, that the party had orders to avoid the ordinary road, and to travel through Terracina and Anagni.

The Dominicans were established in Rome during the time of S. Dominic. The old church of S. Sixtus II., in which lay the relics of six martyr-popes, must have attracted the attention of the Saint. It stood opposite the gigantic ruins of the Baths of Caracalla, and at the foot of the Celian Mount, upon the Appian Way. The convent attached to the church must have been ample, for S. Dominic, by his eloquence, in the space of a few months had filled it with a hundred disciples. Here it was that he worked some of his most famous miracles—raising the dead, multiplying bread and wine, and bringing angels in human form into the presence of the community.

But the Dominicans had left S. Sixtus for Santa Sabina before the time of S. Thomas. Honorius III., desiring to establish a community of nuns at the convent of S. Sixtus, offered to the friars the convent of S. Sabina, situated close to his palace on the Aventine.

The church seems to have been founded, as early as the fifth century, by an Illyrian priest, in the Pontificate of Celestine I. It stood boldly on the highest verge of the Aventine, and overlooked that classic spot, where Horatius Cocles, with a prowess which immortalised his name, defended Rome against Porsenna. The church was built on the plan of the old Basilicas. Two rows of ancient pillars, supporting a plain roof, divided the church into three naves, each terminated by an altar. Here, under the high altar, rested the relics of S. Sabina, who had suffered under Adrian. Close at hand stood the palace of the Savelli, occupied by Honorius III. The Pontiff made over a portion of this noble residence to the friars. From the windows of this palace convent, the eye stretched over Rome, and, passing over towers and domes, rested on the Vatican Basilica. Two flights of steps led to the city, one running to the Tiber, the other to a corner of the Palatine, near the church of S. Anastasia.

The convent, which had been a workshop of saints, was, even in S. Thomas's time, full of touching reminiscences. Here Hyacinth and Ceslas, two of the most successful missioners who ever laboured for the love of God, received their inspirations of devotedness and sacrifice. Here Henry of Moravia, and Hermann of Germany, lived, and studied, and prayed. Here it was that 'Mary, in the person of Reginald,' once Doctor of Law in Paris, and Dean of S. Argnan d'Orleans, 'girt the reins of the Order with the girdle of chastity, and prepared its feet for the Gospel of peace.' Here it was that S. Dominic, being rapt in spirit, 'saw the Lord with the Blessed Virgin on His right hand, clad in a cope of sapphire.' Here it was that he had the vision of S. Mary, S. Cecily, and S. Catharine. Here, to this day, may be seen in the church, upon a pedestal, the great, black, shining stone, said by the legend to have been hurled by the demon at the Saint, to interrupt him in his nightly meditations. Here is shown the narrow cell where he prayed, the hall in which he gave the habit to S. Hyacinth, and an orange-tree in the garden, which, to this day, tempts, with its golden fruit, the piety of citizens and strangers.

I need not attempt a description of the emotions of young Aquino on approaching the Eternal City, and on entering that venerable church where the bones of S. Sabina rested, and the great S. Dominic had loved so much to pray. Doubtless, wonder and devotion were mixed with sad thoughts about his mother, and with strange anticipations about his future life. Doubtless, long and earnestly he prayed before the altar, and begged of Christ to fill him with S. Dominic's spirit. This much is certain, that the young man gave himself up to study and to contemplation—to prepare himself for that mighty mission which he was afterwards to fulfil.

But his repose was speedily disturbed. Theodora, with the fire of her nature thoroughly stirred up, finding that her son had been carried away from Naples, set out forthwith for the Eternal City. She was extremely angry with the friars. In vain the Countess called at their convent; in vain she begged admittance, by entreaties the most imploring, and by threats the most indignant; in vain she protested that, far from wishing to trifle with her son's vocation, she simply desired to confirm it all the more. Thomas did not appear; the doors remained shut; the Dominicans would not be moved. She then bewailed her hard lot amongst the Roman nobility, and denounced to the Pope the rapacity of the cruel friars, who, in spite of her position and all her promises, had robbed her of her boy.

The Dominican superiors, perceiving how excited Theodora was, and dreading her influence in the city, sent S. Thomas off from Rome, with four others, to travel by secret roads to Paris. Whilst the party was making its way towards the frontier, Landulf and Reginald (the Saint's two brothers) were actively engaged ravaging Lombardy with a band of Frederick's soldiers. Theodora, who had heard of the young Dominican's departure, despatched a courier to the brothers, beseeching them to secure the fugitive. They set the military at once to watch the passes through which the Dominicans might escape. Meanwhile, the friars, fagged with the journey, which they had made on foot, halted near Acquapendente, between Sienna and Lake Bolsena. Here, as they lay resting under the shade of a tree, suddenly they beheld themselves surrounded by armed men; and, to his intense astonishment, Thomas found himself, without a chance of escape, a prisoner in the hands of his brothers. The two young soldiers behaved with great brutality to the Saint, threatened to tear his habit off his back, and, forcing him on horseback, carried him away to San Giovanni, whilst his companions fled hastily back to Rome.

From the accounts given of Theodora's interview with S. Thomas, some notion can be formed of the energy of the mother, and of the calm determination of the son. She made use of every argument she could invent, and brought into play all the passions of her nature—her tears, her entreaties, her prayers, her fierce anger, her threats, her hatred, her love—but without effect. She argued that obedience to parents is a law of God, that filial piety is of strict obligation, that youth is easily deceived, that what inexperience admires is condemned by mature reflection, that Thomas would ruin and disgrace his father, and bring upon the family the anger of the Emperor—and so on in a similar strain.

But Thomas was immovable. Though full of tenderness towards his mother, he had read enough, and had thought enough, and had been visited by God too often, to abandon a call which he deemed Divine. Perceiving that neither threats nor blandishments could effect her purpose, Theodora threw Thomas into prison, fastened the door, and set guards to watch outside. She then sent godless young men in to him, to argue him out of his resolve. His sisters seconded their foolish mother. They alone were permitted to serve the prisoner; and they practised all their arts upon him, to turn him from his high vocation. But the calm deportment of the future Angel of the Schools, his resignation, his tenderness to his sisters, his tranquil mind ever fixed on things Divine, were more powerful, in the end, than creature stubbornness, or human passion. The impress of heaven ever overpowers, in the issue, the instability of human influences. The two girls by degrees ceased their talking, and began to listen, and finally rendered themselves up to the mastery of a superior power; their hearts expanded, their minds enlarged; they listened, they believed, they acted, they were subdued—in a word, S. Thomas converted his sisters; his prison became a hallowed spot; his habit, an earnest of high heroism; his obstinacy, a note of predestination; and his life, a pattern of perfection. They were no longer his guards and his seducers, but his companions, his helpmates, his dearest sisters, and his constant friends.

They put him in a position to communicate with his brethren. The monotony of confinement was broken by study, prayer, and contemplation. The Saint procured a Bible, the 'Sentences' of the Lombard, and some of the works of Aristotle. His memory, which was so retentive as never to forget anything he once had read, is said to have got these books by heart. Thus it was that he prepared himself for his mighty labours in the future.

But this comparative repose was broken in upon rudely enough by the perseverant brutality of his brothers. They still persisted in their determination to force him from religion. After they had delivered him to his mother, they were called away into active service under Frederick. But, when the troops had been brought down to Melfi, and were encamped near Ciprano, they had an opportunity of visiting the prisoner. Possibly they imagined that, through the influence of the family, he had already changed his mind. If so, they were bitterly disappointed. For they found that, far from being changed himself, Thomas had converted both his sisters. They were furious. They forbade the girls to approach him, and, forcing themselves in upon the boy, they insulted him with brutal jests and oaths, and ended by tearing his habit piece by piece off his back.

Meanwhile, his sisters informed the Dominicans outside of what the Saint was undergoing. Br. John of S. Juliano brought another habit for him from Naples. This made Landulf and Reginald worse than they had been before. They fixed upon a most infamous expedient for shaking their younger brother's vocation. They hired a bad woman of the neighbourhood, and sent her secretly to his cell, to tempt him to sin. Whilst waiting the issue, a fearful shriek, proceeding from the direction of the prison, rang from one end of the castle to the other. A rush was made by Landulf and Reginald to their brother's cell. They saw the door burst open, and beheld the girl rushing away in an agony of terror, and the young man chasing her with a blazing brand, which he had just plucked out of the fire. Even the brutality of the two rough young soldiers was overcome by this; and from that day forth, they ceased to persecute their gentle, younger brother.

Just before his death, the Saint told his familiar brother, Rainald, that no sooner had the girl been driven out, than he made a cross with the charred brand upon the wall, and, casting himself upon his knees before it, made a vow of chastity for life. Whilst thus praying, he fell into a calm gentle sleep, and was ravished by a heavenly vision. He saw angels descending from the clouds, and they came and bound his loins with the girdle of continence, and armed him for life as a warrior of heaven. The pain of this binding roused him up with an unconscious cry of suffering. On hearing it, his guards entered the cell, but he carefully concealed his favour from them. He declared to Rainald that never, since that time till his death, was the spirit of darkness suffered to approach his person, to seduce him from that heavenly-mindedness which is one of the characteristic notes of his gentle, meditative character.

The girdle was worn by the Saint till his death. Afterwards, it was given by John of Vercelli to the Dominican Convent of Vercelli, in Piedmont. With what jealousy the friars preserved the relic, is evident from heir refusing to part with it, even at the request of a Sovereign Pontiff. A holy confraternity was speedily established, called 'The Angelic Warfare.' Its object was to preserve purity, or to restore it, if unhappily it had been forfeited. Cords, made after that given to S. Thomas, were worn by members of the institute. And

Innocent X., in a Brief of March 21, 1654, and Benedict XIII., in a Bull in favour of the University of Toulouse, enriched it with many signal favours.

The confraternity spread rapidly and widely. Rich and poor were anxious to place themselves under the protection of this glorious Saint. Students of the University were glad to possess a token of his triumph, and an earnest of their own success in resisting one of the most seductive enemies of youth growing to maturity.

But, though his relations had ceased to persecute S. Thomas, they kept him in his confinement, some say, two years—and they would, no doubt, have detained him longer had it not been for the influence of the Dominicans with the Pope. It was an unheard-of thing for an ecclesiastic to be set upon, and cast into prison, by a band of ruffians in the Papal States—particularly when those ruffians were in the pay of the Emperor; it was an affront to the Pontiff, as well as an infringement of the law. The Dominicans did not represent their grievance in vain. The Holy Father was roused. He not only brought the case before the Emperor, but he ordered him to let the prisoner free, and to visit the perpetrators of the outrage with condign punishment. Frederick, having latterly been humiliated by the *Viterbesi,* and having, in consequence, been abandoned by some of his supporters, was not sorry for an opportunity of gratifying the Pontiff. Orders, accompanied by threats, were at once sent to Landulf and Reginald to set the captive free. Still, these stubborn soldiers, with their haughty mother, would take no active steps to give Thomas his liberty. However, his sisters informed S. Juliano of the position of affairs, and he at once hurried to the castle, accompanied by one or two companions. And finally, the girls let their brother down, through the window, like another S. Paul, into the hands of his delighted brethren. The party at once set off for Naples, and our Saint found his rest once more amongst those chosen souls, who had so deeply impressed him at the outset of his university career.

Who, at this period, was Superior of the convent, and received our Saint's profession, is uncertain. Many, following Tocco, say it was John of S. Juliano, the old adviser of S. Thomas; others, such as Bernard Guidonis, S. Antoninus, and Malvenda, say that Tomaso d'Agni di Lentino was the Prior—a man second to none at that day in virtue, energy, and zeal. He joined the Order during the lifetime of S. Dominic; founded the convent at Naples (1231); ruled over it, some say, till 1255; and then became, successively, Bishop of Bethlehem, Archbishop of Cosenza, and Patriarch of Jerusalem—in which capacity, like another Peter the Hermit, with fiery eloquence, he preached, from kingdom to kingdom, and from court to court, the deliverance of the Holy Land out of the hands of the infidel.

A prelate of this temperament would be but too glad to engraft into the Order a young man who had already, in a marked degree, manifested a character promising the unusual combinations of genius with humility, of sweetness with firmness, and of an almost womanly gentleness with a more than manly courage.

But Theodora and her soldier sons, unfortunately, took a very different view of the case. The mother bitterly repented having permitted Thomas to escape at all, and blamed herself for culpable weakness in having suffered him to be carried away to Naples. She accused the Dominicans of dishonesty, and, assisted by Landulf and Reginald, applied to Pope Innocent to annul her son's vows, and to set the young man once more at liberty.

The Holy Father sent for the young Dominican, and questioned him in presence of the Court. Thomas, with his natural modesty, and yet with gentle firmness, told the Pope how S. Dominic had called him to religion, how unmistakable was the voice, and how he attributed his present difficulties, not to the violence of his brothers, or to the loving indiscretions of his mother; but to his own many sins and imperfections. He implored the Pope to protect him in his one desire of embracing Jesus Christ, and of walking with sure step along the road of perfect charity. Innocent and the Prelates about him could not suppress their emotion whilst witnessing so unusual a manifestation of heavenly purity and grace. We are told that after the young man had finished his appeal, they turned to Theodora, and with congratulations mixed with tears, comforted her; and whilst they lauded Thomas to the skies, they could not bring their hearts to blame a mother, who had made such giant efforts to regain so loving and so admirable a son.

The Holy Father, too, acted with great benevolence. Knowing Theodora's weakness, he proposed to make Thomas Abbot of Monte Cassino, whilst still allowing him to wear the habit of S. Dominic, and to partake of the privileges of the Mendicant friars. The court extolled this generosity of the Sovereign Pontiff. His brothers and relations implored Thomas to accept the tempting offer ; and to their prayers, his mother joined her warm entreaties. The one long desire of her heart seemed about to be fulfilled. But Thomas had made his resolve. He was inexorable. He implored the Pope to leave him alone, and begged that he might be permitted to abide in his vocation. He was so overpowered by the thought of being dragged from his position of a simple friar, that he spent his nights in tears and prayers, begging for graces necessary for salvation ;—the principal one of which, it seemed to him, was that of being permitted to live without charge or dignity, whether in the Cloister or in the Church.

Such was the termination of the conflict which S. Thomas had to sustain whilst carrying out the strong inspiration that possessed him. His mother now no longer worried him, his brothers left him alone, and he was permitted to begin that career of usefulness, which was the source ultimately of such blessings to the Church.

Not long after this, Reginald and Landulf had a disagreement with the Emperor. Frederick took his revenge. He destroyed their stronghold, and cast them into prison. Theodora spent the remainder of her life in prayer, and the practices of an ascetic life—making up in a short time for that too strong human element which she had suffered to possess her heart. Though not without blame, one cannot help looking with some sympathy at her strong passionate nature, her violent devotion to her child, and her love, vehement and ardent too, for God, which ended in her giving herself entirely to Him.

CHAPTER VI.

ALBERTUS MAGNUS.

Now that S. Thomas was free from the persecutions of his family, his superiors began to form plans for developing those conspicuous abilities which had created so great a sensation in the schools. Thomas was the very man that the keen eye of the General would fix upon as likely to profit largely by the most perfect education. From the very first, knowledge was taken by the Dominicans as a principle of power: not knowledge buried in seclusion, or antiquated in its form, but knowledge which would tell upon mankind, and raise up humanity from the egotism of nature to the standard of the Cross. This instinct is manifested in a remarkable manner by the Acts of the first general

Chapter of the Dominicans, by the *dicta* of their greatest men, and by their authorised exposition of the rule of St. Augustine. From the first, they seem to have had a kind of fore-knowledge of the great combat that would have to be waged in the arena of human reason. From the first, with prudence, forethought, and wise economy, they prepared a system for turning the abilities of their members to the fullest account. With them, no intellect was lost. Power was recognised, trained, and put in motion. Those who were less gifted were set to less intellectual employments;—those who had great powers were, with care and patience, by time and the best professors, fitted to become lights of the world and ornaments of the Order.

The interest taken by the friars in the studies of their rising men is clearly seen in the case of S. Thomas himself. He had already received a good education at Monte Cassino and the University; so much so, that, as has been seen, his name was mentioned by the learned in the city with mingled awe and admiration. With such an intellectual capital as our Saint possessed, he might fairly have been set to work in the active ministrations of his Order. But fortunately, his superiors were men who looked into the future, and knew how a present sacrifice would be repaid. They were aware that a young man, carefully built up, fully formed by a process of so much study, and so much training spread over so much time, would be as a fortress for defence or for attack. These men were aware that *time* is as essential a condition for maturing a man, as it is for ripening a fruit; you may bake an apple, but you cannot ripen it at pleasure. To force nature beyond its pace, be it in man or beast, is not to build nature up, but to pull nature down. Time, and trouble, and expense—patience, and confidence in the result—these were the secrets of Dominican success. Like the great material buildings of those days, they built up—stone upon stone, in labour and toil, in process of time—men, full of light and intellectual activity, with their moral nature trained and consolidated in stability. Thus it was that instead of looking on S. Thomas's education as finished, they considered it as only just begun. His mind was now in a position to imbibe the knowledge of scientific things. It was open: light could be poured in with advantage. Who was the master capable of bringing it to its perfection?

This question, no doubt, John of Germany, fourth General of the Dominicans, must have asked himself; it was not a question of distance or expense, but a question of doing the best for the Order. So he at once set off with the Saint, on foot, for a three months' journey, from Rome to Paris, and from Paris to Cologne, where Albertus Magnus was lecturing. When the reader calls to mind what kind of undertaking such a journey must have been, especially when made with no other assistance than a prayer-book and a stick, and that by an old man and a delicate youth, he will begin to realise one of the causes of the rapid development of the Dominicans, who could, even at this date, number eight provinces, sixty convents, and nearly thirty thousand friars. What was easier than for the General to have saved himself this tedious journey? Why could he not have sent S. Thomas to Bologna, or to Naples, or to Paris, where there were teachers renowned for learning and ability? The reason is simple as the principle is golden. Because, at that date, no scholar was so promising as S. Thomas of Aquin, and no master had so high a reputation as Albertus Magnus.

Unfortunately, historians have left us no account of the incidents of the journey of the young student with the venerable General.

The modesty of the Saint himself, his horror of being talked about, and the natural reserve of a lofty mind, has deprived posterity of much that, undoubtedly, would have been full of interest, and have tended to edification. One anecdote is however told of the Saint and his companion which shows how, from his early days, he had learnt to love the great fathers of the Church. It is related that, as they were approaching their destination, and they descried what appeared a distant town, and as the beauty of the city of Paris grew upon them with their advancing steps, the General turned to Thomas and said, 'What would you give, Brother Thomas, to be king of that city?' 'I would rather have S. John Chrysostom's treatise on the Gospel of S. Matthew,' replied the young man, 'than be king of the whole of France.'

The life of S. Thomas of Aquin would not be complete, were I to omit a brief notice of that extraordinary man whose teaching exerted so profound an influence upon him. If Thomas surpassed his Professors at Naples and Cassino, at all events, he now met his match in a teacher, whose breadth of knowledge and wide experience must have convinced him that there was something yet for him to learn. Nothing is a greater blessing for a master-mind, than to come in contact with another master-mind, more highly educated, and with a more matured experience than itself.

Albert was born of the noble family of Bollstadt in 1193, at Lavingen, on the banks of the Danube, in Bavarian Suabia. Some of his historians say that, like S. Isidore, he was dull as a boy. Others tell us that he was so dissatisfied with his tutor at home, that, accompanied by an uncle, he was sent to study under the most famous dialecticians at Paris. The next we hear of him is at Padua, applying himself to medicine and mathematics. Here it was that he was persuaded by Br. Jordan, the General of the Dominicans—who had already, by his eloquence, attracted one thousand young men out of the universities of Paris and Bologna—to join the Order. At once the Dominicans, seeing what a prize they had drawn, set about making the most of it. Albert must complete his education. He was sent at once to Bologna, the second centre of the then intellectual world. Next he began to teach. As lecturer, he was unrivalled. People went in crowds to listen to him as to an intellectual wonder. Princes, Bishops, Prelates, nobles, rich and poor, laymen and clerics, all thronged into the hall of this extraordinary man. The logic, ethics, and physics of Aristotle, and portions of the Holy Scripture, were the subject-matter of his lectures. He put a new impetus of intellectual life into a body of men who would seem to have been intellectual enough before, and was looked upon as a second founder of the Order. He went from Freiburg to Regensburg, and from Strasburg to Cologne, always begging his way and travelling on foot, giving lectures in philosophy and theology. In 1228, he was sent to Paris to look thoroughly into the studies, and to put them on a footing to meet the requirements of the age. Then he returned to Cologne. It was at this period that he first met S. Thomas, who became his favourite disciple and to whom in private he opened the stores of his capacious mind.

Albert's life looks as if it were wholly taken up in travelling and talking. In 1245, he was again sent to Paris to take his Doctor's cap, and to give public lectures in S. James's. It was at this period that he attained the height of his reputation as a professor. Some of his later historians declare that so great was the press to hear him, that no building in Paris was large enough to contain his audience, and that thus he was forced to lecture in the open air. In 1248, he was once more sent back to Cologne, to become *Regens* and *Primarius Lector* of the school. In 1254, he was elected Provincial. The year after he was called to Rome, and made Master of the Sacred Palace. In 1260, he was made Bishop of Regensburg, and then Papal Legate in Poland by Alexander IV. Any one of these offices would have been full occupation for any ordinary man. When it is remembered that Albertus Magnus held each of them with credit—that as Professor he surpassed all his contemporaries; that as Regens he was a zealous and prudent reformer; that as Bishop he left a mark which remains to this day; that as Master of the Sacred Palace he astonished his hearers by the wisdom of his discourse; that as Papal Legate he did more than any man of his period towards mitigating the ferocity of barbarians, and encouraging a Christian spirit—when it is remembered how in those troubled times he was occupied in defending his Order, in making peace, in acting as arbitrator between rivals, for instance, in 1249, 1251, 1258, and that over and above the performance of all these active duties, he repeated the entire Psalter every twenty-four hours, and wrote twenty-one folio volumes upon every then known subject that can be put under logic, metaphysics, psychology, natural science, ethics, theology, chemistry, botany, and the rest, we begin to get a glimpse of what manner of a giant S. Thomas had for his professor. Is there any man in the whole range of history who has manifested in equal proportions such practical ability, such speculative power, and indefatigable industry? Well may his contemporaries have called him the 'Doctor Universalis,' and Engelbert have written of him, 'Vir in omni scientia adeo divinus, ut nostri temporis stupor et miraculum congrue vocari possit.'

There is no doubt that Albert took a wide and profound view of the conditions of the intellectual world of his day. A man does not labour as he laboured, nor strike out a novel course of teaching, with the likelihood of being misunderstood, without having a grave reason for doing so. The very task which he set himself to accomplish, points to the depth and the wisdom of his appreciation of the times. He saw clearly the immense influence which had been, and still was being, exerted by those vast intellectual powers represented by the Koran, the Talmud, and the Stagyrite. Much truth thrown into philosophic form was on the side of the enemy. The power of Greek thought, its precision, its clearness, its order, its logical force, together with the traditionary teachings of men of intelligence, as subtle as profound, could always make a respectable appearance, and often confuse those who were really seeking after truth, and keep them from perceiving clearly the philosophy and beauty of the Christian religion. Besides, not only had the enemy to be attacked, but the whole body of Catholic teaching, like some vast city, had to be defended—and defended not merely against the assaults of her own children, but against the clever insinuations, the artful fallacies, the philosophical systems of men with intelligence every bit as powerful and as educated as her own. All this was clear to Albertus Magnus.

The two grand objects he kept in view during his brilliant career as Professor, and his long labours as Theologian, were, first, that the influences of philosophy, the wisdom, clearness, and systematic methods of the powers of Paganism, should be brought over, and turned round for the defence and glory of the Church,—that Aristotle should be Christianised; and, secondly, that faith should be thrown into the form of a vast scientific organism, through the application of Christianised philosophy to the dogmata of revealed religion. Thus would the Church possess all the highest truths of Greek philosophy in the purest form, without the alloy of error that is generally encrusted round the noblest of human speculations. Thus she would present an impregnable barrier to the efforts of pride of intellect, when endeavouring to overset the framework of the Church. Thus, also, would that almost endless array of points of belief, of which religion is composed, be united in the oneness of a philosophic form, and instead of being objects of difficulty to the inquirer, in reality, startle his mind, not only by their reasonableness, but by their strict relationship to one another. What could be more Divine than the conception of salvation as reflected in that splendid *Summa* of S. Thomas, which, humanly speaking, would never have existed had it not been for Albertus Magnus?

It was not without causing astonishment, and I may say, not without some scandal, that Albert set about this great work of bringing Aristotle into the midst of

Christianity. Had he contented himself with hunting up old manuscripts, with laboriously searching out the true text, and still more laboriously, perhaps, eliciting the true meaning, by comparing one execrable translation from the Arabic, with a still more execrable translation from the Greek; or, foiled in this, by comparing one part of the author with another, or with Theophrastus or Avicenna, men might simply have wondered at the extraordinary hobby of an industrious bookworm. But he did far more than this: he actually had the boldness to modify and mould Aristotle, by the right of Christian principles, into a Christian form, to be set before Christian men as Christian philosophy. And what is more, he made use of the position he occupied of Public Professor of Theology and Philosophy to instil his novel views into the minds of the rising generation. Never before this had Aristotle been made the special subject-matter for lectures in the schools, and never before had the disciples of any professor seen their master with such fulness, depth, and comprehensiveness, build up so vast a system of harmonious truth. Albert has, over and over, been accused of 'introducing the philosophy of Aristotle into the very sanctuary of Christ,' of 'allotting to him the principal seat in the middle of Christ's temple;' of being drunk with the wine of secular science, human wisdom, and profane philosophy; of uniting contentious, thorny, and garrulous dialectics with most sacred and most pure theology, and of teaching his followers a new and philosophic method of explaining and teaching the Holy Word. He has been called 'an ape' and 'an ass,' has been accused of sorcery and of witchcraft, and, in fact, has received that tribute from the foolish which all truly superior men are accustomed to receive, and gratefully to acknowledge.

It would be too long, and beside the purpose, to go round the many-sided fabric of theology, and point out the merits of this mighty architect. It will suffice to hint, in the words of an able writer, at one or two of the services he rendered in particular questions. 'He added two new proofs of the existence of God; he exposed the fallacies of pantheism; he completed the Lombard's doctrine on reprobation; refuted with consummate ability the Aristotelian doctrine of the Eternity of the World; introduced the famous distinction ever since employed against optimists; illustrated by ingenious analogies the Catholic doctrine of Justification; and went more profoundly than any of his predecessors into the sublime mystery of the ever Blessed Trinity.'

Besides being a theologian and philosopher—indeed, the first theologian and philosopher of his day—Albert was also great in natural history; he was a botanist, a chemist, a geographer, an architect, a geologist, and a mechanic, besides being an anatomist and an alchemist. He spent thirty years' toil in working at an automaton, which at length he succeeded in making to speak—the same, if the tradition have any truth in it, which so startled S. Thomas when unawares he came upon it in the workshop of Albert, that he seized the first stick that came to hand, and shrieking, 'Salve, salve!' smashed the fearful monster to pieces, thinking it to be some cruel savage who was about to attempt his life. He entertained William of Holland, in the midst of the severest winter, in a garden he had constructed, breathing the softest zephyrs of spring, and filled with most delicate flowers. Humboldt declares that in his *Liber Cosmographicus de natura locorum* he surpasses in many points the age in which he lived. As a botanist, Maier puts him before all the ancients but Theophrastus. Dr. Jesser, who brought out his work *De Vegetabilibus et Plantis* and is a thorough bigot, equals Albert in his Cosmos to Aristotle and to Humboldt. Peter Crescentia popularised his discoveries and views. His chemical knowledge may not have been far in advance of the Arabians, Geber and Razes, whose doctrines he tried to reconcile with Aristotle's teachings on the elementary properties of matter; but he certainly far surpassed all the ancients in the ingenuity of his experiments and in some of his discoveries. He could make gunpowder. His remarks on gems would repay the perusal of the student at this day. He was the first to perceive the chemical affinities of bodies, and to detect various relations of metals to each other, while he greatly increased the practical utility of chemical materials. Even the Jews looked upon his writings and discoveries with respect. A certain Abraham translated into Arabic his *Summa* of natural philosophy; while the learned Jewish physician Portaleone (1542-1612) pays a handsome compliment to Albert's treatment of 'precious stones,' in that portion of his scarce and celebrated work, שִׁלְטֵי הַגִּבֹּרִים, which touches on the subject. Then, as a geographer, Albert is said to have anticipated the discovery of America; and, as an architect, he gave plans for several churches; and the first design of the stately cathedral of Cologne is said to have been copied from his drawings.

What is as remarkable as anything in this extraordinary man is, that though he knew neither Greek, Arabic, nor Hebrew; though he was very feeble in history; though he is simply ludicrous when he attempts to trace the etymology of words; still, on the authority of one of the most able writers of the history of philosophy, it may be said that he understood Aristotle better than our great modern philologists; and added to all this versatility was a simplicity, a modesty, a gentleness, a piety, a love for the Blessed Sacrament, a love for our Lady, a devotional spirit, a moral sublimity of character, which has ranked him justly among the blessed, and made him a fit companion for the saints. So great was his piety and learning, that some writers declare that his knowledge was infused into him by heaven.

One can well imagine him swaying the minds of his disciples by the marvellousness of his many-sided knowledge. One can see now, in imagination, that placid figure: those features, beautiful in their regularity;

those eyes, singularly meditative and profound; those lips, speaking of gravity and energy; and that general impress of calm genius, with passion altogether conquered, or, at all events, entirely controlled; as, surrounded by admiring and loving eyes, he unfolds the hidden science of the saints, or dwells upon the origins and springs of God's beautiful creation.

He continued teaching till he was eighty-five years old, and ended his laborious and saintly life in 1280.

Such was the master selected by John of Germany for young Thomas of Aquino. Such was the chance given to the young Dominican for bringing to their highest perfection those extraordinary gifts of nature and grace intrusted to him by God. When the genius of the Italian is directed and fostered by the genius of the German, the result cannot but be a glorious manifestation of cultivated ability and power.

CHAPTER VII.

S. THOMAS AT COLOGNE.

WHEN S. Thomas arrived at Cologne, the Dominicans had already been some time settled there. S. Dominic, who always had an eye to great centres, must have observed that the fact of its being a great commercial city, with its one hundred and fifty thousand inhabitants, and three thousand soldiers, would make it a fair field for work; and its intimate relations with Italy, its reputation for science and art, would tend to elevate the mind, and make it a natural centre for Dominican activity.

In the year 1221, those dear friends, Jordan of Saxony and Henry of Cologne, the former who owed his singular conversion to his love of the poor of Christ and of the Holy Office, and the latter whom Jordan declared to be 'the most gracious creature he ever saw,' established the Order at Cologne. They began in a very humble manner. They opened a *hospitium*, near the Cathedral, in the Stolkstrasse (*vicus Stolcorum*), and served a little chapel dedicated to S. Mary Magdalene. Their gentle, devoted lives struck the people of the town, who, unfortunately, had been accustomed to receive very little edification from many of the clergy. Their little chapel quickly filled. The clergy of the town were ill-pleased at this. Invidious comparisons were instituted by the people between the meek, shaven friars, with their extreme simplicity and poverty, and the sleek, well-fed, and sometimes disedifying clergy. The clergy begged the Archbishop to remove the friars. The venerable Engelbert gently answered them, that as long as the little convent of Dominicans did nothing but good, he preferred to allow them to remain. But the clergy replied that the warning-note had already been sounded against them by a saint. It was of these men, with their strange costume and shaven crowns, that Holy Hildegard had prophesied when she spoke of men who would bring danger on the priests, and destruction on the city. Well, then, replied the Archbishop, 'If it be a Divine revelation, it will certainly come to pass.' The Dominicans remained, flourished, taught; and under Albert the Great the little convent became a nursery of saints.

When we consider three things which must have exerted a great influence on S. Thomas, it will not appear surprising that he should have given himself up to silent meditation in the school of Albert. In the first place, a mind so noble and so delicate would be subdued by the force of the master-mind with which it came in contact, and would feel far more inclined to think and listen than to talk and to dispute. Secondly, the knowledge which the young student must have possessed of those great questions which had agitated the schools for so many years—questions intimately bound up with the first principles of Christianity, nay, even with the dogma of the existence of God Himself—could not but affect most deeply his mind and imagination. And, lastly, he may have felt, in his extreme modesty, that his mind had not arrived at that maturity which makes the ventilation of difficult problems of much advantage; and that now was the time to listen and learn, not to talk and teach: and that truth is arrived at by slow degrees, through patient, unwearied thought, and through the laborious comparison of a thousand experiences. Besides, naturally, the Saint loved contemplation. His life, from the beginning, had been formed in a monastic mould: and the impress of S. Benedict made him strange, at first, to the activity and excitement of the modern methods of the mediæval world.

His companions in the school of Albert belonged to quite another class. Whilst Thomas was living in the varied world of abstract thought, of problem, and question and probability—with its labyrinths of truth; with its fitful, eccentric fires; with sombre avenues opening into terrific pitfalls; and vast stretches of clear certainty, with its far-distant peaks, reflecting the light of the good, the beautiful, and the true—his companions were living amongst material things. His world was not only hidden from them, but was beyond their powers of realisation. He was amongst them in body, but that was nearly all. Yet they were occupied with discussing great questions also. But they were young men who thought themselves capable of handling any question; and would argue a point with very slender knowledge of its bearings. They were young men full of activity, intelligence, and life, buoyant with animal spirits, and filled with the impression that to exert the reasoning faculties in debating scholastic questions was one of the principal ends of all philosophy. They had been told of the splendid talents of Abelard, of that brilliant school of intellectual chivalry which he established, and which had made its name famous throughout Italy, Germany, and France.

It is not extraordinary that such young men as these, when they saw young Aquino so silent, should imagine that nothing occupied his thoughts, especially when they perceived that he was equally reserved in the school as he was in conversation. Whilst his companions boldly disputed, and waxed loud and noisy, this imperturbable youth remained in his place without a word and without a sign. They soon came to the conclusion that he was a naturally dull, obtuse lad, who possessed no powers of appreciation. They must have known that he came from the South. Probably they knew that the General had brought him to Cologne; but it is evident that the fame he acquired in Naples had never reached them. What is more strange is this, that Albertus Magnus held the same opinion as his pupils regarding the dulness and deficiency of the young Aquino. Thomas was ridiculed publicly for his intellectual shortcomings, and was called, by master and by pupils, the great, dumb, Sicilian ox. That they all taunted him publicly, and called him by his nicknames to his face, is evident from the surest testimony. But the Saint had been well broken to suffering, and he bore it all without a word. And being a youth of real breadth of mind, he knew how much all this was worth, and took it at its proper valuation.

Still there is no doubt that he must have keenly felt the roughness, vulgarity, and noisiness of his associates. Without doubt, one fully formed in the retiring school of quiet, who had lived in the company of the gentle, silent Benedictine monks at Monte Cassino, and had learnt to fix his mind on the one great object of all man's striving, on the Supreme Good—and that in speechless contemplation—would be scared and shocked by the unrestrained and sportive garrulity of quick-tongued and offhand young logicians—fledglings who were ever piping, and crowing, and flapping their young wings, and bouncing at each other around him, ever trying the strength of their spurs and the sharpness of their beaks and claws, in those dialectical encounters which were the natural consequence of the principle of motion. He must often silently have smiled at their blunders whilst they were thinking to dazzle him by their talent and acuteness.

The four great pillars of the monastic school of quiet: love, reverence, purity, adoration, that is, the principles of contemplation—manifested in the writings of S. Anselm, S. Bernard, Hugh and Richard of S. Victor's—had so firm a foundation in the heart and mind of S. Thomas, that even had he tried, he could not have forced himself into sympathy with the flippant, thoughtless emptiness of his companions. His life had been fixed in another set of principles. He was like the lighthouse, in a noisy, washing sea—calm and steady—and, in the midst of the whirling and seething, the rising and breaking, the lashing and sinking of the objectless waters—ever biding in one place, ever consistently fulfilling one appointed mission, ever throwing the light that was in him upon the instability of all around. It takes some little time for a character like his to make itself felt with all its weight, amongst a school of unreflecting students. But constant, silent pressure, the pursuance of one unbending course, at length produces its effect.

In fact there is little doubt that, from time to time, the young Aquino amused himself quietly at his companions' expense, or, at all events, took them somewhat by surprise. Once, when studying in his cell, he heard a voice crying to him from outside the window: 'Brother Thomas, Brother Thomas, here! quick, quick—look at this flying ox!' With all simplicity, Thomas went to the window, and no sooner made his appearance, than he was saluted with shouts of derision. Those who had played the trick upon him asked how he could be so simple as to imagine that an ox could fly? He answered in his own gentle, yet incisive way, 'I did not believe that an ox could fly, nor did I, till now, believe that a religious could tell a falsehood.' Some of his companions who did not despise him felt compassion for him. One of these offered to assist him in his lesson. Thomas accepted the offer with gratitude. He allowed his companion to proceed, and attentively listened to his explanation. At length the young professor came to a difficult passage, which was beyond his depth, and which he was unable to explain. Thomas quietly took the book from him, and, to the amazement of his companion, explained the entire passage with greater lucidity and precision than could have been done by an experienced professor. All his companion could do was to mix confusion with astonishment, and implore the young Aquino to become his instructor for the future.

Thomas quietly declined; but, being pressed, he consented, on the strict understanding that all that had happened was to be kept a profound secret.

At length a circumstance occurred which brought his extraordinary gifts before the notice of the school. Master Albert had selected a very difficult question from the writings of Denis the Areopagite, and had given it to some of his scholars for solution. Whether in joke or in earnest, they passed on the difficulty to Thomas, and begged him to write his opinion upon it. Thomas took the paper to his cell, and taking his pen, first stated, with great lucidity, all the objections that could be brought against the question; and then gave their solutions. As he was going out of his cell, this paper accidentally fell near the door. One of the brothers, passing, picked it up, and carried it at once to Master Albert. Albert was excessively astonished at the splendid talent which now, for the first time, by mere accident, he discovered in that big, silent student. He determined to bring out, in the most public manner, abilities which had been for so long a time so modestly concealed. He desired Thomas to defend a thesis before the assembled school on the following day. The hour arrived. The hall was filled. There sat Master Albert. Doubtless the majority of those who were to witness this display imagined that they were about to assist at an egregious failure. How could that heavy, silent lad, who could not speak a word in private, defend in public school, against the keenest of opponents, the difficult niceties of theology? But they were soon undeceived. For Thomas spoke with such clearness, established his thesis with such remarkable dialectical skill, saw so far into the coming difficulties of the case, and handled the whole subject in so masterly a manner, that Albert himself was constrained to cry aloud, 'Tu non videris tenere locum respondentis sed determinantis!' 'Master,' replied Thomas with humility, 'I know not how to treat the question otherwise.' Albert then thought to puzzle him, and show him that he was still a disciple. So, one after another, he started objections, created a hundred labyrinths, weaving and interweaving all manner of subtle arguments—but in vain. Thomas, with his calm spirit and keen vision, saw through every complication, had the key to every fallacy, the solution for every enigma, and the art to unravel the most tangled skein—till, finally, Albert, no longer able to withhold the expression of his admiration, cried out to his disciples, who were almost stupefied with astonishment: 'We call this young man a dumb ox, but so loud will be his bellowing in doctrine that it will resound throughout the whole world.'

He who takes the pains to dip into Denis the Areopagite, *De Divinis Nominibus*, will see at a glance what sort of a test Albertus Magnus must have applied to young Aquino. The easy passages in that work are hard enough; what then must it not have been with the more involved? The explanation of this work was thought so difficult by the scholastics, that there is a legend extant to the effect that Albert, when expounding it, received assistance immediately from heaven. Throughout the middle ages it was supposed to have been the composition of a convert of S. Paul's; and such being the case, it was handled with great reverence, deeply studied, and much written upon. Men thought by commenting upon it to elicit out of its Neoplatonism the hidden mysteries of the Christian faith. The work may with safety be put down to the latter part of the fifth century. It is full of fundamental thought, and has a mystic savour which gained it many admirers and commentators in the middle ages; but its explanations are sometimes arbitrary, its thoughts occasionally unworthy, and it contains passages which border very closely upon error.

It is remarkable that the first question in which S. Thomas appears in the capacity of disputant should have been so intimately connected with the cry of his young heart, *Quid est Deus?* It was in the *Divinis Nominibus* that a profound and mystic attempt was made to give a solution to that question, and the fact of its having engrossed the thoughts of the Saint from his earliest years no doubt assisted him in solving the difficulties presented to him by his master. Minds that principally live in external facts and relations are little conscious of that world of wealth which lives in the contemplative spirit, nor of the vivid light that illuminates so many problems, which could not otherwise be unravelled except by the patient labour of love and thought.

Like his father, S. Dominic, young Aquino loved to study the Collations of the experienced Cassian. When studying, he kept this one volume by his side; and he found that such spiritual reading was of assistance in purifying his heart and mind to see more clearly into the depths of theological and Scriptural science. He combined, in fact, the fulness of the monastic temper with a soaring power of speculation. At this very period, besides explaining the mysticism of the Areopagite, he is said to have commenced a work founded upon Albert's lectures in the schools, namely, an explanation of Aristotle's Ethics.

But this same year a change was made by the Twenty-third General Chapter of the Dominicans, held at Cologne (1245). Here it was determined that Albert should leave Cologne and go to Paris. His superiors decided that he should occupy the professor's chair in that capital, and take his doctor's cap; and Thomas was to finish his three years under him at S. James's.

The reputation of many famous men was still fresh in the memory of scholars when young Aquino came to Paris. William of Shyreswood, whom John of Salisbury declares to have been greater than Albertus Magnus; William of Paris, who had fully mastered the doctrines of Plato and Aristotle, and in his great work, *De Universo*, had dealt a mortal blow to the Arabian philosophers; Robert of Lincoln, the learned mystic expounder of the Stagyrite, the deadly enemy of the Holy See; Vincent of Beauvais, who had no doubt spent years in the great library of King Louis, with its one thousand two hundred precious volumes, and who wrote an Encyclopædia of Universal Knowledge; and Alexander of Hales, the great Franciscan light, who manifested such keenness and breadth of reading in his Commentary on the Lombard, and whose stoutness in debate earned him the title of 'Irrefragable Doctor,' and who had just died when Thomas came to Paris—all these had been students and teachers in the University. Paris must have been pregnant with the odour of an hundred lofty names; and those halls and colleges, those monasteries and hostels—in which so many had gained a brilliant reputation, and then had become popes, statesmen, bishops, theologians, poets, philosophers—must, in the mind of the student, have been clothed with a species of mystic awe, from the oppressiveness which so many memories must have brought over the imagination. The homes of genius and the haunts of learning, where men of great brain have worked out the salvation of their fellows by the breadth of their attainments and the vigour of their minds, affect the spirit with a species of fascination; and, whilst overpowering it by their greatness, seem, at the same time, to kindle within it a kindred inspiration.

When a short sketch has been given of the authors and text-books used by students during the thirteenth century, and the condition of the University of Paris has been touched upon, then the way will be clear for entering fully into the great work of S. Thomas; so that, whilst the reader bears in mind the struggles and theological and philosophical positions which preceded him, he will be able, not only to appreciate what the Saint actually did, but, what is of great importance, the relation in which he stands to the intellectual world that went before, and the influence he exerted over the teaching of the future.

CHAPTER VIII.

INSTRUMENTS OF KNOWLEDGE.

Before proceeding to show the work that S. Thomas did, it will be well to give a short account of the instruments that he had to do it with.

The one absorbing science of the middle ages was theology. The whole form of learning pointed to the study of religion as the great terminus of the human mind, and the one right road from earth to heaven. The liberal arts were but a careful and laborious preparation for philosophy or logic; logic, in turn, was only valuable inasmuch as it was an instrument for the ordering, defending, and proving the great truths of revelation. The great object of life was to know God. James de Vitry beautifully says, 'Omnis scientia debet referri ad cognitionem Christi'—all science should be referred to the knowledge of Christ. Again, more clearly still: 'Debet scolaris ire per viam ad puteum (ut Isaac), id est per scientias adminiculantes ad theologiam.' The scholar should go along the road to the well (like Isaac), that is, through the assisting sciences to theology. ‘Logic is good,’ he says, ‘which teaches us how to separate truth from falsehood; grammar is good, which teaches us to write and speak correctly; rhetoric is good, which teaches us to speak with elegance, and to persuade; geometry is good, which teaches us to measure the earth on which we dwell; so is arithmetic, or the art of reckoning, by means of which we can convince ourselves of the small number of our days; and music, which teaches us harmonies, and makes us think of the sweet song of the “Blessed;” and, finally, astronomy, which makes us consider the heavenly bodies, and the virtue of the stars, darting forth splendour before God. But much better is theology, which alone can truly be called a *liberal* art, because it frees the human soul from its miseries.’ Arnoul d’Humblières, Bishop of Paris, thus speaks in his *Summa:* ‘Is it permissible to associate philosophy and pagan letters with the study of Divine sciences? Yes, when this accessory erudition is only employed for the better interpretation of the Sacred Scriptures, for the fuller understanding of prophecy, for comprehending and strengthening faith, and as a help towards creating detestation for false doctrines, and towards more solidly refuting them. But if, on the contrary, one takes pleasure in the fables of the poets—in the worldly ornamentation of their style—such philosophy becomes an impious and corrupting science.’

It may be laid down, roughly, that the Holy Scriptures, the Lombard, and Aristotle, were the three great bases on which the active intellect of the thirteenth century rested, in its development and analysis of truth. The subject-matter of its efforts was revelation—and philosophy also, but only in so far as it had a bearing on religious truth; and the form became more and more perfectly Aristotelian, as the learned gained a more perfect acquaintance with the whole mind of the Stagyrite, and with the immense usefulness of his system, for ordering and systematising the multitudinous teachings of the Church. Not, of course, that the Doctors of the Church of the middle ages became enslaved to the Stagyrite: they had a brighter and stronger light than his shining over their heads, and, by its guidance, were able to do what neither Jew nor Arab had yet succeeded in, viz., to handle so sharp and dangerous an instrument, without cutting the fair form of religion with it, and to turn it with edge and point in the right direction. It will not, therefore, be altogether out of place to give a short account of the opportunities the student had of learning both the sense of Holy Scripture; the theology of the Church; and the method of dealing with revelation, through the influence of the Stagyrite. To begin with exegesis.

The Church of God is principally founded in Holy Scripture. Hence, it follows that, at all times, theologians have given themselves with earnestness to the study of the Word of God. Now, there are several sources to which the student might apply whilst prosecuting such a study. He would first procure the Commentaries of the Fathers—though they were difficult to obtain, except piece-meal—and then he might consult Venerable Bede, Alcuin's Revision, Rabanus Maurus, and Remigius of Auxerre. The student, as a matter of course, would carefully peruse the *Glossa Ordinaria* of Strabo, and, if he lived at a somewhat later period, would manage to procure the *Glossa Interlinearis* of Anselm of Laon. If he were anxious to study the more literal meaning of the sacred page, he could borrow Hugo of Amiens' work on the Hexameron, and choose between the Gospel harmonies of Zachary of Besançon and Odo of Cambrai. For mysticism, he would be at no loss; there would be, at once, S. Bernard the mellifluous, and the beautiful writings of the monastic theologians of S. Victor's. But, if he were of a more strictly scientific turn, he would be recommended to study carefully, as the best treatment of the original Bible text, the writings of Remigius of Auxerre and Rupert of Deutz; or, better still, perhaps, if he could procure a copy, would be the criticism of Abbot Stephen of Citeaux on the text, who had not only taken the trouble to compare the generally received version of the Vulgate with more accurate readings; but had also collated it with the original Hebrew and Chaldaic, which he had somehow succeeded in getting from the Jews. And, in point of fact, the student could not do better, if he were anxious to know something of the traditional interpretation of the Old Testament, than consult such men as Ben Esra, David Kimchi, and Moses Maimonides. Justin's Dialogue with Trypho shows, clearly enough, how much there is in common on this point between the Christians and the Jews. Then, finally, he might dip into the *Clavis* of Melito, which inaugurated a special tradition of exegesis, and can clearly be traced from the fifteenth century upwards, through the late and earlier scholastics, to the days, inclusively, of the great Fathers of the Church. This, together with the ponderous work written by Hugh of S. Caro, assisted by five hundred friars, the *Correctorium Bibliæ Sorbonnicum,* with its concordance, would go a good way towards giving the student a fair knowledge of that science which was called by Rabanus Maurus the four daughters of wisdom, and by Hildebert of Mans, the four feet of the Table of the Lord.

There is extant a very interesting little volume, written at this period, by an unknown hand, and dedicated to a monk called Hugh. The author, in the first place, gives a complete list of the Canonical and Apocryphal books of Scripture. Scripture, he says, must be read in a three-fold manner—'secundum historiam, allegoriam, et moralem instructionem, seu magis dicendum, tropologiam.' Then the whole Bible must be gone through three or four times in its historical sense, and those portions of it be marked which are not capable of literal interpretation. What would be false, unbecoming, unmeaning, and opposed to true morality, if interpreted literally, must be mystically understood.

At first, the student ought to confine himself to the Books of Moses, and the historical books of the Old Testament, and study them with Josephus or Hegesippus open before him. If he cannot make out a word, let him look at Isidore's work on Etymologies, Jerome's Explanation of Hebrew names, the *Liber Derivationum*, or the *Partionarius vel Glossarius*. The principal facts should be committed to memory; for instance, the details of the Creation, the history of the building of the Ark, the names and number of the Patriarchs, the plagues of Egypt, and such like. Next, S. Augustine's work, *De Quæstionibus*, can be read with great profit. After this, the student may begin to read the prophetical books of the Old Testament; paying attention to the fulfilled, and to the unfulfilled, prophecy. Then the rest of the Bible may be read. S. Jerome's work on the localities of Palestine is to accompany the reading of the Gospels. When the Bible has been mastered, the student is to study the Sacraments of the Church. These he will find fully treated by Hugh of S. Victor's. Then he is to study the principal virtues, and the opposing vices. If he wants a history of the Church, there is the *Candela Gerlandi;* or, if he likes, the *Quare* of Simon the Theologian. Next to this, the works of S. Augustine, the *Doctrina Christiana* and the *De Civitate Dei*, are to be mastered. After this preparation, the student is in a position to take up any book of Holy Scripture, and study profitably its allegorical and moral meaning.

With respect to theological authorities, the great basis of all teaching and learning at this period was the *Book of the Sentences*. To master this work, the student would have to apply himself to the Scriptures and the Fathers. It was especially necessary for him to know something of the latter, since the greater part of the *Sentences* were composed of extracts from their writings—so that some knowledge of them became an integral portion of the education of an ecclesiastic. He could study them in two ways: either by procuring copies of their writings—a difficult thing for the generality of students—or by reading the works of Isidore of Seville, Cassiodorus, and Venerable Bede. The translation of the writings of the Greek Fathers into Latin was promoted through the commerce of the East and West, brought about by the Crusades; through the high influence of the Popes, who were always patrons of ecclesiastical learning; and through the enterprising energy of religious Orders. Yet some knowledge of the Greek Fathers seems, at a very early period, to have been possessed by Western scholars. Rufinus did most valuable service. Through his industry, Western Christendom obtained a more accurate and extended knowledge of the works of Origen, S. Gregory Nazianzen, and S. Basil; as also of the History of Eusebius, the pseudo-Clementine Homilies, and Flavius Josephus. Then, Denis the Less translated some of the works of S. Gregory of Nyssa, of S. Cyril, and of Proclus. Cassiodorus compiled his *Historia Ecclesiastica Tripartita* from

Socrates, Sozomen, and Theodoret; and translated several of the works of Josephus, Hippocrates, and Galen. Later on, Scotus Erigena did the works of Denis the Areopagite into Latin. Then, the Orders of S. Dominic and S. Francis had amongst them many linguists of extraordinary ability; and they took every advantage of their missionary opportunities in the East for acquiring a more intimate knowledge of Oriental tongues. Robert of Lincoln translated the *Testamentum Duodecim Patriarcharum;* and, according to his friend Roger Bacon—who laments that more work, and more satisfactory work, had not been done in this way—he also translated many of the other Greek Fathers. The Popes caused the Acts of the Greek Councils to be rendered into Latin. And, lastly, Burgundio of Pisa, at the request of Pope Eugenius III., translated many of the Greek Fathers, and amongst the rest, the celebrated work of S. John Damascene, *De Fide Orthodoxa*.

Besides the writings of theologians and the labours of compilers, there was a rich vein of tradition, of theological teaching, running through the Paris schools. What Bologna was for law, what Salerno was for medicine, that Paris was for the study of divinity.

With regard to the form of teaching in the schools, or the study of dialectics, scholars, up to the first half of the twelfth century, had only such traditions of the later Roman civilisation as could be gathered from the writings of S. Augustine, from the pseudo-

Augustine treatise on the *Categories*, and the sketches of Aristotle's Logic by Cassiodorus, Capella, and Boethius. The student might have picked up some fragmentary knowledge from the writings of Cicero, Lucretius, and Apulejus. Some affirm that extracts from the physical and metaphysical writings of Aristotle were in use as early as the days of Venerable Bede; nay, even as far back as the time of Cassiodorus and Boethius. But it has been shown by Prantl that such could hardly have been the case. This is certain, that the student, at the time of Henry of Auxerre, who had been educated by Haymo at Fulda, would have had access to the *Categories* of the Stagyrite. He would be able to use those strange compendia, thrown together from every source imaginable; and those crabbed commentaries, which were more difficult to understand than the original matter they pretended to elucidate. By degrees, works of Aristotle, which had been translated, but had never been used, were brought into the schools; a more perfect and clear knowledge of the method of the Stagyrite was acquired by the student, when, in the thirteenth century, a pretty full analysis of his principal works had been made by the scholastics. Something of this kind is to be found in John of Salisbury's *Metalogue;* which, though it omits none of the logical writings of Aristotle, leaves out all the rest. Still, there are many more names besides his which might be mentioned; for instance, the labours of Antoli, of John of Basingstoke, and of Henry of Brabant; the Byzantine

Logic of Psellus; the Latin labours of Shyreswood, and of Lambert of Auxerre; and the *Summulæ* and *Translation* of Peter of Spain. Then another constellation of writers, compilers, and translators, such as Alexander of Hales, the Gloucestershire man; William of Auvergne; and Vincent of Beauvais, with his Universals, might be named; whilst the developments of the *Categories* by Gilbert de la Porrée, and the efforts of Robert Capito of Lincoln, carry the science on to the time of Albert, Thomas, and Bonaventure.

Of course, it stands to reason that, so long as the scholars of the West were confined within the narrow compass of the *Dialectics* of Aristotle, they were able to do little else than regulate the practices of dispute. It was a barren and contentious gift at best. Still, such as it was, men hailed it with delight. Rabanus Maurus was about the first to comment on the *Introduction* of Porphyry, and on portions of the *Organon*. In the year 935, whilst Reinard of S. Burchard, in Wurtemburg, commented on Aristotle's *Categories*, Poppo was elucidating, at Fulda, the *Commentary* of Boethius. Notker Labeo, who died in 1022, translated into German the *Commentary* of Boethius, and the *Categories* and *Interpretation* of the Stagyrite. Abbo of Fleury (1004) wrote a clever and original work on the *Conclusions*, and Adalberon, Bishop of Laon (1030), disciple of Gerbert, wrote a dissertation *De Modo recte Argumentandi et Prædicandi Dialecticam*.

But the time at length came when men got tired

of chopping logic. From time to time, circumstances occurred which called for the application of the forms of logic to the methods of metaphysics. The celebrated question put by Otto III. to Gerbert occasioned that subtle work, so far in advance of its period, *De Rationali et Ratione Uti*, which goes into the relations of possibility to reality, and of substance to accidents, upon the right meaning of which the solution of the royal difficulty depended. Then comes another step, and not a small one, from the work of Gerbert to that of S. Anselm. His dialogue *De Grammatico*, in which he treats of the categories of substance, quality, &c., is written with great ability, and with so firm a grasp of those difficult and abstract subjects, as manifests what an advance had been made upon the speculations of his predecessors. The scientific results of the contest of Berengarius with Lanfranc have already been hinted at, and thus, as the knowledge of philosophy, through the streams flowing into Europe, from Constantinople and from Arabia, became more extended and less fragmentary; and as men, by degrees, were able to gaze on the full orb of truth, as expressed in the splendid mind of the Greek philosopher, and to see that the whole *scibile* of human cognition could be reduced, from a comparative chaos, into system; they doggedly and laboriously set about piling together, under headings and divisions, the whole mass of information that was extant at their day. This, Hugh of S. Victor's attempted—this was the work that immortalised the name of Vincent of Beauvais. Men had studied reasoning, and the laws of order and arrangement, and they naturally brought their knowledge to account. But systematising is not science. An encyclopædia, however much matter may be thrown into it, and however cleverly it may be put together, is not the highest result of the efforts of the human mind. In a corpse, the anatomy remains as marvellous, in the economy and wisdom of its order and arrangement, as in a living body; but a corpse represents the silent power of death. Anatomy must be animated by a living spirit, and then the relations of its parts will manifest their power, and be able to act upon the world. This men gradually began to see. The masses of knowledge must receive the animation of an intellectual life. The *spiraculum vitæ* must be breathed into the ready clay—S. Thomas must turn the Encyclopædia of Albert into the power of an intellectual life. The one, long ago, has been dead, strangled in the mightiness of its own birth—a monster accumulation of all human knowledge of that day, thrown into order and division, but dead. The other, a clear, scientific exposition of the truth of God, animated throughout every portion of its organism with the vitality of a scientific life; of a life that has lived, and fought, and conquered, from that day to this; a life which is so living, that it has possessed the minds of the most consummate masters of human thought, and, through the strength of its vitality, has given intellectual vigour to men, who, unexercised in its power, would have remained comparatively feeble all their lives.

The quiet monks in the peaceful Benedictine monasteries, who introduced the study of dialectics into the schools, little knew what they were about—that those imperfect translations of Boethius were to be the beginning of a movement which would shake the Catholic intellectual world. It was all well enough for men busied in the love of God, and balanced in the contemplation of the Day of Judgment, to exercise their minds upon literary remains, saved from the wreck of Greek and Roman letters. But all the students at the monasteries were not monks; or, if they were, there were not wanting those whose ardent natures would find greater pleasure in intellectual contest, than in the quiet monotony of religious routine. Such youths, when they had learnt to use the weapons which had been put into their hands, awkward and clumsy as they might have been, were bent upon leaving the retirement of the cloister, to brandish them in the world. Dialectics soon began to be applied to faith. The Church had grown into vast and stately proportions. Her creed had to be defended, illustrated, proved; her rights had to be maintained. Philosophy, theology, and law were to be mastered by those who were to be her champions; and dialectics were the most powerful weapons in the hands of the dispensers of her gifts. The stream of learning from the East, tinged with its Oriental fanaticism, and the principles of Greek thought, which sharpened still more the keen edge of the mind, entered into the soul of European society. This, added to the mysterious influence of supernatural faith, the marvels performed by saints, and the extraordinary interference of the unseen in human affairs, worked the mind into enthusiasm. The spirit was ready to be acted on throughout its circumference, by the unimpeded influence of truth.

The Church was far too wise to allow instruments, so finely strung, to waste all their power in personal displays. She was the *Ecclesia Docens*, and she undertook their direction. She knew the task of governing minds, and felt her responsibility in guiding them in their fiery impetuosity—in their headlong speed—to the gate of truth. Ever looking into the future, with an eye that sees farther than human vision, she perceived her opportunity, and seized upon it.

The Sees of the Bishops were centres of her influence. Endless branches radiated from them, as they themselves seemed to radiate from the Apostolic See. Or again, they form the knots in the vast net-work of the Hierarchy spread throughout the world, and maintain its whole complexity in power, unity, and order. The Council of Rome, in 1078, took a broad and masterly view of the necessities of the times, and met the wants of the age. By the side of every Episcopal Cathedral it placed a school of liberal arts. It stands to reason, that the most important capitals would be the first to grow into a larger life. Rome, being the seat of the Papacy, was ever the first seat of authority; but Paris may be said to have been the capital of intellectual Europe. Its position, its resources, its healthiness, the balminess of its air, its traditions—which ran back to Charlemagne and Alcuin, and had not been altogether extinguished—point to it as the natural centre of university activity.

CHAPTER IX.

PARIS, THE UNIVERSITY.

LIKE the solar system, according to the theory of La Place, the Universities were not organised in a day. Both were developments out of chaos and confusion, into order. Power and method had to expand into a vast system of intellectual activity; and the greatest minds of the new world were to be exercised in the highest and most splendid forms of human thought. This, of course, took time. A few teachers came as adventurers, or to assist in the Episcopal schools. Then, some took lodgings, and hired rooms. Others, having received a good education, and being active, enterprising fellows, pushed their way, in spite of poverty and obscurity; drew young men under their influence, and made a name. Godfrey of Boulogne, the Bishop of Paris, saw which way the current was running. He at once founded, towards the end of the eleventh century, a high school in the capital. Now the great development began in earnest. Here, Lanfranc taught; and astonished his hearers by the grasp of his intellect, and by the splendour of his eloquence.

There were not only deeply-learned men acting as doctors in the schools of Paris ; but young men with no learning, and little experience, would undertake to collect students around them, and to teach a class. Cardinal de Vitry speaks of these conceited young professors, and warns the inexperienced against them. He says that all their learning was in their copy-books and text-books, and that by force of prayers, caresses, and even money, they strove to gather about them a crowd of curious young men, and encouraged them to waste their time in futile questions. Some young men are mentioned, as being so dull and negligent, as to learn nothing, even under the ablest masters—continually on the move, never resting with this master or that, ever changing their books and their course of studies ; sometimes attending lectures in winter, and giving them up in summer. Some did only barely enough to secure to them their titles of scholar, or to preserve the stipend which was given to poor students. They would be seen sitting on the benches of the lecture-hall two or three times a week, perhaps ; and were said to prefer to attend the lectures of the decretists, because they took place at three o'clock, and thus they were enabled to sleep all the morning. However, they made up for their idleness by their ostentation, employing men to carry enormous volumes before them through the streets, so that people might take them for excessively learned and studious young men. Others, on returning home, in order to make their friends imagine that they had been working hard, would carry with them a large parchment book, full of blank leaves, and very elegantly bound in red.

The turmoil and excitement of a city of students from every part of the world can be imagined. The narrow streets swarmed with clerks and students, brandishing their weapons, and ever on the alert for the pleasures of some fresh intellectual excitement. Then came Abelard and William of Champeaux, with their noisy, boisterous following. Paris had by this time obtained a name for depth and activity of theological display. What Bologna was, and Modena and Orleans became, for law; Padua, for liberal arts; Salerno, for medicine; and Toledo, for mathematics—Paris now became for theology,—the *Summum Scientiæ*. She decided cases of conscience, and was consulted by Popes and Kings. The third Council of Lateran helped the movement on. Paris became the centre of an attraction, which possessed the power of drawing everything like intellectual life, however distant, into itself. Crowds of students, from every portion of Europe, filled the city, already half inhabited by Jews. It was impossible for such a multitude to exist, or to be taught on any rule, without some permanent arrangement for the schools. This pressure gave rise to the University. The Episcopal Seminary, S. Victor's, S. Geneviève, and S. Germain's, which alone, at this period, had permanent professors, formed the basis of this splendid institution.

The natural laws of demand and supply waited on the intellectual market of the University. Men would arrive, perhaps from Salerno, and give lectures on medicine; then others would set up and descant on civil and canon law, until Paris became crammed with a diverse population of boys and men from every quarter of Europe, and even from the East—eager, excited, full of animal spirits and animal passion, half civilised, and glowing with an indescribable desire after knowledge and after fame. At length, some of these teachers put themselves in connection with the Chancellor of Notre Dame; and the University thus took a wider development. All kinds flocked to the schools. There were starving, friendless lads, with their unkempt heads, and their tattered suits, who walked the streets, hungering for bread, and famishing for knowledge, and hankering after a sight of some of those great doctors, of whom they had heard so much, when far away in the woods of Germany or the fields of France. Some were so poor, that they could not afford to follow a course of theology. We read of one poor fellow on his death-bed, having nothing else, giving his shoes and stockings to a companion, to procure a mass for his soul. Some were only too glad to carry holy water to private houses, *selon la coutume Gallicane*, with the hope of receiving some small remuneration. Some were destitute of necessary clothing. One tunic sometimes served for three, who took it in turns—two went to bed, whilst the third dressed himself and hurried off to school. Some spent all their scanty means in buying parchments, and wasted their strength, through half the night, poring over crabbed manuscript, or in puzzling out that jargon which contained the wisdom of the wisest of the Greeks. Whole nights some would remain awake on their hard pallets, in those unhealthy cells, trying to work out some problem proposed by the professor in the schools. But there were rich as well as poor at Paris. There was Langton, like others, famous for his opulence, who taught, and then became Canon of Notre Dame; and Thomas à Becket, who, as a youth, came here to seek the charm of gay society.

Indeed, all eyes, even those which had been accustomed to spend the greater portion of their time in following the Psalms of David, and the remainder in resting on quiet woodland, and placid stream, and solemn mountain, and those, too, which had been practised in more active work, all turned to Paris, all gazed on that busy, eager swarm, which was ever working at, and purifying, and taking possession of, the learning of the past. These silent thinkers, at first, were mystified, and then were sad. The dry seed which they so gently had sown in the mind of a former generation had taken a terrific growth. Those chance words of Porphyry had set on foot a revolution in the intellectual world. Who would care to study at Fulda, at S. Gall, at York, or at Citeaux; or to dwell amongst the hills of Germany and France, when Anselm, William, Abelard, or Hugh, were dazzling the world in intellectual Paris? Who would care to go to the tricklings on the mountain side, when large draughts could be imbibed from the great reservoir itself? Hence, in the desert, on the hill-top, and in the fruitful valley, a gradual movement might have been discerned. Solitude and peace join in the uproar of a vast city! The Trinitarians had launched into the troubled sea, and were lecturing at S. Mathurin's as early as 1209. Then Stephen Lexington, stung by the satires of the Mendicants, brings in the ascetic children of S. Bernard, and the Cistercian drops his pick and spade, and is on his way to Paris; the Carmelites, too, are seen clustering with their sandalled feet at the foot of S. Geneviève and the Augustinians at Montmartre; then, there are the Black Monks of S. Benedict, who are heavy at heart, and quietly hide themselves away near the great Abbey of S. Germain, to watch and take advantage of the movement; Cluny is there, and even the silent and solitary Carthusian, struck by the pulse that throbs in the heart of the outer world, throws himself into the whirl of intellectual activity. Provincial schools cease to satisfy. Bishops forward their contingents to the growing city of science; and we read of the seminaries of Laon, Narbonne, and Bayeux, taking their place amongst the rest.

It will be well rapidly to touch upon the foundation of Notre Dame, S. Geneviève, and S. Catharine's; on the colleges of the Premonstratensians, the Carthusians, and the Cluniacs; on S. Martin's; and on that influential college which opposed the Regulars so violently, the famous Sorbonne.

The oldest and most celebrated school of Paris, that of Notre Dame, owes its origin to the enlightened influence of Charlemagne. It was when he met that able Yorkshireman, Alcuin, in Italy, that he first entertained the idea of systematically bringing the light of learning into France. He founded the Palace school, which was Peripatetic, following him wherever he went; and he loved to join his sons and his daughters in taking lessons from its learned men. Then the Emperor ordered the Bishops under his influence to erect free schools in connection with their cathedrals. This may be said to have been the origin of the school of Notre Dame. The cloister of the metropolitan church, for some centuries, continued to be the centre of public instruction. Even when S. Geneviève became most influential in the teaching of science, the reunions of the Faculties took place at Notre Dame. As late as the eighteenth century, the Chancellor of Notre Dame had the privilege of being one of the Chancellors of the University. What Charlemagne and Alcuin began was continued by the successors of both. Clement of Hibernia, Claud, Aldric, Amalarius, Peter of Pisa, Paul the Deacon, John Scotus Erigena, and Mannon, carried on the work. But it was the Benedictine Monk, Remigius of Auxerre, in the ninth century, who started the first really public school in Paris. Its reputation grew steadily under Adam the Englishman, a professor at a school at Petit-Pont; and under that extraordinary book-worm Peter Comestor, and under Peter the Cantor and Michael de Corbeil—till the contests of Abelard and William of Champeaux drew upon it the concentrated notice of the Paris public. The Cathedral, in Abelard's time (*Sacro-Sancta Ecclesia Civitatis Parisiorum*), was composed of two distinct churches, one dedicated to S. Stephen; the other, to the Blessed Virgin. The present magnificent structure was begun in the year 1163, and was finished about the close of the thirteenth century. In all the old plans of Paris, that grand, sombre temple seems to overtower, and, by its majestic proportions, to overshadow, the churches that surround it. Its cloister, with its dependencies, extended to the north and east of the church on to the banks of the Seine. The present street of Cloître-Notre-Dame occupies a portion of the old foundation. In the fourteenth century, it enclosed thirty-seven houses, which were occupied by as many Canons. The school was fixed in the enclosure, in the portion called 'Tresantiæ,' and the scholars, till the year 1127 (when the privilege was taken from them), had a right to live in the houses there. There was one favour accorded to its students by Notre Dame, which was not given by other colleges till a considerably later period. Notre Dame not only possessed a valuable library, composed of books, the gifts, amongst others, of Bishop Gilbert (991), Bishop

Theobald (1157), the Lombard (1160), Aubert the Cantor (1180), Dean Barbedor (1182), Eudes Sully (1208)—who had so much to say to the building of the Cathedral—and of Bishop Peter (1218), and Bartholomew (1229), and many others; but the poor students had these works put at their disposal—an immense advantage in those days before printing was invented. The Chancellor had the general superintendence of the library. The library had *in communem usum* forty-two annotated volumes, besides the *Sentences* of the Lombard—which Peter seems to have presented himself—and the *Quæstiones* of Peter of Poitiers, which consisted of commented extracts from the Sacred Text, forming a pretty complete treatise on the Bible. The necrology of these large establishments, where the names of benefactors were written down to be remembered and prayed for, shows how thoughtful Bishops and friends of learning were, in those days, of the wants of needy students.

The Chapter of the Cathedral was composed of a dean, a cantor, three archdeacons, the sub-cantor, the chancellor, the penitentiary, and fifty-two prebendaries.

Let us now glance at S. Geneviève. S. Gregory of Tours relates, that Clovis and Clotilde founded, at the solicitation of S. Geneviève, on Mount Leucotitius, the Basilica of S. Peter's. All three—the King, the Queen, and the Saint—were buried in the church. The establishment connected with it was soon turned into an Abbey. Between the ninth and eleventh centuries, it was several times ruined by the Normans, and the tombs of the saints were rifled, and their ashes scattered to the wind. The increase of students carried the University in this direction, and the Canons, being connected with France and Denmark—into which they sent a colony—soon gained a high reputation by the eminent abilities of their scholars. As has been seen, it was in the time of William of Champeaux that its reputation was greatly raised, by the influence of Peter Abelard. In 1790, its library consisted of fifty-eight thousand volumes, and two thousand manuscripts.

The college called 'S. Catharina Vallis Scholarium' was established by four celebrated professors—Richard, Everard, William, and Manasses. These men, wishing to renounce the world, in 1201, retired into a valley surrounded by woods and fountains in the diocese of Langres. But they soon got tired of this, and longed after Paris again. So Manasses procured some land from a man named Gibouin Baudet; and a sergeant of the guard of King Louis, in fulfilment of a vow (1214), built them a church, of which the King laid the first stone (1229), and made them an offering of forty livres.

In the year 1247, Abbot John de Roquignies, of the Premonstratensians, an Order founded at Premontré by S. Norbert in 1120, established a house for his young men in Paris. In 1252, he purchased a great building in the Rue Hautefeuille, close to where the Franciscans built their immense church and quadrangle. Sister Guillerma, three years later, let him have three other houses, and thus the great College of S. Norbert began its useful work. Any one entering the present Café de la Rotonde, at the corner of the Rue Hautefeuille and the Rue d'Ecole-de-Médecine, would find Frenchmen sipping their coffee and reading their papers in the very sanctuary of the church of the Premonstratensians.

The Chartreux was one of the largest establishments in Paris. In 1257, King Louis placed five monks in the Château de Vauvert, which was supposed to be haunted by evil spirits, but which were effectually dispersed by the piety of the monks. Louis held these men in highest reverence, and treated them with kingly generosity. Their building and dependences covered nearly all that space in the gardens of the Luxembourg, lying now between the Boulevard S. Michel, formed by the Rue d'Enfer and the Rue de l'Est, and the first of the three great new streets that have been cut across the great *allée*. The Cruciferi, like so many others, were called to Paris in 1258 by King Louis, and they settled on the right bank of the Seine.

Cluny founded its college here in 1269. Ivo of Vergi bought land on the left of the present Place de la Sorbonne, surrounded it by a wall, built a kitchen, refectory, dormitory, and a portion of the cloister. S. Martin des Champs was situated in a most beautiful position, with oak-trees and windmills on an eminence to the north—on the one side, a stream winding its way through a valley to the Convent of the Filles-Dieu, and, on the other, fertile fields and bright courses of water.

It was first the property of the Canons Regular, till the Monks of Cluny took possession of it.

There were innumerable foundations, which it would be tiresome to mention—the Collége du Trésorier, founded by William de Saône, in 1268; the Collége d'Harcourt, by Ralph d'Harcourt, in 1280; the Collége des Cholets, by Cardinal John Cholet, in 1292; the College of Cardinal Lemoine, founded in 1302; that of Navarre, by Johanna, Countess of Champagne, in 1304; the College of Laon, by Guy of Laon, in 1313; of Narbonne, by Bernard de Farges and the Archbishop, in 1316; the Collége du Plessis, by Geoffrey du Plessis Balisson, in 1323; the Collége de Cornouailles, in 1317, by Galeran de Grève; the Scotch College, by David, Bishop of Murray, in 1323; and the Collége de Presles, by Guy de Laon and Ralph de Presles; and so on.

But there is one institution which, though established at a later date than Notre Dame and S. Geneviève, still, perhaps, in the long run, has exerted a greater influence upon the intellectual world than any other seat of learning in Paris. And since it seems to have been established as a check upon the predominance of the religious Orders, and since one of the great opponents of S. Thomas was educated there, it will be well to give a somewhat fuller sketch of its origin and development.

The Sorbonne, then, owes its origin to the great overflow of students during the time of King Louis.

Both in S. Victor's and S. Geneviève the students had increased three-fold, whilst the cloister of Notre Dame, like a hive of bees, could not possibly contain the multitudes that desired to take up their abode within its precincts. The Dominicans and Franciscans, of themselves, attracted hundreds of eager youth. Geoffrey of Poitiers, William of Autun, William Lenoir, Gerard of Abbeville, Gerard of Courtray, and others, opened new establishments. Paris was still full to overflowing. The terrible dangers of city life, the continual broils between the students and the lodging-keepers about their unhealthy rooms—broils which necessitated the intervention of the Pope himself, and of which more will be said afterwards—made a deep impression on that thoughtful and kind-hearted Robert of Sorbon, chaplain of King Louis. He was not a man, perhaps, of first-class talents, but he certainly was unrivalled in his knowledge of the world and as a man of business. The idea struck him of bringing together professors and students into one establishment, and thus saving both from many difficulties and temptations. Some affirm that his object was to create a power to balance against the Regulars; others, that he wished to give poor scholars facilities for taking degrees, which they greatly required under the regulations of that period. Whatever were his reasons—and why could not all these motives, and others besides, have influenced him?—his idea, when realised, became the type upon which all future colleges were established.

Robert was born October 9th, 1201. It is generally believed that he first saw the light at Sorbon, near Rethel, in the diocese of Rheims. He became Canon of Cambrai. He was presented at court by the King's brother. The King seems to have liked him, and though of lowly family, he was often invited to the royal table, and became confessor to his Majesty. He made use of his influence with Louis for advancing his favourite design. In 1250, he persuaded the King to help him with his college. Louis let him have, 'ad opus scholarium qui inibi moraturi sunt,' a house and stables in the Vie de Coupegueule, 'ante Palatium Thermarum.' It was called Coupegorge, on account of the frequent murders and massacres that were known often to have taken place there. The authorities of the college, later on, obtained permission to close at night the two ends of this dangerous street, and thus it came to be called Rue des Deux-Portes (Vicus ad Portas, or ad duas Portas). But, when the establishment had made its reputation, the street's name was absorbed into that of the college, and it was called Vicus de Sorbonia, or de Sorbonio. Others, however, do not agree with this explanation, and say that the Rue Coupegueule went down from the Rue des Poirées to the Rue des Mathurins, between the Rue de Sorbonne and Rue des Maçons.

Here Robert tried to collect the ablest men he could induce to help him at the college. He found many of his friends at the court well disposed. There was William of Chartres, Canon of S. Quentin and Chaplain to the King; Robert of Douai, Canon of Senlis and physician to Margaret of Provence, wife of King Louis. Then there were Cardinals Geoffrey de Bar, Dean of the church of Paris; and William de Brai, Archdeacon of Rheims —these men offered him money and advice. Others gave their brains: above all, William of Saint-Amour —the great enemy of S. Thomas and the Regulars; there was also Odo of Douai, the Englishman Lawrence, Gerard of Rheims, Gerald of Abbeville, Ralph of Courtray, Reginald of Soissons, Godfrey Desfontaines—a man of great learning—Henry of Gand, Peter of Limoges, Odo de Castres, Siger de Brabant, Poncard, and Arnulf de Hasnède. The college was opened in 1253.

As may easily be conceived, such a beginning as this would naturally grow. In less than five years the buildings had to be enlarged. S. Louis, wanting to establish a convent of Brothers of the Holy Cross in a house contiguous to the college, exchanged with Robert some houses in the Rue Coupegueule for some property in the parish of S. John de Grève. Five years later, the King made another exchange. He gave Robert a new house in the Rue Coupegueule and all he had in the Rue des Maçons for some property in the Rue de l'Hirondelle and the Rue Saint-Jacques (1263). Robert was already a Doctor of Divinity, but, in the deed of transmission, he is called a Canon of Notre Dame of Paris—'ad opus Congregationis Pauperum Magistrorum Parisiis in Theologia Studentium.' Robert of Douai died, and left the new college 1500 livres—a considerable sum in those days. Alexander IV. (1259) recommended it to the generosity of prelates, abbots, and the faithful generally. Clement IV. (1268) approved of it, and regulated its relations with the Holy See, showing how keen an eye Rome kept, even in those days, upon the great fountains of science and education. Robert naturally was officially recognised as head. But the Pope insisted upon his successors being nominated with the approval of the Archdeacon and Chancellor of the church of Paris, of the Doctors of Theology, the Deans of the Faculties of Law and Medicine, the Rector of the University, and the Procurators of the four nations.

Robert died in the year 1274, after having been head of the college for twenty years. About the year 1270 the Faculties were established in different places: law was at Clos Bruneau; arts were at Rue du Fouare; and the Sorbonne itself remained the chief place for the faculty of theology. To be admitted to the college, a man had to be a bachelor; to defend a thesis, called the Robertine; and to obtain the majority of votes in three *scrutinia*. The members of the community comprised two classes, viz. Hospites and Socii. The former had all facilities for study provided for them, and had nothing to do with the administration; they were allowed to work in the library, but were not trusted with the key. When they became doctors they had to leave the establishment. The administration was carried on by the Socii, who maintained a strict equality amongst themselves, according to the saying of the old Sorbonists,

'Omnes sumus sicut Socii et æquales.' The Socii who were well off paid exactly the same sum to the college as the poor Socii (Socii Bursales) received from it. Originally the number of Socii was thirty-six. Some of the doctors were obliged to apply themselves to the study of Cases of Conscience. People, after a while, sent cases for solution from all parts of Europe, and thus the Sorbonne gained a wide-spread reputation.

The Provisor was the highest dignitary. The active duties fell upon the Prior, who was generally taken from amongst the younger members of the Socii, and his term expired at the end of twelve months. Four seniors were appointed to regulate difficult questions, and to maintain the ancient traditions of the place, thus forming seemingly an equal—though it hardly seems practical—check and countercheck of old and young. The meeting of the Socii, which was held the first of every month, was called the *prima mensis*. The establishment most probably was under the protection of S. Ursula.

The Paris students may roughly be divided into three classes: those who lived in seminaries, those who lived in monasteries, and those who lived as best they could. The principal inhabitants of the city appear to have been at first tradesmen, publicans, furriers, jewellers, barbers, cutlers, mercers, tavern-keepers, and sellers of tapestry and parchment, who made their money by the students; with thousands of Jews and women of ill-fame. Paris, in early days, must have presented a spectacle of great public disorder, debauchery, and crime. The professors, in great part, were reckless adventurers—a sort of wild knight-errants, who scoured the country in search of excitement for the mind and money for the pocket. The students were, in the main, disorderly youths, living in the very centre of corruption, without control, loving a noisy, dissipated life in town. Some were destitute, quarrelling with prostitutes and varlets, and filling the tribunals with their scandals and litigations, living on charity or in *hospitia;* others were rich and lordly, great spendthrifts and swaggerers, and devoid of every virtue except perhaps the gift of faith, studying, if at all, to know—from mere curiosity; or to be known—out of pure conceit. They would rollick, and row, and stream in and out of the schools, like swarms of hornets, buzzing and litigating and quarrelling with one another, upsetting every semblance of discipline and order. They simply went to Paris for excitement and adventure, to fill their bodies and minds with whatever could minister to their cravings. These young martinets, as they were called, would acknowledge no master but the impulse of the moment; and their conduct at length became so unbearable that by charter they were excluded from all the privileges of Paris students. In the evenings and towards nightfall the taverns in those narrow crooked streets would be filled with the fumes of their liquors, and the streets would echo again with their boisterous mirth and to the sound of the voices of troubadours, minnesingers, and minstrels, who loved good cheer, and were never so happy as when gaily singing love-songs or dealing out satire upon people in high places to the ring of the joyous thoughtless laugh of the Paris student. As the drink passed round the mirth would become more pronounced. Words would be dealt out, interspersed with knocks and blows; the tavern would become a scene of indescribable uproar and confusion, with students and women and noisy rakings of the town, till the mass of them would swarm out irregularly and choke the narrow street, shouting and yelling and brandishing their daggers, as they parted company, some to their lodgings, others to crown their night's debauch by waking up and insulting the sleeping citizens. Bloodshed was frequent in these brawls; death was not uncommon. The confusion would at times spread to the people. There would be a general town-and-gown fight. Pegge, in his life of Bishop Grossetete, speaks of a tumult at Oxford in the thirteenth century, in which the brother of the Papal Legate was struck down by a bow-shot, and which was of so violent a character, even for those reckless days, that the numbers of the University dwindled away from thirty thousand to six thousand.

The elections of professors gave a great opening to bitterness, jealousy, and contention. The custom at Paris was at one time for the different 'nations' to elect a reader of ethics; but this practice led to so many brutal outrages that it had at length to be done away with altogether. There were plenty of occasions for faction fights without such direct encouragement as the public election of professors. After one of these contests the students appealed against the Parisians to the king. Philip Augustus took their part. He transferred them from the jurisdiction of the civil arm to that of the ecclesiastical courts. He placed a member of the University upon the bench, and great advantages resulted to both sides from the relations thus introduced. Having been recognised by the King, the University was now recognised by the Pope. Innocent III., who had been a student there, formed it into an ecclesiastical body. He deputed Robert Courçon, his Legate, to draw out a set of statutes. In these, the qualifications of professors, the books to be used, and the relations of the students to each other, were stated. To teach arts, a man must have had a six years' course, and had to be at least twenty-one years old. To teach theology, an eight years' course and thirty-five years of age were requisite. Just as Bologna became the model of Italian and Spanish universities, so Paris became the model for those of Germany and England. In Italy, law, almost exclusively, was taught; in Paris and Oxford there was no neglect of theology.

Paris seems to have taken the lead in influence and numbers. The distracted state of England induced scholars to leave Oxford and Cambridge and fix themselves in Paris. So multitudinous was the number of students that they were divided, not according to schools, but according to nations. Whoever came were classified, either as Frenchmen, which included Spaniards, Italians, and Orientals; as Englishmen or Germans, including the Hungarians, Scandinavians, and Poles; or as Picards or Normans. So great was their number at one time that, in a procession, the first rank had entered the church of Notre Dame whilst the last rank was still leaving S. Mathurin's. Kings would assist at their splendid pageants, and would honour by their presence five thousand graduates. On one occasion the University promised to send twenty-five thousand scholars to increase the pomp of a funeral. In 1262, Olfred himself gave his lectures to ten thousand scholars in Padua. In the sixteenth century there were forty thousand students. Bologna, Padua, Salamanca, Naples, Upsal, Lisbon, and Rome followed suit. In 1260 there were ten thousand students at Bologna; in 1262, some say, there were twenty thousand. In 1200 there were four thousand scholars at Oxford; in 1231 thirty thousand; and in 1263 fifteen thousand. We read of five thousand being at Cambridge. Toulouse was equally flourishing with the college of Guienne at Bordeaux, which was able to muster two thousand five hundred students. The University of Louvain, later on, had as many as forty colleges attached to it, whilst before the Reformation Europe could boast of as many as sixty-six universities, sixteen of which belonged to Germany.

Such was the marvellous influence of knowledge in

the middle ages. Nor was the enthusiasm of individuals of short duration. In these days a lad has finished his education at twenty-one; in those days he had not done much more than begun it. The mind, through the drill of the schools, was fit and ripe for manly thought, for abstract speculation, and for grasping with firm hold the form of truth. No pains were spared to obtain good professors, and to economise them. Even in meditative Cluny there was a ten years' course; three years of *logicalia*, three of *literæ naturales et philosophia*, and five of theology. It was not at all unusual for a man to spend ten years over philosophy. Men studied philosophy and theology at Paris fifteen or sixteen years, and continued scholars till between thirty or forty years of age. Grown men, and men with wives and families, were not ashamed—were proud to sit by the side of striplings, and learn the wisdom of the schools. Then they finished their education by attending different centres, and travelling to different countries; for instance —Innocent III. was at Rome, Bologna, and Paris; Alexander V. shone both at Paris and at Oxford; John of Salisbury studied under many masters; so of Vacarius, Lanfranc, and many others.

It was only in process of time that the true division of science began to be understood. At first, all things were taught together. By degrees, men saw from Aristotle that method and order conduce to clearness and grasp. It was only in the middle of the thirteenth century that theology was made a separate faculty; that medicine was divorced from art, and law from theology. The rector could be chosen only from amongst the Artists. Their privileges were numerous. For, if their vacation only lasted one month in summer time, they seem to have possessed all, and more than all, the privileges of citizens, without being subject to their responsibilities. They seem to have held somewhat the same relation to the students that townsmen do to soldiers quartered on them during war; with this difference, that the soldier is under strict discipline, whilst the student was hardly under any discipline at all. It can well be conceived how independent—nay, overbearing—so vast and powerful a body of young men and professors could easily become. De Vitry says that their bitterness and contentions were the result of three causes, viz. because they belonged to different sects, and so reviled and irritated each other; because of the school disputes, which were fruitful parents of hatred, envy, and sometimes bloodshed, and even death; and because of their different temperaments and nationalities, which were ever a standing excuse for indulging the instincts of the animal. Certainly there could not have been better ingredients for mixing up into a quarrel, if the view they held of each other's characteristics was founded upon fact. The Englishman was a sot; the Frenchman, effeminate and proud; the German, furious and obscene; the Norman, vain; the Picard, a spendthrift; the Burgundian, stupid and brutal; the Lombard, a miser and a coward; the Roman, violent, seditious, and a thief; the Sicilian, cruel and tyrannical; the Brabantine, a man of blood, and an incendiary; the Fleming, prodigal, a glutton, and soft as butter. It is not astonishing that, with such elements as these in a state of constant friction, there should have been little peace, and periodical explosions. Then, when it is considered how the application of the faculties in search of truth and the exercise of the reason in logical display heats the brain and renders the whole being full of a nervous excitability; when it is remembered with what brutal loyalty some of the half-barbarians of these days maintained the teaching of their master, and held to creation of the fantasy with much more keenness than they would have held to life; when it is remembered that the living voices of the most eloquent men were continually ringing in their ears, and often carrying them away in the flow of their impetuous rhetoric against some other professor, who was, very probably, acting exactly a similar part in another school; when it is remembered that there was little self-control in those days, that they were days of singular enthusiasm, of emotion, of passion, of ecstatic display, and maddening life, some notion may be formed of the moral position of those thousands who poured into Paris from every country of Europe. Many almost killed themselves by over-work, and the tiny light, when the morning broke upon the city, could be seen flickering from their windows as they still pored over the books which they had opened with the setting sun. Others despised study altogether. They expressed the reaction against the overstrain of intellectual life. They went about talking loudly, and boasting that it was absurd to take lessons in logic and in learning; that teaching was waste of time and of no account at all; that man was quite sufficient for himself; that if he had talent enough to go to school he had ability enough to make his own logic; and that if he was too dull to frame his logic for himself, he was far too stupid to do any good at school. It may be imagined how eager scholars, whose hearts and intelligences were engrossed by the fascinating problems of the schools, would be irritated and maddened by these coxcombs; for the Cornificii were only too glad to put a bilious student in a passion and then turn round and laugh at him. The Cornificii, we imagine, were the most rollicking, independent, useless set that ever drank or sang—that ever disputed for the sake of pastime, and frittered away their time in the amusements of the gay city. They would be troubled by no dyspeptic melancholy; they would not be peevish, as is the sickly student who passes his days and nights in poring over parchment as yellow nearly as himself. The violence of the students sometimes led to strange results. In the time of Gregory IX. a fatal brawl took place in a tavern and much blood flowed. The authorities interposed. The University resented the interference. It was maintained that the civil authority had no right to meddle. It was for the University to settle its own quarrels and punish its own misdeeds. Redress was demanded. None was forthcoming. So students and professors at once *en masse* left Paris, and went off to Rheims, Angers, Toulouse, Orleans, Italy, and Spain, and left the 'Mistress of the World' almost a ruined and a silent city. The Pope looked on this as a calamity. He impressed upon King Louis the importance of conciliation. Louis took Pope Gregory's view. The professors and students were recalled, and the work went on as busily as before. But Gregory would no longer suffer the students to carry arms. The Bishop of Paris was empowered to punish and arrest; but the like liberty was not conceded to the Chancellor. Other decrees relating to the better order and greater safety of the University were issued at various intervals, and many privileges were accorded to the students.

But fortunately for science and religion, there were in Paris other students, besides those who represented the element of disorder and human passion. In the midst of this heaving ocean, which was seldom calm, and at times lashed into tempestuous fury, there were islands, centres of stability, where the thunder of the ocean could scarcely be heard; at least, against which the sea might beat, but certainly to break. These centres were the monastic convents, where men advanced in knowledge in proportion as they sunk in humility and rose in love. There were exceptions, but to speak broadly, they were the instruments of power against the mass of humanity, that was heaving and sinking, and swaying to and fro, in the outside world.

The founders of these colleges were keenly alive to the immense danger, for young men, in the proximity of so much corruption. The plaintive cry of those simple monks is the voice of the old method expiring away. Peter of Cells complains bitterly; Matthew of Paris, that keen observer, sees how the tide is turning; and Philip, Abbot of Goodhope, expresses the full feeling of that school, when he exclaims, 'Blessed is the man, not who hath heard Master Anselm, or who hath studied at Paris, but to whom Thou, O Lord, dost teach Thy law.' Those who bent to the pressure of the times felt quite as keenly. The regulations for students coming to study at Paris were very stringent. It was strictly forbidden, for instance, in the Cluny convent, for a student to go into the city without an express permission, and, even then, always in the company of a master.

Robert of Sorbon gave a very interesting instruction (*De Conscientiâ*) concerning what the student should do to profit by his study. This is a *résumé*:

The scholar, who would profit by his position, ought to observe six essential rules:

1. He ought to dedicate one certain hour to one specified piece of reading, as S. Bernard advises, in his letter to the brethren of Mont Dieu.

2. To fix his attention upon what he is going to read, and not to pass on lightly to something else. There is the same difference, says S. Bernard, again, between reading and studying, as between a host and a friend—between a salute exchanged in the street and an unalterable affection.

3. To extract, each day, one thought, one truth of some sort, and to engrave it in the memory with especial care. Seneca has said, 'Cum multa percurreris in die, unum tibi elige quod illâ die excoquas.'

4. To write a *résumé*—for unwritten words are blown away like dust before the wind.

5. To join with his companions in the 'disputations,' or in familiar conversations—this practice is even of greater service than reading, because it results in clearing up all doubts, and all the obscurities which have been left by reading on the mind, 'Nihil perfectè scitur nisi dente disputationis feriatur.'

6. To pray — for this is, in point of fact, one of the best means of learning. S. Bernard teaches that reading should excite the affections of the soul, and that such influences should be turned to advantage in elevating the heart to God, without, on that account, interrupting study. . . . . In the acquisition of knowledge, the pleasures of the flesh must be abstained from, and creature-comforts must not be embraced. There were at Paris two masters, bound together, of whom one had seen much, read much, and remained bent day and night over his books—hardly did he take time to say a single *Pater*. This man had only four disciples. His companion had a worse-furnished library, was less carried away by study, hearing Mass every day before giving his lesson: and, nevertheless, his school was full. 'Now, how do you manage?' the first asked him. 'It is simple enough,' the second replied, smiling; 'God studies for me; I go to Mass, and when I return, I know by heart all that I ought to teach.'

Meditation is not only becoming in the master: the good student ought to take a walk in the evening on the banks of the Seine, not to play, but to repeat his lesson, or to meditate.

Robert ends by blaming those who content themselves with incomplete instruction, and know not how to utilise their knowledge.

'Grammar,' he says, 'forges the sword of the word of God; rhetoric polishes it; and, finally, theology makes use of it. Bu there are some scholars who are always learning to fashion it, and to point it, and keep on sharpening it till they have sharpened it all away; others keep it shut up in the scabbard, and when they want to draw it out, they themselves are old, and the iron is rusty, and they can make nothing of it. With regard to those who study, in order to become dignitaries and prelates, they are very much deceived, for they hardly ever obtain the end of their ambition.'

But to revert to the Dominicans. S. Dominic had his eye fixed on Paris, from the first. He sent seven brothers there, divided into two parties: the first being three Spaniards; the second, three Frenchmen and an Englishman. They rented a house in the middle of the city, close to the gate of the Episcopal Palace. They were all, except Matthew, utter strangers to the town, and had it not been for the Englishman, whose name was Lawrence, they would have abandoned their foundation in despair.

Now, John of Saint Alban, who was physician to the King, and connected with the University, and a man of considerable influence, had founded in the 'Magnus Vicus Sancti Benedicti' an *hospitium* for pilgrims. The chapel was dedicated to S. James, the favourite Apostle of Spain. Somehow, John got to hear that members of a new institute had made their way to Paris, and that they professed to preach the Gospel of Christ, in imitation of the Apostles of the primitive Church. He saw them, was excessively impressed, and at once handed over to them the half-ruined pilgrim-house dedicated to S. James (1218). In 1221, he legally transferred it to them: the University, at the request of Pope Honorius, transmitting to the friars the right to the land and house, with the condition that yearly, the day after S. Nicholas, a solemn Mass should be sung for the living members of the University, and a solemn requiem on the day after the Purification, for its departed members. For a master, the same offices were performed as if he had been a member of the community. If a theologian died during his professorship at the University, he could claim to be buried in the Chapter-room: a professor of any other faculty might be buried in the cloister. Thus, from the beginning, the Dominicans came into contact with the University. Indeed, from the first, they attended the theological schools of the church of Paris. Though excessively poor, they soon made themselves known. S. Louis looked upon them with great regard, for he saw that their poverty was the poverty of Christ. He built them a convent after a time, chose three confessors from amongst their body; and, at his death, left them a portion of the library he had collected at the Sainte-Chapelle. But, before this, students came to hear them, and several joined the convent. In the year 1219, they could muster as many as thirty in community, one of which was the famous preacher, and friend of S. Louis, Henry Marburg. Here they worked steadily with pen and ink-horn and copybook. Here they weighed and studied the Lombard, the Bible, and the Gloss. Novices were taught Latin grammar and logic; and disputations—unlike Monte Cassino—could be heard echoing in the cloister. Meditation was made a counterbalance to the excitement of study; and the friars, who mostly had been professors in the schools, were particularly cautioned not to become too eager after learning, or to be carried away by the applause and temptations of the schools. S. Dominic himself visited them, and 'set in order a regular house, with cloisters, dormitory, refectory,' and especially cells for study. Honorius called them 'The Brethren of the Order of Preachers studying the Sacred Page in Paris.' They were watched over with extreme care, and were guarded with great strictness. The *magister studentium* had a certain discretionary power, and could allot cells to them for private study; could give them lights—for reading in the night; and other privileges. Prayer, holy office, humiliation, contemplation, silence, love—these influences maintained the even balance of the mind. The course of studies at one time was very strictly confined to theological works; it was decreed that students should not make a study of the books of heathens and philosophers, even though they might look into them from time to time; nor study the arts which were called 'liberal,' unless the Master of the Order, or a General Chapter, or the Provincial Prior, should see fit, in certain cases, to grant a dispensation—'Let none,' says the decree, 'be they young or otherwise, read any but theological books.' After three years at Paris, the young men could return to the convent where they had made their vows.

It was in this convent of S. James that Albert and Thomas wrote their *Commentaries on the Sentences.* Here S. Thomas came, at the end of his life, to write his Summa against the Gentiles. Cardinal Hugh of S. Caro—a contemporary of Lawrence the Englishman—selected the Dominicans of S. James to assist him in making his concordance of different Bible texts, so that the work became known as the *Concordantia Sancti Jacobi.* A little later, Richard de Bury speaks of the immense activity and labours of these men—'Qui diversorum voluminum correctionibus, expositionibus, tabulationibus, ac compilationibus indefessis studiis incumbebant.'

No doubt, the grand results which flowed from the Dominican labours are due, in great part, to the system they adopted. A greater portion of knowledge in those days entered through the eye and the ear than has been the case in our education. In the first place, the lectures were given in large halls. In the middle, generally, stood the chair of the master, with another seat below, and in front of him, for the bachelor who was going through his training. The walls of the lecture-room were often covered with inscriptions from the Fathers or from Scripture—for instance: 'Ama scientiam Scripturarum, et vitia carnis non amabis. Qui addit scientiam, addit dolorem. Videte ne quis vos decipiat per philosophiam, secundum elementa mundi, et non secundum Christum ;' and so on. Around the hall and across it benches were placed for the students. If there was not room, they got into the hall as well as they could, and sat on the ground. In Paris, the students often sat on the straw which was under their feet. There were no writing-desks or conveniences for putting down the lectures. The teaching was principally done by question and answer, by exposition, repetition, and disputation. Sometimes the professor's chair had an inscription on it, to keep the mind sober, like that on the chair of Albert the Great—'Timete Deum et date illi honorem, quia venit hora judicij ejus'—though possibly this chair may be of later date. Neither the master nor his assistant used a book ; no reading was allowed ; professors might have the text, perhaps, before them, but nothing more ; occasionally, a student might, with permission, take a few notes ; many, especially if they had memory and parts, would commit the lectures to writing on their return from the school. Some were able to take down almost *verbatim* the lectures of the masters. Like the ancient Greeks, mediæval students —at all events, students of the thirteenth century—made use of a kind of shorthand, which, after they had taken down the master's lecture, they turned into the *littera legibilis* at their leisure. Doctors and masters themselves were sometimes in the habit of writing their works or lectures in shorthand ; and their admirers or disciples, who knew how to read their characters, threw their compositions into the common form for the benefit of the public. Thus, it appears, S. Thomas wrote his *Contra Gentiles,* as well as his *Exposition on Isaias.* Some young men, in the time of Albertus Magnus, are spoken of as excessively ready with their smartness in taking down a lecture.

Then the bachelor who was working under the eye of a master had to teach the Introduction to the Books of Aristotle or the *Sentences* of the Lombard; and to take the students through their repetitions and disputations. But even he was not permitted to have a book. This, no doubt, had something to do with the influence of the schools. The power of an individual mind, the moral weight, the tone and inflection of voice, the glance of the eye, the whole bearing of the professor, if he be a superior man, must, of a necessity, act with great force upon the mind of youth. It makes the difference—so well understood, and so philosophically spoken of, by some mediæval writers—between dead and living words. A profound knowledge of Scripture is what was most sought after. On it rested the fabric of theological knowledge. It was carefully explained in its various senses, and the love of the marvellous tended to make the allegorical method of interpretation—by which men seemed to sink into the mysteries of God—the most common and most esteemed. Some young men were kept exclusively to this, and were denominated *Biblici.* The middle age was one of great simplicity. Men oftentimes studied the Scriptures for years, and nothing else, with great energy and earnestness. The *Sentences* of the Lombard were also expounded *viva voce* from the chair, and this went on for several years, the students going by the name of the *Sententiarii*.

The abandonment of Paris by the students and professors in 1229 left all the professorial chairs completely empty. William of Auvergne began to be apprehensive that the study of theology would come to an end altogether. It would be better, he thought, to give a chair of divinity to the Dominicans than to have none at all. So he invited the brother of S. James to fill that honourable post. Having some exceedingly able men amongst them, the Order closed with the offer. When the students and professors returned to Paris, they found the children of S. Dominic in the theological chair. The friars continued lecturing, and even possessed themselves of another chair (1230), to the great disgust and envy of the members of the University. The secular elements came to an agreement amongst themselves that no religious community should have more than one chair in the University. The Dominicans would by no means consent to carry this resolution into effect. For several years they had been in quiet possession of these chairs, and no opposition had been made to them; and, since they had right on their side, and taught with eminent success, they did not intend to move, simply to satisfy the spitefulness of party feeling. They were left for the time alone. It was afterwards, in a contention which will be touched upon, that they lost their hold upon the University.

Had the philosophies and theologies of the Arabians remained in Arabia, or been confined to Spain, they would not have influenced the universities of Europe. But that terrible intellectual pestilence which came out of India and Egypt—which was partly imported from Greece, which was rampant in Bagdad, Mecca, and Damascus—was carried from Spain, to France and Italy. Those learned men, who, with such ardour, hurried off to Moorish academies, Jewish colleges, and Spanish universities, instead of taking home a new illumination of the human mind, carried back with them, in reality, an infection which was to taint with its deadly poison the highest seats of learning in Italy and France. The Arabs seem to have invaded, and almost taken possession of the schools of Paris. The practices of dialectical fence, and the overweening yearning after natural science, made men abandon the more serious studies of theology, and they became so blasted with intellectual conceit, that, if what we read be true, not only the judgments of the Holy See, but the anger of God Himself, visited some of the professors with terrible severity. The startling history given by Bulæus, of Simon of Tournay, and his disciple Silo, is too well known to require repetition. Then, when the Glosses of such men as Theophrastus, Aphrodisius, and Philoponus, came into the hands of the teachers in the schools—full of all manner of detestable philosophy, and yet, somehow, by a certain charm, recommending themselves to their eager intellects, a new peril made itself evident. Aristotle was dangerous enough, when rightly understood; but Aristotle, tinged with the fatal doctrines of Eastern superstition, with the pantheism, mysticism, Gnosticism, and materialism of Arabia, was more than a danger—it was absolutely, in many cases, a destruction. The blasphemous teachings of the Eastern mind appear to have had a certain unaccountable attraction for the professors and the students. Theology was neglected; intellectual excitement became the order of the day; men in high place gave a cry of warning. The Pope, Gregory IX., himself declared that his soul was filled with bitterness in contemplating such a state of things. Curiosity, vanity, love of mere physical science, absorbed men's hearts and minds. It was but a natural consequence that, when the queen of sciences was put on one side to gratify the greed of novelty, men would rise up, and boldly tread under foot what others secretly contemned. Blasphemous tenets were taught scientifically from the chairs. Amalric of Bena, a professor of logic and theology (1205), fearlessly taught, in his public place, that human nature could be identified with the Divinity; that the Eternal Father became incarnate in Abraham; the Eternal Son in Mary; and the Holy Ghost in us; and that all things, in reality, are one; because all things, in reality, are God. Nor was he alone. David of Dinanto taught, as his first principle, 'Quod omnia sunt Deus'—that God is the primary substance of everything. If such teachings as these were to continue, the Christianity of thousands of young minds would be thrown into fearful jeopardy. The high authority of the Church had to interfere. David was condemned at the Synod of Paris (1209). The same Synod commanded the bones of Amalric to be dug up, and to be buried in unconsecrated ground—ten of his disciples were burnt alive, and others condemned to prison for life—whilst Aristotle's books on natural philosophy, and the comments on them, were forbidden. But even this did not check the virulence of the poison. The East had entered, not only into Aristotle's natural speculations, but into his metaphysics. Robert Courçon, the Papal Legate, in 1215, had sufficient grounds for forbidding the Aristotelian metaphysics to be read, as well as the writings of Mauritius Hispanus—who some say was no less a man than Averroës. But the tradition of a false principle clings to a school, and blinds scholars and professors. The faculty of arts seems to have been most damaged. Albertus Magnus, though at this period a feeble old man, had to write his *Liber Determinativus Adversus Parisienses*. The schools were in great peril. Not only blasphemous and false doctrines were maintained publicly, but the articles of Christian faith were discussed, proved faulty, and rejected with scorn, and, in their place, the rankest and crudest forms of pantheism were professed. In many private schools, heresy was freely circulated. S. Thomas says that, in his time, some taught that the *intellectus agens* was nothing less than God Himself; and that followers of Averroës lectured in the public schools—which is equivalent to saying, that Christianity was banished to one side, and that the hideous blasphemies of Eastern dreamers were set up in place of the revelation of Jesus Christ. It is almost inconceivable that the state of Paris could have been so bad. For a man to teach *ex professo* in an university city, in a Catholic country, and in the ages of faith, the most revolting tenets of the East, is something that is difficult, all at once, to realise.

Amongst other theses, these were maintained: that the will is not free; that there is but one intellect for all men; that all lower things are under the necessary influence of the heavenly bodies; that the world is eternal; that there never was a first man; that God cannot bestow immortality; that the soul corrupts; that God does not know individual things; that the acts of man are not governed by a Divine providence—and many others, equally startling. William of Auvergne was bound to censure a string of propositions, which were taken from the worst Arabic commentators on Aristotle, or from that deadly book, *De Causis*, which had so baneful an influence in the middle ages. Shortly after this, a strict decree was issued, to prevent discussion of points of doctrine and philosophy amongst the Artists, but without much effect, to judge from propositions taught but shortly afterwards—for instance: that the teachings of theologians are founded on fables; that the philosopher is the only wise man of this world;

that there is no more excellent state than to be called a philosopher; that continency is not necessarily a virtue; that the world is eternal; that a future resurrection is not to be believed in by a philosopher, because it cannot be investigated by reason; and many more propositions, equally false and destructive. Nor were these deadly heresies confined to Paris. Being the centre of learning, it is but natural that its teachings should have exerted their influence throughout civilised Europe. The doctrines of the Arabs, and the heresies springing from them, had to be combated in Ireland, as early as the ninth century. In England, the pantheistic bias of the East is clearly evident, particularly in the teaching of the Franciscans at Oxford, regarding the human soul. Robert Kilwardby, Archbishop of Canterbury, condemned a set of propositions, which had had the run of Oxford—similar to those which were branded by authority at Paris (1277). Avicenna seems to have had great influence on some of the theologians of S. Francis. Roger Bacon declares that it was the traditionary teaching of the Oxford schools, that the active intellect exists separate from the soul of man; and, moreover, that it was generally held that the active intellect was, in reality, identical with God. William, Bishop of Paris—he maintains—publicly declared before the University of Paris—and was supported by no less an authority than Robert of Lincoln, and Adam of Marisco—that the active intellect could not be a portion of the soul. Marisco, on being asked—'What, then, is the active intellect?' replied, 'The chariot of Elias,' meaning either God or an angel.

So corrupted had the University become at one period, that it limited the number of its doctors in theology to eight. The infection spread, from the learned and the students, amongst the general population. Several fanatics of low rank had to be burnt, because they went about protesting that the most depraved of mankind had an equal chance of salvation with S. Peter and S. Paul, on the principle that, since the intelligence of mankind was one, all mankind would be where that one universal intelligence was: and hence good and bad would live an equal life. Even ecclesiastics—ribald clerks, with tonsure and priest's habit—scoured the country, and travelled about amongst country towns and villages, proclaiming to the ignorant people that all souls were merged in one, and that therefore it was a delusion to preach the doctrine of future reward or punishment. Though S. Thomas turned the tide, it was not till long after his time that these phantasms were thoroughly destroyed.

From all this, it is evident that the University of Paris—whose vocation it was to teach the world—was deeply tainted with the most frightful intellectual corruption, and that the plague, which had been brought by the Moors into Spain, had seized upon the centre from which radiated the light of science, sacred and profane. It was not a mere surface attack, or passing epidemic, but a deep-seated corruption that had taken possession of men's minds, and had to be met, combated, and overcome. Islam and Christ could not live together in harmony, for Christ must reign, or the moral and intellectual degradation which springs from a false philosophy must eat out the heart and intellect of men.

What added to the excitement of this period was the influence of the world of spirits upon the imagination. This is not the place for speaking about the truth of those marvels. True or false, the present point is that they were believed in, and had all the effects, at all events, of reality. For instance, a recluse at Bonn saw a light through a chink in her cell, which looked over a churchyard; she went to the window, and perceived a woman, surrounded by a blaze of glory, hovering over a grave, and heard a voice saying, 'This is the Mother of Christ, come to take away the martyr.' We read of people seen in the air, writing by some celestial light. Thomas of Cantimpré saw, in 1246, just before S. Louis started for the Crusades, a luminous cross, eight cubits long, standing in the air. William of Auvergne heard distinctly voices weeping and sobbing when his sister died. John of Salisbury relates how, when a boy, a magician tried to use him as an instrument of his dark art. When Robert of Lincoln died (1253), the Bishop of London heard sounds like the deep toll of some superhuman bell; and some friars, who were journeying that night, heard in the air the harmonious sounds of bells. Innocent III. seems to prophesy his own demise in his allocution at the opening of the Lateran Council. Balls of fire, chalices surmounted by Hosts, half-moons, stars, aërial crucifixes, all manner of strange sights and awful interpositions, were continually spoken of. The *Magnum Speculum* is full of them. Matthew of Paris, John of Salisbury, Cæsar of Heisterbach (1240)—in fact, all the voluminous writers of the middle ages—carry one into a state of things in which the spirit-world was far more mixed up in human affairs than it is in our days. Then the actions of men themselves were often very startling. Alanus de Insulis was struck dumb (they say), for not having invoked the Blessed Virgin at the beginning of a sermon. Fulk, coming to Paris as an illiterate man, and then being waited on by professors, and by scholars with note-books in their hands, ready to take down the extraordinary wisdom that poured from his lips; John of S. Giles, the famous university professor, preaching to an immense audience in S. James's, suddenly, after speaking of perfection, descending the pulpit, and, in the presence of the astonished multitude, begging for the habit of religion, are simply specimens of what I mean. Brother Guerric, the first prior of the Dominicans at Metz, was converted by a few simple words. One day, as he was studying at his window in Paris, he heard some one singing this refrain in the streets below, which at once made him enter into himself:

> 'Tempus vadit,
> Et ego nil feci;
> Tempus venit,
> Et ego nil operor.'

Such occurrences were frequent. The minds of men seem to have been excessively excited by the effects of the new learning, and by the supernatural influences that worked so strangely upon them. The legend of Alanus de Insulis is a fair type of this state of things. He was one of the most famous professors of the University. On a certain day he promised his pupils to give them a perfect knowledge of the Blessed Trinity. The day before the lecture, while walking by a solitary stream, he saw a little boy trying to fill a trench of sand with water. 'What are you doing, my sweet child?' said the professor. 'I am going to put the river into my trench,' he replied. 'Do you think you will succeed?' said the philosopher. 'Before you keep your promise,' was the reply. 'What have I promised?' asked Alanus. 'You said you would explain the Trinity of God.' Alanus was terrified and overcome. He saw his pride. On the morrow a vast crowd had assembled, and Alanus ascended the pulpit, and having uttered these words, 'Sufficiat vobis vidisse Alanus,' came down, hurried out of the church, went off to Citeaux, and became a shepherd lay-brother. After many years he came to Rome to take charge of the horses of the Abbot, who went there to attend the Council against the Albigenses. As a great favour, the Abbot permitted him to sit during the council at his feet. At one moment the heretics appeared to triumph. Alanus rose up from beneath the Abbot, and, to his intense surprise, bowed, and said, 'Jube Domine Benedicere!' 'Madman, what art thou doing?' said the Abbot. 'Jube Domine Benedicere!' meekly replied the brother; and so he went on, till the Pope commanded him to speak out. Then he began, and with such marvellous keenness of dialectical skill did he press the enemy that, overcome with fury, the heretics exclaimed, 'Aut Diabolus est aut Alanus.' 'Non sum ego Diabolus, sed Alanus!' gently replied the man of genius. From this time forth the clerks were in attendance on him to write down his dictated wisdom. Endless stories might be repeated to prove the extraordinary activity, power, passion, and fermentation of the human mind before, and during, and some little time after the period of S. Thomas of Aquino. This leaven runs through and tinges with its unearthly colouring the mass of humanity in the middle ages. It is possible also that the extraordinary ignorance of history and geography which generally prevailed tended to develop the faculties of wonder and admiration, and to prepare the mind for almost any marvel that might be announced. When the keenness of the vision into things unseen is not checked by the practical realities of creation, it is a comparatively easy thing to lose the just balance of the mind. When we are assured that Francus was son of Hector, and that the Franks came over from Troy; that the history of Spain begins with Japheth, that of England with Brutus, and that of Scotland with Fergus; when historians always begin history from the creation of the world, pointing out Babylon, which had been destroyed centuries before, as existing—now identifying it with Cairo, and now with Bagdad; when Priam is dressed in ermine, with armorial bearings; when Nabuchodonosor is favoured with a seneschal, and surrounded by a court of barons; and when names are clipped and altered to suit the peculiar ear of the historian, and all manner of liberties are taken with fact, and allegory and invention are served up in the place of proofs—we can partly understand how the mind, living so much upon fantasy, became excessively impressionable to the eloquence of rhetoricians, to the brilliancy of debate, and to the action of the marvellous in both the plane of magic and religion.

It will be well now, for a passing moment, to turn to another Order—to which reference has already been made, and with which S. Thomas of Aquin had an intimate relationship—that is, to the Franciscans. When S. Thomas came to Paris, they had been some time settled in the city, and were in a very flourishing condition. Sometimes as many as seven hundred friars were in Paris at one time. The halls in their convent were particularly fine. The greater school was not exceeded by any other in the University. It was seventy-six feet long, forty-eight feet broad, and had eleven large windows. Two lectures were given every morning—one on speculative theology, the other on various points requiring explanation; and in the afternoon there was a lecture on Holy Scripture. From four to five in the evening the Fathers held discussions, affirming, denying, and clearing the subject-matter, whilst it was open to any one to contend against them or answer their objections. In this seminary two hundred and twenty-two youths were educated. Every night two of the younger brethren repeated, in the graceful hall of the seminary, portions of the Divine Office; and on festivals all were required to be present together in the church. Here there were four schools: one for grammar, another for rhetoric, one for logic, and the fourth for the *Sentences* of the Lombard and the Physics of Aristotle. It was to these lowly Franciscans that that celebrated Paris doctor, Alexander of Hales, betook himself, in consequence of his tender love to our Blessed Lady, hoping thus, not merely to secure his own salvation, but to labour in a mortified life for the good of others. He appears to stand in the same relation to the friars of S. Francis, as that in which Albert stands to the Dominicans. Here, too, S. Bonaventure, the dear familiar friend of our S. Thomas, received his illuminations and helped to build up the Church of God.

The first Dominican who publicly professed theology in Paris was that enthusiastic Englishman, of whom mention has been made, John of S. Giles. So high a reputation had he acquired during his career of doctor of theology, and the Paris students clamoured so loudly for his reappearance in the chair after he became a Dominican, that the friars were constrained to consent to his giving public lectures. His was not a local reputation; having taught in three or four foreign universities, his name was famous throughout the learned world. It was in this school that the great encyclopedic writers Alanus de Insulis and Vincent of Beauvais laboured over their gigantic tasks. Here that humble religious, afterwards known as Innocent V., was trained. Here Roland of Cremona and Hugh of S. Caro accomplished the difficult task of maintaining that high name for wisdom which S. James's had acquired through the genius of John of S. Giles. When S. Thomas arrived at Paris, John of Paris occupied one of the Dominican chairs, and Albert was sent, as bachelor, to occupy the other—for, according to a special statute, the chairs had respectively to be occupied by a Frenchman and a foreigner.

In the natural course of things, our Saint would have had to be presented by the General Chapter, or by the General of the Order, to some master in the schools—as, in fact, he was presented to Albert by the General. With the master, he would go through the *Sentences* of the Lombard. After a year's drill, he would be presented to the Chancellor, by the Prior of the Paris house, in the presence of all the actual professors of the University. The *magister* then took an oath that he was competent to teach, upon which the Chancellor would confer on him the *licentia docendi*. But a stiff trial had to be given him before he actually began his work—that he might give a clear proof to the entire University that he was fit to instruct others in theology and philosophy. The *magister licentiatus*, as he was styled, would have to hold a solemn disputation in the Episcopal Aula. Hence, of one who had passed through that ordeal it was said—*aulam suam habebat.* If he passed with credit, he became Laureate. Now he might teach a school himself, and the *magister laureatus,* consequently, having been trained by an experienced professor, commenced to comment on the *Sentences* of the Lombard. This he would continue doing for twelve months. After that time, just as, two years before, he had read the *Sentences* under a master, so now some young man reads the *Sentences* under him, whilst he—thorough master of his subject, experienced in the technicalities of disputation, and well-seasoned in the schools—holds *disputationes generales* upon any difficult points that may turn up. Besides this, he would also handle the *quodlibeta.* On the completion of his third year, he would present the bachelor who had had the advantage of his experience—just as he himself had been presented—for his licentiate. Thus it was that the efficiency of the teaching body was maintained. These grades were not gone through as a matter of form. To succeed in the grand disputation in the Aula; to lecture before a crowd of the keenest minds, without a book—the students all the while marking every word—required talent and readiness of logic; memory, and power of analysis; besides presence of mind, and sufficient fluency of speech. When it is remembered what William of Champeaux had to suffer from Abelard, and what Abelard himself had to suffer from his opponents, some idea may be formed of the requisites of a doctor, lecturing publicly before all the learning of the Paris world. The Dominicans were excessively particular about efficiency. Unless a man had formerly lectured with *éclat*, or was a person of evident distinction, they were loth to place him in the chair. At first, the majority of those who joined the Order were experienced professors, who had made their reputation, and at the calling of Jordan and others, had left the dangers of the University for the security and peace of religious life. Reginald, Jordan, Henry, Roland, Humbert, Raymund, Conrad, John of S. Giles, and more than can be mentioned, were of this class.

Albert went through his course in the ordinary way: in the second year, being master with John of Paris; and in the third, *primarius regens* with Stephen of Auxerre, who had succeeded John. It was under the influence of these men, but especially of Albert, that S. Thomas finished his education. Wadding has endeavoured to prove that S. Thomas had studied under that brilliant commentator, Hales the Minorite. But Touron and Bareille have shown, conclusively, that Alexander had died before S. Thomas reached Paris, and that, some little time before his death, he had ceased to attend the schools. If he had studied under a Franciscan at all, it would have been under John of Rochelle, who succeeded Alexander, and who was the master of S. Bonaventure.

But we left our Saint under the tuition of Albert, at

Paris—I now must carry on his history during the quiet time of his pupilage.

At this period, his favourite book was Cassian—as at Cologne—and the writings of S. Augustine. His biographers relate an anecdote of him which is also told of Lanfranc. He was reading in the refectory. The Prior, thinking he had made a false quantity when he had not, corrected him. Thomas, with great humility, pronounced the word wrong out of obedience. On some of the friars expressing their surprise at this, he said to them, 'It makes little difference how a word is pronounced, but it is of great importance for a religious to practise humility and obedience.' When at table, he knew not what he eat. Abstraction, contemplation, silence—these composed the atmosphere in which he dwelt.

It is often the custom of good men to moralise upon the beauty of peace and gentleness—on the charm of solitude and silence; but they do not often go beyond this; they do not often sink into the depth of the human spirit, and seek to discover the hidden spring which produces the great effect. He alone who has lived to God and to himself can fully realise the strength and vigour produced within the soul by prayer, silence, solitude; by dwelling under One Eye alone, and communing with One Only Spirit, and by opening out the whole man—the entire being—like a flower to the sun—towards the light and warmth that is produced by heaven. Great souls, souls made of fine and noble elements, have it in them; it is their nature, when alone, to seek Him who is above, and to find their freedom and their companionship with the world that is unseen. Open the life of any saint: speak to any man who has really given himself to God. Ask him of his silent, solitary hours—whence come all his sweetness and his spiritual light—and he will have but one answer to give. It comes from basking and living in the sun, and by letting the spirit expand itself, and grow, with its own spontaneous rectitude, towards Him who made it; from Whom it originally came; and to Whom, finally, it will have to go. Ask the gentle, silent, young Aquino how he spent his time. He spent it drinking in the brightness of heaven, and filling himself with the strength of God. But this is a digression.

Nothing has been handed down, of any moment, regarding the teaching of St. Thomas at Paris during this period. Albert was in the height of his reputation. The days of Abelard and William of Champeaux seemed almost to have returned. Neither the accommodation at S. James's, nor the hall attached to the University, was large enough to contain the crowds of students. It has been said, in another place, that, on account of want of room, Albert was forced to lecture in a square still pointed out to strangers, near Notre Dame, and which, ever since that day, has been known as Place Maubert (*du Maître Albert*). Albert, having finished his course, took his Doctor's cap.

The success of the Dominican professors at Paris

induced the friars to extend the field of their labours. The same year in which S. Thomas finished his studies (1248) a General Chapter was held at Paris. Here it was ruled that four new schools should be started, on the model of S. James's :—Bologna, for the Lombard Province; Montpellier, for Provence; Oxford, for England; and Cologne, for Germany. In spite of Albert's great fame at Paris, both he and Thomas were ordered to Cologne. Albert was to take the chair, rearrange the studies, and be Regent; whilst Thomas—who was not twenty-three—was to be second professor, and *magister studentium*.

The old city of Cologne, which was frequented by pilgrims from all the world, was moved when the return of Albert and Thomas was announced. Albert's name, his ancient reputation, and his new dignity, attracted crowds. Thomas had as yet to make his powers known.

CHAPTER X.

S. THOMAS MADE BACHELOR.

It was not long before the young *magister studentium* acquired a brilliant reputation at Cologne. Here it was that he began to make a name which eventually became more than European. It is natural that this sheer purity and saintliness should draw young men around him. But he had other attractions. He possessed the keenest of minds, the most capacious of memories; he could, with facility, take up any tangled skein, unravel it, and, with a mastership that might make ordinary men despair, display its whole complexity in such a manner that the student could, with the greatest ease, take in the entire bearing of the question.

His distinctions, even compared with those of Albert, were so new, his arguments so ingenious, that all were dazzled at his great ability. It was in the school of Cologne that he first gave evidence as a teacher of that depth, balance, and expansion which, in after life, made him the weightiest of authorities on the most momentous of religious questions. In his treatment of the Lombard, and in handling of Scripture, he had ample opportunity for displaying his many-sided gifts.

Nor did he confine himself to teaching in the schools. He preached and wrote. His first pieces were *De Ente et Essentia* and *De Principiis Naturæ;* in which, following the leadership of Albert, he lays down fundamental principles of philosophy—principles which were afterwards developed, and which thread his entire teaching in metaphysics. He also composed several minor papers which point to his mastery of Aristotle; to the frame-work which he afterwards put together for sound scholastic teaching; and to the subtlety, lucidity, and grasp of his intelligence. His two first pieces contain the germ of a future system, and are remarkable productions for a youth of twenty-two.

No doubt the Saint's practice in teaching, and the accuracy he acquired by writing from an early age, were of great assistance to him in developing his powers. Then he possessed another gift, very valuable in the middle ages, particularly so in the thirteenth century, and more especially useful to a religious man—a changeless calmness and self-possession. Partly through education; through the vicissitudes of life; greatly by character; partly through breadth of mind; and principally through grace—he possessed his soul in patience. He, if any man, could say, 'Anima mea in manibus meis semper:' for it was never known, even under the most trying provocation, that he lost his gentle self-control. His humility and sweetness came out strikingly when arguing in the schools. Though his opponent, in the heat of disputation, might forget himself, yet Thomas never did so. He answered meekly, and with benevolence—steadied by the light from which his every action sprang.

On one occasion, when a certain student arrogantly defended a thesis, of which he knew the Saint disapproved, he was suffered to proceed without remark. Asked why he did not check the youth, the Saint replied that he could not bring himself to put the young man to shame. Next day, emboldened by the silence of the previous evening, the student continued his argument with still greater arrogance. The Saint now thought it time to interfere. So, with infinite sweetness, yet with crushing power, he put a few questions, made some distinctions, and upset the student with such ease, first on one point, then on another, that the whole school was in an uproar of admiration. Both the youth and his companions were thus taught a lesson of gentleness and power, which they did not easily forget.

On another occasion he was preaching to a crowded congregation at S. James's. It was Palm Sunday. During the discourse an official, sent by the Senate of the University, walked up the church. He beckoned to the Saint to stop, and then read out, before the astonished people, with S. Thomas standing silent in the pulpit, an offensive document, drawn up by the secular party, in opposition to the Friars Preachers. When the man had finished, and the congregation had recovered from their surprise a little, S. Thomas proceeded with his sermon, with the same calmness with which he had commenced it. No human influence, however sudden or distressing, seemed to have any power over his extraordinary mind.

Corrado de Suessia, who knew him intimately, gave a most interesting testimony on oath to the simplicity and purity of his life. He declared him to be 'a man of holy life and honest conversation, peaceful, sober, humble, quiet, devout, contemplative, and chaste: so mortified, that he cared not what he eat, or what he put on. Every day he celebrated, with great devotion, or heard one or two masses; and, except in times proper for repose, he was ever occupied in reading, writing praying, or preaching. I saw him,' says Corrado, 'leading the above life.' To this was joined a great confidence in spiritual illumination. 'His science,' says Raynald, 'was not acquired by natural talent, but by the revelation and infusion of the Holy Ghost, for he never set himself to write, without having first prayed and wept. When he was in doubt, he had recourse to prayer, and with tears he returned—instructed and enlightened in his uncertainty.' A letter, attributed to the Saint, gives his views on the temper of a Christian student. It is addressed to a certain 'In Christo Carissimus Joannes.' John is not to plunge all at once into the sea of science, but to approach it by degrees, as water does along the beds of rivers, beginning with easy things, and then advancing to more difficult ones; talking too much must be avoided; purity of conscience, prayer, and solitude, are to be cultivated; John is to be amiable to all, familiar with none, for familiarity produces contempt, and stands in the way of study; he is to avoid mixing up with the affairs of seculars; he must shun vain conversations, and walk in the footsteps of the saints; he must not concern himself whence good comes, but treasure it up in his memory; he must try and know what he does, and try and understand all he hears; rid his mind of doubts, and fill the chamber of his intelligence with knowledge; and never aim at knowing what is beyond his reach.

It was about this period that S. Thomas was ordained priest. It is mortifying that no certain information can be procured regarding the time at which it took place. To him it must have been an occasion of extreme joy and overwhelming awe. His treatise on the dignity of the Christian priesthood, his illuminated tract on the Blessed Sacrament, and his writings on the Mass, besides other references to the Real Presence, manifest the temper of his mind. All his biographers lay stress on his great devotion while celebrating. He was frequently rapt in spirit whilst at Mass, when the tears would spring to his eyes and flow copiously. This happened to him also at other times. During Compline, at the words, 'Ne projicias nos in tempore senectutis cum defecerit virtus mea,' he was frequently thus carried away. After he had said Mass, he prepared his lectures, and then went to the schools. Next he wrote, or dictated to several scribes; then he dined, returned to his cell, and occupied himself with Divine things till time for sleep; after which he wrote again, and thus ordered his life in the service of his Master.

The duty of preaching also fell upon him. A man so filled with the Spirit of God would, almost of necessity, manifest the passion which ruled supreme. His reputation, even at this period, was great enough to draw a large congregation into the Dominican Church. He preached with the fervour of a true man of God. His learning, his piety, his extraordinary gifts, then his nobility, and his commanding yet gentle appearance, must have produced a deep impression.

But, before speaking of his sermons in particular, a general view of 'preaching' in the thirteenth century will not be unacceptable.

Sacred eloquence from the time of the Apostles till the fourth century, consisted principally in homilies and in popular harangues. Then we come upon the days of the great columnal Fathers, whose eloquent thoughts have a power still to move men's hearts, and whose methods influenced those lesser lights who followed them. S. Basil, S. Gregory, S. Chrysostom, and S. Augustine—looking back even from our day—occupy a position which could be filled by no other four. They were succeeded—worthily indeed, but were not approached—by S. Gregory the Great, S. Isidore of Seville, and Venerable Bede: just as in turn S. Gregory, S. Isidore, and S. Bede were succeeded, but were not surpassed, by Alanus of Farfa, Rabanus, Heric, Alcuin, and Paul Warnefrid. The scale of excellence seems gradually to diminish, till we come to such stirring times as the Crusades, or to days of contest against the violence of heretics, which, from the very nature of the case—from the force of circumstances—caused earnest men to speak with vigour and with enthusiasm, if not with the elegance and polish of academicians. There was Ralph Ardent, for example, now almost forgotten, who anticipated the great Dominican in his eloquence and power; then S. Bernard, and Peter the Hermit—

whose unction and earnestness and fire are well known as exerting a great sway over the masses—and Hugh of S. Victor's, and Comestor, and Fulk, of whom mention has been made before; and Maurice de Sully, and John of Nivelle—mighty orators in their day, but now forgotten with the rest—bringing us down to the great revival in the Orders of S. Francis and S. Dominic.

James de Vitry, Maurice de Sully, and William of S. Amour say quite enough about the boldness of such heretics as the Catharites and the Vaudois to give a clear notion of the energy with which the children of S. Dominic would follow out their special vocation. The preaching of the Word of God, with school learning, was their one object in life. They opposed with fire and eloquence the truth of the Gospel against the errors and blasphemies of fanatical performers, who, in the streets or in the country places, would collect the simple-minded around them and pour into their ears all manner of detestable teaching.

The language in which at this period sermons were preached was French—that is, when given out from the pulpit. Even when written in Latin—and this was generally the case—they were delivered to the people in the people's tongue. S. Bonaventure is said to have preached in French. S. Bernard even preached his Crusades in the vulgar tongue. Jordan of Saxony and John of Wildeshusen also preached in French. In 1213 the Abbot of Jumièges had to explain the Gospel in French for the sake of the less instructed (*simplicioribus fratribus*). But, as a rule, the clergy were addressed in Latin. It was not thought complimentary to do otherwise. The epitaph of Abbot Notker (998) shows what the custom was, even as early as his time. Some had a fancy for making sermons in rhyme—*sermones rimatos*—which seem to have had a strange attraction for many amongst the people.

The sermon generally took place—if it were an ordinary Sunday, and the preacher addressed the people in an instruction—after the Gospel, as is still the custom to this day. But special sermons preached on state occasions, such as at marriages or funerals, were delivered after Mass. There were sermons *in mane*, in the morning; and *post prandium*, after dinner. Then there were Collations, or Conferences, which were generally delivered by the same person who spoke to the congregation in the morning. The people were arranged with the men on one side, and the women on the other; and ladies of distinction came to church preceded by their valets carrying cushions for them to sit upon during the discourse. The preacher was in the habit of addressing the people as 'Fratres,' 'Fratres Carissimi,' 'Bele Gens,' 'Bele Segnors,' 'Douce Gent,' 'Signor et Dames.' Sometimes, if the preacher said something offensive, or made use of unsound or heretical expressions, there were not wanting those who would interrupt him and call him to order. Robert of Sorbon gives a very interesting account of an instance of this. A learned clerk preached before the King of France.

During his sermon he went on to say that all the Apostles, at the moment of the Passion, abandoned Christ, and that faith became extinguished in their hearts; the Blessed Virgin alone kept it from the day of the Passion to that of the Resurrection, in commemoration of which, in the Holy Week of penance, at matins all the lights, one after the other, are put out, except one, which is reserved for making blessed fire at Easter time. A solemn ecclesiastic of higher rank rose up to reprehend him; for the Apostles, according to this censor, had abandoned Jesus Christ in body, but not in heart. The preacher was about to retract, when the King (Louis), getting up in his turn, intervened. 'The proposition is not false,' he said; 'it is to be found clearly expressed in the Fathers. Bring me the Book of S. Augustine.' The book was brought, and the King pointed out a passage in his Commentaries on the Gospel of S. John where, in point of fact, S. Augustine expresses himself in these words: 'Fugerunt, relicto eo corde et corpore.' Sometimes, if the preacher said hard things about the ladies—like S. Bernard's saying that the first time a woman opened her mouth she upset the whole world—the women rose up and protested before the congregation against the unfairness of such imputations. Nepotism, riches, pluralities amongst the clergy, cheating in trade, usury, immorality, and vanity and love of dress, and of adorning their heads—especially amongst women—were constant subjects for the preacher.

Of course sometimes the congregation would not properly attend to the discourses. At one time complaints were made that the men left the church just as the sermon began and only came back when it was over. Cesarius of Arles, to put a stop to this kind of abuse, had the doors of the church closed after the Gospel. Robert of Sorbon, with the same end in view, adopted different means. One Easter Sunday he told his congregation that he would be short, like the Gospel of the day. 'I know,' he said, 'that on this day you must have a short sermon and a long dinner; but it is to be hoped that the Mass is not too long for you.'

When the preacher found some of his congregation asleep he did not experience much difficulty in addressing himself to them pretty directly. Many anecdotes are given to this effect. For instance, the preacher would cry out, 'He who sleeps in the corner there does not know the secret I am going to tell you.' Another, seeing persons fast asleep, left the immediate subject of his discourse, and said with a loud voice, 'Once upon a time there was a king called Arthur;' upon which the sleepers awoke, and the orator said to them, not without irony, 'When I speak of God you sleep, but immediately I talk of fables you awake.' De Vitry's plan was to cry out, 'He who sleeps there in that corner does not know my secret!' And on another occasion, when an old woman was asleep, 'Would you have me speak of the honest woman? I will talk, then, of the old woman fast asleep there. . . . Those who sleep at sermons take good care not to sleep at table.'

With regard to subject-matter, sermons depended upon the state of society, and the different classes into which men were divided. There were sermons *ad cleros* and *ad populum;* then sermons *ad status,* addressed to the different wants of various sections—*e.g.* 'Dolentes de morte propinquorum,' 'Majores civitatis,' 'Familiæ divitum,' 'Mulieres meretrices.' Then there was the *dilatatio,* or the method of spinning out and making the most of a few ideas; and the *sermo communis,* or common sermon, which was so constructed as to fit in with almost any occasion, and was intended to prevent the preacher ever being taken by surprise.

Of Englishmen, Stephen Langton and S. Edmund were both noted for their preaching. The former, on account of his powerful voice, was called *Stephanus Linguæ-tonantis;* the latter was famous for his zeal. But of all, whether secular or religious, the Dominicans were without doubt the great preachers of the thirteenth century. In 1273 sixty preachers were employed in the principal churches of Paris, and of them exactly one-half were Dominicans. In the early part of the century the style of preaching was earnest, simple, and natural. There must have been eloquence and fire to have effected what the Dominicans achieved. Later on the manner changed, the method became too dry and scholastic, and the spirit of analysis that did so much harm to theology entered into sacred eloquence.

But it is time to return to the preaching of S. Thomas. His sermons can be judged by what he has written, and by the history of their effects. His biographers speak of their simplicity, depth, and balance. Several anecdotes related by Touron prove the power he possessed over his audience. On one occasion, in a sermon on the Passion in St. Peter's during Lent, he so vividly brought home to the congregation the sufferings of the Cross, and drew so touching a picture of the compassion, mercy, and love of Christ, that his words were interrupted by the passionate crying of the people. Then, on Easter Sunday, his sermon on the Resurrection filled the congregation with such jubilant triumph that with difficulty they were restrained from giving public expression to their feelings.

It was not after the modern fashion that the Saint preached. His power did not proceed from violence of manner, fierce gesture, theatrical display, or artificial warmth. There was nothing of brute - oratory about him. The exaggerated and excited method of announcing the Gospel, imported from the Continent—and which might suit the market-place, but ill-beseems the dignity of the pulpit—was unknown to the great Dominican. Doubtless he felt that the truth of God is too sublime to admit of much human heat in its expression; that a loud manner does not tend to make proof more cogent; and that the Spirit of the Gospel is gentle, calm, and self-possessed, yet firm, earnest, and commanding. Tocco says that he preached all one Lent at

Naples on the one text, 'Ave Maria gratia plena, Dominus tecum,' and that during the whole time he was seen to keep his eyes closed in the pulpit, and his head in such a position as if he were looking into heaven. Yet it does not follow, because his eyes were closed, that he did not give full expression to his thoughts. Bourdaloue recited his master-pieces with his eyes shut; but, as Schleiniger assures us, he by no means was wanting in animation and variety of manner. Our Saint preached ten years in Naples, as well as in Paris, Rome, Cologne, and other places. The people reverenced his word as if it had come direct from the mouth of Christ. 'Tam reverenter audiebatur a populo,' says Tocco, 'quasi sua prædicatio prodiret a Deo.'

The sketches he has left of his sermons are a valuable index to his method. In the fourth Opusculum (according to the Parma edition), there are one hundred and forty-two skeleton-sermons for Sundays and eighty-three for festivals. The former on the Gospels, and the latter upon our Lord and upon the Saints—forming a very complete and useful set of discourses, even for the present day. Whether our Saint confined himself to these 'notes' and extemporised the words cannot be known with any certainty. Probably, having great practice in speaking and in writing, he felt no difficulty in clothing his thoughts in appropriate language, and with his prodigious memory a very meagre skeleton would suffice. In the notes he divides the meaning of his text into three or four grand divisions, and each of these he subdivides into three or four portions. The divisions are expressed with exceeding brevity, and yet with so good a choice of words that the whole pith becomes evident at a glance. To each division or subdivision is attached a text to the point from Holy Scripture, with the proper reference. The skeleton is so well organised that, when once fixed in the mind, there is no difficulty in diversifying each portion into one very clear and consecutive discourse. To those who seek for plans of sermons these notes would be very suggestive. One often sees 'notes' for sermons, but not often such as these, where the divisions are in keeping with the subject and form a portion of its unity, and do not represent a heterogeneous admixture of unharmonious ideas.

Here is a specimen taken at random of the method of the Angelical.

Homily CXXV.

TRUE AND FALSE RICHES.

'I give thanks to my God always for you, for the grace of God that is given you in Jesus Christ; that in all things you are made rich in Him.' 1 Cor. i. 4, 5.

The Apostle in giving thanks that they were enriched 'by Him,' indicates that there are certain riches which are to be desired; and in threatening the rich, Christ shows that there are certain riches which are to be avoided. Whence we learn that there are *temporal* riches, *spiritual* riches, and *eternal* riches. Of temporal riches it is said: 'If riches abound, set not your heart upon them.' Of spiritual riches: 'Blessed is the man that feareth the Lord,' and 'Glory and wealth shall be in his house.' Of eternal riches: 'With me are riches and glory; glorious riches and justice.' 'With me are riches,' *i.e.* the better goods; 'And glory,' *i.e.* ineffable; 'glorious riches,' *i.e.* such as are exalted; 'and justice,' *i.e.* such as is according to merit.

I. In the *first* place it is to be noted, that *temporal* riches are to be despised chiefly for four reasons. (1.) On account of their uselessness: 'He that loveth riches shall reap no fruit from them,' *i.e.* the fruit of eternal life. 'Riches shall not profit in the day of revenge.' That is, temporal riches do not avail for the salvation of man in the day of judgment; 'But justice shall deliver from death;' *i.e.* the good works of justice deliver from eternal death. 'Set not thy heart upon unjust possessions; and say not, I have enough to live on. . . . For it shall be of no service in the time of vengeance and darkness.' 'We brought nothing into the world, and certainly we can carry nothing out.' (2.) On account of the necessity of leaving them: 'They have slept their sleep; and all the men of riches have found nothing in their hands.' 'The riches which he hath swallowed, he shall vomit up, and God shall draw them out of his belly.' (3.) Because they lead the unjust possessor to perpetual poverty: 'The rich man when he shall sleep shall take nothing with him: he shall open his eyes, and find nothing. Poverty like water shall take hold on him.' (4.) Because the contempt of them leads to eternal life; 'And every one that hath left house, or brethren, or sisters, or father, or mother, or wife, or children, or lands, for My Name's sake, shall receive an hundred-fold, and shall possess everlasting life.'

II. On the *second* head, it is to be noted, that by riches man sins in four ways. (1.) By acquiring them unjustly: 'He that heapeth together riches by usury and loan gathereth them for him that will be bountiful to the poor.' 'He that oppresseth the poor to increase his own riches shall himself give to one that is richer,' that is, to the world, 'and shall be in need.' (2.) By possessing them avariciously: 'Riches kept to the hurt,' *i.e.* to the peril of the owner, 'are lost with very great affliction.' (3.) By being badly spent: 'Give not thy substance to women,' *i.e.*

to the corruptions of sin; 'thy substance,' *i.e.* thy body and the riches of temporal things. Mystically it signifies do not contaminate your whole store of virtue by the corruptions of vice. 'The younger son gathering all together, went abroad into a far country, and there wasted his substance living riotously.' (4.) By trusting in them, and becoming proud of them: 'He that trusteth in his riches shall fall,' *i.e.* from eternal life. Gloss: 'He who thirsts after present goods, neither thinks nor reflects on the future, so that in the end he will lack eternal riches: "Charge the rich of this world not to be high-minded, nor trust in the uncertainty of riches, but in the living God . . . to lay up in store for themselves a good foundation against the time to come, that they may lay hold on the true life."'

III. On the *third* head, it is to be noted, that *spiritual* riches are knowledge and virtue: 'The riches of salvation are wisdom and knowledge: the fear of the Lord is his treasure.' 'Through fear sin is driven out.' 'They that fear the Lord will prepare their hearts, and in His sight will sanctify their souls.' The root of wisdom is to fear the Lord. . . . For he that is without fear cannot be justified.' Discretion and honest conversation are the result of knowledge; for it is by knowledge that man knows what is due to God, to his neighbour, and to himself. God teaches us this knowledge, being weaned from the milk, and drawn from the breasts of pleasures and desire. Isaias by the Holy Spirit, the Lord, asks, saying: 'Whom shall he teach knowledge? And whom shall he make to understand the hearing?' And then He answers: 'Them that are weaned from the milk and drawn from the breasts.' It is strange, when man finds bitterness and burning in these breasts, that he does not withdraw from them. As S. Augustine says, 'O Lord, Thou hast mingled my delights with bitterness that I might seek to live without bitterness.' Thou, O man, if thou wishest to be taught by the Lord, separate thyself from these breasts, because it is said: 'Wisdom shall not enter into a malicious soul, nor dwell in a body subject to sins.' But by wisdom the love of God enters into the soul; hence S. Bernard says: 'Let a man learn what he will; I will not call him wise who will not fear nor love God.'

IV. On the *fourth* head it is to be noted, that these *spiritual* riches are to be sought for three reasons. (1.) On account of their immensity: 'For she is an infinite treasure to men: which they that use become the friends of God.' 'For God loveth none but him that dwelleth with wisdom.' 'She is more precious than all riches, and all the things that are desired are not to be compared with her.' Gloss: 'Charity is to be preferred not only before earthly but also before heavenly riches; nay, even before the very sight itself of the angels, so that none need dread poverty who have acquired the riches of wisdom.' (2.) On account of their utility: 'The ransom of a man's life are his riches; but he that is poor beareth not reprehension.' 'Depart from Me, you cursed, into everlasting fire.' 'Beareth not.' Gloss: 'Let him who wishes to redeem his soul from future wrath gather together the riches of good works; for if he lack these he will not be able to bear the reprehension of the just Judge. There the poor shall not be rebuked, but they shall partake of the blessing of the inheritance.' (3.) On account of their dignity: 'The crown of the wise,' *i.e.* the eternal crown in reward of their virtue, 'is their riches,' *i.e.* true riches, and not earthly gain; whilst 'the folly of fools is imprudence.' Gloss: 'Though they have a certain emolument as their riches, the wise will still share in the eternal crown, on account of their virtues; whilst the stupidity of fools is most glaring in this, viz. that through improvidence they sacrifice eternal gains for present satisfaction.' For imprudence is often called improvidence.

V. On the *fifth* head, it is to be noted, that *eternal* riches are to be sought for three reasons. (1.) On account of their truth, for they are true riches: 'If, brethren, you wish to be truly rich, love true riches,' S. Bernard. (2.) On account of their joyousness: 'The saints shall rejoice in glory: they shall be joyful in their beds.' 'His eyes shall see the King in His beauty.' (3.) On account of their eternity: 'But the just shall live for evermore.' 'And of His kingdom there shall be no end.' 'Lay not up to yourselves treasures on earth, where the rust and moth consume, and where thieves break through and steal.' The Lord showeth by these three (rust, moth, and thieves), that there is no safety in the possession of earthly riches; for there are certain things which rust devours, such as silver and gold, and other metals. There are others which not the rust but the moth destroys and eats, such as silken and precious garments; there are other things which neither rust nor moth eat, but which thieves steal and dig up, such as gems and precious stones; whence it is manifest how uncertain are the goods of life, and the possession of all things. The Lord persuades us to lay up to ourselves treasures in heaven, saying: 'Lay up to yourselves treasures in heaven; where neither the rust nor moth doth consume, and where thieves do not break through, nor steal.' But how can any one lay up treasures in heaven, unless by first making riches in time? By rust, moth, and thieves, we may understand spiritual wickedness. By rust pride is signified; for pride, when it takes possession of the soul, turns it from the 'path of justice.' As rust shows itself openly, so pride ever spreads itself abroad after human praise. By the moth envy is signified; for like the moth it destroys what it fixes itself on, and gnaws it to pieces. By thieves evil spirits are understood, who are on the watch to dig up and steal the treasures of the soul. In heaven there is no rust; for there is no place there for pride, since the devil and his followers were cast down from thence. In heaven there is no moth, no envy, because no one there will envy the happiness of another. In heaven there are no thieves or demons, because they with their chief have fallen from thence. S. Chrysostom says: 'There is one only thief who steals the treasure laid up in heaven, and that thief is vain-glory.'

Whilst Thomas was thus occupied Frederick II. was carrying out his policy of violence in Italy. His excommunication, and the way he had been abandoned by the Italian nobility, added to his exasperation. In his striving after the dominion of the world, and in his endeavour to usurp power belonging to the Holy See, he treated with brutal cruelty those who did not fall in with his unscrupulous ambition. Many noblemen, outraged by his arrogance, and fearing the spiritual weapons of the Church, openly declared against him, and sided with the Guelfs. This was the case with the two rough brothers of the Saint, who, through the prayers of the Angelical, were brought to see the error of their past course. The loving heart of Thomas never forgot them. No sooner did he become a priest, than he offered the Holy Sacrifice, with many tears, begging the Lord to change them into other men. They turned against their powerful relation, and espoused the cause of the Pope. Frederick then destroyed their stronghold at Aquino, and they died at last in the cause of truth. In reward for his earnest prayers, and tears, and simple faith, S. Thomas was favoured by a heavenly revelation, which assured him that his brothers had received forgiveness.

After four years at Cologne, our Saint received orders to prepare to take his degrees at Paris. This move was made, no doubt, with full deliberation. The Superiors of the Dominicans were merely carrying out a preconceived plan for strengthening the Order. And how was this best achieved? By placing their most promising subjects at Paris, and by earning so unmistakable a name for depth, accuracy, and brilliancy of teaching, that men would be constrained to acknowledge their superiority. Jealousy might be strong, but never so powerful as to overset an institution which, according to the unanimous voice of learned scholars, held the palm for doctrine in the most deeply theological university in the world.

Albert, and Cardinal Hugh of S. Caro, were instrumental in getting our Saint to Paris. Albert had had a life-long experience of the difficulties which beset a professorship; of the qualifications required for success; and of the work which had to be accomplished in the future—a work requiring something more than learning, viz.: tact, temper, coolness, and caution. He saw all these qualities combined, in an unusual degree, in Thomas of Aquino, and founded on a basis of supernatural love. Then Hugh had been present when the young man implored the Holy Father to let him follow Christ in humility and poverty—and had not forgotten it. He had watched, ever since that occasion, the career of the young Dominican, and became more firmly convinced every day, that he was destined to perform some great service for the Church.

Thomas, when he heard his fate, was much concerned. His pronounced distaste for honours and position made him wish to be left alone. But, in obedience to authority, he set out on his journey from Cologne, and begged his way to Paris. Some say he stopped at Louvain, but of this, the evidence is insufficient

It is certain that he passed through Brabant and Flanders, and preached before the Duchess Margaret. Probably the Duchess was acquainted with his family; and since she encouraged men of letters, possibly she had heard of his reputation, as a teacher in the schools. She conceived the warmest admiration for his saintliness and genius; and, subsequently, was in the habit of consulting him in her difficulties relating to the well-being of her people.

Not only the Duchess, but the learned men of Paris had been told of his successes during his four years at Cologne; and he was received by them with marks of unusual distinction.

There were many young Dominicans, who, if age counted for much, had a greater claim to be sent to Paris than Thomas of Aquino. But they were all passed over by the General: and Thomas, on account of his talents and activity, was admitted—though below the legal age—amongst the Bachelors (1248).

But it was not at his own request that he was promoted. On the contrary, his deep humility, and the greatness of the responsibility, tempted him to refuse the proffered honour. However, holy obedience constrained him to obey. The Dominican professors of theology at this time were Hugh of Metz, and Elias Brunetus. It was as teacher in the school of Elias that S. Thomas, according to the custom, now began to expound the Holy Scriptures, and the writings of the Lombard. He was no sooner made Bachelor, and it became his duty to speak, than his silence abandoned him.

The quiet, meek young man—so mortified, so recollected—began to let flow that fountain which had been filled with 'the waters of wisdom' during his long and deep meditations. His influence over young men was very remarkable. It far surpassed, as will be seen, that of any other master. He could, beyond other teachers, inflame the minds of his disciples with an ardent love of study. They were conscious that his teaching had something about it of another world; and the feeling crept over all, and finally mastered them, that he spoke as one 'having power.' The opinions which he formed at that early age, with few exceptions, he committed to writing; and held them, and defended them, with little change, in his maturer years. From his youth he had dedicated himself to wisdom as his spouse. The Bollandists say that this spouse of his drew him to herself in such a manner that nothing could overcome a mind which, in the possession of one reality, possessed everything. Only one thing he asked for—that was wisdom. Even in conversation his mind clung to its One only Rest—though speaking to man, his eye was fixed on God.

Rainald, his confessor, knew, for certain, that the Saint gained everything by prayer. On one occasion, during class, the conversation fell on the great Angelical. Rainald burst into tears, and exclaimed, 'Brothers, my master forbade me, during his life, to tell the wonderful things he did:—one thing I know of him, that it was not human talent, but *prayer*, that was the secret of his great success. He never discussed, read, wrote, or dictated, without begging with tears for illumination.' Tocco says that he thus acquired all he knew. This was his daily prayer: 'Grant me, I beseech Thee, O merciful God, ardently to desire, prudently to study, rightly to understand, and perfectly to fulfil that which is pleasing to Thee—to the praise and glory of Thy Name.' When a child, if conversation did not turn on God, or on matters which tended to edification, the Angelical would go away. He wondered how men, especially religious men, could talk of anything but God or holy things. He was 'Miro modo benignus in animo, qui totus suavis erat in verbo et liberalis in facto.' He wept for the sins of others as if they had been his own—yet so spotless was his mind, that he could hardly bring himself to think that man could sin. No one could look on him in conversation without receiving the grace of a special consolation. To meet his eye and to hear his voice, was to warm the heart and to elevate the soul.

The young professor had reason to throw himself earnestly into his work. Though ever dwelling in the unseen kingdom, as is evident from his history, he was keenly alive to the tendency of the intellectual world around him. His saintliness, his character, and his parts, seem to have pointed him out as destined to sway the philosophical and theological teachings of an age, in which the human mind appeared to be in a very dangerous state of flux. The rationalism of the Abelardine school—the corroding mysticism of the East, and depravity of morals—had to be faced, and to be withstood. Thomas fixed himself, therefore, on the immovable basis of authority, and grounded his teaching on the monastic methods of the *Sentences* of Peter the Lombard. It can hardly be doubted that the surprise caused by his distinctions, and the admiration created by his novelty in argument, proceeded, in great measure, from his vivid appreciation of the work he had to do—of the enemy he was contending with, and of the powers by which alone that enemy could be overthrown. Frigerio says he was looked upon *quasi divino oracolo*—as a heavenly oracle. He followed Albert, but his teaching was more incisive, more definite, and more strictly to the point.

It will be seen, later, how he met dominant errors, and gained the confidence of those who naturally would have looked upon him with jealousy or suspicion. Many of his disciples became distinguished men. Ægidius Romanus, of the Colonna family, was his pupil for eleven years, and became famous for his acquaintance with theology, philosophy, and law. Ægidius was a vehement defender of Thomistic traditions, and wrote voluminously on morals and scholastic theology. Eventually he joined the Augustinians, was made General, then Archbishop of Berry, and acquired the title of *Doctor Fundatissimus*.

S. Thomas assisted others besides his own pupils—sovereigns, cardinals, bishops, superiors of Orders, and professors, besides inquisitive young men, wrote to him for advice, and for solutions to their difficulties. For instance, a professor, of Venice, sends him a paper of thirty-six articles, to which he desires a response in four days. The Saint answers him with great courtesy, saying how occupied he is, still promising to do his bidding. Each question is first stated by S. Thomas, and then he gives the answer as briefly as is compatible with clearness. He is asked whether the angels move the heavens; whether they do so *suo imperio;* if there were any method of proving this infallibly; and whether these spirits belong to the order of heavenly Virtues. The answers given by S. Thomas show how great an influence the writings of the Areopagite had had upon him. Then Br. Gerard of Besançon, a Dominican, writes asking six questions, which hardly show that Br. Gerard had either a very practical or a very scientific turn. He wishes to know, amongst other things, whether the star which appeared to the Magi was like a cross, or a man, or a crucifix; whether the little hands of Jesus created the stars; whether the words of Simeon—'thy own soul a sword shall pierce'—were remembered by our Lady with vehement grief seven times a day till the Resurrection; and lastly, there is a somewhat inane question about Confession. Br. Gerard asked these questions with an eye to the pulpit. The Saint treated them as they deserved—showing that he was not given to scholastic subtleties. He tells Br. Gerard that he thinks, when indubitable truth offers so much matter for sermons, frivolity should be avoided: still, what has been said need not be recalled, unless scandal has arisen. The Opusculum, on the difference between the Divine and human word; and the somewhat larger treatise, on the nature of the intellectual word, are full of close reasoning, and state principles which are fundamental, regarding the method of human knowledge. They show a deep study of the Stagyrite, and, though Albert and S. Augustine are kept in view, they manifest marks of powerful and independent thought.

One of the most important of his treatises is that addressed 'ad Fratrem Reginaldum socium suum carissimum,' on the nature of the angels; a favourite subject in the middle ages. It was begun during the Saint's Bachelorship, but he never got beyond the thirtieth chapter.

In this treatise, he exhibits a familiar acquaintance with the systems of Thales, Diogenes, Heraclitus, Empedocles, Democritus, Anaxagoras, and others. He shows his mastery of Arabian philosophy, and of the teachings of Porphyry and Avicenna. He compares Plato with Aristotle, and brilliantly refutes the doctrine of Avicebron. He oversets the pantheism of Avicenna, the untenable doctrines of the Platonists, and the equally dangerous, but perhaps more remotely destructive tenets of Origen. He establishes the Providence of God over the angels, with the assistance of Aristotle's metaphysics; and proves, with an argument full of ingenuity, that the same Providence extends its beneficent influence to the smallest creature. Finally, the Manichean error is disposed of, and the *substantiæ separatæ* are proved to have been created; whilst the last chapter treats of the condition and distinction of the angels. The Areopagite, S. Basil, S. Augustine, S. Gregory of Nyssa, S. Jerome, S. Gregory Nazianzen called *Theologus*, S. Chrysostom, and S. John Damascene, are used in a manner which makes it evident that S. Thomas must have been extensively read in the Fathers, even so early as this in his career. The treatise shows the Saint's grasp of some of the cardinal questions of the day, and how masterfully he dealt with errors which, had it not been for him, might have stained the most promising minds in the Paris schools.

There are some other Opuscula which are put down to this period—writings of less importance in themselves, but interesting in as far as they point out what kinds of subjects occupied the thoughts of scholars in the thirteenth century. There is the Tract against those who maintained the eternity of the world, and which strikes at the root of the Eastern systems. Here the Saint follows his favourite, S. Augustine, and shows his acquaintance with the writings of Boethius, S. Anselm, and Hugh of S. Victor's. Then there is *De Sortibus*, which rests principally upon the common assumption that the heavenly bodies exerted immense influence on terrestrial affairs; *De Fato,* in which the Saint shows that he is well acquainted with some of the Latin poets; and finally, a treatise on the *Essence of Matter and its Dimensions,* in which, in nine chapters of subtle arguing, the errors of Averroës are combated. The *Exposition* of the two decrees of Innocent III. for the Archdeacon of Trent, an *Opusculum de motu cordis ad Philippum Magistrum,* and another *De Potentiis Animæ,* seem also to have been written during this period.

But, whilst thus engaged upon the Scriptures and the Lombard, S. Thomas was frequently in the pulpit; he zealously observed the duties of conventual life, and regularly delivered lectures to the crowds that pressed around his chair. His versatility, his power of abstraction, his astonishing memory, his jealous husbanding of time, carried him with ease through works which would have broken the spirit of any ordinary man. He possessed that marvellous gift, which Origen and Cæsar are said to have displayed, of being able to dictate to three, and even four scribes, on different and difficult subjects, at one time, without for a moment losing or entangling the thread of each separate question—dictating to each as if he alone was exclusively the object of his attention.

There are one or two points in S. Thomas's answer to the Duchess of Brabant, about the Jews, which are of interest. He begins, as was his custom, by saying how overpowered he was with work, but that charity would not suffer him to keep silence. The Duchess asked whether she could make exactions from the Jews? Absolutely speaking, he thinks she could; still, according to the Apostle, we should be without offence to Jew and Gentile, and the Church of God. Nor is it permissible for her to turn to her own account money which the Jews acquired by extortion. She may not receive ill-gotten goods; they must be returned to the lawful owner. If this cannot be effected, they must be converted to some pious purpose, at the suggestion of the Diocesan, or some other worthy person. Can Jews be punished by fine, seeing that their money is acquired by usury? Some penalty should be added, since money thus obtained does not belong to them. The Saint blames princes for not constraining the Jews to take to some honest occupation, as had been done in parts of Italy; and observes that if princes are defrauded of their rights it is their own fault, for not acting with greater vigour with the Jews. Can presents be taken from Jews? Yes: but if the gifts have been acquired by usury they should be returned to the owner or converted to pious purposes. What is to be done with the residue if more is received from the Jews than is required? The answer is given in the principle already stated. Is it lawful to sell places to bailiffs and officials? Many inconveniences would follow from such a practice. The worst men—the ambitious, and the avaricious, would be purchasers; and having once obtained position would abuse their power, and become overbearing and tyrannical. Is it lawful to impose taxes on Christian subjects? It must be borne in mind that princes of the earth were instituted by God, not that they might seek themselves, but the common utility of their subjects. For it is said in Ezechiel, 'Her princes in the midst of her are like wolves ravening the prey to shed blood, and to destroy souls, and to run after gains.' And in another place, it is said, by a certain prophet, 'Woe to the shepherds of Israel, that fed themselves; should not the flocks be fed by the shepherd? You ate the milk, and you clothed yourselves with the wool, and you killed that which was fat; but My flock you did not feed.'

Hence princes receive their rents that they may not despoil their subjects—according to the Prophet, 'He shall have a portion of the land of Israel, and the princes shall no more rob My people.' Still, if the revenue be not sufficient for supporting their position, princes may exact what is necessary. Those who live for the common good should be supported by the people. So, also, extra expenses for the common good are to be defrayed by the public purse. But it is unlawful to tax the people to meet inordinate outlays, or for the lust of personal gain. The seventh question is: what is to be done with money extorted by officials? To be returned to the rightful owner. Lastly, should the Jews have a badge to distinguish them from Christians? Both according to the General Council (of Lateran), and to their own law, they should wear some distinctive mark on their dress.

Such is the manner in which the Angelical treated political questions of no little difficulty in his day. Any person carefully reading the advice given by the Dominican to the Duchess will, at once, perceive with what prudence, tact, and judgment the Saint viewed the difficulties in which she was placed. It will, moreover, be observed that he possessed a spirit of justice and a love of freedom, tempered by wisdom in its widest sense, which was not as general as it might have been in the middle ages. The views of the Angelical become all the more striking, when it is borne in mind that he was a friar, and had had no practical experience of government. In a man of genius intuition and instinct often serve in the place of study; and what ordinary men only acquire by laborious application, he is enabled to grasp by reason of his extraordinary gifts. Such seems to have been the case with the Angel of the Schools.

It is, of course, impossible, by means of extracts, to show, as one would wish, the great mastery that our Saint attained over theological and philosophical problems. To thoroughly understand the great intellectual gifts of the Angelical his entire works must be laboriously studied. By boldly placing theology as a queen reigning paramount amidst her vassals—a queen not only holding her own, but, with a fearless and uncompromising voice, declaring that all were made to be her ministers—the Angelical sets himself wholly against the encroachments of human reason; and takes up ground, which he never ceased to defend, and to maintain, during the whole of his intellectual career.

There is also another fact which must be borne in mind, when weighing the influence of the Angelical upon theological thought, viz., that he was not a man to indulge in dangerous originality of thought or theory; nor was he ever seduced by a delusion common to many able thinkers, that man, of himself, is able to give law to the world. He had sufficient greatness and clearness of mind, sufficient intellectual modesty, to assure him that his triumph would depend upon adhering to the traditional teaching of the Church; and that, if his fame and power were to go down to posterity as a lasting influence, it would be on the condition of his interpreting, not *self*, but the living voice of an infallible Guide according to its truest meaning; and of enforcing, with arguments which could not be overthrown, the saving revelation of Jesus Christ. He felt that to leave the Church, and to trust to self, would be to rely upon a support that lacks stability; whilst to adhere to the one Living Voice, and to sink human ingenuity, would be to identify himself with a power which has God for its stay, and everlasting truth for its support. It was because the Angelical was a true interpreter of Church doctrine that his name has come down to us; and, because he was the most accurate of interpreters, that his name still holds the foremost place amongst the doctors of Christian theology.

It is hardly possible, in looking at the position

attained by the Angelical in the Church, and at the general bent and tenor of his mind, not to perceive that, in great part, his success was owing to the marvellous stability of his character, and to the extraordinary manner in which the grand monastic principles of love, reverence, purity, and adoration, had taken possession of, and had coloured the whole of his intelligence. To see him prostrate before the altar, with all the abandonment of a little child; to see him lifted up to God, in ecstasy of spirit, in his prayers; to think on his spotless purity of heart and mind, and then to call to memory his genius, is to account, in part at least, for the depth, balance, and steadiness of his method, and for the singular influence of his mind upon the Catholic religious world. When a perfect Doctor is also a perfect Saint, then the world receives not merely a fading light, but a lasting illumination.

CHAPTER XI.

S. THOMAS MADE LICENTIATE.

According to the usual custom, S. Thomas would now become Licentiate, and perform the necessary acts which led to the Doctor's cap. But an impediment, created by one of those University brawls for which Paris had an unhappy celebrity, stood in the way of his promotion to that distinguished honour.

The facts of the case were these. During the Lent

either of 1250 or 1253—authorities are not in accord—a party of tumultuous University scholars came into collision with the night patrol. The students, no doubt, were noisy and violent, and the patrol was no less determined to perform the duty of its office. Most likely the students—as was often the case in their night carousals—were none the better for drink. Anyhow, they were very unceremoniously attacked; one was killed outright, and three others, after having been heavily mauled, were hurried off to jail.

The authorities of the University, who were excessively jealous of their rights, were greatly ruffled; they demanded the instant release of the incarcerated youths, and insisted upon those brutal keepers of the peace who had murdered one student, and misused the others, being visited with condign punishment. The civic authorities let the students free, but did not seem at all inclined to punish the patrol, which, according to their notions, had simply been carrying out its orders. But the University authorities thought otherwise, and resolved to abide by their opinion; they swore a solemn oath not to rest till justice had been done; and refused, for two whole months, to lecture in the schools. They considered it their bounden duty thus publicly to protest against a gross infringement of their rights; and against the insult offered to their body by the officials of the town. This stand, made by the professors, brought into flame a fire which had long been smouldering—and which burnt fiercely for forty years—between the Mendicant Orders and the secular element of the University. The explanation of the case is simple. The object of the professors in shutting up the schools was, evidently, by force of pressure, to compel the town authorities to bring the patrol to justice. The more effectually the schools were closed, so much the greater probability of the pressure taking effect. Hence, they were excessively mortified to find that the Mendicants by no means took the same view as themselves. For the friars to go on teaching when the seculars were silent was to suffer the infliction of a double blow. The professors felt, first, that their protest would lose the greater part of its force; and, secondly, that the friars would be daily gaining in popularity, and drawing crowds of their own students under the influence of S. Francis and S. Dominic. Whether the astute superiors of S. James's and other thoughtful men had any eye to this, of course one cannot tell. But this much is certain, that while the secular professors were silently waiting for their pressure to take effect, the Dominicans and Franciscans—the sole mouthpieces of learning—were lecturing away in the various chairs of the University. They simply did what they had done some twenty years before, when, during the regency of Blanche, the secular doctors, irritated by a similar provocation, had abandoned Paris altogether, and had settled themselves down to teach at Angers, Rheims, and different towns of Europe.

But the doctors of the University were not easily

discouraged, and stood true to their first resolve. They finally obtained the redress they sought. The beadles had to expiate their rashness by punishment according to the customary law. Two of the patrol, who had been actively instrumental in killing the student, were condemned to death; the others, who had laid violent hands upon the three, were banished from the kingdom.

The doctors, having thus far achieved their end, determined to draw up regulations for future emergencies; and did their utmost to bring the friars, whose stubbornness had nearly upset their plans, into agreement with their views. They called a meeting, at which they drew up an instrument, declaring that, for the future, no one could be admitted as master who had not sworn to observe all the laws of the University: and that law in particular which met the case in point. The doctors knew well what they were about. They made up their minds either to include the regulars in the oath, or to come to an open rupture. That no scruple should stand in the way of the Dominicans, this clause was inserted in the oath: 'Provided there be nothing in these statutes forbidden by the rules of the Friars Preachers, of which I make profession; or contrary to honesty, or the salvation of souls, to human and divine right, to the public good, or to the Holy Church of God.'

But the regulars had no idea of taking the law from the authorities, and wished to maintain liberty of action. They felt no inclination to interfere with the views of the secular doctors, and expected the same liberty to be granted to themselves. In a word, they refused to take the oath: some say because they did not wish to compromise themselves: others, because they could not, being religious, take any oath at all.

This brought things to a climax. Since they would not accede to the oath, the University issued a decree, declaring the friars excluded from its body, and deprived of their chairs.

The regulars appealed, as is natural for regulars to do, to Rome; and did not omit to place their case before the brother of S. Louis, who governed France in the absence of the sovereign. But the viceroy could effect nothing. Pope Innocent sided with the friars, and commissioned the Bishop of Evreux to reëstablish them in their chairs, and to visit with ecclesiastical censures any who should presume to oppose such a design. To make things all the more securc, the Holy Father addressed a Brief to Master Luke, Canon of Paris, to the same end; and the Canon, without waiting the issue of a counter appeal to the Holy See, carried out, without delay, the instructions he had received.

Meanwhile, the University was not idle; it published its decree of exclusion, and addressed a long letter to the French bishops, describing the state of affairs at Paris, and begging for their protection. At this juncture, things were complicated by the death of Innocent IV., at Naples. However, the Cardinals assembled, without delay, for the election of a successor, notwithstanding the unsettled state of the country, in consequence of the victories of Manfred, son of Frederick II. The new Pope took the name of Alexander IV., and, naturally, was desirous to inaugurate his reign by an act of clemency and justice. Feeling all the charity of a common father towards the contending parties at Paris, and being conscious that, as long as learned ecclesiastics spent their energies in mutual recriminations, the cause of charity and science could not possibly be served, he published a Bull, by which he hoped to bring about a reconciliation. This Bull begins with the words: 'As the Tree of Life,' and speaks in glowing terms of the services rendered by the University of Paris to the Catholic world. He compares it to the Tree of Life, planted in the midst of a terrestrial paradise; to a lamp of brightness in the House of the Lord; and declares that from it, as from a source, flow the waters of wisdom over the face of the sterile earth. Having thus paved the way, he enters into business, and says that, having heard the Procurators of both sides, he judges it expedient to modify the statutes of the University according to a Constitution of Gregory IX. He then prescribes in what way the Chancellor is to give licenses, and leaves him to determine, both with regard to regulars as well as seculars, the number that it may be advisable to admit. Regarding the main point, he makes use of the usual *mezzo termine:* for, whilst he confirms the decree of the doctors, binding al to stop teaching in case of insult—if satisfaction be not afforded—he reëstablishes the Dominican and Franciscan professors; revokes all decrees issued against them; commands the secular doctors to receive them, and to live with them in peace. To insure the operation of this Bull, the Holy Father commissioned the Bishops of Orleans and Auxerre to see it put in execution; and, above all, to restore to their professorial chairs the two Dominican doctors, Bonus-homo and Elias Brunetus.

It would naturally be imagined that so explicit a pronouncement as that of Pope Alexander would have removed all possibility of mistaking his meaning; but men who have started on a wrong course, especially when it is a course mixed up with pride, and pushed forward by passion, often cannot bring themselves to see the clearest orders of the Holy See, when they militate against their own idea. The celebrated William of S. Amour, who, with his followers, was the originator of this attack upon the Mendicants, persuaded his conscience that his party, in spite of the Papal order, could still oppose the reëstablishment of the friars in their academic rights. The sophism he and his followers used was this: they withdrew for a time from the colleges in which they had been accustomed to teach, and then declared that since they had left the University, the Bull of Pope Alexander did not apply to them. The two Bishops had a mind to visit them with censures; but they made an appeal to the Holy See, which, it must be confessed, bore very much the appearance of a threat: they protested that they would either transfer their schools elsewhere, or altogether retire from the responsibilities of teaching, to the liberty and repose afforded by their own country, rather than acquiesce in a measure which met their wishes in no way whatsoever. They begged the Holy Father to remove the excommunication which was upon them, and to restore them to their former position. But Pope Alexander would not hearken to them. He was determined to have the *quasi lignum* put in force, and to that end, issued orders more stringent than those he had given before.

At this juncture, King Louis returned, after six years' absence, from his first expedition against the infidel. The troubles of the University were quickly brought before him. It pained him excessively to hear of the scandal of priests and religious carrying on uncharitable war. He especially felt it in this instance, since his two favourite Orders, the Dominicans and Franciscans, were compromised in the matter. Naturally, he at once set about trying to bring all parties to an accommodation. He stopped the execution of the Papal Briefs. He hoped, without appealing to force, or to his kingly authority, by means of the joint remonstrances of the bishops, to prevail upon the litigating parties to settle their quarrels by arbitration—putting the whole case into the hands of the Archbishops of Bourges, Rheims, Sens, and Rouen. These four prelates declared themselves willing to carry out the wishes of so holy a prince—of one who not only had ever shown great esteem for the Episcopate, but had so tender an affection for the Orders of S. Dominic and S. Francis, that he is said to have declared that if he were able to divide himself in two, he would give one half to S. Dominic, and the other to S. Francis. The archbishops, in due course, assembled, and having heard each of the opposing parties, and having called in the assistance of other distinguished ecclesiastics, brought things, as they imagined, to an amicable arrangement. The conditions which they thought fair were as follows: The Dominicans were to be permitted, by the secular doctors, to possess, *in perpetuum*, their two chairs of theology, but upon three conditions—first, that they should give up the Bulls which they had obtained from Rome; secondly, that they should not procure any others which were hurtful to the interests of the University; and thirdly, that they should use all their influence with the Pope, to induce him to recall all the edicts which had been issued in their favour by Innocent IV. and by himself, since the beginning of the disturbances. To these conditions both the seculars and the regulars agreed. And it is alleged that the Dominicans, in the fulness of their gratitude for the benefits which the University had lavished upon them in the past, did all they could to induce the Holy See to recall the instruments it had published in their favour.

Whether they knew the character of Alexander IV. sufficiently to read what course he would pursue, it is impossible to know for certain. It is, no doubt, a far easier thing to give way, if one's interests are attacked, when it is pretty certain that a stronger power will be ready to support them, than to give way when there is no prospect of any help at all. The Dominicans could afford to act a graceful part, as long as Alexander was in reserve. Their interests, by such a policy, far from being put in danger, would become infinitely safer than before; and it is hardly imaginable that men so intimately connected with the Court of Rome would not have made a pretty shrewd guess, that Pope Alexander would hardly consider himself respectfully treated, when his own business was taken, unasked, out of his hands; his rescripts abolished; and petitions made to him to reverse a method of procedure which, with full deliberation, and in a most formal manner, he had thought it his duty, as father of the faithful, to adopt.

Whatever shrewdness the friars may have possessed, the Holy Father took that course of action which, under the circumstances, alone was open to him. He issued a new Bull (June 17, 1256), in which he freely spoke his mind. He declared that the whole matter of the accommodation had been carried through without his having been consulted, and in the teeth of his express decrees. And he declared William of S. Amour, Odo of Douay, Nicholas of Bar, and Christian, Canon of Beauvais—whom he looked upon as the originators of this disorder—by name, deprived of all their grades and benefices; and he forbade them to teach, and inhibited any one from taking lessons from them. Moreover, he ordered them to be driven out of the kingdom, and instructed the Bishop of Paris to confer their benefices on other subjects; and threatened their adherents with a like penalty, if, within fifteen days of its publication, the Bull were not obeyed. At the end of the same month, the Holy See issued two other decrees, confirming the action that had already been taken.

These measures of Rome may look to some as bordering on severity; but, in reality, they were acts of the greatest and wisest mercy. It was an assertion of the first principle of order, and a blow at the principle of anarchy. King Louis, in his charity and haste, overstepped the bounds of his authority; and the bishops who fulfilled his behest trenched upon the prerogatives, and interfered with the right, of the supreme power. Without a bold, unflinching assertion of his position, Pope Alexander might have brought such difficulties upon the government of the Church, as would have hampered its free action, and so have injured the noblest instrument of justice and humanity on earth.

Meanwhile, the regulars continued their public teachings in Scripture and theology. Since the beginning of the year 1256, S. Thomas had been lecturing as Licentiate, and his great reputation drew to his schools the most promising intelligences of the day. The way in which he was introduced to his new office, speaks for the high esteem in which he was held, both at Paris and at Rome—not only by the Chancellor, but by the Pope. Without waiting for the Papal Rescript, the

Chancellor appointed him to lecture in the schools; upon which, the Holy Father addresses a letter to that dignitary, expressing his satisfaction that he has anticipated the Apostolic wishes by bestowing the Licentiate upon 'Brother Thomas of Aquino, of the Order of Preachers, a man eminent for his birth, and for his virtues, and for the treasure of science with which God has enriched him.' The Saint took no notice of the contests raging around him. Not that he was callous to what was going on; not that he did not pray, and inflict penance upon himself, to the end that all might coöperate to the advantage of religion; but he never entered into strife, without being forced to it by obedience and necessity. His only reply to William of S. Amour and his associates, and to the violent onslaughts that were made upon the Order, and upon himself, was that of modest silence and humility. He lived in a region far more serene than that of ecclesiastical jealousies; and treated with disregard the bitter and perseverant assaults made upon his character. As long as he was permitted to occupy his professorial chair, to preach, and to use his pen, he suffered little from the most vehement denunciations of passion and unreason.

In fact, whilst others were wasting their energies in mutual recriminations, he was enjoying the sweetest and deepest of human gifts, the friendship of one, if not as able, at least as full of love as himself. Born at the foot of the beautiful mountains of Tuscany and Calabria, S. Bonaventure, like S. Thomas, was an Italian saint.

They were both about the same age—Bonaventure not being more than a twelvemonth older than his companion—and they both had dedicated their lives to God in the same year; the one joining the chivalrous S. Dominic, the other, that flame of love, S. Francis of Assisi. Both, at this period, were engaged in a similar pursuit:—S. Thomas lecturing under a Dominican professor, and S. Bonaventure under the Franciscan, John of Rochelle. Both men exhibited, in a striking manner, the fundamental quality of the Order to which they respectively belonged. They were eminently representative men. In them, dogma in its purest, and mysticism in its best, met, and embraced, with something like that transport which draws natures, as nearly as possible, into one. Whilst both were founded on the same Catholic principles; whilst both had the same aim—earnest, utter love of the One Supreme—each was different from the other, and each found in the other that which was wanting in himself; and in that sweet discovery, experienced the full harmony of his entire being. Bonaventure loved to look into the placid, earnest soul of Thomas, as into a deep glassy sea, with its marvellous transparency, and awful stillness; whilst Thomas was roused and brightened by the ardent, outpouring nature of his friend. S. Thomas was Angelical, S. Bonaventure was Seraphic—the one, the deep thinker; the other, the tender poet. Thomas was famous in the schools for the keenness of his thought, and for his depth and clearness; Bonaventure, for his eloquence and vivacity in exposition. Thomas, abandoning a high position and bright prospects, hid himself in solitude, and sought an humble life; Bonaventure was born among the poor, and was elevated to the highest dignities of the Church. Thomas was, essentially, a child of contemplation; Bonaventure, of activity. Two characteristic and beautiful traits are related of these men: S. Thomas was in the habit of visiting, from time to time, his friend Bonaventure, and of discussing with him various religious questions of the day. On one occasion, as he entered Bonaventure's cell, with his *socius*, he perceived the Saint, deeply engrossed, writing at his table. S. Thomas knew at once that he was composing the life of S. Francis, so, turning to those present, he said to them: 'Come away; let us not disturb a Saint, writing the life of a Saint.' On another occasion, S. Thomas called upon S. Bonaventure, and, during conversation, said to him: 'Show me, my brother, the books out of which you get those sublime thoughts in your writings.' 'There is the book,' replied S. Bonaventure, pointing to a figure of the Crucified, which hung before him. Then S. Bonaventure, on returning the visit of S. Thomas, perceived what none of his companions were privileged to see—viz., an angel actively assisting the Angelical in the composition of his treatise on the Blessed Sacrament. Rejoiced at beholding so beautiful and touching a picture, in order to attract his attention, S. Bonaventure said to the great Dominican: 'Are you writing, my brother

Thomas?' 'Yes,' replied the Angelical, 'and I am writing about the Most Holy Body of Christ;' and from this answer, Bonaventure got to know that S. Thomas, besides being gifted with great natural talents, was illuminated also by a supernatural light.

Just as both Saints received their doctor's diploma on the same day, so both, after twenty years' labour for the Church, died in the same year; each giving his last energies in furtherance of that Council over which Bonaventure presided in the flesh, and over which, no doubt, S. Thomas presided in the spirit. If S. Thomas was called Angelical, in the words of Alexander of Hales: 'Adam does not seem to have sinned in Bonaventure.' Doubtless, Staudenmaier had such men as these before his mind when he said that: 'The acute and deep scholastics were, at the same time, high moral characters, pure, and in harmony with nature—exhibiting the wonderful phenomena of an interior Christian life.'

Nor was S. Thomas idle with his pen during the contests which were being waged by the University authorities. The Exposition of the Symbol of the Apostles, the Exposition of the Lord's Prayer, and the Angelical Salutation; one Opusculum, on the Ten Commandments, and the Law of Love; and another, on the Articles of Faith, and the Sacraments of the Church, fall within this period. Then there is a Commentary on Isaias and Jeremias, on the work of Boethius, *De Hebdomadibus*, and on the pseudo-Dionysian work, *De Divinis Nominibus*. These five theological tractates, in reality, form a logical unity, which is expressed by the author himself, when, in his tract on the Precepts of Charity, he affirms that three things are necessary for man's salvation: a knowledge of what has to be believed, to be desired, and to be done. The first is taught in the symbol; the second in the Lord's Prayer; the third in the Law—that is to say, in the Commandments and in the two precepts of charity.

There are some few points which it will be interesting to dwell upon, and some few expressions of the Saint, full of depth and brilliancy, which will require no apology for their introduction. As a general critique upon these instructive portions of his writings, it may be said that they touch upon fundamental Catholic thought, and that the individuality of the writer is carefully kept out of sight. All flows from the Gospel, from the Fathers, and from the traditionary teaching of the Church, and there is no appearance of any other effort except that of placing orthodox doctrine upon a firm basis, and making its truth and utility apparent, by lucidity of style, logical division, and apt illustration. To those who have the cure of souls, who have, Sunday after Sunday, to instruct half-educated people, and sometimes the learned too, in the first principles of Catholicity, these tractates would be of value. It is a misfortune that the teaching of the Angelical on these matters should have been so much neglected. Perhaps it may be partially accounted for by a growing tendency to preach long, elaborate, and 'fine' sermons, instead of breaking the bread of simple, homely, and familiar instruction to the people.

In the exposition of the first article of the Creed, the Saint draws from his store-house some telling and deep thoughts. The first thing necessary for a Christian, he says, is faith. Faith produces four good effects. First, by faith the soul is joined to God. S. Augustine, on these words of S. Paul: 'Whatever is not of faith is sin,' says: 'Where there is no recognition of the Eternal and Immutable Truth, virtue is counterfeit even in the best men.' The second effect of faith is the beginning of eternal life in us; for eternal life is nothing else than to know God: 'This is eternal life to know Thee, the only true God.' The third effect is, that faith directs us in our present life. No philosopher, with all his efforts, could discover, before the coming of Christ, as much about God, and the conditions of salvation, as a poor old woman knows, by means of faith, now that our Lord has come. Hence, Isaias: 'The earth is filled with the knowledge of the Lord.' The fourth effect is, that by faith we overcome temptations: 'The saints through faith conquered kingdoms.' And this is evident, because all temptations proceed from the devil, the world, or the flesh; and faith offers arguments which are more powerful than any these can bring forward.

Some people affirm that it is foolish to believe what cannot be seen. But not so, if the imperfection of the human mind be considered. The mind is so weak that no philosopher was ever able perfectly to investigate the nature of the merest fly. But, if this be so, is it not foolish to believe only that concerning God, which the human mind is able to elicit of itself? In the second place, it may be replied, if a countryman denied the truth of a proposition stated by an expert in science, on the ground that he did not understand it, would not that countryman be considered a fool? But it is certain that the intellect of an angel surpasses the intellect of the greatest philosopher in a higher degree than the intellect of the scientific man surpasses that of the rustic. Therefore, that philosopher is a fool who rejects what angels say; and far more so, if he refuse to believe the Word of God. Just as a king puts his seal to an instrument, and thus it is known to be the king's, so all that has been handed down to us by the saints is stamped with the seal of God. This seal is formed of those miracles by which Christ confirmed the works and words of His Apostles.

The Saint goes on to treat of the first article of the Creed: 'I believe in one God.' He says there are four causes why men have been drawn into adoring many Gods. The first is the weakness of the human mind, which has never pierced beyond visible things; the second arises from that spirit of adulation by which kings and potentates have been turned into gods; the third, from over-weening affection for children and relations—men having first erected statues of them, and then, in course of time, having fallen down and adored them;

and the fourth comes from the malice of the devil. S. Thomas likens the feeling of a man looking on the beautiful order of the Creation to one entering a house with a fire in the centre. He feels different degrees of warmth, and though he may not see the fire, he knows that different degrees of heat proceed from it. So man recognises God in His works, and perceives them to be more beautiful the nearer they approach to Him. He compares the Manicheans, who said that visible things were created by the devil, to a man going into a carpenter's shop, and, in his stupidity, wounding himself with one of the tools, and then crying out against the carpenter. He likens those who declare the world to be eternal to that boy spoken of by Rabbi Moses, who was born on a solitary island, and left by his mother, and, after he had grown up, would not believe that man begins by being conceived, is carried in the womb, and is born of a mother. It was impossible, he said, that man could dwell in his mother's womb. So, these men, looking upon the world in its present stage, cannot believe that it ever did begin. The Saint then combats the error that God did not make the world out of nothing, and concludes the article by pointing out five moral consequences, most consoling to the Christian, which flow from such considerations. In the second article, he manifests his acquaintance with the master-heresies of the past ; and indicates how this second article bears on Photinus, who denied Christ's divinity; on Sabellius, who declared the Eternal Father became flesh ; on

Arius, who denied the divinity and the eternity of the Son, and His oneness of nature with the Father. He then proceeds to explain the difference between the Divine and human word, and states somewhat the same principles which he had laid down in his special treatise. In the third article, he shows how the words: 'He was conceived of the Holy Ghost; born of the Virgin Mary,' strike down the heresies of Photinus, Manes, Ebion, Valentine, Arius, Apollinaris, and Nestorius, and then finishes with useful, practical reflections. In the fourth article, he speaks of the guilt of the Jews, saying, that the Son of God is the Word of God; and the Word of God became incarnate, just as the word of a king is written down upon paper. If any one should tear up the royal document, it would be equivalent to tearing to pieces the royal word. And so the sin of the Jews was as great as if they had murdered the Word of God. Before the Passion of Christ, few lived out of mortal sin; but since His Passion, many have lived, and continue to live, in a state of grace. He who would live a perfect life, let him only contemn what Christ contemned whilst on the Cross, and desire what Christ desired. There is no example of virtue which is not given us by the Cross. If you seek an example of patience, you will find a most excellent one in the Cross. Patience is shown in two ways: when heavy trials are borne with resignation, or when those things are suffered, and are not avoided, which can be avoided. And Christ did both these. 'If thou seekest an example of humility, look on the Crucified.' He was, moreover, an example of obedience, and an example of contempt of earthly things. The fifth article is full of beautiful and profound instruction. It touches on praying for the dead. S. Augustine says they can be helped principally in three ways: by masses, prayers, and alms-deeds; S. Gregory adds a fourth, namely, fasting: 'Nor is it strange, for in this world also one friend can satisfy for another.' S. Thomas then speaks of the Resurrection, of the pious belief that our Lady, as well as S. John the Evangelist, rose from the dead. Then come four practical points, with a quotation from Venerable Bede, regarding the difficulty of shaking off the devil after he has had long possession: 'The longer the devil has hold of a man, the more difficult he is to get rid of.' The sixth article is short, and consists of three heads, with their subdivisions. The seventh would be a useful study for those who are in the habit of giving Spiritual Exercises, as it treats, with great power, on the Last Accounting Day. The Divinity will appear, on that day, in the form of a man; because not even the damned could look upon the Godhead without being seized with joy. The Judgment is to be feared for four reasons: on account of the wisdom of the Judge; on account of His power; on account of His inflexible justice; and, fourthly, on account of His anger—'How strait are the ways of Judgment for sinners,' says Origen. Against this fear there are three remedies: good works, confession, and alms-deeds, which make all things clean. The eighth article, on the Holy Ghost, is full of Scripture quotation. The ninth, on the Church, contains matter worthy of remark. As in one man there is one soul and one body, and yet there are many members; so in the Church there is one body, but it has divers members. The soul animating this body is the Holy Spirit. The Church of God has four conditions: it is one, holy, catholic—that is, universal; and it is strong and firm. In this Church alone man can be saved; just as outside the ark of Noah nobody could help perishing. The Church of Peter, alone, was always steadfast in faith; and whilst elsewhere there is no faith, or little faith mixed with many errors, the Church of Peter is strong in faith, and is clean of errors. Nor is this astonishing, since our Lord said to Peter: 'I have prayed for thee, Peter, that thy faith fail not.' The tenth article, on the Communion of Saints, and the Remission of Sins, draws out a striking and well-known analogy between the effects of the Sacraments and the requirements, wants, and necessities of the soul and of the body; illustrating the spiritual by means of the material. Regarding the state of grace, we are told that not only the virtue of the Passion of Christ is communicated to us, but also the merits of the life of Christ. Whatever good the saints have done is participated in by those who dwell in charity, 'because we are all one.' And, hence, he who abides in charity, is partaker in all the good that is done throughout the world. So, the merits of Christ are communicated to all, and the virtue of one man has its effect upon his neighbour; thus, those under excommunication, being out of the Church, lose a share of all the good that is done, which is a greater misfortune than the loss of any temporal possession. And there is this other consideration, namely: by these suffrages the devil is prevented from tempting us; whilst, on the contrary, when a man is excluded from them, Satan easily overcomes him. Hence, when, in the early Church, a man was excommunicated, the devil immediately began worrying him in the body. In the eleventh article, on the Resurrection of the Dead, we are assured that all will rise at the mature age of about thirty-two or thirty-three; nor will those who had been blind, or halt, rise with their defects. In the twelfth article, on Life Everlasting, these beautiful words of S. Augustine's are quoted: 'All joy will not enter into those who rejoice, but all those who rejoice will enter into all joy.'

One or two points may be mentioned in the treatise on the Lord's Prayer. The 'Our Father' has five excellences which belong to prayer: for prayer should be confident, becoming, well-ordered, devout, and humble. These qualities, in a special manner, are found in the 'Our Father.' Nobody recites this prayer without fruit; for by means of it, says S. Augustine, venial sins are forgiven. It is a most difficult thing to know what to ask in prayer, because it is most difficult to know what we ought to desire. Here, Christ is our Teacher, and we are safe. Nor is prayer to be long, for too great prolixity interferes with devotion; hence, our Lord says: 'When you are praying, speak not much;' and S. Augustine: 'Let there be few words, but much earnestness, in prayer, if the object be ardently desired.' In the first petition, a touching anecdote is told of S. Ignatius, who, when Trajan ordered him to deny the name of Christ, said, that it could not be driven from his mouth; and when threatened with death, if he should persevere in using the Holy Name, said: 'If you take it out of my mouth, you will never be able to draw it from my breast; for I have that Name engraved upon my heart, and hence, I cannot cease calling upon it:' and it was found by Trajan, written in letters of gold, on the martyr's heart, after his death. Holy means firm: the Blessed are called holy, because they are fixed in eternal felicity. On earth there can be no perfect holiness, for all is in continual motion; hence, S. Augustine: 'I have turned away from Thee, O Lord, and have erred exceedingly; I have wandered from Thy stability.' Under the second petition, we read, that man will find all he seeks from the world in God; but in a more perfect and more excellent manner. If you desire pleasure, you will discover its perfection in God; if riches, in Him you will find all fulness; hence, S. Augustine: 'The soul, when it departs from Thee, seeks out of Thee those things which it does not find pure and spotless, save when it returns to Thee.' In the third petition, our Lord did not say 'Do,' nor 'Let us do;' but He said, 'Thy will be done,' because two things are necessary for eternal life: the grace of God, and the will of man; and though God made man without man, He does not justify him without his concurrence. Presume not then of thyself, but trust in the grace of God; and be not negligent, but perform thy share. For He did not say: 'Let us do,' lest it should seem that the grace of God achieved nothing; nor did He say 'Do,' lest it might appear that our will and endeavour were wholly idle; but He said: 'Let it be done,' expressing the grace of God, and the coöperation of the human will. In the fourth petition there is nothing very striking. In the fifth: 'Forgive us our trespasses, as we forgive them that trespass against us,' the Saint says that we owe to God that which we receive from Him, and which is His possession by right. His right is that we should do His will, and prefer it to our own. We therefore take away His right when we prefer our own will to His will, and this is sin. Sins, therefore, are 'our trespasses.' It is, hence, a counsel of the Holy Spirit that we should beg God's pardon for our sins; therefore we pray, 'Forgive us our trespasses.' Two consequences follow from this petition: first, that man should be ever humble, and should fear. Some so far presumed as to say that, of himself, man could avoid sin. But this grace has been given to none but Christ, who had the Spirit, not according to measure; and to the Blessed Virgin, who was 'full of grace,' in whom no sin was found; as S. Augustine says: 'Concerning whom (viz., the Blessed Virgin), I do not wish to speak, when there is question of sin.' The other consequence is, that we should always live in hope. The Novatians sinned against this hope, because they taught that whoever fell after Baptism would never rise again. The sixth petition gives a definition of temptation: 'To tempt a man is to test his virtue.' A man's virtue is proved in two ways: by avoiding evil and by doing good. The seventh petition: 'But deliver us from evil,' is a general petition against evils of all kinds—sins, infirmities, and afflictions, according to the teaching of S. Augustine. At the conclusion of this treatise there is added a short Exposition of the entire prayer.

The Tractate on the 'Angelical Salutation' has some points of interest. For instance, in the Blessed Virgin's case we have the first example of an angel doing reverence to man. Men used to show angels reverence, and for three reasons: on account of their dignity, their familiarity with God, and on account of the plenitude of their splendour, and of their grace: for the angels participate in the Divine light in the completest fulness. Hence, as the act of reverence was reversed in our Blessed Lady's case, it follows that she surpassed the angels in these three gifts. This the Saint goes on to prove by many texts of Holy Scripture. Hugh of S. Victor's is quoted in testimony to her intense love of the Almighty: 'Because the love of the Holy Spirit,' he says, 'burned in a special manner in her heart, wonderful things were done in her flesh, things so wonderful, that of her was born God and man.' In all danger, safety can be found in this glorious Virgin. She exceeds the angels in plenitude of grace; hence she is called 'Mary'—which is interpreted to mean, illuminated with interior light. She is called 'The royal dwelling-place of the Blessed Trinity.' The word 'Mary' also signifies 'Star of the Sea,' because, as those at sea are directed into port by a star, so Christians are led to glory by Mary. The Blessed Virgin, in the Fruit of her womb, found all that Eve expected to find in the apple of sin; for she hoped to be as a god; to have pleasure; and to look upon beauty. All this our Lady experienced, in possessing the Fruit of her womb, Jesus.

Under the heading of the two precepts of charity, and the ten Commandments of the Law, there are some noteworthy thoughts; in fact, the whole of these Opuscula of the Angelical are so studded with noble ideas, and so interwoven with Scripture, that it is difficult, by a few extracts, to give an adequate idea of them—let us look at his theory on the Law: 'The Law' teaches us how to act, and it is fourfold; the Law of Nature, which is nothing else than the light of the intellect placed in us by God; by it we know what to do, and what to avoid. God gave man this light, and this Law, when He created him. The Law of Concupiscence destroyed the Law of Nature; so there was given to man the Written Law. Then came the Law of Charity and Grace, which is the Law of Christ. But since all men cannot be learned, Christ has instituted a short Law, which all may know, and from which no one can be held excusable on account of ignorance: and this is the Law of Divine Love, 'A short word shall the Lord make upon the earth.' This Law should be the rule of all human acts, and, as the Angelical teaches, it produces four effects: first, it causes spiritual life—as S. Augustine says: 'For as the soul is the life of the body, so

God is the life of the soul.' As a corpse dressed up with gold and precious stones would not be living; so the soul, had it all the gifts of the Holy Spirit, to the exclusion of charity, would be dead. S. Gregory says: 'The love of God is never idle; if it really exists, it works great things; what does not work, cannot be love.' The second effect of love is the observance of the Divine Commandments; the third is that it guards us against assault; and the fourth, that it leads to happiness. Love is the measure of bliss. Then comes the explanation, development, and illustration of the first great Commandment, in which man has to give to God his heart, soul, mind, and strength. The 'heart' which is given to God, is the good intention with which a man acts. Frequently, however, men act with a good intention, but without fruit, because an upright will is lacking. For instance, were a man to commit a robbery to feed a beggar, he would have a good intention; but the rectitude of a right will would evidently be wanting. A good intention is no excuse for doing evil: 'Who say, let us do evil that good may come; whose damnation is just.' A good will is joined to the intention when the will of man is in harmony with the will of God. The Saint then shows that the other conditions which make up the full rendering of the whole being to the Almighty should so combine, as to tend towards that one consummation. There are four influences which urge us to practise charity towards man, viz.: the Divine love, the Divine precept, and the communication of nature: 'Every animal loves its like;' and finally, the utility that follows from such a course. Two things tend to the consolidation of friendship: patience, and humility, from which patience springs. He who thinks much of himself, and lowly of another, cannot bear with the defects of that other. God loves and hates—loves man's nature, but hates his vice. Blessed Stephen, in praying for his enemies, did a great service to the Church—he converted Paul.

Now, just to touch upon the ten precepts of the Law, simply culling out, here and there, some striking thoughts:—

1. The Law of Moses is founded on the two precepts. They were engraven upon two stone tablets. On the

first, three of the Commandments are inscribed—these belong to the precept of loving God: on the second,

the seven remaining ones are written, and they are included in the second precept, of loving our neighbour. The greatest and most horrible of all sins is the worship of devils. There are five reasons why we should adore one only God: on account of His dignity, His generosity the stability of His promises, the slavery of diabolical domination, and the immensity of the reward: 'They will be like the angels of God in heaven.'

2. Swearing is like medicine, only to be made use of in case of necessity. Our Lord insists upon this teaching, on account of a man's tongue being his most unruly member; for nobody has thoroughly mastered it. The name of God can be used under six circum-

stances: in confirmation of what has been said, as in an oath; unto sanctification, as in Baptism; for the expulsion of adversaries, like the devil; in confession of the Name itself; as a defence: 'The name of the Lord is a strong tower;' and in the completion of any work.

3. In the first Commandment, we venerate God with our heart; in the second, with our mouth; in the third, with our work: 'Remember thou keep holy the Sabbath Day.' There are five reasons for this: first, the destruction of the error of those who would teach the eternity of the world. The Sabbath was kept by the Jews in memory of the Creation. Christians keep Sunday in memory of the New Creation by Christ, who rose gloriously from the dead. Then, secondly, as a testimony of faith in the Redeemer, for the flesh of Christ did not corrupt in the tomb; thirdly, as a confirmation and figure of the truth of the Promise. We expect rest from three things: from the labour of the present life; from the temptations of concupiscence; and from the servitude of the devil. Fourthly, the precept was given to inflame love: 'For the corruptible body is a load upon the soul:' fifthly, that those who are subject, might have an opportunity for works of piety. Work may be done on the Sabbath under four circumstances: through necessity; for the benefit of the Church—as the priests did all that was necessary in the temple on the Sabbath; in rendering a service to one's neighbour; and, finally, by the authority of a superior. S. Jerome tells Rusticus to be ever occupied with some good work, so that the devil

may always find him busy. There are three things which we ought to do on the Sabbath: to offer sacrifices of our soul, our body, and our goods; to study the Word of God; and to perform spiritual exercises. But, before the soul can really rest, three kinds of repose must precede: repose from the unrest of sin, from the passions of the flesh, and from the occupations of the world; and after this has been done, the soul can rest freely in God.

4. Now commence the seven precepts of the second tablet of stone. Man must fly evil, and do good. So in the precepts, some of them lead to good, and others prohibit evil. Above all, we ought to do good to those who are our relations. 'First, we should love God,' says S. Ambrose; 'and then our father and mother.' For, from our parents, we receive three things: our being, our food and support, and our education. Five desirable promises are made to those who honour their parents; that they shall have, first, grace in the present life: and, secondly, glory in the future: 'He that honoureth his father shall enjoy a long life.' But, bear this in mind, that a life is long, when it is full; and fulness, according to the philosopher, is not measured by time, but by action; and a life is full, when it is virtuous. But they that injure their parents shall die: 'The eye that mocketh at his father, and that despiseth the labour of his mother in bearing him, let the ravens of the brooks pick it out, and the young eagles eat it.' The third promise is, that they shall have grateful and acceptable children; the fourth, that they shall have a

praiseworthy fame; and the fifth, that they shall possess riches: 'The father's blessing establisheth the houses of the children; but the mother's curse rooteth up the foundation.'

5. We have not only to do good, but to avoid evil. One of the greatest evils we can inflict upon our neighbour, is to kill him. Regarding this fifth precept, there is a three-fold error. Some have said that it is not lawful to kill even brute animals. But this is not so; all animals are subject to man. And the philosopher says, in his Politics, that 'hunting is like a just war.' 'Whatever is sold in the shambles, eat, asking no questions for conscience sake.' Others have declared it to be unlawful, under any pretext, to put a man to death; so that, according to them, judges, and others, are murderers. But S. Augustine is against this, when he declares that 'God does not deprive Himself, by this precept, of the power of putting to death.' What is lawful to God, is lawful to His ministers, when He orders them to execute His law: 'I will kill, and I will make to live.' Others have said that this precept does not include suicide: and therefore, that suicide is lawful. But S. Augustine answers them, when he says: 'He who kills himself, without doubt kills a man.'

Is all anger contrary to virtue? There are two opinions. The Stoics taught that true virtue consisted in peace of mind: the Peripatetics held that a wise man might be moderately angry—and this seems nearer the truth, and is evident, from the Gospel, from the example of Christ, and from reason; for the irascible power would have been given in vain, were no anger ever permitted. So, anger is sometimes a virtue, and sometimes not a virtue. Anger may be considered in three ways: when it resides only in the judgment of the reason, without any disturbance of mind, and then it is not, in reality, 'anger,' but 'judgment;' and it is in this way that God is affected, when He punishes the wicked. Next, it may be considered as a passion, and then it resides in the sensitive appetite, and is two-fold —for sometimes it is regulated by the dictates of reason; when, for instance, a man is angry when he should be, and as much as he should be, and no more—and then, anger is a virtue. At other times, man's anger gets the better of his reason, and then it is sinful. The difference between anger and hatred is this, that the former is soon over, whilst the latter is abiding; and, therefore, a mortal sin. 'He who hates his brother, is a murderer.' S. Augustine says in his Rule: 'Have no contentions; or if you have any, end them as soon as possible; lest anger develop into hatred, and the mote be turned into a beam; and the soul become guilty of murder.' In all our doings, we should observe two things: justice, and mercy. Anger prevents us from so doing. Hence, a philosopher said to one who had offended him: 'Were I not angry, I would punish you.' Christ wishes us to abstain from the beginnings of evil; anger is the beginning of homicide; therefore, our Lord warns us against anger.

6. Adultery is forbidden after murder, and fitly, for man and wife are, as it were, one body: 'They shall be two in one flesh.' A wife seems to be guilty of a greater sin in committing adultery than a husband. She commits three grave sins. The first is incredulity, because she misbelieves the Law; she sins against the ordination of God, and also against the Statutes, or Sacrament, of the Church. The second, treachery, for she abandons her husband. The third consists in the commission of a theft; and it is the greatest theft, for she gives the whole inheritance to the children of another. The woman, therefore, who is an adulteress commits sacrilege, and is a traitor and a robber. Nor do husbands sin less than their wives, and this on three accounts: because of the equality they enjoy; on account of the superior strength of the man; and on account of his authority—for the man is the head and the teacher of the woman. But the sin of a priest is greater than that of a layman, and that of a bishop greater than that of a priest. Similarly, a husband committing adultery is guilty of a breach of faith. But let wives attend to that which Christ says: 'All things, therefore, whatsoever they shall say to you, observe and do: but according to their works do ye not, for they say, and do not.' S. Gregory says that carnal sins, though less culpable, are more infamous than spiritual offences; and the reason is, because they render a man like to a beast.

7. The Law forbids injury, first, to persons: 'Thou shalt not kill;' secondly, to the married: 'Thou shalt

not commit adultery;' and thirdly, in respect of goods: 'Thou shalt not steal.' S. Augustine says that, 'All unlawful possession is a theft.' This precept forbids all unjust taking away. And there are many reasons to induce us to avoid this sin. First, on account of its gravity, for it is likened to the crime of murder: 'He that sheddeth blood and he that defraudeth the labourer of his hire are brothers.' Secondly, on account of the ruinous danger it implies; for no sin is so insnaring, since it cannot be remitted without satisfaction and penance. A man may quickly repent—just as a man's anger subsides after a murder, or his passion ceases after his sin; but here, though a man may repent, he does not so easily make satisfaction, since he not only has to restore the goods, but to repair the damage done. And, besides all this, he has to do penance for his sin: 'Woe to him that heapeth together that which is not his own; how long also doth he load himself with thick clay?' Thirdly, on account of the inutility of such a sin; and fourthly, on account of the singular harm which results from it, for it brings destruction along with it, like fire when thrown upon straw: 'Fire shall devour their tabernacles who love to take bribes.'

8. We have seen that God forbids man to injure his neighbour by deed; now He commands that he should not injure him by word: 'Thou shalt not bear false witness against thy neighbour.' This may be done in two ways: in giving judgment, or in common conversation. In judgment, three sins may be committed: by

accusing falsely—and, remember, that as you cannot say what is false, so you must not conceal what is true; then, by witnessing to a lie; and, finally, by an unjust sentence. In common conversation five kinds of persons sin against this command: detractors, who are hateful to God; those who freely listen to them; gossips, who relate all they hear; flatterers, that is, adulators; and murmurers. By this Commandment all lies are forbidden, and for four reasons: because lies render men similar to the devil—a liar is the devil's son: 'For thy speech doth discover thee;' on account of inveracity tending to bring about the dissolution of society, for men could not live together, if the truth were not told; because lies destroy a man's reputation; and, finally, because they work the perdition of the soul: 'The mouth that belieth killeth the soul.' The Saint then gives some of the principal causes which lead men to tell lies, ending with the case of those who tell lies in fun. And of this we must be careful, lest, through custom, we be led on to mortal sin: 'For the bewitching of vanity obscureth good things.'

9. This is the difference between the Divine and the civil law, viz.: the civil law only judges words and actions; the Divine law judges thoughts also; and the reason is because the former is made by man, who judges things from the outside; the latter is from God, who sees both within and without: 'Man seeth those things that appear, but the Lord beholdeth the heart.' With God the 'will' is equivalent to the action; not

only are we not to steal the property of another, but we are not even to covet it. And there are many reasons for this: first, on account of the infiniteness of concupiscence. And the reason why covetousness is never satiated is because the heart of man was made for God; hence S. Augustine: 'Thou hast made us, O Lord, for Thyself, and our heart is not at rest till it rests in Thee.' What is less than God cannot fill the heart. Secondly, because it disturbs repose, which is very pleasant; for the covetous are eager to obtain what they do not possess, and to preserve what they have got hold of. And on this account Christ likened riches to thorns, as S. Gregory tells us. Thirdly, because it makes riches useless to the owner, as well as to others, for all he does is to hoard them up. Fourthly, because it does away with the equity of justice. Fifthly, because it destroys charity; for, according to Augustine, 'the more charitable a man is, the less covetous he is, and conversely.' Sixthly, because it brings forth all iniquity, and is the root of all evils.

10. On account of the corruption consequent on sin, Christ and the glorious Virgin alone escaped concupiscence. Sin reigns in the flesh, first, when concupiscence, by consent, domineers in the heart. Secondly, when it rules in the mouth, by giving expression to the concept of the mind; so, even according to the philosophers, they are not without sin who compose wanton songs, for poets who wrote love-songs were driven out of the cities. Thirdly, when it is put into act—and these are

the three degrees of concupiscence. Much labour must be expended in conquering this sin, for it is intrinsic to us, and a domestic enemy is conquered with difficulty. But there are four ways of overcoming it. By flying external occasions: 'Can a man hide fire in his bosom, and his garments not burn?' Secondly, by not giving admittance to thoughts which are an occasion of exciting concupiscence; and this is done by punishing the flesh: 'I chastise my body, and bring it under subjection.' Thirdly, by being constant in prayer. If two men are fighting, and you wish the one to conquer and not the other, you must strengthen the one and weaken the other; hence, if you want the spirit to be victorious, you must assist it, and this is done by prayer. And you must reduce the flesh, and that is done by fasting, for by fasting the body is weakened. Fourthly, by persevering in lawful occupations: 'Behold this was the iniquity of Sodom thy sister—pride, fulness of bread, and abundance, and the idleness of her and of her daughters.' Amongst all occupations, the best is the study of the Holy Scriptures. S. Jerome writes to Paulinus: 'Love the study of the Scriptures, and thou wilt not love the vices of the flesh.'

The reader must now be left to form his own judgment upon the minor works of the Angelical, written at this period. Some of the most telling thoughts have been selected, and the general tone and method of the Saint's mind have been displayed. But it stands to reason that, fully to appreciate the depth and solidity of his mind, and the consecutive chain of his reasoning, the works themselves must be studied in their relation of part to part. What, perhaps, is more striking than anything else in these Expositions is this—that, in the entire handling of each subject, the profoundest theological science is made manifest, and an acquaintance with Holy Scripture is evinced, which shows at once what a deep knowledge and what a complete grasp the Angelical had of the Sacred Text. It is difficult to say which is the most extraordinary, the ingenuity with which he illustrates the minutest point of morals with passages of Holy Writ; or the memory which he displays in the number of his quotations; or the readiness of his resource in bringing them to bear; or, finally, the vividness with which he appears to perceive an association of ideas where less elastic minds would never have discovered any at all. Then, again, what is particularly valuable in these Expositions is, that the analysis of the various virtues and vices and passions which come under discussion is made with extreme care and with undoubted success. The Saint's appreciation of the human heart, his singular clearness of mind, his logical directness of expression, and his thorough mastery of the moral theory of the Stagyrite, fitted him in a remarkable degree for such undertakings. Then, once more, his great purity of life, his intense power of prayer, his associations with the unseen world, his intimate relations with his Maker and his Master, and the calmness of his intellectual vision, which was never disturbed by prejudice or by passion, by narrowness or by feeling, but was always fixed gently yet steadily on Truth, gave him a steadiness and a force, a brilliancy and a depth, which has made him the light of the Church, as well as the Angel of the Schools.

Many more points of great interest might of course be touched upon in the writings of our Saint at this period; but there are other events, of a less peaceful nature than the learned disquisitions and tracts of the theologian, which must not be passed over. In times of tranquillity the Angelical manifested high and splendid virtue; but, after all, it was in days of contest, and amidst the jarring of contending parties, that his greatest nobleness was shown, for this simple reason, that such occasions offer the most favourable opportunities for the practice of distinguished virtue, and for the display of true heroism of soul.

CHAPTER XII.

WILLIAM OF SAINT-AMOUR.

WHILST S. Thomas was busily engaged in teaching, preaching, and writing, those antagonistic elements which can be traced in the history of every thinking race were fermenting and preparing for a great explosion. The condition of the Paris University has already been dwelt upon—how the rationalism and irreverence of the disciples of the school of Abelard had spread abroad;

how the Eastern heresies had lodged in the heart of the University; how the whole intellectual atmosphere of the greatest theological centre of the world was charged with principles of misbelief; how a fanaticism of a singular nature had possessed many minds, and had driven them into all manner of spiritual insanities; and how, in fine, the fierceness of the political order added fuel to the general excitement.

As the religious Orders, particularly those of S. Dominic and S. Francis, seem to have been raised up to create a barrier to this press of unreason and disorder—and by holy vows, by abrogation of private judgment, abandonment of family ties, and renunciation of worldly goods, to become organised witnesses to stability of faith, to subjection of will, and to control of mind and imagination—it stands to reason that they would be the first to be attacked. There is a subtle instinct in man, as there is in the animal, by which, with the rapidity of infallible intuition, he detects at a distance and at once those who are his natural enemies, however artfully they may have endeavoured to simulate friendship or to hide their hostile dispositions. Then antagonism on one side elicits opposition from the other, till what were at first almost imperceptible germs grow into vast organic and conflicting powers. If it be truth against error, or against truth mixed with a little alloy, or, again, against error mixed with a little truth, the battle may be protracted, and the fight at times may seem doubtful; but in the long run the stronger prevails, the weaker is overpowered, is cast to the earth, decays into it, and at length disappears altogether.

Now at this period rationalism and irreverence had been worked up to a vigorous display of themselves through the successes of their rivals. That frame of mind which belonged to the liberal school could not endure to behold men whose very appearance preached veneration, reverence, self-control, and custody of tongue and eyes, by degrees gaining a firm hold on the minds of youth. Men can bear with comparative patience a word or a blow, but nothing is so mortifying, because nothing is so withering, as the silent condemnation of a living principle which, without the effort of words, by simply letting itself be seen, scourges folly, rebukes pretence, and shames the shallowness of self-assertion, and the emptiness of self-conceit. The noisy and the thoughtless are never more at ease than when with men of the same build as themselves, and never less so than when there happens to be in the company some quiet thoughtful man, who says perhaps nothing, but who nevertheless is known to be a critic and an observer of his kind.

Much more reason had the liberals to dislike the Mendicants, who were guilty of two unpardonable faults: they were religious, and they were successful. They had already penetrated into the University. They had, in a few years, expanded into powerful corporations; and, like a network, had spread their meshes over the surface of the Church. Their mortified appearance, their unmistakable rejection of the world, their eloquence in the pulpit, and their influence in the confessional, drew thousands under their control; and thus they did away with the prestige, and lessened the power, of the secular clergy, and the secular professors. There was, for instance, Albert, called the Great, who drew such crowds that he had to lecture in the open air; and he was but one amongst many more who caught the ear of the promising student, and drew him under monastic influences, and often into the Order itself. And now, Thomas and Bonaventure were imitating Albert, and were blighting, by their brilliancy, the reputation and the prospects of less able men.

Then, it was not forgotten that, when the Doctors were unanimous in their desire to assert the dignity of the University, the Mendicants stood aloof; and, in fact, ever seemed to keep their right eye steadily fixed on the advancement and reputation of their own Society. Again, besides being living protests against Abelardine principles, the Mendicants were *successful* protests, inasmuch as they counted amongst their number men who, into whatever position they were cast, would, from their own intrinsic merit and ability, act as leaders of the world.

Still, light, however brilliant, is not without its shadows. The most splendid and perfect institution, if it grow and occupy a large space, if many join it, will have amongst its members imprudent, ardent, and therefore dangerous men—men, who through their very love of their religion, by trying to elevate it rashly, bring it to the verge of ruin: or, at least, offer so fair a pretext to the malevolent for attacking it, that the combined learning and prudence of many years will hardly make good the damage done. The mass of men do not deal in fine distinctions; they see only broad outlines; to distinguish, with them, is casuistry; and casuistry they consider to be next door to systematised imposture. Point out some telling scandals against some member of a large organised body; be they only three or four, or true or false, repeat them often enough, couple the name of that organised body with them; and the 'public' will pass the verdict of guilty upon the whole, and condemn both the system and him who sins against it.

So was it with the Dominicans and Franciscans at this period. They represented the great principles of monasticism, as opposed to the liberalism and irreverence of that day. But the Dominicans and Franciscans formed a powerful and influential body of men. There were spots amongst them—and some very large and ugly spots. There had been, and still were, abuses amongst them—and large and ugly abuses too—in a word, they were human, and they lived in the thirteenth century.

Now, the great practical work which S. Thomas did against rationalism and irreverence was to save the religious Orders from being wholly overpowered. He has, in his writings, laid down the principles of true reason, which, when developed and applied, overset the rationalistic spirit. Had he not possessed a clear head, and had he not been gifted with extraordinary genius, in all probability the cause of monasticism would have suffered a very terrible blow. One thing is a set of principles buried in a book, or taught even in the chair; another thing is the organised power, or system, which embodies them, and expresses their energy and power. The high motives of love, reverence, purity, and adoration, in their noblest form, would soon disappear from the consciousness of men—would soon, indeed, be wholly misunderstood, and then be hated by society—if their living exponents were thrust on one side; that is, if men who felt themselves called to devote their whole beings to the Divine service were thwarted of their purpose, and forbidden to carry out, in their lives, the highest teachings of the Cross.

S. Thomas must clearly have seen that the adversaries of the religious life—that rationalism and irreverence, in one word—were bent upon sweeping away, not simply the theoretical teaching of the principle of reverence and authority, not merely monastic theology, but monastic *men*. The liberals perceived, shrewdly enough, that if the Mendicants were deprived of that training which gave them half their power, the world would soon abandon them, and then despise them, and rob them of the other half; that, if it could in some way be shown that the fundamental truths of monastic life were vain, or absurd, or unbecoming; that freedom, and independence, and self-assertion, were more worthy than subjection and self-repression, and an humble life; then, those promising young men who formed the rising generation, would forsake the cloister, join in the struggles of the world, and become the admirers and slaves of irreverence or infidelity.

There is no doubt that the contest which eventually raged in the Paris schools between the two great parties—beween the secular element and the regulars—was no sudden creation of mutual antagonism. The University, ever since these two elements had grown into anything like a powerful life, had been the scene of much rivalry, and no little jealousy and ill-feeling. Principles cannot possibly assert themselves, in the shape of living, active men, without very soon coming into collision; and of all principles, religious principles, as far as the experience of history goes, appear to be the most inflammable and explosive. Often two opposite parties smoulder, and smoke, and threaten, for a long time, before actually encountering each other. Much depends on the accident of individuals. It happens, at times, that in either party no one rises up who can be chosen as a centre, or can be trusted as a leader. As long as there is no one to take this initiative the fire spreads, steadily and gradually, but silently, and without being seen. The principles which are eating their way into the minds of many, and every day fixing themselves on some new subject on the one side, at length come in contact with the antagonistic principles which have been advancing unimpeded in exactly the same way upon the other: till, finally, on one side or the other, some man who has energy, talent, and enthusiasm, is roused into activity by the influence that comes suddenly upon him, and at once, like a spark amongst prepared combustibles, the whole material, on either side, bursts out into flame.

In the present instance, S. Thomas and William of S. Amour were the representatives of two sets of principles, which, for a long course of years, had been growing in opposition—S. Amour combating on the rationalistic side; S. Thomas on that of authority.

The work S. Thomas did, in this respect, cannot be understood without a reference to the rise, progress, and close of the great University struggle in which he had to take a leading part.

William of S. Amour is a fair specimen of one of those conceited and turbulent men who seem never to be wanting in the Church—possibly to teach her pastors to watch, and to be patient. Without Abelard's brilliancy or gifts, without his polish or generosity, he possessed, in an exaggerated degree, his contentious spirit and rationalistic malady. He was master of all that astuteness, cunning, and elasticity of conscience—all that talent for throwing a trifling difficulty into a distorted form, and that ability in playing the injured man, which seems, by a sort of fatality, to accompany a self-sufficient and an irreverent teacher. And William of S. Amour was also a violent man; and, it is to be feared, he was hardly honest. He may have had his own reasons for what he said, and his own explanations—doubtless, he had—but he did not always strictly tell the truth. Morally, very possibly, he may have been innocent enough. He had a vast and an unruly imagination, and, when on fire, it blazed without control. To have thrown water upon it—to have dropped into it a truth here and there—would only have been to have created noise, to have multiplied confusion, and to have generated much more smoke than before.

Some writers, who do not seem to look much below the surface, have ventured the opinion that William's quarrel was simply a personal matter. Is it not more philosophical to suppose it to have been the first note of a war of principle? Had it been merely a private difference, the whole world of Catholic thought at Rome and Paris—popes and kings, bishops and generals of Orders, professors of Universities and students of the school—would not have been set so violently in motion. No, it was the call of the bugle; the shrill clarion, sounding for a charge, which was the prelude to a general engagement.

The fact is, before William of S. Amour had penned the first line of his celebrated *Perils of the Last Times*, he had incurred serious suspicion on account of his unorthodox beliefs and teachings. He had not only been charged with divers errors before the Bishop of Paris, and in the presence of several attendant prelates; but he had also, through the influence of the Papal Legate, been accused of holding dangerous views, before the

King of France himself. William, with that cunning which generally accompanies misbelief, turned all this to the best possible account; and played the part, so often acted since his time, of making himself out to be a martyr. And very likely he might have been privileged to remain one, had he not been so imprudent as to publish a great many of his errors in his notorious attack upon the Mendicants. He penned it, he declared, at the request of the bishops; an assertion as unjustifiable as gratuitous, for the bishops were excessively scandalised at the appearance of the book, nor had a single one of them ever given to it the slightest indication of approval, either before or after its condemnation by Pope Alexander.

The ostensible object of the work was to draw out, by means of Holy Scripture, the character of those false prophets who are to appear at the end of the world; and who are spoken of by S. Paul, in his second Epistle to Timothy: 'Know also this, that in the last days shall come on dangerous times. Men shall be lovers of themselves, covetous, haughty, proud, blasphemers, slanderers, incontinent, unmerciful, without kindness. Traitors, stubborn, puffed up, and lovers of pleasure more than of God.' The author undertakes to prove that the Church was to be exposed to great vicissitudes. He says, he will show what kind of men they are who are to bring these perils upon her, and will make known the nature of the perils. He says that they are close at hand, and must be faced; and that those who are too blind to foresee them, or fail to take precautions against them, will perish. He explains who those are who ought to foresee them, and put the faithful on their guard; and indicates what punishment they will be visited with, who are wanting in this important duty. And then he points out how these evils may be warded off; and how those dangerous men, who are to draw them upon the Church, may be clearly recognised.

Then, as if knowing full well in what sense his work would be understood, he artfully protests that he is simply treating the matter in the abstract; that he refers to nobody in particular; nor does he allude to any religious Order approved of by the Church. Yet, without exception, when the book came out, and it was translated into French to increase its circulation, the whole world declared, with one accord, that it was aimed straight at the Mendicant Orders, and at the Dominican Order in particular. In point of fact, William of S. Amour had simply committed to writing, and had published, opinions, accusations, libels, slanders, and lies, which had been heard coming from his mouth incessantly, against the religious principle with which he was ever implacably at war. He was saying nothing new; he was simply giving in the gross, what he had poured out in detail, in his public and his private life. He, with his fierce, 'liberal' spirit, and his over-bearing arrogance, fumed in presence of the poor and humble followers of S. Dominic and S. Francis. He saw all their actions through a distorted and a coloured medium

—they possessed, in his eyes, all those qualities and attributes by which the false prophets, who are to seduce men during the last days of the world, are characterised in Holy Writ. What he appears to have hated most, seems to have been their poverty. He did not content himself with striking at abuses, but he launched out at the very principle itself upon which regular life was founded; and at that Rule, and at that authority which approved of it. In fact, he would have blotted out the whole Order of friars, if he could have done so; and would have broken down the entire organism, by means of which, alone, the monastic principle could be upheld. 'It is true,' he says, 'that the Church permits, or at least has, for some time, tolerated the practice of begging in some regular Orders; but it does not follow that she ought to permit it always, for that would be against the authority of S. Paul. If she has countenanced it through error, she ought to recall her concession, when she has recognised the truth.'

Besides writing this book, William of S. Amour made free use of his tongue in propagating all manner of libellous stories against the Mendicants. He said they were hypocrites, who were greedily scraping wealth together, whilst they were making a great profession and display of poverty; that they made profession of humility, and aped the externals of that virtue; but that, in reality, they were steeped in satanic pride. Such accusations as these, quite in keeping with the cravings of what, in these days, is called 'the public,'

ence of the meekness, poverty, and religious spirit of the Dominicans. If what he says be true—and it is scarcely probable that he did not know the real position of affairs—there is little doubt that the successes, and the earnest piety, of the religious Orders, the name they had acquired, and the influence they were exercising, formed the one deadly sin for which the University was punishing them. Jealousy and brutality go often hand in hand; and in this case, it is difficult to tell which was the more pronounced. The popular feeling, and the feeling of the schools, had been worked upon, and unless something were done, the friars were likely to lose their hold on the University.

Again, William of S. Amour was not content with doing all he could to turn the Parisians against the Mendicants; he also tried to play upon the secular clergy, and through them upon the Bishops. He said that the Church should be on her guard against false prophets; that those prophets were false who preached without being sent; that the Mendicants had not been sent; and, therefore, that they were false prophets—for preaching belongs to bishops, as the successors of the Apostles; and to parish priests, as the successors of the seventy-two disciples of the Lord. Moreover, what is contrary to the Canons, and what infringes on the rights of the Episcopate, cannot be permitted, even by the Pope. The Bishops should stop the Mendicants from begging; for begging makes flatterers, blasphemers, and liars. It is false that our Lord and

His disciples lived only upon alms. S. Paul, for instance, preferred working with his hands to being a burden to the community. The Mendicants think to excuse themselves by alleging that they are engaged in study—study which results in their obscuring the true teaching of the Church by their pedantry and hair-splitting, and serves to keep them in a state of permanent damnation. In fact, there was nothing too bad which could be said or written of these men by William of S. Amour; and no trouble was too great, to ingrain into the minds of rich and poor, high and low, a detestation and an abhorrence of the principles of monastic life.

When the reader calls to mind the excited condition of society at this period, he can imagine for himself the turmoil which was created by William of S. Amour flinging down the gauntlet in the way he did. The friends and the foes of the Mendicants had been worked into excessive irritation, and a fierce contest was ready to be waged.

S. Amour and his party were keen enough to be aware that the book on the *Perils* was too flagrant an attack upon powerful and holy institutions, approved of by the Holy See, to be left alone. The work would, sooner or later, they must have felt pretty sure, be sent to Rome for examination and for condemnation. But they were not the men to be behindhand in tactics of that description. If the friars got the *Perils* of S. Amour condemned, S. Amour would get the *Introduction to the*

Eternal Gospel of the friars condemned. If he was to be stained, they should be stained as well. Such was the view of the liberal party which made contention in the Church at that day.

And it cannot be denied that the *Introduction to the Eternal Gospel* offered to the enemies of the friars a terrible weapon wherewith to castigate them. Whatever the Mendicants might say of William of S. Amour and his *Perils of the Last Times*, William and his friends could retort with equal violence upon the Franciscans respecting the *Introduction to the Eternal Gospel*, which was so intimately connected with one of their Order. For, in fact, the *Introduction to the Eternal Gospel* was, if possible, more fundamentally opposed to the principles of Christianity, than were the writings of the secular professor himself; and it certainly was more blasphemous and infidel. Carried away by the reveries of the Abbot Joachim, and by the heretical spirit of Amaury, whose memory and whose doctrine had been condemned, the author of this work filled his pages with impious and destructive propositions. Just as the book of William, whilst pretending to attack theoretical abuses, and touch upon theoretical mistakes, was, in point of fact, a violent onslaught upon the existing Orders approved of by the Church, so the *Introduction to the Eternal Gospel*, whilst it simulated the defence and glorification of the regulars, was, in reality, upsetting the first principles of Christianity, and bringing again into life the effete and exploded follies of an earlier age. Some of the propositions contained in the *Introduction to the Eternal Gospel* are as follows:

The doctrine of the Abbot Joachim is more perfect than that of Jesus Christ; and hence more perfect than that contained in the Old and the New Testaments. For the Gospel of Jesus Christ, or the New Testament, does not lead to perfection: like the Old Testament, it will be abolished; and will only remain in force till the year 1260.

At this period, the third era of the world will commence, which will be the era of the Holy Spirit. Those who live during this time will be in a state of perfection; and there will be another gospel, and another priesthood. The preachers of this third era will be men of still greater authority than the fathers of the primitive Church. The understanding of the spiritual sense of the New Testament was never confided to the Popes, but only a knowledge of its literal signification. The Greeks did well to separate from the Roman Church; and they walk more according to the Spirit than the Latins. As the Son works the salvation of the Latins, so the Eternal Father works the salvation of the Greeks. Whatever afflictions God may send the Jews in this world, He will still protect them, and deliver them, in the end, from all the attacks of their enemies, although they remain in their Judaism.

Jesus Christ, and the Apostles, were by no means perfect in the contemplative life. It was only since the time of Abbot Joachim that contemplation commenced to bring forth fruit. Up to his time, men were engaged in the active life, which was useful then, though now it is no longer so. Hence it follows, that the clerical Order will have to perish. And from amidst the religious Orders, one Order will rise up more worthy than all the rest; and this was predicted by the prophet, when he said: 'The lines are fallen unto me in goodly places.' No man, purely a man, is capable of instructing others, if he does not walk about barefoot. Persons who go about barefoot are not obliged, as other men are, to expose their lives in defence of the faith. They will pass over to the infidel, when they are persecuted by the clergy; and it is to be feared that they will induce the infidel to make war against the Roman Church, as is written in the Apocalypse.

These propositions are sufficient to show the drift of the *Introduction to the Eternal Gospel*, and how, even in the severe religious Orders, spirits can break forth which, overpassing every legitimate control, commit those very errors which the religious Order to which they attached themselves was instituted to repress. A kind of coarse Manichæism seems to have pervaded many minds about this time. The smoke of the contest which was going on about them blinded men's vision. Some imagined that they could see on earth two powers—two militant churches: one, carnal, under the dominion of the Pope; the other, spiritual, rejoicing in all the liberty which is given by the Spirit of the Almighty.

No doubt, the dominant tendencies of the day were

fully appreciated by the authorities at Rome. The *Introduction to the Eternal Gospel* would certainly be looked upon as the exponent of a large class of dazed fanatics and heated dreamers. If the anti-regular party could only manage to fasten the *Introduction to the Eternal Gospel* on the backs of the Dominicans and Franciscans, and compromise those two powerful bodies with its corrupting errors, the Holy See would not be in a very great hurry to maintain their chairs for them at the University. If such an issue could be brought about, William of S. Amour, notwithstanding his book on the *Perils*, would thus achieve the victory he so ardently desired.

Whilst William and his party, on the one hand, were preparing their attack upon the friars, on the other, the question of the condemnation of the *Perils* was being discussed with considerable agitation. The professors and students of the University were in a state of great excitement. The religious, even those living in the distant provinces, were thrown into painful suspense with regard to their future prospects, seeing themselves opposed by such unscrupulous and such formidable enemies. Scandalised at the turn things were taking—good men deeply lamenting such divisions in the centre of Christian learning, and rationalists and libertines making a mockery of religious persons—the bishops of the provinces of Sens and Rheims, who happened, at the time, to be in Paris, proposed to assemble in council; to call together the most able theologians from the provinces; and, once for all, put an end to these scandalous disputes. But the past had taught the Dominicans a lesson. There was very little to be gained by coming to a judgment which might, in a few weeks, be altogether reversed by a higher authority. King Louis, this time, was more circumspect in his dealings with the Holy See. Instead of deciding the whole question off-hand himself, he set about accomplishing his good intentions through the proper channels. He sent two doctors of theology to the Court of Rome, who were duly instructed, and who took with them the *Perils of the Last Times* for the Pope's examination. The Dominicans also sent their representatives, who were to support these doctors, and to defend the Order against the threatened onslaught.

Nor was the University idle. It despatched a powerful deputation to Rome, to represent the interests of the seculars, and to make the Holy See fully acquainted with that terrible book, the *Introduction to the Eternal Gospel* of the Franciscans, which had been adopted by members of the regular Order. William of S. Amour was the leader of this deputation; then, there was Odo of Douai; Christian, Canon of Beauvais; Nicholas of Bar-sur-Aube, together with John Belin, and the Englishman John of Gecteville, Rector of the University.

It can be imagined what sort of excitement prevailed at Paris when these two antagonistic parties were on their way to the Eternal City. They were both powerful. Both appeared to have strong reason for acting with energy. Each was intent upon procuring from the Holy See the condemnation of the other. Both were represented by men of great acuteness and ability; and it remained to be proved whether the Mendicants would be driven out of Paris, together with the *Introduction to the Eternal Gospel*, which was connected with their name; or whether William of S. Amour and his followers would have to submit to the condemnation of the *Perils of the Last Times*, and be obliged, after all, to work side by side with the despised children of S. Francis and S. Dominic.

The solemn deputation of the University, as became grave and learned doctors, after long and careful preparation for the journey, finally set out for the Eternal City; and, after a somewhat slow advance, at length reached Anagni, where the Pope, Alexander IV., was holding his Court. It found that the envoys of King Louis, and the representatives of the Dominicans, had arrived before them, and had already brought under the attention of the Holy See the incriminated book of William of S. Amour. Alexander at once appointed four Cardinals to examine it: Eudes de Châteauroux, Cardinal-bishop of Tusculum; John Francioge, Cardinal-priest of the title of S. Lawrence; Hugh of S. Caro, Cardinal-priest of the title of S. Sabina; and John de' Ursini, Cardinal-deacon of the title of S. Nicholas.

The Holy Father was not content with one commission. He instructed the General of the Dominicans, Humbert de Romanis, to have the work thoroughly examined by theologians of the Order; and expressed a wish to see Thomas of Aquino employed amongst the number.

The Saint had, during all this time, been continuing his labours of teaching, preaching, and private sanctification, undisturbed by the noise and turmoil that raged round him. He had his duty to do, and he did it. He did not look beyond it. He was employed in what obedience had placed before him; and he was in his vocation. But in the midst of these peaceful occupations, the command came to him to gird himself for the strife. The General sent him orders to leave his routine of occupations at Paris, and to come at once to Italy to engage in the great contest that was at its height; and to defend, by his extraordinary ability, the honour of the Order in which he had made his vows.

S. Thomas, without delay, set about obeying the injunctions of his superior. The Franciscans also were in full activity, and sent their best men forward to Anagni, to defend the children of the Seraphic Father. They, as well as the Dominicans, could not conceal from themselves the peril of the attack to which they were exposed. S. Bonaventure was sent on the same errand as S. Thomas. The venerable Albertus Magnus had, a year ago, gone from the depths of Germany to take the post of danger, and to be ready, with his vast learning and experience, to maintain the cause of holiness and truth. However great the dangers may have been with which the Mendicants were threatened, one thing is certain, viz., that they had most able and most saintly defenders on their side. For their champions were filled with truth, and justice, and heroism; they were gifted with high and noble natures; and they were animated with the true spirit of sacrifice, for they had been trained in the science of the Saints. It is evident that this was a supreme moment for the religious Orders, and for the principle of monastic life. The rationalistic and the dogmatic principle were coming into collision. The serious view taken by Pope Alexander; the care of the regulars to select their best men for their defence, and the very fact of calling them in from Germany and France; then the efforts of the University, with its powerful deputation, all point to an important and acknowledged crisis. How did the contest end? Its history will not take very long to tell. Three able pens were employed in the defence of the regular Orders—that of Albert, that of Bonaventure, and that of Thomas of Aquino. But of the three, that of S. Thomas was the most powerful, in logic, lucidity, and method; and to him may fairly be attributed the final overthrow of that arrogance and despotism which the Paris professors had ever displayed in their relations with the Mendicants.

The General of the Dominicans was exceedingly troubled when he saw the tempest which threatened to burst over those gentle and loving beings confided to his charge. And even had not the Holy Father sent him a command, he would, without doubt, have called to his assistance, at this hour, the most learned and acute doctors belonging to the Order. Now the General seems to have placed his greatest trust in the genius and address of Thomas of Aquino. There was not one in the whole range of the Paris schools who had so swift an eye for error, such self-command, such lucid power of exposition, and such boundless gentleness and charity. He would be the man to unmask, and thoroughly to expose, the sophisms of S. Amour.

The Dominicans had a house at Anagni; and the friars-preachers there were, as may be conceived, in great agitation respecting the issue of the trial which was coming off. On the arrival amongst them of S. Thomas from Paris, the General summoned a Chapter of the brethren. He wished to do all in his power to cheer and encourage them in their suspense. He called the Angelical from his place—and we can see the brothers, in imagination, with their loving and wondering eyes fixed upon the Saint, whilst Humbert addressed him thus: 'Behold, my son,' he said, 'behold the Order of S. Dominic, attacked by powerful enemies, is left to your lights and to your zeal for its defence. Take, therefore, this fatal book, which has excited or has added to the storm which rages against us, and which appears likely to give trouble to the Church for some time to come, and to stand in the way of that fruit which would otherwise spring from our preaching, and from the example of lives which are without reproach. Read it, examine it, and see, before God, how it had best be answered; not in order to keep alive, but to bring to an end, the scandal into which the Church is plunged. I here unite my own prayer to the command which comes to you from the Vicar of Jesus Christ.'

When the General had made an end, S. Thomas approached him, and received out of his hands the book of William of S. Amour; and then, turning to his brethren, he implored them to assist him by their earnest prayers; and having left the Chapter-room, he quietly retired to his cell.

But before S. Thomas set himself down to the task appointed to him, according to his invariable custom, he sought for light and strength in prayer. He humbled himself before his Lord, and after having poured out his whole soul before his Master, and begged for help and guidance, he sat down in his place, drew the book before him, opened it, and examined it, from beginning to end, with that quickness and penetration for which his intellect was justly celebrated. As by intuition, when he had once grasped his plan, he saw through the entire fallacy of his opponent, and detected all the trickery whereby William thought to substantiate and bolster up his allegations. We are assured that the Angelical had mastered the whole work, and had formed in his mind a complete refutation of it, in less time than a professor of ordinary ability would have required for understanding its drift, and for discovering its leading artifices.

It can well be imagined how eagerly the convent awaited the issue of the young professor's studies, and how both young and old prayed fervently to God to give him the grace to overthrow his adversary. The following day the General again assembled the Chapter. Thomas appeared once more in the midst of his brethren, like an angel of peace, bringing joy to their hearts. 'Fear not,' he said to them, 'let us place our confidence in His powerful goodness Who has drawn us to His service. The book which has caused you so much anxiety will not bring upon you the evil it announces. God has given me the grace to discover whatever is false, captious, erroneous, and impious in it. With our Lord's assistance, I shall bring into such clear light the faults with which it is filled, and shall make it to be so sensibly felt that the doctrine contained in it is contrary to the grounds of faith, and to the true sense of the Fathers —whose writings the author has misused—that, after the judgment which the Holy See will then pronounce upon it, the faithful will take no more notice of it; or, if they do, it will simply be to condemn its teaching, and to reject it, with all the contempt which it deserves!'

These words must have greatly consoled and encouraged those who heard them. Few men, who have not devoted themselves to serve God in religion, under certain conditions of heroism, can wholly realise the sovereign love which religious men feel for the religious state. There is the love of husband and wife, strong, tender, enduring; there is the love of son for mother, boundless and pure, as it is mighty and sweet; there is the love of brother for brother, equally enchaining, mutually close and uncompromising; there is the love of country, vague perhaps, yet, in spite of its want of outline, all-pervading in the spirit: but there is a love which, when once it has fastened its grapples in the heart, more fully masters the human spirit than all of these together—for it is more powerful in its grasp of the entire man, it more completely satisfies the highest cravings of his being, and binds itself, with more heroic bonds, about his heart—and that love is the soul's love of Christ, intensified by the vows of religion. It is the passion of the Saints. Its condition is sacrifice of self—and by that sacrifice, by that one moral death, the spirit rises up in the love of Christ. A true monk is a man who is dead, and out of whose perfect self-annihilation, out of the tomb of whose royal sacrifice, the glorious spirit of Christ is born. Such a man, in one word, no longer lives, but Christ it is who lives in him.

Now it was for this principle of life and death that the Angelical had to combat. Was this principle to be cut out, root and branch, and to be dragged away and buried in the earth, or charred in the kiln of human passion, till all life was extinct—till it was withered, and all its sap was dry? Were love, and adoration, and reverence, and purity, to rule? or were conceit, and pride, and self-assertion, and carnality, to domineer? Were old standards and patterns to be torn to shreds, and new ones to take their places? Such questions as these must have occupied the minds of many holy men, whilst S. Thomas was penning his reply to William of S. Amour.

In the space of a few days, the Saint had time fully to prepare his defence of his Order, and his answer to the book of William of S. Amour. He was called upon to plead before the Pope, surrounded by his Court. Displaying his own inimitable lucidity, logic, and arrangement, the Saint read through his apology for the religious life, in the presence of the most august assembly in the world. He not only poured forth a continuous stream of argument and learning, but he was also ready to reply to all objections, and to solve them to the satisfaction of those by whom they were advanced. It must have been a glorious moment for S. Thomas when he found that, by degrees, the force of his reasoning, and the simplicity of his eloquence, and the earnestness of his purpose, were beginning to tell upon his learned audience; and when he felt assured that he was carrying with him the hearts and intelligence of the learned Cardinals of the Sacred College, as well as the good-will of the Pope himself. Touron says that the Holy Father admired him, the Sacred College applauded him, and the whole Roman Curia now saw clearly what would be the issue of that mighty struggle which had occupied so much of its valuable time, and which had kept minds in a state of continual agitation, both in Italy and France.

When the Angelical had concluded his discourse, the four Cardinals who had been commissioned to examine the *Perils of the Last Times* gave in their report. The document was drawn up with that perspicuity and order for which the Roman mind is celebrated. It declared that, in the work which had been sifted, there were to be found sentiments which were perverse, many propositions which were absolutely false, scandalous, erroneous, contrary to the maxims of the Saints and to piety, injurious to the authority of the Pope and of the bishops, and to the honour of several religious Orders approved of by the Holy See, which had produced much fruit for the Church, by eloquently preaching the Word of God, and by manifesting zeal for souls.

Having read this report and examined the principal propositions which the Cardinals had considered worthy of reprobation, the Holy Father passed sentence upon the book in the form of a Bull, dated the fifth of October 1256. This Bull declares the entire work to be condemned as iniquitous, criminal, execrable. It commands all who possess the same to burn it within eight days, under pain of excommunication; and it forbids any one, whoever he may be, to read it, to approve of it, or to sustain it in any way. This condemnation was pronounced publicly in the Cathedral Church of Anagni, and the book was burnt in presence of the Pope.

The deputation from the University arrived after the work of their leader had been given to the flames in the sight of the Roman Court. They protested against the act, and tried to bring their influence so to bear as to restore the honour of their party; but, far from obtaining the revocation of the condemnation of the *Perils*, they were forced to take pen and ink to subscribe to it themselves. There never was a more complete and absolute overthrow. Odo of Douai and Christian of Beauvais promised with an oath, in presence of Cardinals Hugh of S. Caro and John de' Ursini, and several other witnesses, to obey the Bull *Quasi lignum vitæ*. They swore, moreover, to receive into their society and into the body of the University the Dominican and Franciscan friars, mentioning specially by name Thomas of Aquino and Bonaventure. They promised neither to further nor to permit the breaking up of the Paris schools, nor to countenance their removal to any other place, without the express permission of the Pope. They swore to preach and to maintain publicly, both in the Roman Curia and in Paris, that the Mendicant state, when embraced for the love of Jesus Christ, is a state of perfection; that those religious who have made profession of it may live lawfully on alms without the necessity of manual labour, especially if they dedicate themselves to preaching and to study; that the Orders of S. Francis and S. Dominic are in themselves good, and are approved of by the Church, as God Himself has declared through the miracles worked by the saints of each Order legitimately canonised by the Apostolic See.

The two doctors made these promises publicly, in the Papal Palace at Anagni, on the twenty-third of

October 1256. No stronger evidence could be given of the view taken by the Holy See respecting the doings of the Paris University. Here the instinct of Rome comes out regarding the merits of religious life, its scope, and its obligations; and here, too, is manifest the Christian spirit of submission which animated some at least of those fiery doctors of the schools, in spite of their bitterness and want of charity.

William of S. Amour, however, was not quite so easily worked upon as his companions. Though abandoned and condemned by them, he defended his book with great shrewdness and ability, and some assert—though they do not prove it—with considerable success. The Holy Father addressed a letter to him, forbidding him to enter France under pain of excommunication and of privation of all his benefices, and inhibiting him for ever from teaching and preaching, as a punishment for his various faults, particularly for having composed that detestable and pernicious book, the *Perils of the Last Times.*

Though William did not possess the humility or the good sense to submit to the judgment of the Holy See, this strenuous action of the Pope did much towards strengthening authority and towards supporting the true spirit of Catholic morality in Italy and France. Forbidden the kingdom of France, William retired, full of spleen and disgust, to his estate of S. Amour in Burgundy, waiting for the approach of better times. A few years later (1263) he was permitted by Urban IV. to return to Paris, and was triumphantly received by his party. His detestation for the Mendicants lasted his lifetime. His eagerness in maintaining the privileges of the University and in defending its immunities seems to have blinded him to the rights of every other society. After ten years had elapsed since the condemnation of his work, he tried to revive the old dispute, and sent to Clement IV. a new brochure, entitled *Collectiones Sacræ Scripturæ*, which in reality was nothing else than his *Perils* thrown into another shape and headed with another title. The Holy Father caused a letter to be written to him, omitting reference to his book, and recommending to him docility and peacefulness. The new brochure was sent to the General of the Dominicans, John of Vercelli, who forwarded it on to S. Thomas. The Angelical recognised his old enemy instantly, notwithstanding its disguise, and thought it would be quite sufficiently answered if he published his *Contra Impugnantes* in the shape in which it has been handed down to us. Then came his tract, *Contra Retrahentes ab Ingressu Religionis*, in which he makes mention of an earlier work, *De Perfectione Vitæ Spiritualis*. Both are to be found amongst his minor labours, under the heading of Opusculum XVII. and XVIII. respectively.

To S. Thomas's last work William of S. Amour made no reply. He died shortly after its publication in 1270, having acquired unenviable notoriety by the split he made amongst the doctors of the greatest University of Europe, yet having achieved the lasting fame of being considered a fellow-founder with his friend Robert of Sorbon of an institute which for its theological ability became famous in the Church as well as in the schools.

Such is a brief outline of the animated contest which was carried on in Paris with respect to the monastic principle. It is simply a repetition of the war which had been waged years before between Abelard and S. Bernard. The very condition of the mind of a man who could write as William of S. Amour wrote, points markedly to the rampant spirit of irreverence which must have infected a large section of intellectual Paris. It is abundantly sufficient to read through a portion of the list of accusations made by S. Amour, and to weigh a few of the principles which he endeavoured to establish, to become convinced that the moral and religious position of an influential body of men—in fact, speaking broadly, of the secular element of the University—was critical in the extreme. The evident bias—indeed, the unmistakable hatred, entertained against the Mendicants, and against the sacred principles of religious life, betoken a corruption which, doubtless, owed its origin, in part, to the poisonous philosophies which had entered into the schools; and in part, also, to the traditional rationalism and irreverence which had been handed down from the days of William of Champeaux.

False philosophy, and the monastic principle, have ever been in antagonism. The moral effects of the monastic training on the reason and the heart is something distinct and specific. When the eye of the heart and intellect has been cleansed of creatures, when the imagination has been purified—in a word, when the mechanism of the mind has been put thoroughly in order, and has been directed aright, the delusions of error, or the phantoms of philosophers, are almost powerless against it. Blindness and passion are the causes of error—these are the springs of false philosophy: clean them out; open the eye clear to the light; calm the mind; let it steadily, without fear of disturbance, fix itself on Truth, and its judgment will be upright, and its conclusions will be sound.

Here it was that the Angelical came in. He opposed the light of his elevated intelligence to the blindness of carnal men; he opposed the marvellous calmness of his whole being—a calmness which was the effect of nature as well as of grace—to the violent vapourings of the passionate and the proud, who seemed bent upon destroying that one grand set of principles which alone could keep the excitable and savage mind of youth within reasonable bounds. The very way in which the Angelical began the work of defending the principles of religion, speaks of the self-possession of his nature—a self-possession which did not spring from the virtue of mere human constancy, but which he acquired by throwing himself before the crucifix, and by asking it from Him who hangs upon the Cross.

To appreciate fully the intellectual labour he went through, and to comprehend adequately his view of religious life, those two celebrated tracts on the monastic state must be studied, of which a rapid outline shall be attempted in the coming chapter. And it may be premised that the principles of religious life are so profound, and are pregnant with such fruitful consequences, that he who would really understand them must not simply read them, but he must study them, meditate on them, and let them sink into and saturate his mind. One simple religious maxim, which can be thrown into a single line, may contain a germ within it capable of revolutionising the mind and heart of the ablest and most gifted man. There is no power like the power of truth, when the soul has once fully taken possession of it.

CHAPTER XIII.

S. THOMAS MADE DOCTOR.

In looking back upon the differences between the Angelical and William of S. Amour, what is to be seen save a repetition of that contest, which had been waged so many years before between the austere S. Bernard and the brilliant Abelard? The same principles of antagonism had survived after the death of their respective champions; and when two fresh spirits, sufficiently active and interested in the subject, became animated with their vitality, the same battle again commenced, differing only inasmuch as it took its character and direction from the divers natures and talents of the combatants—William, proud, sour, and not wanting in artifice and talent; S. Thomas, meek, gentle, and overwhelming from his intellectual weight, and overpowering in his grasp of truth, and in his dexterity in the use of it. Yet the Angelical does not appear before the mind's eye as an antagonist of error so much as an august arbiter of truth. Fighting implies, if not anger, certainly passion. In him, there was destroying force, but never violence; there was intensest power, but passion never. With calm forcible exposition, with inimitable skill, with cautious reserve, with entire self-control, yet with unruffled confidence, he displays the full form of truth, and is victorious. Yet *he* does not triumph; he does not advert to his own successes: it is truth, and reverence, and authority which are lifted up in victory; and if he be lifted with them, he spares not a thought for self.

And it was this sublime self-repression, or rather self-forgetfulness (for self-repression implies self-consciousness), which was the secret of the Angelical's extraordinary discriminating power—of that keenness and security with which he could put his finger straight down on that minute thread at which truth and error seem to meet, and separate them clean. And this high gift it was which secured to him so vast a sway over the deepest minds and the hardest students of the Paris University. Passion, prejudice, small, narrow, self-seeking ways, and miserable blindness, were unknown to him, except in theory, or in his having to suffer from the action of such agencies in others.

The history of the *Introduction to the Eternal Gospel* illustrates his impartiality.

It will be remembered that, whilst the Angelical was earnestly engaged in bringing the *Perils* of William of S. Amour to condemnation, William, on his part, was doing his utmost to secure the same fate for the *Introduction to the Eternal Gospel.* In the former work, the secular party of the University was compromised; and in the latter, the regulars were unpleasantly mixed up. In fact, the *Introduction to the Eternal Gospel* was the composition of a certain Br. Gerard, who was a Franciscan friar. This friar, urged on by a fanatical monk, a native of Calabria, named Leonard, and Leonard, in turn, being urged on by him, both of them worked on one another to such a degree, that they finally became possessed by the conviction that the *Ordo Parvulorum*—that is, the Order of Minorites—was to form the one great absorbing spiritual power in the world; and that all those inanities and follies, written down by one of them in the *Introduction,* would come to pass amongst mankind. Now, the influence of men who are verging on insanity, and yet can hardly be called mad, is proverbially great. The proverb is illustrated by the case in point. For Br. Gerard and Br. Leonard, fired by their belief in the glorious future of their Order, and disordered in brain by the reveries of Abbot Joachim, soon made many converts. Men starting in life with an intense devotedness to their Order, men who could not help seeing how great a work had been done already, were soothed and flattered by the vivid pictures presented to them by these new apostles. Weak minds, and pious minds too, were tinged with the new fanaticism. Not only the silent novice and the active preaching friar, but men of great authority in the Order, could not resist, altogether, the fascinating influence of forecastings and prophecies which foretold the future splendour, and imperial advance, of the institute they loved so well. Even the General of the Franciscan Order had himself, eventually, in consequence of his being compromised in the affairs of Br. Gerard, to resign his high office, and hide himself away in the obscure retirement of conventual life.

But the keen eye of that hawk, William of S. Amour—as has been said in another place—at once perceived its opportunity. He who would take the trouble to write and publish, far and wide, a book against the Mendicants, would be only too charmed to snatch their own weapons out of their hands, or to make them slay themselves with their own sword. The *Introduction to the Eternal Gospel* became as popular as the book of the *Perils*. Men who were glad to ridicule the friars, and turn them into mockery by means of a book which was written purposely against them, found their zest sharpened when they were able to laugh at them, and turn them into foolery, by means of a book which they had written in favour of themselves. Possibly, the people living in a university city in the thirteenth century may have had their wits exercised more than others, and may have been trained to appreciate more keenly the humorous and the severe, through their constant intercourse with noisy students and sharp-set professors. Anyhow, the populace in Paris always seems to have been on the *qui vive* to catch at anything that might create a laugh, especially if they thought they saw the glancing edge and the keen point of genuine satire, or hoped to witness an interchange of caustic repartees and pungent sarcasm. Though few of the population could read or write, all of them could hear and see. They were quick, observant, full of vivacity, easily provoked, easily carried away, impetuous, and overflowing with *esprit*; and bright, ready, and free as summer birds.

The song of the minstrel, the play of the buffoon, the constant presence of the Paris student, had developed their intelligence beyond all power of books. What better material to work upon could William of S. Amour have desired? Could only the laugh be turned against the friars—could they only be made the objects of ridicule and wit—then they would speedily lose their power. The enemies of the Minorites set about their work, not only in earnest, but in the right way. Copies of the *Introduction to the Eternal Gospel* were sold and distributed in the public market-places. They were used as quivers, out of which to draw all manner of barbs—small, sharp, swift-flying shafts, and poisoned arrows too. The grave professor would draw from it, and fire off his learned disquisition ; the quick-witted student would pour out his voluble mixture of ready wit and ready nonsense ; the tumbling buffoon would join the chorus, and cause a crowd of listeners to set up a shout of boisterous laughter ; whilst the troubadour would throw into song, partly playful, partly spiteful, always telling, that general sentiment which glowed in the imagination of the people, but had not the gift of breaking into words. It is sufficient to read Ruteboeuf's *Complainte de Constantinople* to be convinced, not only of the damage which the *Introductorius* had done the regulars, but also of the bitterness and mockery which, in consequence of it, were poured upon them. John de Meung, another caustic satirist, a few years later proves, in his *Roman de la Rose*, that the strong feeling of the people had by no means died away.

The activity of William of S. Amour, the energy of the buffoons and singing minstrels, and the hostility of party feeling, created so strong a bias against the *Introductorius* and those connected with it, that Rome was called upon to interfere. As she had condemned the *Perils* of S. Amour, so now, though the honour of an Order which was one of her strenuous supporters appeared to be at stake, she would not shrink, as she never has shrunk, from dealing out to all men even-handed justice.

The Holy See commissioned the learned Cardinal, Hugh of S. Caro, and the Bishop of Messina, both of them Dominicans, to study and then report upon the work. The result of their labours was what could only have been expected. The *Introductorius*, like the *Perils*, was sentenced to be burnt by the common hangman; but with this reserve, that it should be given to the flames in private—not in a public place—as a mark of delicacy to that Order which had always stood so firmly by the Church, and with which, unfortunately, it was in a certain way connected.

This vigorous action of the supreme power deeply affected the General of the Franciscans. He had, by some mischance, compromised himself with the reveries of the *exalté* friar and the imaginative monk. John of Parma was, no doubt, a pious man, but he hardly had shown himself a prudent one. He tendered the resignation of his office, and then suggested S. Bonaventure as his successor. The Order received his resignation; and, though only four-and-thirty years of age, the seraphic friend of the Angelical was elected General of the Order, by the Chapter which met in Rome at Aracœli.

S. Bonaventure's dignity brought with it a heavy crown of thorns. He found himself in a position of great difficulty and delicacy. Those who were determined to keep the Mendicants straight were by no means contented with the resignation of the General, and the burning of the book. A clamour was raised for investigation. S. Bonaventure did what he could to prevent things running to extremes. But the opponents of the regulars had got hold of too fine a bone to be easily dropped until it had been thoroughly well picked. A process was instituted against Gerard the Franciscan and Leonard the Monk. As ringleaders and originators of the scandal of the *Introductorius*, they were sentenced to imprisonment for life. But even this was not sufficient to satisfy the craving of the public feeling. Why should so great a prize as the General of an Order be suffered to escape? In vain the gentle, loving Bonaventure pleaded for his familiar friend; in vain he tried to pacify the eager, greedy crowd of persecutors. The cry was too powerful. John of Parma had to stand his trial like the rest. It must have been a bitter, heart-destroying blow to that pious man, when he presented himself before his judges. But, fortunately for him, he was not without his friends. Cardinal Cajetan de' Ursini who afterwards became Pope Nicholas III., presided at the trial; and, through the energetic and powerful protection of Cardinal Ottoboni, nephew of the reigning Pontiff, and afterwards Pope himself, under the title of Adrian V., he was allowed to depart without any sentence of condemnation being passed upon him. His public career was at an end. All he looked for was to prepare for death. Bonaventure permitted him to select a convent, to which he was suffered to retire. He chose one at Greccio, near Rieti; and when the tomb closed over him, he left, as a legacy amongst the brethren, the odour of a saintly name.

Such is a brief account of the fate of the *Introduction to the Eternal Gospel*, of its authors, and of those who were smitten by its prophetic dreams. What had the

Angelical to do with it? He had been a strenuous adversary of William of S. Amour, and all that violent party of which he was the spokesman. He himself wore the regular habit, which he loved and prized above all earth could give. S. Francis and S. Dominic were bound together with chains of tenderest love and fellowship; the honour of the one was the honour of the other: what stained S. Francis left its mark on Dominic too. Then, the Angelical had fought and conquered in the same combat, for the same victory, and almost with the same weapons, as the Minorites. S. Bonaventure was his nearest familiar friend. His whole spirit and sympathy leaned towards those preachers of poverty and lovers of the Cross of Christ. How did he act regarding the *Introduction to the Eternal Gospel*? That he would defend the wrong done, no one could suspect or could believe. But might he not shield the authors? could he not explain away? might he not at least be silent?

He who would understand the conduct of the Angel of the Schools must calm his spirit, cleanse his intellec tual eye, fix it upon the truth, and follow it. Small men engrossed in earth, men spoilt by dealing with creatures, men blinded by looking only on clay, and deaf from the whirl and din of perishing humanity, easily become confused and scared when two great roads open suddenly upon them, and they are obliged to choose the way. The promptings of passion and the idle voice of sloth, the command of pride or the fascinations of ambition, heat their brain, and parch and warp their judgment. The Angelical had cast all this on one side; he had flung self and all its chains from him. 'Wisdom' was his passion; Truth was his goal; God alone was his reward; and God's larger glory his one aim in life. As a bird bursts its way out of a thicket into the expanding blue of heaven, and can then look down on earth without impediment, so was it with our great Angelical. He rose above all human littleness and party feeling, and lived with that Truth which alone he fought for and defended.

Hence, far from justifying the errors of spiritual men, he at once acknowledged them. He saw clearly that there is nothing more dangerous than a false philosophy, or a false mysticism, amongst the clergy. That which is their daily food—their staff of spiritual life—ought to be wholesome. And no taint is more difficult wholly to expunge, than the stain imprinted on the minds of holy men by a highly-wrought spirituality based upon an unscriptural foundation.

This, the clear mind of the Angelical must have vividly perceived. His love for the Religious Orders of the Church, especially for the Minorites, spurred his zeal to do all he could to apply an antidote to the poison which had been introduced into many minds. He could not help feeling that the Fraterculi, and other Apocalyptic enthusiasts, who rested their fanatical teaching on the theories of Abbot Joachim—theories which they had distorted into a mixture of wildness, wickedness, and blasphemy, essentially their own—would, unless sharply checked, spread like fire, without being as easily extinguished. True charity and wise love does not conceal the flaw, but points it out, and makes it good.

And the Angelical took the best possible means for doing this. Tocco tells us that he absolutely 'destroyed' the heresy in question. And how? Whilst still in Italy, he went to a certain monastery—indeed, some say he travelled about to many monasteries on the same errand—and asked the Abbot for the writings of Abbot Joachim, which formed the basis of the fanaticism which then was rife. He studied them from end to end. When he had thoroughly mastered them, then he took his pen, and marked those portions underneath which were erroneous, or savoured in any way of error; and drew his pen across other portions which should neither be read nor be believed in. And thus he restored the book to the Abbot, touched and corrected with a master's hand. There is little doubt that the work thus altered served as a guide and test to hundreds of spiritual men. For the Angelical's reputation was very high for learning and acuteness. And there is little doubt that religious men, living in days of violent spiritual delusions, were only too glad to obtain a work which would be at once a sure guide and a useful warning. One small effort of a master-workman exerts its influence and power—not because of the size of the volume, but on account of the skill and reputation of its author. It seems but a trivial undertaking to mark with a pen the errors in a spiritual book. It was the high reputation of the Saint that made his work of deep importance.

The fascinating influence exerted by the Saint on all who were drawn within his power seems to have been the product of a most unusual synthesis. Since his real life-spring was fixed in the unseen world, his whole method before men spoke of that intellectual might, and that Divine tenderness, which is an expression of the most perfect form of supernatural strength. Immense weight of character, surpassing grasp of mind, and keenness of logical discernment, added to a sovereign benignity and patience, and to a gentleness and grace, which spoke from his eyes, and thrilled in the accents of his voice, made men conscious, when in contact with him, that they were in the presence of a man of untold gifts, and yet of one so exquisitely noble as never to display them, save for the benefit of others. Men knew that he had the power to crush them; but since he was so great, they knew also that he never would misuse it; they found him ever self-forgetting and self-restrained. A character with such a capability of asserting itself, and yet ever manifesting such gentle self-repression, must have acted with a singular fascination on any generous mind that came into relation with it. It is evident, from Tocco and S. Antoninus, that the one abiding specialty, which receives an illustration in every chapter, nay, in almost every paragraph of their biographies of the Saint, is that of his possessing vast power, combined with a royal gentleness in the use of it. Largeness of mind and self-control—those two great Benedictine characteristics—separated him off, with marked distinctness, from the common herd of students and professors in the thirteenth century.

Indeed, one of the great works which he was raised up to accomplish, was to bring into the midst of the heats and disputations of the University a portion of that lofty spirit of serene self-government which sat so naturally upon him.

Comparing the character of the students and professors of the Paris University with that of the Angelical, no greater contrast could possibly be imagined. Only in one thing he seemed to resemble that turbulent society, and that was in his quick logical mind, his swift intellectual vision. But even here, on their own strong vantage-ground, dialecticians were little better than untrained children in comparison with him; and they felt it—they were forced to acknowledge his superiority. He was undisputed master; he was the 'Angel of the Schools.' And when once his place had been secured—and it was universally admitted that no one could approach him in proof, or defence, or in accuracy of judgment, or in store of learning, or readiness of resource, or power of logic, or breadth of vision, or in any kind of mental or moral eminence—then his influence in the University, which naturally adored great genius and unlimited success, became supreme.

Besides, men knew that he was a saint. His high perfection of soul could not have been concealed. Those four rivers which made him what he was made the students also what they were in relation to him—something not very far short of worshippers. Tocco does not say as much—but there is a thread running through his *Life* which witnesses, even at this day, to the vast impress of the Saint's character. When S. Antoninus writes of him, there is a fragrance about his whole tone which has to do with the *odor suavitatis* of the Blessed.

Fancy this great Angelical logician, whose one idea was to enlarge Christ's glory, sitting in the chair of science with those hundreds of youths around him—not only youths, but bearded men, and possibly prelates and bishops, and other persons of distinction! Think of his familiar contact with them all—of his mighty gentle mind day by day pouring forth, from the vast chamber of his memory, 'new things and old' for their instruction, and flooding them with light! He who as the merest child was ever asking, *Quid esset Deus?* he who as a stripling in the schools of the gay city of the South had surpassed his own professors; he who under Albert at Cologne had struck wonder into all by his profound defence of the Areopagite; he who had commented with such brilliant success upon the Lombard—now as a finished student in his early prime, leaving out all other reasons, was, as the natural consequence of his successes, King of the noisy schools!

He who has met a man of powerful intellect can make some estimate of the mysterious influence of mental power, and of the fascinating slavery of being enthralled by it. He may form a conception of how far-reaching it is. He may recollect how everything that drops from the tongue of such a man, or comes from his pen, has that indescribable sweetness and attraction about it which belongs to the temper of his mind ; and how scores who have never seen his face, to whom he is an utter stranger, defend his cause with as much jealousy as they would the honour of their mother or the reputation of their dearest friend. And if such be the effect simply of the writings of an able man, how paramount must not be his sway, when the glance of his eye, the accents of his voice, the charm of his manner, and the whole stamp of his character and genius, combine in one harmonious influence to illustrate and recommend his doctrine, and to subdue and captivate the heart! How mysteriously great is not the force of intellect over the generous, confiding, impressionable heart of youth!

Yes, see the great Angelical in the midst of the thronging schools. Brilliancy, depth, tenderness, and eloquence—all the force he had of mind and manner was exerted by him to further the one cause he had espoused upon the earth : to advance the imperial cause of Wisdom. How he must have shamed many of those ungovernable Doctors ! With what awe must not the shallow teacher have looked on him and heard him ! What a lesson to the vain dialectician—the lover of intellectual display—to be constrained to beat his breast and say : 'Verily, that man aims at one thing only—self-forgetting, to make Truth known and loved!' What a new sensation for the students when he serenely took his place amongst them, and held them spell-bound by his lucid, eloquent, simple exposition; by his brilliant, quick defence; by his modesty and gentle kindliness! No wonder Tocco declared his influence to have surpassed that of every other Doctor; no wonder that his school was crowded as no other; no wonder that at last all recognised the Divine Hand which was upon him, and that he was finally declared by the Holy See itself to be 'The Angel of the Schools.'

Several examples are given, in different lives of the Saint, of his remarkable gentleness and self-possession. On one occasion a young man was being examined before an imposing meeting of professors and a large assembly of students for his Licentiate. During the course of the defension he advanced a proposition which was decidedly unsound. The Angelical saw the flaw at once. He, in his own masterly way, entered into the lists with the young man. To him, of course, it was merely like the play of a child. However, the student, with that arrogance belonging to his class, thought to maintain his proposition: but the poor fellow was as a bird in the hand of the fowler. The Angelical pressed him, using as his lever a certain Council of the Church, which was wholly opposed to the proposition which the student had undertaken to defend. In vain the young man tried to extricate himself from the dilemma: his most artful efforts simply entangled him the more

The Angelical pushed him still further, till finally he was constrained by the sheer force of logic to own himself beaten: his pride was broken; he sunk to his proper place; and begged the Angelical, with a very different air and with expressions of genuine humility, to enlighten him upon the subject. 'Now you are speaking properly,' said the Saint sweetly to him: and then he began to unfold the true thesis to him with such a store of gentleness and sympathy, that all the Masters were carried away with admiration of him: 'Magistri omnes,' says Tocco, 'admirati sunt de tranquillitate mentis ejus et verbi'—showing, by the very fact of their being so much surprised, that he was introducing a new element amongst them.

Another time he had occasion to engage in a formal defension with the Minorite friar John of Pisa, who eventually became Archbishop of Canterbury. Great was the concourse to witness this passage of arms. It was what Frigerio calls a *solenne congresso*, and no doubt there were many eager Franciscans with their picturesque rough habits, and many Black Friars, as well as Augustinians and Trinitarians, seated in the great hall of discussion, waiting to see the issue between S. Francis and S. Dominic. To hear Brother Thomas of Aquin defend a public thesis, even in great intellectual Paris, was a treat which no man who had a taste for exquisite dialectic art, or for displays of crushing power, would be willing to throw away. Even to look on that man, with his meek princely bearing and his finely developed brow and serene countenance, would have been enough delight. Well, the assembly met and the contest began. We are not told the subject of dispute, but—which is more interesting—we know what was its issue. John of Pisa, though a keen and learned man, had no chance with the Angelical. It would have been folly for any one, however skilled—yes, for Bonaventure, or Rochelle, or even Albert the Great himself—to attempt to cross rapiers with Brother Thomas. He was to the manner born. Brother John did all that was in him—used his utmost skill—but it was useless : the Angelical simply upset him time after time. The Minorite grew warm ; the Angelical, bent simply on the truth, went on completing, with unmoved serenity, the full discomfiture of the poor Franciscan. John of Pisa at length could stand it no longer. In his heat he forgot his middle term and forgot himself, and turned upon the Saint with sarcasm and invective. The Angelical, in his own gentle, overpowering way, giving not the slightest heed to these impertinences, went on replying to him with inimitable tenderness and patience ; and whilst teaching a lesson which, after so many hundred years, men still can learn, drew on himself unconsciously the surprise and admiration of that vast assembly.

Such was the way in which the Angelical brought the influence of Benedictine *quies* and *benignitas* into the boisterous litigations of the Paris schools.

And what is more, Frigerio tells us that the Saint

taught the great lesson of self-control, not only by the undeviating practice of his life, but also by his writings; that he looked upon it as an 'ignominy' (*ignominia*) to soil the mouth with angry words; and contended that 'quarrels, immoderate contentions, vain ostentation of knowledge, and the trick of puzzling an adversary with sophistical arguments—such as is often the practice of dialecticians—should be banished from the schools.' Still he did not at all object to argumentation when carried on pacifically: 'Utilis est autem humilis collatio, et pacifica disputatio.'

It may be imagined by some that the singular grace of the Angelical proceeded simply from a happy gift of natural character. To take that view would be to misunderstand his life altogether. A man may naturally be of a graceful and amiable disposition—doubtless: and such was the Angelical; but to bear affronts meekly, to be patient under bitter injury always, under all circumstances to be the same, cannot be nature; such stability as this can only come from grace—can only proceed from having conquered nature by practising it in virtue and treading it under foot. Had the Angelical not been a mortified man he certainly never would have been a meek one.

Those who have not been behind the scenes, but simply gaze on the results of heavenly labour—on the issue of heroic suffering and heroic love as it manifests itself abroad in the world—will most assuredly wonder at it, but they cannot possibly comprehend it. An outside carnal man looks on a saint as some strange foreigner, whose ways perplex him, and whose character he cannot understand. He looks on him as a species of moral enigma, of which he has no attraction to discover the solution.

But let him, after looking on the sweet Angelical fascinating the crowded schools, take the trouble to follow him, as silently, after the day's work, he retires to his cell, seemingly to rest; let him watch him bent in prayer; see him take from its hiding-place, when all have gone to sleep, that hard iron chain; see him—as he looks up to heaven and humbles himself to earth—without mercy to his flesh, scourge himself with it, striking blow upon blow, lacerating his body through the greater portion of the sleepless night: let the carnal man look upon this touching sight; let him shrink back in horror if he will—still let him look on it, and he will learn how the saints laboured to secure a chaste and spotless life, and how a man can so far annihilate self-seeking as to be gentle with all the world, severe with himself alone. If in human life there is anything mysteriously adorable it is a man of heroic mould and surpassing gifts showing himself great enough to smite his own body, and to humble his entire being in presence of his Judge.

And whilst S. Thomas punished the flesh our Lord, who desired him to advance from glory to glory towards his reward, allowed him continually to be molested in the spirit by the enemy of man.

It seems that most of the mighty men of God—those men of awful soul, those abysses of passion, and those flames of fire—like Hilarion and the giant Fathers of the Desert—had it as their lot to wrestle with the frightful powers of hell, to see the fiend, to strike at him, to strive with him, to be worried, and even smote by him. Our Lord Himself, in His gracious mercy, allowed His sacred Person to come in contact with, nay, to be pressed in the foul arms of the arch-fiend, and to be borne through the air by him. The greater the stake the more terrific the battle. To destroy a rational creature, which is a whole *cosmos* of love and heroism, to drag it down and plunge it into the burning lake as a damned soul for evermore, is the highest ambition of satanic enterprise. No trouble is too great; all arts must be practised to secure that end; no years are too long for perseverance in the struggle. Did the Angelical escape this trial of lofty souls?

Satan had made, as has been seen, one great assault upon him when a boy-prisoner at San Giovanni, and he had been victoriously repulsed; nor was he again permitted to try to enter by that door. One of his three great weapons was thus struck from him. What of the concupiscence of the eyes? Here Satan was powerless again. The Angelical had grown up from youth to manhood with so keen a vision into the Unseen that deception was impossible. His heart and intellect had no part with what is made of clay, or falls to dust and quickly perishes. Pride? The monastic principles on which his life was fixed, out of which grew his moral man, were so firmly set in him that the suggestions of pride simply created a jar in his intellect, which shook and resounded in his heart. The ring of light around a life of purity and love kept the polluted fiend at bay. However, if Satan could not touch the Saint, he had the power to annoy him; and his spiteful and venomous hatred at being foiled and rendered helpless expressed itself in all manner of frightful apparitions. 'Satan,' says Frigerio, 'often appeared to him in horrible shapes in order to terrify him.' But the Angelical feared him not: directly the Saint cried out to him and made the sign of the Cross he instantly disappeared.

John of Blase, a judge in the courts of Naples, and attached to Queen Mary of Sicily, gave his testimony on oath respecting a fact which came within his observation as to the terrible spiritual trials which the Angelical had to undergo. This learned judge does not appear to have been a man of imaginative mind; his evidence speaks of clear, hard common sense—and he knew the Angelical well; he seems to have been quite familiar with his habits of life; he speaks of his great piety, uprightness, and sobriety. He had attended his sermons for upwards of ten years, and had lived with him as an intimate friend for more than five. He was the same who had watched the Saint during his Lenten discourses preaching on the simple text *Ave Maria*, with his eyes ever closed, and his face directed towards the heavens.

His evidence was as follows. The Angelical was

staying in the convent of his Order at Naples, and it seems to have been the habit of the judge to pay him visits in his cell. Now, not far from his cell there appears to have been an open place or verandah, such as is often seen attached to foreign convents, where the friars, after the toils of the day, could meet in the pleasant evening air, and edify each other in holy conversation. The judge declares that whilst he was engaged in the cell of the Angelical the Saint went out, intending to go to this verandah, and that whilst on his way, Satan suddenly appeared to him in the shape of a negro, dressed in black. Immediately S. Thomas saw him he knew it to be the arch-fiend, and at once rushed upon him with his arm raised ready to strike at him with his fist, exclaiming at the same time, 'Why dost thou come here to tempt me?' But as the Saint came upon the apparition Satan vanished, and never again appeared to him there.

Being asked by the commissioners how he acquired this information, the judge answered on oath: 'Quod interfuit et vidit'—that he was present, and witnessed the occurrence with his own eyes.

The biographers of the Saint declare that this was the only occasion when he was ever known to have been roused to anger. Not like the old sailing ship, which, whilst it can be steered, yet depends upon the wind, but just as one of those mighty vessels of modern construction, propelled through the dancing ocean with a strong steady course, taking its own line, and going on its own way, in spite of the heaving troughs of the sea and the treachery of the wind—so the Angelical seems to have had within him a force so mighty that it bore him through the lifting ocean of life, with its storms and currents, cutting through them all, ever bearing up swiftly and grandly in one direction, towards the lights flickering in the distance at the entrance of the port of the Spiritual City. What man in history, saint or not saint, has ever shown, in the midst of so many trials, from infancy up, so marvellous an equanimity, so unruffled a self-command?

And, in point of fact, an event took place about this period, which perhaps gives the most telling witness to the chivalrous bearing which was so noble a trait in his many-sided character.

When the great contest which had drawn the Saint from his life of study, prayer, and preaching, to take a prominent part in defending the Religious Orders in Italy, had come to a close, he received instructions from his Superiors to return once more to France. The deputies who had been sent by King Louis, as well as the representatives of the University, who had been mixed up in the affair of William of S. Amour, appear to have started about the same time. Whether they travelled with S. Thomas, does not appear. It is very probable that the Angelical went on foot, begging his way, as he had been accustomed to do from his early religious life, accompanied by his *socius*.

Before he set out on his journey, he was admitted to an audience with the Holy Father. With what marks of deep esteem and admiration he was received may be left to the imagination of the reader. In the first place, Pope Alexander had ever been a friend to literature and men of letters; he himself was an author, and he freely promoted learned men. Henry, Cardinal of Ostia, who had been a renowned lawyer and a deep divine, was placed by him in the Sacred College; whilst his royal munificence to the great Canonist, Bartholomew of Brescia—who wrote so much on the Decretals—might be remembered. If such was the bias of the Sovereign Pontiff, what an exceptional interest must he not have felt for the great Angelical! Even quite recently he had reason to look on him with unfeigned tenderness and regard. His fame, his name, the work he had already done for the Church, his last brilliant victory—so modestly yet so crushingly achieved—all this, no doubt, filled the mind of Pope Alexander, as the Angelical knelt down at his feet, and received, with the loving reverence of a little child, the Apostolical benediction. It is a touching picture to paint in the imagination—the great light and pillar of the Church bending down with all humility, whilst he to whom the care of all the Churches is confided spreads his hands over him, looks up to heaven, and invokes the Spirit of God upon his head. These acts of reverence and of authority are not without their intrinsic efficacy as well as their external worth.

Then he had to take leave of those loving beings who had watched him with such longing when he was being commissioned by the General of the Order to defend their holy cause. They too had much—indeed, it may be said, *all*—to thank him for. He had saved them. They were still to live in honour. They were still to keep possession of their privileges. In fact, he had raised them up, and given them a position, and lent them a *prestige* which they did not possess before. See them there, all around him, with their shaven heads and circling crowns of hair, the gentle novice and the deep-eyed professor;—there they are in their neat white habits, pressing about him as he stands, higher, greater than the rest, a larger man, one of themselves, but yet, in spite of himself, a King amongst them all. Sweet is the sorrow that they feel—for religious men know nothing of the world's bitterness in parting. They are persuaded, as they look on him with their mild, pure, loving eyes, that they will surely see him once again, whatever happens, come the worst. They know that life in reality is not life; but after death is Life—and then comes joy and calm repose, with all pangs of parting over. Such is their gentle, firm conviction, lending a light to the darkest shadows, and touching earth with a ray from heaven. And they embrace, and say, 'Addio carissimo,' sadly, perhaps, but hardly sorrowfully. And so he parts with them; they accompany him, it may be, to the convent door, as he and his *socius*—most likely Reginald—start on their journey; and then the 'Brethren,' having watched him out of sight, after saying to each other all manner of loving things of him, retire, one to his study, another to his cell, all to their work, to their labour till the evening-tide.

One of the reasons why the Angelical and his companion left Italy so soon, was in order to get settled down in Paris before the severity of the winter should set in. Besides, they had to make part of their way by sea. But their forethought did not save them from trouble here. The treachery of the ocean can be trusted in no season of the year. The Angelical embarked. There appear to have been many passengers, and a good ship's crew on board the boat, such as boats were—poor craft for sailing—in the middle ages. After a favourable run out to sea, the wind suddenly shifted, and became violent and contrary. Black murky clouds spotted the horizon, and gradually bulging out into all manner of fantastic forms, blended and spread themselves like a curtain over the sky, whilst a violent tempest, with shock and flash, burst across the waters, carrying the ship bodily upon a girdle of thundering breakers, which were madly bursting and seething over the half-hidden rocks which seemed to guard an island beyond. Every moment that island became more visible through the darkness as the boat was hurried along; every moment the passengers could hear more distinctly the deafening agony of the waters, as they threw their spray and spent themselves against the rocks, or rose and fell around the island; every moment the details of their awful position revealed themselves with all their varied noisy horrors. The sailors had done their utmost—they could not stop the boat; she was borne away towards the reef in spite of sail and helm, in spite of master and sailor, in spite of the shrieks of the women, and the prayers and the curses of the men. It is but natural, when all seems lost, when all has been done, and all has failed, that terror and despair should take the place of hope and courage. So was it here—captain, crew, and passengers, seeing that their doom was sealed, became petrified with terror. There was, however, one exception; there was one calm self-possessed being, whom no power on earth or in the waters seemed capable of ruffling, and who—when the ship was being carried away violently by the hurricane to inevitable destruction, when the ship's company as well as the passengers were altogether paralysed with fear, when the agonies of death seemed already to be at hand—turned gently and confidently to his Lord, as he would have done in his little cell at Anagni or at Naples, and begged of Him to stay the tempest and save the foundering ship. His prayer was heard at once, the wind changed, the boat was borne away from the breakers, the awful island diminished gradually to a speck, and at length was lost in the distance, as the craft ran quickly along before the wind, and sailed gaily and gallantly into port.

O, how deeply set in the centre-soul of the Saint must not have been his trust in the power of the World Unseen! How great a gift, in real peril, to have Christ for one's stay, and His Cross for one's support—to be ever one, in storm or shine, like the great Angelical!

Tocco tells us that he had his own way of meeting

'the terrors of the air.' He doubtless remembered how narrowly he had escaped, when the fork of lightning searched out and killed his little sister sleeping by his side at home in early childhood. His sword was the sign of the Cross; and the shield which covered him the words: 'Deus in carnem venit: Deus pro nobis mortuus est!'—'God came in the flesh; God has died for us!' as if he should say: 'I fear you not either for life or death. He who bore our clay and died our death, He will be the shield of my help and the sword of my glory, whilst underneath are the Everlasting Arms.'

Great must have been the excitement in the University on the return of the two parties which had been sent forth to fight their respective battles. Great the sadness of the one, great the exultation of the other. Irreverence and rationalism had not for many years, perhaps never since Remigius started the Paris schools, received so severe a check. The battle had been a bold, open, uncompromising contest. Both sides did all that was in them to overset the pretensions of the other. Both were sanguine. And had not the Holy See been the arbiter, things might have gone very differently. But her principles are fixed; her laws are sure, definite, and easily understood by those who care to read. The secular party had been blinded through conceit, and had lost themselves through insubordination, and therefore did not rightly interpret the signs of the times: they had played a losing game, and their champions returned to them simply to relate how Bonaventure,

Albert, and Brother Thomas of Aquino, by their learning, keenness, and moral weight, had carried everything before them at the Court of Rome.

The Angelical meanwhile found his way through the narrow crowded streets of the great city—streets he had travelled along years before, when quite a stripling, with the venerable General—and no doubt was glad, after the turmoils and excitements of discussion, after the perils of the deep, and the fatigues of a long land journey, to shut himself up in his cell in S. James's, and enjoy, away from tongues, some of the sweets of holy solitude. But it is hardly probable that he was allowed to have much repose. He was the hero of the triumph which had been achieved. He was looked upon, by that powerful body representing the party of discipline and order, as having, by his extraordinary gifts, saved from destruction those principles for which they would readily have sacrificed their lives. He had left Paris on his high errand, followed by the admiration and blessing of all who loved religious life and desired order to be preserved. They knew from his antecedents that he was a great and powerful reasoner, and a pure and spotless man of God. The crowded convent itself to which he belonged, the grave Cistercian, the solemn Carthusian, the ascetic Bernardine, the active Trinitarian, the children of S. Augustine, and the meditative Benedictine, all with any interest in the maxims of perfection, must have welcomed the Angelical as citizens welcome the return of a chief from battle—from a war on which their all was staked, and in which he, through his superior generalship and presence of mind, had been victorious. And in proportion as they realised the benefit he had conferred upon religion, so much the more fully did he gain an influence over their hearts. It was no small matter, in days when Religious Orders were so powerful, to have achieved a position which secured to him their united countenance and support.

And whilst the Regulars were congratulating one another on the favourable outcome of their common trials, the Holy See, with that sagacity which sees too far for human eyes, was preparing to follow up strenuously the action it had from the first determined on. Pope Alexander felt that there would be very little use in issuing decrees and fulminating anathemas at Anagni, very little profit in burning heretical books there, and severely punishing their composers, unless something were done to secure the realisation of the Pontifical wishes in the theological capital of the intellectual world. If Paris still walked in the old courses, all the energy of the Italian Doctors would be simply thrown away. If the Dominicans and Franciscans were still to be insulted, ridiculed, lampooned, starved, cudgelled, and driven out of the seats of learning; if the ground-principles of religious life were still to be scorned and scouted—things would not simply be as bad, but they would be absolutely worse than they had been before.

To save all possibility of cavil, therefore, the Holy See directed a Bull to the University of Paris, requesting the members of that distinguished body to carry into effect the commands which had been issued at Anagni. Any one who has a curiosity to see this instruction, and a host of others, will find them drawn out in the *Bullarium* of the Dominicans. The Holy See was excessively active. It felt the enormous power of the Paris University for greater good or evil. The only chance of putting and keeping so large a concourse of learned, acute, and turbulent men in the right way, was to persevere till all those improvements had been effected which seemed called for by the nature of the case: for the Paris Doctors still shrank from admitting the Mendicants to their chairs. It is said that, counting from the beginning to the end of these disturbances, no less than forty Briefs connected with an adjustment of the subject were issued by the Holy See. Bulls were directed to the Chancellor; Briefs were written to the Bishops; Briefs were sent to the Professors and to those connected with the University; three Briefs were sent to the Ordinary of the city; King Louis himself was addressed at length on points concerning difficult questions bearing upon university discipline and education; some Bulls were issued forbidding any one to be promoted who refused obedience to the *Quasi Lignum;* others to check dangerous communications between that firebrand, William of S. Amour, and certain impressionable Doctors; others giving instructions that the pestiferous book on the *Perils of the Last Times*, together with all other publications which had scandalised the faithful during the great dispute, should be burnt publicly in Paris. And indeed so carefully did the authorities of Rome enter into detail—so anxious were they to annihilate, once for all, the seeds of disaffection, that a special Brief was published, punishing with exile and excommunication Guillot, that wretched beadle of the Picards, who had so brutally interrupted, with his insulting document, the preaching of the Angelical during the previous Lent.

Though there were many turbulent spirits in Paris, and many subtle minds which could always frame a plausible excuse for refusing to perform a patent duty, still the energy and determination of Pope Alexander in the end prevailed. The doctors, bachelors, and scholars of the secular party found themselves firmly met at every point; they found that resistance and subterfuge simply brought Bull upon Bull and Brief upon Brief upon them from the Roman Curia; and that in proportion to their efforts to shake themselves free was the vigour with which the Italian authorities bound them, by excommunications and anathemas, to carry out the law. Finding that opposition was useless they submitted with a generosity and manliness which did great credit to their hearts and to their heads. Though turbulent and obstinate, though many of them were as conceited as well could be, and stone-blind with the crassest species of prejudice, still they were not openly contumacious. They had studied history enough to be convinced that opposition to Peter is as truly intellectual as it is moral suicide. They had read the fate of many men more learned than themselves, and the lesson had not been thrown away. They believed in the authority of the Holy See: they might try to evade it, but they would never question it, and when once fully confronted by the vision of just, though it may have been sometimes stern authority, they turned round and did their best to follow its commands.

Very possibly the tact and piety of the king, S. Louis, who took the liveliest interest in the prosperity of the University, and who did his utmost to bring the contending parties to a peaceful understanding, helped materially to create a more charitable and generous tone of mind. Whatever the causes may have been, the authorities of the University determined to prove, by an act of largeness which was as gracious as it was noble, that all the past had been forgotten, and that they had made up their minds for the future to live with the Religious Orders in the city on the most friendly and harmonious terms. They consequently invited the two great champions who had not only fought against them, but had moreover utterly defeated them, to prepare themselves forthwith, and by a public Act, before the assembled doctors, bachelors, and scholars, to earn the highest grade which a seat of learning can bestow upon its children—that of Doctor of Divinity. By this, not only would the Mendicants stand before the world in their due place of honour, but the very men who had been contending, and contending successfully, in defence of their privileges, would be the two first persons to enjoy them.

This well-timed and noble act on the part of the University gave an almost universal satisfaction. The king, who loved Thomas very tenderly, and who seems to have drunk at the same spiritual fountain, had long ardently desired to see him and Bonaventure in a leading position in the schools. He knew what two men of deep mind and saintly life can effect, and how such characters as theirs would act as a leaven amidst the crudities and freedoms of scholastic life. How earnestly the See of Rome longed to place S. Thomas and Bonaventure as leaders of thought, as *candelabra lucentia*, in the metropolis of theologic learning, is evident from many Bulls and Briefs; and by degrees the public opinion of the noisy city worked in the same direction. The general feeling recognised the merit of the men, and possibly also the splendour and soundness of the principles which they represented. In proportion as light fell upon the people, they became zealous, and, at length, even clamorous, for the appearance of Thomas and Bonaventure in the *Aula*. The Mendicants had had a hard battle to fight. But they had fought and had won it. Irreverence, for the time at least, had to retire. William of S. Amour ceased to be the idol of the hour. A reaction had set in. The friars were in favour. They had succeeded, and—with the herd of men at all events, even in the thirteenth century—nothing was so successful as success.

It was said just now that the action of the University 'gave an *almost* universal satisfaction.' There was, however, one notable exception. There was one man who did all that lay in him to hinder the champion of the Dominicans from being raised to the high honours of the Doctorate, and that one solitary man was the great Angelical himself.

We have seen, on more than one occasion, how his gentle sensitive mind withdrew with spontaneous horror from anything that looked like honour to himself. Not even to soothe his mother after all she had gone through, nor to please his brothers, nor his friends, nor even the Pope, could he be brought to accept the high dignity of Abbot, and to maintain the family traditions on the mountain. When made Bachelor, it was against his will. He had to be forced into his Licentiate. How then could he, who had been shrinking back all his life from titles and positions, make up his mind to the dignity and the responsibility of Master in Theology? And here there was something besides honour from which he fled—he thought he was too ignorant; he felt he was too young. With his heart all on fire, he went to his Superiors. He explained to them his case. He spoke of his slender parts, his lack of knowledge, his inexperience, and urged how difficult he found it to bring himself to take the dreaded step. There is something almost awful in the way he was overpowered by the consciousness of his own unfitness, and in the sickness which crept over him when he thought he was going to be made something of. 'Leave me,' he seems to say; 'let me serve God in peace: drag me not out into the sight of men: let me have Him alone for my reward!'

But his Superiors, in spite of his earnest representations, went quietly on their way. They listened to all he had to say, and ended by telling him to prepare for his degree.

Here is evident the wisdom of living under the authority of religious life. Though a saint, the Angelical was no fit judge on practical matters in his own case. As the reader feels full well, he was neither too ignorant nor too young. This manifestation of his deep humility proves his worthiness all the more, and the whole of his action in this affair evinces the profound character of his mind. He did not arrive at his conclusion because he compared himself with other men. Saints are not in the habit of weighing themselves against their neighbours. But he weighed himself as he knew himself—against his duty to our Lord, and against his view of the requirements and offices of a leader of thought in the schools of Paris at that day. And as it is the case that in proportion as a man's soul is illuminated with supernatural light, in that same proportion he sees vividly, and appreciates keenly, his own shortcomings and imperfections; and in proportion as he is gifted with a master-mind, in that proportion he grasps the full weight of responsibility, and the full significance of the word *position*—so it follows that the

Angelical, being exceptionally illuminated by grace, and exceptionally gifted by nature, recoiled from that which common minds are ever craving for, and craved for that which they would do anything to escape. His humility was no foolish, mawkish, sentimental effeminacy; not the result of a weak constitution or of a softening brain; no hollow pretence or unreality—but the issue of deep supernatural vision into self, and of the workings of an exalted mind upon the lofty theory of human obligations. Men of this class, when directed by the light of supernatural obedience, are led to the highest heroism before God, and become the greatest champions of the good, the beautiful, and the true, in the sight of men.

This fear of being made something of, which was the one great anxiety of the Angelical through life, seems to have grown upon him as he grew in years. It was the fruit, as he teaches himself, of that 'Reverence' which is one of the great pillars of the Benedictine temple of perfection. Frigerio says that in his tender infancy at Monte Cassino, the Saint manifested this ruling sentiment. Under Albert at Cologne it was the same. He drew back quite wounded and sad; a cloud would come across his brow if it were hinted to him that he ought to be noticed or placed in some position. The Benedictine love of retirement, of being left alone, of being permitted to live to God undisturbed by the worry of men, seemed at times almost to have borne upon him with too powerful a sway. It is the mightiness of his modest, loving, contemplating character that makes him so deep a mystery of moral loveliness, and that ranges him so far above the category of ordinary men.

Even the commands of his Superiors, who marvelled at his soul the more they knew of it, did not relieve him from any of the pain—did not break the cloud, or dispel the terror, with which his whole being was encompassed. The very thought of what was coming seemed utterly to prostrate him. Strong and brave as he was, chivalrous as the noblest of knights, knowing no fear, and fearing no danger, he could not find the nerve to bear up against the thought that *he* was to be dragged from his quiet resting-place, and to be thrust into a public position of grave responsibility, and to be held up before the eye of intellectual Paris, as one worthy of high dignity. As the bat, when being drawn out of its dusky hiding-place into the light of day, shrinks away further into its obscurity, terrified and scared by an overpowering sensation, so did the Angelical shrink, or so would he have shrunk, as S. Anselm did before him, had he not been steadied by the express wishes of his Superiors.

What did he do? He knew whence alone he could draw comfort. He knew where alone, if he did not get comfort, he was certain, at all events, to find strength.

It had been his custom ever since he came to S. James's, when all had retired to rest, to slip out of his cell, and to steal quietly among the shadows of the empty church to pour out his spirit before our Lord. Christ was his one great Love—the seat of all his 'Wisdom.'

Our Lord fired and warmed him, and made his whole soul glow with a heroism which alone can spring from the Sacred Heart. The thought of our Lord humbled him to the dust, when he turned to the Agony and the Death. It broke him utterly to think of *his* being honoured, being made the object of the admiration of hundreds, and in so emphatical a manner, when his Love was smitten with a reed, and stood crowned with thorns! He could not endure to feel that he was to be rewarded for a service which, when compared with what was really his Master's due, was, at the best, but the effort of an unprofitable servant. How could he put out his hand for recompense, how could he consent to receive the applause of men, when his whole life was but one act of selfishness, compared with the outpouring love of Christ for him? How could he be bright and gay, and highly placed, when his Master was broken and sorrowing, and reputed with the wicked? No; he could not stand so terrible a stroke as that. His large, throbbing, sensitive heart, worked upon by his vast intelligence and glowing imagination—the one drawing out before him the mysterious scheme of Christ's self-annihilation, the other imaging the Passion with the vividness of light—seemed filled like a fountain, as he threw himself before the Crucified, and gazed fixedly upon the Cross. There he looked, and knelt, and prayed; there he held himself half-stunned in the presence of his Lord, till the large tears gathered to his eyes, and flowed down copiously, as he prostrated himself at full length upon the ground, crying his heart out like a little child, before his Saviour, and begging of Him for the knowledge and grace necessary for acquitting himself of the duties which were to be thrust upon him. Then, as if overpowered by a consciousness of the immense work which was to be done, and calling to mind the terrible condition of the schools, and his own weaknesses, he broke out into the Psalm which begins: 'Save me, O Lord, for there is now no saint; truths are decayed from among the children of men.' And so he prayed and wept for a long time, praying till he could pray no more, and weeping till he had no more tears to shed; till finally, thoroughly exhausted, he fell into a deep sleep, as he had done once before after the excitement of temptation at San Giovanni. And behold, as he lay upon the pavement before the altar, an old and venerable-looking man, dressed in the habit of S. Dominic, appeared to him in vision. And the old man said to him, 'Brother Thomas, why do you sob, and for what are you praying to our Lord?' And he answered, 'Because they are going to make me Master in Theology, for which I am quite unfit; nor do I even know how to choose a thesis for my public act.' The old man replied, 'Behold, thy prayer is heard; accept the office, for God is with thee; and for thy thesis, take no other words than these: "Thou waterest the hills from Thy upper rooms: the earth shall be filled with the fruit of Thy work."' Upon this, the Angelical awoke from his sleep, rose up, and thanking our Lord for having heard his prayer so speedily, retired, strengthened and comforted, to his little cell. Such are the dealings of Wisdom with the elect soul: 'She will bring upon him fear, and dread, and trial; and she will torture him with the tribulation of her discipline till she try him by her laws, and trust his soul. Then she will strengthen him, and make her way straight to him, and give him joy.'

The Angelical that night had crept into the church with a dead weight upon his spirit, and oppressed with an indescribable anxiety; he returned a strong and valiant man, with his whole heart expanding towards his work, with his mind free with a Divine elasticity, 'rejoiced as a giant to run the way.' In proportion as he distrusted self, he reposed confidence in God. When he felt that he was fighting our Lord's battle, at our Lord's desire, and enlightened and held up by His Holy Spirit, no power could stand against him—he knew not what it was to fear. Self, even his fear and horror of self, sunk away out of sight, vanished, as the splendid vision of Wisdom, beautiful and strong, seated as a queen securely amongst men, fastening herself on their hearts, and sealing herself on their intelligences, seemed to rise up before him, and occupy his mental vision. Could he but draw aside the veil, and make men, once for all, gaze upon the majesty, the constraining loveliness, the entrancing beauty of the world in which he himself habitually lived—could he but show them the Face of his Christ—then would his life not have been spent in vain ; then he would, perhaps, have achieved a work not unworthy of a recompense.

But the Saint now had little time for reveries, or for indulging in anticipations of the future. As the gray morning broke into his little cell, as he entered it on coming from the church, he felt that before that day was out his great Public Act would have been made, and that he would have been invested with the insignia of a Master in Divinity. He had been all confusion, he could not collect his thoughts, even a subject upon which to speak would not suggest itself—so much was he upset, so crippled and bewildered were all his faculties—till our Lord lifted him up, and the old man said to him in the dream, 'Take no other words than these: "Thou waterest the hills from Thy upper rooms: the earth shall be filled with the fruit of Thy work."' Now all was changed. The powers of his vast intelligence were summoned by his commanding will to carry out each its allotted task, and they willingly obeyed the order. So rapid was his mind, so powerful his grasp, that in a few hours he had thoroughly prepared himself to expand, and then defend, against the keenest intellects in Paris, a subject so large that it may be said to have included the greater portion of the theological teaching of that day. Doubtless on account of his vast memory, and his exquisite gift of order, and the far reach and piercing force of his intellectual vision, embracing the widest range, whilst fixing itself on every detail—mastering the parts together with the whole—he was enabled to study his thesis mentally, as ordinary men study a map rolled out ready-made before the eye, with every minute river and tributary, with every sea and bay, with every town, village, and hamlet, with the very nature of the soil and character of the vegetation, fixed and marked in its proper form and colour. He took in, and adjusted, and retained the entire plan, without effort and without confusion; and, through his accurate appreciation of the whole, and of the mutual value and relations of its component parts, he was ready to defend, with sound and incontrovertible arguments, any portion of his thesis which might be assailed by an opponent. It was the gift and genius of his mind to see no portion of philosophic or theologic truth in isolation. He saw each member in its relation to the entire organism, and he knew how to bring the power of the whole to bear on its defence. Aristotle and Albertus had but fostered in him a gift which was a splendid natural endowment, now developed in its range, and multiplied in its power—not only by constant exercise, but also through the abiding influence of grace; and sealing itself eventually upon the recognition of the world, for all time to come, by the glorious synthesis of the immortal *Summa*. But the world as yet had only witnessed him display some small portion of his power; it had reason to remember him as a boy; it had not forgotten his brilliancy as Bachelor and Licentiate; it was now full of his masterly defence of the principles of evangelical perfection: but the sun in its meridian splendour had not yet burst through the surrounding clouds, though it was sufficiently strong to draw an immense concourse to the episcopal *Aula* where the Angelical was to make his Public Act for his degree.

And in point of fact, not merely the talents and reputation of the Saint, but a series of circumstances which was inseparably bound up with this defension, created an interest, and kept up an excitement, which could not have been produced by any ordinary occurrence. It was the grand act of triumph of the Regular party. It was the crowning victory of the Dominicans and Franciscans. The University had sworn to oust them from its chairs; and now that same University, in the most public and emphatic manner, was about to reinstate them therein, and to confer the highest academical honours upon those two very men whom it had been specially bent upon excluding.

Let the reader imagine for himself the agitation which prevailed in Paris on the morning of that day. If he know anything of academical life, of doctors and professors, of students and religious, of those whose energies are devoted to literature or learning, and of the texture of their minds, he may draw for himself a picture of many a preliminary gathering in the narrow streets of the University town, as men formed in groups and knots to discuss the general question of the Regulars, or to canvass the relative merits of the two candidates for the degree. He can see the troops of Black Friars proceeding from the Convent of S. James's, with an elastic step, and an unmistakable expression of satisfaction, as they wind their way through students, professors, and gaping crowds, towards the Episcopal Palace, where they are off to see their brother Thomas receive his ring and cap. The children of S. Francis, too, with their coarse brown habit and their knotted girdle—men who look as if they knew what a rough life was—move their pink sandalled feet somewhat more briskly than is usual, as they thread through a herd of staring citizens who seem bent on feeding their eyes without stint to-day, and turn out of sight amongst the streets, evidently working in the same direction. They, too, feel a special interest in this occasion. If Brother Thomas was to do honour to S. Dominic, Brother Bonaventure—of whose birth they had heard strange tales, who was ever tending the leper when he was not attending the schools, who had amongst them the reputation of a saint—was to maintain their credit as learned men, and to do honour to the seraphic S. Francis of Assisi. And if the other Orders had not so immediate an interest in the Public Act, they all must have felt that this day was their day, inasmuch as it was to inaugurate the solemn triumph of those fundamental principles on which their religious life depended. No wonder then that the children of S. Bernard, of S. Augustine, and of S. Norbert, that the black Benedictine and the gay Trinitarian, and even, perhaps, some lonely hermit attracted from his solitude by the din of the city—no wonder that all men who had abandoned earth for heaven should be astir this day, and that hundreds should be pressing in the same direction, following S. Francis and S. Dominic into the great hall of the Bishop's Palace. S. Martin's and S. Germain's, S. Victor's and Clairvaux, have emptied themselves into the busy streets of the city, and all seem animated by one dominant idea.

Nor were the great Orders alone in their interest in the coming pageant. Doubtless there was many a gallant knight and many a goodly citizen, many a thriving merchant and many a grasping Jew, many an honest artisan and bright minstrel and noisy *jongleur*, who would willingly throw himself into the motley stream which flowed steadily towards the Palace, feeling that his trouble would surely be well repaid before the day was done. As to the students themselves, crowds of them from the four great nations had hung charmed on the lips of Thomas of Aquino, when in times past he had poured forth his wealth of learning in the Convent of S. James's. His novelty of proof, his calm eloquence, his divine fire, his inimitable simplicity, had filled the schools as they had never been filled before, and the students had not forgotten it; and now, what would not be their joy, their curiosity and unfeigned delight, knowing that they were about to witness the great master make his solemn Act—to see him perform a *tour de force* in which he would be almost obliged to display (what he ever tried so modestly to conceal) the wide circumference of his knowledge, the matchless grace of his dialectical skill, and the full swing of his gigantic intelligence! Doubtless, on this day,

Sainte-Geneviève, Saint-Germain-l'Auxerrois, Saint-Nicolas-du-Louvre, Saint-Julien-le-Pauvre, and many other colleges besides, sent forth each its contingent of joyous students to take their places, if places they could contrive to find, in the large public room where the Faculties were assembling.

At length the great hall is full. On a raised position, in sight of the whole multitude, sit in their chairs the solemn and august authorities of the University—the highest exponents of learning in the then civilised world—decked out with the various robes representative of their office, and the different insignia of their several degrees. Bishops and Doctors of Divinity, Jurists and Canonists, Rectors and Provosts, Bachelors and Licentiates, heads of religious houses and Generals of Religious Orders, the secular element and the regular, the hood and the gown, all are represented here. There, at a convenient distance from them, yet full in the public gaze, is the chair, that centre of attraction, in which the Licentiate is to defend his thesis before the assembled fathers. On taking his place, he perceives that the authorities of the University are behind and partly around him, whilst below him moves a sea of eager faces and curious eyes—the bright, quick-witted audience, ever ready generously to applaud a brilliant pass, but still more ready, it must be owned, to catch the Licentiate tripping, and with noisy laughter and sharp and caustic words to afford merriment to the whole company at his expense.

To defend a wide field of theological and philosophical truth before such an assembly, and against the longest and keenest heads, and the most skilful and practised dialecticians—against the *élite* of every faculty—required a stout heart, a clear intellect, and an imperturbable coolness and self-possession.

But the Angelical had no cause for apprehension. Whatever his own humility may have thought, there was no man in Paris, Naples, Bologna, or Cologne who could have stood against him for one moment. The mastery of his genius alone would have protected him against the efforts of the keenest of antagonists. Besides, it was not simply with the power of a gifted man, but through the inspiration of the Spirit Himself, that he was about to address the meeting.

Some authors relate that before the Seraphic Franciscan and the Angelical Dominican began their defensions, a holy rivalry of modest courtesy took place between them. Thomas could not be brought to take precedence of Bonaventure; whilst Bonaventure of the Ordo Parvulorum—belonging to that society which called itself 'the least of all'—shrank from the thought of being foremost in accepting an honour which ought by right to be first conferred on a child of the chivalrous S. Dominic. What they were unable to arrange between themselves was settled for them by their friends. Since S. Bonaventure was older than the Angelical, it was determined that he should be the first to occupy the post of honour.

We can see him in imagination as, with modest self-possession, he advances to take up his position in the chair, feeling that the attention of that great assembly is concentrated upon him. He, too, has had his antecedents. Favourite child of the great Alexander of Hales and of Rochelle, he must already have earned a reputation for fiery eloquence, for scholastic lore, and for Platonic elevation of intelligence. Representing the sweet, soaring, passionate mysticism of the seraphic S. Francis, he knew how to control love's darting flames, and to bring theologic science to bear upon the highest aspirations of the heart. His intensely affectionate nature, his warm Italian fantasy, and his yearning love of the wounds of the Crucified; his tenderness and compassion to the suffering and the poor, and the poetical bent of his mystic mind, which made him love and defend Plato as a father,—all this, there is little doubt, had before this day stamped his true image on the plastic and appreciative mind of the Paris University.

Look at him as he sits there in the sight of all. If it resembled the picture drawn of him by Galesinius, the very appearance of that man—the dear familiar friend of the Angelical—must have caused for the moment a quickened beating in the hearts of those who beheld him for the first time. He is above the middle height, and of noble personal bearing; and, unlike most men of ascetic habits, his frame gives indications of strong health and a robust constitution. His garb is the brown picturesque costume of S. Francis, the tunic of coarse serge, the sharp-pointed hood, the white twisted cord, the wooden sandals. He is shaven, save a circle of hair over the ears, running around the head. His face is grave, yet so tender an expression beams forth from it that men, when they once come under its influence, are seized with a feeling of indescribable sympathy. There is one special mark upon him which seals a supernatural impress on the whole character of the man—his cheeks are furrowed with the courses made by frequent tears, springing from his burning love of the wounds of his Saviour. To live in those wounds, to make them his one meditation, was the joy of his life; and the flames of a burning compassion, and the fires of a consuming charity, raging within his soul, caused those waters to well up from his heart which were constantly gushing to his eyes and flowing in streams down his corrugated cheeks. Men did not see the furnace that was kindled within him; they only saw what others had perceived, in the days of Abelard, on the face of Bernard—signs of compassion and the marks of tears.

It was men of high character like him—men of large, loving, tender hearts; men of mighty, soaring aspirations, who knew no selfishness, no littleness; men lifted above the world—who were made to raise up earth and make it pure. Though perhaps the students in that hall—the Englishman and the Frenchman, the German, the Norman, and the Picard, the Burgundian and the Lombard, the Roman and the Sicilian, the Brabantine and the Fleming—did not realise that they were looking on a saint, still there is little doubt that there was neither boy nor man there present who was not impressed by Bonaventure, whose heart did not respond to his countenance or eye, and whose nerves were not touched by the accents of his voice. It is but the natural effects of love, and sacrifice, and high humility, to win and captivate the open heart of man.

What subject the Saint selected as his thesis history does not tell us; how he acquitted himself biographers do not relate. But it may be safely said that his lofty mind—which loved to soar with Anselm, and with Bernard, and with Denis—defended, with true Platonic subtlety and elevation, the thesis he advanced. There is little doubt that, when the occasion offered, he held his audience riveted by what Trithemius designates as his *flammantia verba*—his 'flaming words'—whilst he was borne along in the lucid course of his high argument.

After this beautiful mediæval figure, this seraphic friar, who eventually became a Prince, and then a Doctor of the Church, had been clothed with the insignia of his new degree, he was at once conducted to his place amongst the Masters of Divinity, thence to watch, with loving admiration, his dear familiar friend go through a trial similar to his own.

See him then, our great Angelical, as with calm and princely bearing he advances—a mighty-looking man, built on a larger scale than those who stand around him—and takes the seat just vacated by Bonaventure. His portrait as a boy has been sketched already. Now he has grown into the maturity of a man, and his grand physique has expanded into its perfect symmetry and manly strength, manifesting, even in his frame, as Tocco says, that exquisite combination of force with true proportion, which gave so majestic a balance to his mind. His countenance is pale with suffering, and his head is bald from intense and sustained mental application. Still, the placid serenity of his broad lofty brow, the deep gray light in his meditative eyes, his firm well-chiselled lips and fully defined jaw, the whole pose of that large splendid head, combining the manliness of the Roman with the refinement and delicacy of the Greek—impress the imagination with an indescribable sense of giant energy of intellect, of royal gentleness of heart, and untold tenacity of purpose. That sweet face reflects so exquisite a purity, that noble bust is cast in so imperial a mould, that the sculptor or the painter would be struck and arrested by it in a moment: the one would yearn to throw so classical a type into imperishable marble, and the other to transfer so much grandeur of contour and such delicacy of expression, so harmonious a fusion of spotlessness with majesty, of Southern loveliness with intellectual strength, to the enduring canvas.

Perhaps, too, the simple Dominican habit adds a charm to the grandeur of the picture. It seems, when worn by saints, to blot out all idea of mere sensual admiration; it carries the mind into a higher range of thought, and into a more elevated sphere, in which a beauty of a nobler sort finds its natural habitation—a loveliness which excludes all touch of carnal taint, and which, chastened by a flame of hallowed fire, seems to transform the coarseness of human clay into a vision of supernatural gracefulness and of illuminated purity.

Such, anyhow, must have been the impression produced by the 'Angel of the Schools.' And who at this hour would make so bold as to deny that, as he sat there in the midst, his majestic beauty fell upon the eyes and melted into the hearts of those who, Tocco says, could not look on him without loving him? Who does not perceive that all must have been drawn towards him? Men knew enough of him to be aware that he was supernaturally helped. The history of his youth was no secret at Paris. He had been known to cure in an instant a woman who had but touched the hem of his garment. The students themselves, ten years ago, had decided that he was inspired by the Holy Ghost. His torrents of tears, his frequent ecstasies, which increased as he grew older, his raptures, his liftings in the air, were talked of, and awfully remembered. Thus he appeared to them, as he sat there, not so much a citizen of earth as a friend and confidant of the Everlasting King, a high interpreter betwixt earth and heaven, an angelic man who kept Divine secrets, and was assisted by that mysterious power which issues from the upper world. Men were not startled in those days as they are in these by the unusual deeds and privileges of chosen men. They took God's work for granted. They believed what they saw; they did not pry, and test, and examine, and lose their souls. They got nearer the truth than we do. Their minds were not corroded by false science. Anyhow, the natural thought, the spontaneous feeling, of that vast concourse, when looking on the great Angelical as he began to unfold his thesis, was that he lived more amongst the secrets of the Unseen World than in the midst of men; and that he wielded, like a giant, the strength he gained from God, for the sake of perishing humanity. Love, awe, admiration, enthusiasm—these were awakened in the breasts of those in that assembly who had hearts to feel, and brains to reason withal.

And especially would it have been so on this occasion. The audience was ignorant of the supernatural instruction which the Angelical had received. Men did not know, as he sat there 'with the striking elegance of ease,' that in the dark night, amidst the shadows of the church, he had wept his heart out, prostrate before the altar. They were not aware of the fact, but for all that they were impressed by its effects. The supernatural power which was in him spoke to them. And when he began and gave out his thesis, with his deep commanding voice: 'Thou waterest the hills from Thy upper rooms: the earth shall be filled with the fruit of Thy work,' a tremor must have passed across every heart in the great concourse, and men must have looked at each other with awe, admiration, and an unconscious feeling of surprise.

The text was worthy of so great a master of theology, and he used it to advantage. He took a broad and lofty view, befitting the greatness of the occasion, and the learning of the Doctors. His whole plan lay clear before him. His central idea was Christ as the Redeemer and the Restorer of mankind. The 'eternal hills' represent the everlasting Church of God; the 'upper rooms' are the mansions of the blessed—the heavenly Jerusalem; and the 'waters' which are poured out from thence—the waters of the Paradise of God—are the supernatural graces and unctions which proceed from His life-giving Spirit. And as the mists and waters which fall upon high mountains unite, and break, and tumble through a thousand rents and fissures, working their way down, and forcing their way on, till they reach the spreading plain, clothing it with verdure, and fruitfulness, and colour; making it vocal with sheep and with cattle; filling it with fragrance and with flowers, with song of birds and with sunny life—so the streams of the Grace of God, descending on the Church, flow through the channels of the Seven great Sacraments of the New Dispensation, and carry into the parched clay of the souls of men elements of life and strength, of supernatural goodness and of Christian beauty, turning winter into spring-tide, and quickening that with life which before was dead.

Such is an outline of the subject which the Angelical had to develop and defend before the assembled University. It included the entire range of theology—it treated of God and man, and their relations. Of how he expanded it, how he spoke and looked, how he replied to the arguments adduced against him, his biographers say but little; still, enough has already been suggested to convince the reader that he was gifted with surpassing mastership, and that there was not a single man, in any one of the Faculties there assembled, who would have dared to measure his strength against him.

When he had made an end, amidst enthusiastic applause he was declared by acclamation worthy of the Doctorate in Theology, and was invested with the insignia of his office. The head of the theological faculty brings the Doctor's ring, and places it upon the finger of the Angelical, in token of his being espoused to 'Wisdom' as a Bride. Next, the Saint lays his right hand on a closed Bible, as a sign that he is master of the wisdom contained in the Sacred Books. Then one of the Doctors present advances, opens the Book, and delivers it over to him, saying: 'Accipe potestatem docendi ubique terrarum'—'Receive power to teach all nations.' The Angelical now rising, the authorities lead him between them to a seat ready prepared amongst the Masters in Divinity, and place him by the side of Bonaventure, with the words: 'Sede inter Doctores'—'Be seated amongst the Doctors.' After having received the ring, he now receives the cap. It is first placed upon his head, and then immediately removed with the words: 'Te discoöperio'—'I uncover thee'—as a mark that he is not to use the power to teach in his own name, but in the name of the Catholic Church, which alone is the guardian of the truth contained in the Sacred Scriptures. He is then invested with the cap once more; and there, in the august presence of the most learned assembly in the world, the great Prince of Theologians sits by the side of the seraphic Bonaventure, with all eyes fixed upon him, the ring sparkling on his hand, and the Doctor's cap encircling his placid brow—a type of the boundless power of supernatural eminence and of intellectual sway.

When this ceremony has ended, the meeting breaks up. The great Act has been accomplished. The hall is emptied by degrees. The streets hum again with a noisy crowd, and men retire to their ordinary occupations, their hearts soothed with tenderness and warmed with admiration, as they bear away, imprinted on their imaginations like a picture, the graceful and majestic image of the Angel of the Schools.

CHAPTER XIII.

THE POPES ON S. THOMAS.

It may easily be imagined by those who admit S. Thomas of Aquin to have been a blessed Saint and a great Doctor of the Church, that it is quite possible for a fervent admirer of his—one who has for any length of time lived upon his life—to grow gradually into an enthusiast, and to draw a picture of him which is to some extent coloured by warmth of imagination, and represents, at least in part, a perfection and a beauty which an unbiassed judge would not be able to detect in the original.

There is no question at all that such a danger exists in writing the biography of any heroic man. The spirit is drawn to him, and feels lifted and invigorated by him; his presence seems to cheer the heart, and to expand the higher powers of the soul; a familiarity and sweet friendship seems to have been commenced; and just as a true friend fights the battles of his friend, whilst each screens the other's faults, so the writer of a 'Life' may naturally be tempted to indulge the weakness of a similar generosity towards one who can say no word in his own defence, and whose fame and honour are treasures confided to his keeping.

Lest it should be thought that any degree of exaggeration attaches to the picture already drawn of the greatness and loveliness of the Angelical's mind and genius and character, it will perhaps be well to compare him with 'men of renown,' and bring forward the opinions of persons of the highest authority in the Church with regard to his position. He who confidently and thankfully follows the verdict of the most illuminated and most august of the Church's servants, indeed of the Church herself, and simply desires to throw that verdict into clear expression, and to adduce reason for its justice and its truth, will stand little chance of being ensnared into subjective views, or of being carried away by mere emotion.

When a Sovereign Pontiff bears public testimony to the greatness of any man, that testimony carries with it an especial weight. And when his utterance has to do with an eminent teacher; when he who is the shepherd of the flock points out the field, and declares it wholesome food and excellent, then his words, uttered within the limits of his own special illumination, carry with them a conclusiveness beyond those of all other men.

Bacon says that 'the mind is not like a plane mirror, which reflects the images of things exactly as they are; it is like a mirror of an uneven surface, which combines its own figure with the figures of the objects it represents.' And the remark is worthy of the sagacity of such a philosopher. Men are ever mixing their own subjective moods with the objective reality which they contemplate, and a partial distortion is the inevitable result. But if there are any classes of men who reflect the simple truth, and not themselves, those men are emphatically the Roman Pontiffs. Like great polished mirrors, they can be followed by the mind's eye, from Pius up to Peter, through the darkest portions of human history—receiving from above, and ever reflecting upon the world below, a four-fold ray: not that of the Tribe, or the Den, or the Forum, or the Theatre; but of the Good, the Beautiful, the True, and the Just. And perhaps their reflection has never been thrown upon the world with greater force than when the thick darkness which encompassed them seemed to lend, by its intensity, an additional lustre to their solitary shining. What then do the Popes, against whom in doctrine there is no appeal, say of the Angelical?

Pope Clement XII., in a Bull beginning with the words 'By the Word of God,' makes mention of fourteen Sovereign Pontiffs who, in solemn decrees, have passed magnificent eulogiums on the Angel of the Schools. It may be remembered in what terms Alexander IV. spoke of him to the Chancellor of the Paris University, when declaring him possessed, through the grace of God, of a treasure of heavenly wisdom. Urban IV. (1261) and Clement IV. (1267) made use of him as their greatest champion of truth. Gregory X. (1274), in calling him to assist, by his mature experience and theological ability, at the Council of Lyons, declared that the glory of his holiness and wisdom had already spread itself abroad widely in the Church of God. So far for those Sovereign Pontiffs who were contemporaries of the Saint, and who, through their own practical experience, had learned how mighty a power was invested in him.

But there are other mirrors which reflect with still greater brilliancy the form of truth. Take, for example, some of those Pontiffs who occupied the chair of Peter from the death of S. Thomas to his canonisation, that is to say, during a space of nine-and-forty years.

Innocent V. (1276), a man of high education and a Dominican, who had, as Professor at S. James's, lived in intimate familiarity with the Angelical, and who successively became Archbishop of Lyons, Cardinal Bishop of Ostia, and, finally, successor to Gregory X., reverenced him as the profoundest master of human thought. The works of S. Thomas were always in his hands. They were his one delight. He made an abridgment of them with his own pen. He defended them with vigour and warmth; cast his thoughts into the same mould, and studied to acquire their method and their style. Blessed Benedict XI. (1304), who was also a Dominican, a man in character similar in many ways to our Angelical—gentle, courteous, and refined, and who was beatified by his namesake Benedict XIV. —was in the habit of calling S. Thomas 'My Master' and 'My Doctor.' Pope John XXII. (1323), when some persons, referring to the canonisation of the Saint, ventured to suggest that his life had not been illustrated by numerous miracles, exclaimed: 'Tot fecit miracula, quot scripsit articulos'—that he had worked as many miracles as he had written Articles; and though this expression may be looked on as rhetorical, still it emphatically testifies to the high opinion which he entertained of the Angelical. His Holiness solemnly declared to Tocco himself (and we have Tocco's own testimony to the fact) that the knowledge of S. Thomas must have been miraculously acquired. 'He alone,' said the Holy Father, 'has cast greater light within the Church than all other Doctors taken together.' And again: 'A man would make greater progress in science were he to apply himself to the writings of S. Thomas for a single year, than he would were he to study the teachings of other Doctors during the whole course of his mortal life.'

These were not words uttered in private, or in the heat of generous enthusiasm; but gravely, and with caution. They were solemnly pronounced by the supreme judge of doctrine in full consistory; they were applauded by all the Cardinals; and they have since been confirmed by the express testimony of many Popes. And what the Holy Father had said in presence of the Sacred College, he afterwards, in a still more formal manner, promulgated to the Universal Church. In the Bull of canonisation, he declares that the Angelical could not have written what he did write without having received a special assistance from on high.

Clement VI. (1344), who is said to have been a man of profound learning, and (like S. Thomas) never to have forgotten anything he once had read, and to have had a singularly tender conscience, compares the teaching of the Angelical to the rays of the sun which light up the whole earth; or to a mighty spiritual sword, with which men of powerful arm can slash to pieces the vices and errors of the world. He declared that the works of the Angelical never ceased to bring forth to the Universal Church all manner of useful fruits.

Innocent VI. (1360) is said to have declared that, with the exception of the Sacred Scriptures, the teachings of S. Thomas surpass all others in choice of language, in method of expression, and in accuracy of doctrine; so that he who makes them his own is never found slipping, whilst he who calls them in question, *ipso facto* lays himself open to suspicion always. Urban V. (1368), who was a man of princely mind, declared that S. Thomas had illuminated the whole Church by his works, which were filled with light and with truth. He addressed a Bull to the Archbishop, the University, and the faithful of Toulouse, and especially to the Professors, exhorting them to imitate the virtues of the Saint, and to replenish themselves with his loving spirit. 'Calling to mind,' says the Pontiff, 'that he who has been endowed with such profound knowledge by God, has enlightened the Order of Friars Preachers, and the Universal Church; and that, following in the footsteps of S. Augustine, he has enriched the same Church with a store of erudition; we wish and enjoin you, according to the spirit of these presents, to follow the teaching of the said Br. Thomas, as being true and Catholic, and to use all your endeavours to make it more and more widely known.'

So far for the fourteenth century. In the fifteenth, Nicholas V. (1451), who lived in the days of the great restoration of learning, and who was one of the most active founders of the Vatican Library, declared, in a Brief to the Dominicans of Toulouse, that the whole Universal Church was illuminated by the teaching of S. Thomas. Pope Pius IV. (1564), speaking to the University of Salamanca, which held the Angelical in highest estimation, refers to the precious fruit which the Church of God has derived, and every day still continues to derive, from 'the heavenly doctrine of so great a Doctor.'

At the risk of wearing out the reader, I have brought forward these clear testimonies of the supreme authority in the Church, respecting the position and merits of S. Thomas of Aquino. The Sovereign Pontiffs are placed too high, and sweep with too wide a range the plane of theological teaching, to be seduced by party bias, or by mere subjective feeling. Their voice is unmistakable. From the time when the Angelical, as a boy, stood, with his mother and his two rough soldier-brothers, before the Holy Father and his assembled court, and begged to be permitted to follow Christ in poverty, and to live unknown—from Innocent IV. to Benedict XIII., we find one Sovereign Pontiff echoing the voice of the other, the voice becoming clearer and the echo more articulate as it approaches the present day. The gentle boy, so serenely explaining the high heroism of his heart, becomes 'the Prince of Theologians,' the 'Angel of the Schools,' 'another Solomon,' 'the glory of his Order and the ornament of the Church,' 'a Sun illuminating the Universal Church,' 'a mighty Sword dividing heresies,' 'a master and guide in Christian doctrine,' 'exempt from all errors,' 'more brilliant than the sun,' 'ranking with S. Gregory, S. Ambrose, S. Augustine, and S. Jerome;' 'who himself alone has cast a greater illumination on the Church than all other Doctors taken together,' and 'from whose teaching greater advantage may be gained in one year, than would be derived from the writings of any other teachers were they to be studied during an entire lifetime.'

What the Popes have taught, Councils have confirmed. Pope Clement XII. tells us how his teachings have been held in reverence by Œcumenical Councils. Pope Gregory X. looked upon the Saint as the great Latin champion against the Greeks. The learned Cardinal de Cusa was no less favourable to the Saint. He was sent by Pope Nicholas V. into Germany to revive the ecclesiastical spirit of the clergy. He presided as Papal Legate at a Council held at Cologne in 1452. And his view of the best method of effecting his purpose is intimately bound up with the reputation of S. Thomas. He strongly and emphatically recommended the teachings of the Saint. 'We approve and highly esteem,' says the Council, filled with his spirit, 'the teachings of S. Thomas on the Faith and the Sacraments; and we wish and desire them to be read in diocesan synods; and moreover we order all those having the cure of souls to keep at hand, and deeply to study, that portion of the *Summa* which treats of the Holy Sacraments.'

Nor did lapse of time seem to diminish, it appears rather to have increased, the influence of the Angelical. The power of his mind over the Council of Trent (1545-1563) can hardly be exaggerated. And indeed that great Œcumenical Synod, if it is not fanciful to say so, seems to hold amongst the Councils a place analogous to that which the *Summa Theologica* holds in relation to the teachings which preceded it. As the Angelical, with his singularly architectonic mind, appears in his great scientific work to sum up into one all the theology that went before him; so in the Council of Trent we find a synthesis of all the preceding Councils; a masterly summary of all those definitions which had distinctly drawn the line where error was endeavouring to fuse itself with truth—a line which, whilst it encircled round the faith, served to point out the impertinent encroachments of mere human ingenuity. If the Council of Florence is to be considered the summary of Eastern Councils, Trent, surely, is the summary of all. Nicæa, Ephesus, and Lateran, Orange, Vienne, and Toledo, are represented here, and are confirmed. It was the beginning of a new era. The world had sunk into something resembling a spiritual lethargy. Spain and Portugal had become benumbed by material prosperity and commercial rivalries. England was in the arms of heresy and schism. Germany had sent forth its flight of spiritual locusts, which threatened to eat up the fair fields of genuine Christianity. The human element in the Church herself required cleansing and elevating. A new enemy had to be confronted. The supreme authority itself was called into question, and was denied. And thus during eighteen long years, with many interruptions, did the Church labour at her gigantic work, collecting her powers together to meet the world, and preparing herself to issue forth refreshed on her great career of regeneration! For three hundred years the Council of Trent has given rule to the Universal Church; and the Œcumenical Council of the Vatican merely completes a work which was initiated then.

And in fact the ruling minds at Trent were those which had been moulded by the great principles embedded in the *Summa*. The spirit of S. Thomas lived in its Sessions, and seems to have formulated its Decrees. There is a completeness, an unity, a scientific proportion about them, which speak emphatically of the mind of the Angelical.

And there are not wanting weighty witnesses to testify to the influence he exerted there. His Eminence Cardinal Vincent Justiniani, who assisted at the Council, calls the Angelical 'the Oracle of the Fathers.' Pope Pius V., who had been obliged, from his position, to study deeply the action of the Council, affirms that its Decrees are evidences unmistakable of how the teaching of the Angelical was constructed for confronting heresies and dissipating errors. The eloquent Bossuet declares that, on the important question of Justification, the words of the Council of Trent are in reality simply a tissue formed from the writings of the Angel of the

Schools. Cardinal Baronius affirms that it would be a difficult task to throw into words the expressions of admiration which had been made use of by the Fathers of the Council when speaking of S. Thomas, or to recall all they had said with regard to the purity of his scientific teaching.

One fact vouches for itself, and speaks to the whole world. On the table of the Council were placed, conspicuously, three books: the Holy Scriptures, the Decrees of the Popes, and the *Summa Theologica* of S. Thomas.

The honour thus accorded to the *Summa* before the world was simply an external manifestation of the feeling of the Fathers. F. Camblat says that the theologians of the Council made a point of consulting it whenever any difficulty arose. The prelates never dared to come to any decision before they had learnt the mind of the Angel of the Schools, nor would they formulate a single Decree that was in any way at variance with his teaching.

A curious instance of this occurred in the twenty-first Session of the Council (July 6, 1562). At the very moment when the Decrees which had been prepared were about to be solemnly recited before the Fathers, and published in the Council, the Archbishop of Grenada suddenly stopped the whole proceeding. Some theologians wished to append to the first chapter certain views regarding Communion under both kinds, which he considered were opposed to the doctrines of S.

Thomas. This was too grave an objection to be carelessly passed by. The solemn order of the proceedings was interrupted. The *Summa* was called for. The passage referred to by the Archbishop was read out before the Fathers. The case seemed doubtful. They could not come to an agreement off-hand as to whether the Decree was in accordance with the mind of the Angelical or not. As the more prudent course, it was unanimously determined that its promulgation should be postponed to the twenty-second Session. In the mean time the difficulties were solved, and finally, two months later, the Decree was read, confirmed, and published in the precise form in which it has been committed to us. How different a spirit is this from that which animated the father of the Reformation! In the one case the greatest theologians pause, and bow to the teaching of a simple Doctor; in the other an apostate friar defies the Mother which gave him spiritual birth, and raises a revolt, of which he himself did not see the final issue.

What had been taught by the Popes, and had been sanctioned by the practice of Œcumenical Councils, was also taken up and insisted on by the great Universities.

Paris naturally takes the lead. Her Doctors, during the life of the Angelical, refer their disputes to him, and gratefully abide by his decision. At his death they weep and mourn his loss, as men who had been deprived of the joy of their hearts and the light of their eyes. The day-star was quenched which had shone so placidly, and yet with such radiance, in their theological heaven. Then, when his teaching was attacked, they defended it as one would the honour of a friend. Stephen II., Bishop of Paris, instructed by Pope John XXI., had censured, in 1277, two hundred and twenty-two propositions which had been advanced, in one way or other, by the Faculty of Arts. Some malicious men raised a cry that certain philosophical tenets of the Angelical were included in the condemnation. This was too much for the loyalty of the University. Bishop Stephen III. was induced, by the importunity of the Doctors, and by his own sense of justice, to issue a decree altogether clearing the theological character of the Angelical. Indeed, it speaks of him in the highest terms of reverence and praise. He is called 'The most brilliant light of the Universal Church, the radiant gem of the clergy, the flower of Doctors, the most spotless and exalted mirror of our University of Paris: shining, with the effulgence of his life, teaching, and fame, like a resplendent morning star.' And the high reputation which he enjoyed at Paris appears to have remained undimmed during a long series of years. Cardinal du Perron, a man of high intelligence, declared in a public speech, in 1615, that 'the *Summa* of S. Thomas had always been looked upon as the oracle of theology, had always been publicly read, and (if it be permitted so to speak) had always been adored in the schools of Paris.'

The paramount influence acquired by the Thomistic system, especially amongst the Dominicans, can be imagined when it is remembered how vast a sway the Saint exerted over theologians, old as well as young, during his lifetime. Those men who had partaken of his spirit in the schools of Germany, Italy, and France, went forth, like the Apostles of old, full of new fire, bent on spreading far and wide the teachings of their master. Echard assures us that those who had studied under him in due course became professors at Oxford and Cambridge, at Bologna and at Cologne, at Naples and at Rome; and that they were in the habit of drawing all their teaching from the writings of their common master.

It would take a large book to contain the high praises which have been poured out upon the Angelical by theologians, literary men, and saints. His fame is so great, he towers so unmistakably over all others, that not envy itself, no, not even the blindness of bigotry and passion, can deny to him the first rank amongst the scientific theologians of the Church. Simply as specimens a few names shall be recorded, that the reader may clearly perceive how deeply the same impression was sealed upon minds of entirely dissimilar character—upon men of altogether different, indeed of hostile, habits and convictions. The shrewd and sweet S. Philip Neri used the teaching of S. Thomas as his guide, and consulted the Angelical in all his doubts. Pope S. Pius V., S. Charles Borromeo, S. Francis of Sales, S. Vincent Ferrer, S. Antoninus, and more than can be mentioned, looked upon it as an exceptional privilege to have been trained in his school. Pico of

Mirandola, a prodigy of science and the most brilliant scholar of his age, read with avidity whatever was written in defence of the Angelical, and declared the study of his writings to be his one delight. Cardinal Bessarion, a man of splendid and solid learning, is said to have declared that S. Thomas was not only the most saintly amongst the learned, but also the most learned amongst the saints. Cardinal Osius calls him the light and torch of Catholic theology; Baronius, the theologian *par excellence*, and the 'Prince of Theologians;' Bellarmine says that his works are more brilliant than the sun. Cajetan and D'Aguirra speak with still higher eulogy. His own master, Albert, calls him *Flos et decus mundi*, the flower and ornament of the earth. Cardinal Toletus does not shrink from saying that he who has S. Thomas may dispense with all other Doctors. Cardinal Pallavicino, and Gennadius, the Patriarch of Constantinople, speak of him with the profoundest reverence. F. Labbe, the Jesuit, says: 'Thomas Angelus erat, antequam esset Doctor Angelicus'—'Thomas was an Angel before he was an Angelic Doctor;' Suarez, that he surpasses all the scholastics in his explanation of the mysteries of faith, and that he ranks with the first Fathers of the Church.

Then, in England, Fisher, Bishop of Rochester, made use of him in combating Luther; whilst Henry VIII., before he was delivered over to a reprobate sense, had undertaken to write with his own hand an apology for the Saint.

Erasmus, perhaps one of the most critical and fastidious scholars who ever used his great talents against the Church, declared that he was acquainted with no theologian whose diligence was so great, whose judgment was so sound, and whose doctrine was so solid as that of Thomas of Aquino.

And, as if merely human testimony were not enough, there is the testimony of our Lord Himself, who on three distinct occasions expressed His Divine approval of the teaching of the Saint, viz., at Paris, at Orvieto, and in the Chapel of S. Nicholas at Naples. And even those who refuse to believe in the miraculous, at all events will admit this much in evidence, that the Catholic world must have held the Angelical in the highest possible estimation, to have been drawn to invent or to imagine, in his honour, so solemn and unusual a confirmation.

Thus, then, to sum up, we have a series of eminent Sovereign Pontiffs recommending the teaching of the Saint in the highest terms; Councils echoing the words of Sovereign Pontiffs; Universities following the spirit of Councils; Religious Orders going with the rest; and a countless host of witnesses of every country, religion, and character, all declaring this one man to be unique in his own line—in a word the Prince of Theologians and the Angel of the Schools.

CHAPTER XV.

S. THOMAS AND THE FATHERS.

Now that the Angelical had been ranked amongst the Doctors of the University, he commenced to govern in the schools of S. James's as *regens primarius*. Here he would develop the delicate and difficult questions of theology. The Doctor having gone through an elaborate training himself, and having also had many years' practice in dialectical disputation, was ripe for descending into the depths of theological subtilty, and for bringing up and displaying before his wondering scholars the root of some far-creeping heresy, or the seed of some obscure spiritual malady—that element in a system of religion or philosophy which stamps it with a special character, and lends to its propagation a peculiar success. Or he might take up one minute point in philosophy—as a man might select a blade of grass or the wing of a gnat—and, by means of a careful analysis, display, through the microscopic powers of a keen and logical intelligence, the whole complication of its delicate construction. First one line of thought would be brought under observation, then another, and then a third and a fourth; next, various threads which appeared to intersect the main question, or to diverge from it, would be disentangled and explained; till, finally, by the application of a process of masterly synthesis, each several line would be drawn into its position and adjusted; so that what at first, in the eyes of a casual observer, appeared to be an insignificant and inorganic particle or atom lies mapped out before the wondering eye, like those webs spreading in the morning grass, when the dew still lies on the ground, and the fresh beam slopes across the meadows.

After the Angelical had lectured during the course of a year as *primarius regens*, he was obliged, in accordance with the laws of the University, to make way for another Professor. It was contrary to rule that any Master should teach in the same school for more than three years consecutively. The Saint, however, was fully occupied in matters concerning the interests of his Order. He was employed to preach the Lenten Sermons at S. James's. A month later he was summoned to Valenciennes. Here the General Chapter of the Dominicans was being held. One of the principal objects which the Fathers had in view was thoroughly to examine the studies, and to place them in the best possible state of efficiency. A Commission was formed to carry out this object. It was composed of the most prudent and most celebrated Dominicans of the schools, viz.: Albertus Magnus, Thomas of Aquino, Bonushomo, Florence of Gaul, and Peter of Tarantasia. These men soon set earnestly to work. They effected a complete reformation and reorganisation of the course. The result of their deliberations was drawn out at length in the Acts of the General Chapter of Valenciennes—the thirty-sixth since the foundation of the Order by S.

Dominic. Werner assures us that the influences of the change produced by this Commission are felt by the students in the Dominican schools to the present day.

But the University of Paris, which had been at one period so violently opposed to the Dominicans professing divinity at all, now that it had discovered how great a *prestige* the Angelical had given to the schools, implored him to return. The authorities said they were most desirous to set on one side the law which excluded him from the theologic chair, and that no time ought to be lost in his resuming his old position as a Doctor in the schools. The Saint complied with their request. He appeared once again in his former place. The crowds which had pressed around him before, and had, like the tide, receded at his departure, now he had come again, assembled in still greater throngs than ever. And thus he continued pouring out his matured wisdom, forming theologians, and building up the Church of God, until obedience summoned him away to other duties.

A man like S. Thomas could not continue lecturing for any length of time, in a great University town like Paris, without attracting notice, and multiplying fame. The Holy See, which had ever kept a watchful and cautious eye upon this great centre of intellectual activity, which never forgot the deeds of learned men, and which ever knew how to turn such men to the best account, summoned the Angelical to Rome. Whether this order was given by Pope Alexander IV. (1260), or by Urban IV., has never been clearly ascertained. One thing is certain, that the Roman Pontiff desired to have this prudent and mighty counsellor at his side. Where we find the Sovereign Pontiff, there we are sure to find the Angelical. Though he never omitted lecturing, still he continued with the Pope. Not only Rome, but Civitià Vecchia, Anagni, Viterbo, Perugia, and other cities of Italy, received the great theologian, and hung upon his lips. He preached in their churches, he taught in their schools. And thus, either at Paris, or Rome, or Bologna, or Naples, the great Angelical passed away his life, pouring out the golden stream of theologic lore, and silently, and with an heroic perseverance, working out one object, to the realisation of which, since his early youth, he seems to have dedicated his entire life.

There was nothing desultory in the career of the Angelical. The same wisdom which taught him as a boy to abandon the Abbey, and to join the Dominicans, taught him also how to turn his vocation to best account. An ordinary man might have made the same step without foreseeing or looking forward to the like results. But the early development of our Saint's judgment, and his talents, must be remembered.

Excepting the shock he suffered when driven from the great Abbey in early days, and the trials of his vocation, and the annoyance given him by the tumultuous friends of William of S. Amour, his career had been one of peace, contemplation, and uneventful labour in the schools. From the period of his imprisonment at San Giovanni, where he learnt to love the Scriptures, the Stagyrite, and the *Sentences*, till he was raised to the honours of the Doctorate, it may be said, without exaggeration, that his life had been one uninterrupted *curriculum* of study. And then again, from the time he received his Doctor's cap, till he gave himself up, weary and broken, into the hands of S. Benedict, at Fossa Nuova, viz., during a period of about seventeen years, the whole energy of his vast mind was concentrated on deep problems and on intellectual pursuits, on fulfilling that exalted mission which Providence had called upon him to accomplish.

It is scarcely probable that the Angelical left the Benedictines merely to become a Dominican Professor. It is scarcely probable that the *Summa* was a simple after-thought. Whether the Saint was blindly led by Providence, or whether his one great work broke upon him by degrees, we have no means of ascertaining with absolute certainty.

Yet his history, from the very first, points directly to the issue of his life. His course was straight and direct towards one point. Had he possessed, as I feel inclined to think he did possess, an intuition of the future, his preparation for it could not have been more complete. Does not the 'Quid esset Deus?' of his boyhood ask a question which is answered in the *Summa* of his declining age? The very books found in his prison form the broad basis of his greatest work: the

Bible—Revelation; the Lombard—Tradition and the Fathers; Aristotle—Reason. These master-works he is said to have got by heart, or at all events so thoroughly to have grasped, as to have been completely imbued with their spirit and their force. Next we find him studying under Albert the Great, at Cologne, at Paris, then at Cologne again, and at Paris once more. His superiors had discovered the quality of his genius. The versatility, wide information, and many-sided energy of Albert, were brought to bear upon the formation of his character and mind. Unquestionably he had had many an anxious discussion with his master, not only on deep subjects of theology, but also on what was beginning to occupy men's minds—on vast systems and profound methods of organising truth. It would seem almost impossible for a mind like the Angelical's to grasp the *Sentences*, and to comment on them, without being carried beyond the steady, yet narrow and somewhat unscientific, process of their author. If the Lombard had done so much—had raised a breakwater against the rising tide of rationalism and irreverence, could not the highest gifts of reason be turned round in the service of the Church? could not irreverence be shown to be irrational; and the fundamental virtues and graces of a Christian heart to be simply the most perfect development of the noblest moral gifts of man? Could the Angelical possibly have known all he did know, and have lived under the influences which were brought to bear upon him, without feeling a solemn call to sacrifice his life in the prosecution of a vocation worthy of his exceptional abilities?

The hand of Providence, the dispositions of superiors, the circumstances of his life, the very subjects which he taught, the points on which he wrote—all concentrate, like the rays of light on a burning-glass, upon the one great achievement of his life, upon the *Summa Theologica*.

This *Summa* was the destiny of the Angelical. As naturalists assure us that there are creatures whose one simple end in life is to produce another life, and having accomplished that, to die; so, in a measure, was it with our great Angelical. He seems to have been born into this world to achieve one masterful work, to erect his mighty acropolis, and then to be called away. The *Summa Theologica*, though written quickly, and at the end of his career, was his one life's labour. It was his great legacy to humanity. It absorbed all his powers, and used up all his knowledge, and employed all the breadth of his vast mind, and all the illumination of grace, accompanied by a pure and abstracted life, to produce that one result.

What are all his other labours but preparations for this *opus summum?* Without such an explanation, his writings become confused and unmeaning fragments, the scattered fruits of intense thought and study, without any appropriate end. If a man goes abroad, and comes upon a heap of stones here, a column there, here a capital, there the portion of a roof, with wood and quarried work, and tiles, and slabs, and sashes, and all the ordinary signs of building—he at once perceives that these materials, though different in kind, are destined to take their place in giving unity to one grand conception; and if, after a time, he returns and finds some splendid pile there, and recognises in its walls, and roof, and shafts, and capitals, the materials he had before seen scattered on the ground, does he not take for granted that the preparation he had seen was the result of careful calculation; and that the architect, before he had given out a single drawing, had thoroughly matured his entire plan;—that he had a distinct scope in view, and was steadily working towards it; that each board and stone, each tile and frame, did not contain its meaning in itself, but alone could be interpreted when brought into relation with the general design? Would he not say, 'Those were the materials, this is the grand result'?

This is precisely the case with the Angelical. Take all his works, his *Catena Aurea*, his *Commentary* on the Lombard, his *Quodlibeta*, his *Quæstiones Disputatæ*, his *Contra Gentiles*, his *Compendium of Theology*, even his very first brochures, as well as his voluminous writings on Aristotle and on the Gospels, on Job and on S. Paul —take whatever he has written as it lies scattered up and down his life, whether it come under Revelation, Tradition, or Reason, whether it be the foundation, or the columns, or the buttresses, and you will recognise it, though it may be cast in a different form, as occupying its place in the vast creation of the *Summa Theologica*. So true is this, that those who succeeded this great architect were enabled, from the materials which he himself had drawn together, to complete the edifice which he had left unfinished.

Combining the parts is the smallest labour of a great architectonic work. Genius lies, first, in conceiving the entire plan; then, in collecting material in sufficient quantity; and, finally, in fashioning each separate portion into shape. When this has been accomplished, then the work is all but ended. The *Summa* was written in a few years; the preparation for writing it occupied an entire lifetime of uninterrupted thought and study.

What, then, it will be asked, is this *Summa Theologica?* It is the Christian religion thrown into scientific form, and the orderly exposition of what a man should be. The Angelical had studied the mind of the Church. In as far as is given to man he had mastered that Divine intelligence. And just as a Carlo Dolce would pore over some beautiful face, with its sweet modest expression, with its delicate colouring, with its soft-rounded features; just as he would note every shade and tint, to the light living in the eye, and the curve playing on the lips; just as he would photograph all this upon his imagination, and then, with inimitable tenderness and skill, reproduce it upon the glowing canvas—so with the Angelical. He spent his days in the study of the lineaments and expression of the spotless Bride of Christ. To reproduce the likeness of her beauty was the labour of his life; his mind was in harmony with her gracefulness; for her radiance is not corporeal: it is the truth, goodness, and harmony of her high supernatural commission, which lends to her that loveliness which comes straight from the Eternal Throne.

The mind of the Church, unlike the simple face of a Madonna, is vast, deep, and difficult to grasp, on account of its awful oneness and sublime multiplicity. The Church's mind is reflected in her history; there is a human element in it, as well as a Divine. She has her great giants, who are born to her, who fight for her, who die away and are succeeded by others; whilst she, ever young, strong, and beautiful, sweeps on from age to age towards the revelation of her final glory. Unlike decaying and fickle man, her mind is ever one. As she advances, bleeding, out of the first tragic periods of her history, she unfolds her sympathies more and more. Her enemies maliciously strike at her, and her champions ward off the blow. Her voice, shrill as the bugle, speaks by the mouth of a glorious line of Pontiffs, who live and die, whilst the spirit which animates them goes on without a shadow of alteration or vicissitude. She holds in her hand the Book of the Revelation of the Supernatural Life; she appeals to the past as a confirmation of the present, and she fearlessly challenges her opponents to point out a flaw in her heavenly armour—one single seam through which the glittering point of human reason can penetrate and wound her. Her majesty, her grace, her radiant purity, the supernatural character of her whole intelligence and action, the tenderness of her mother's love—all is displayed to captivate the heart of man and to make it fit for heaven. The magic which springs with her elastic step, the beaming of her countenance, the sparkling of her eye—all tell of her Divine Original, of the triumph of a hundred victories, and of the glories of her supernatural crown.

To draw out her picture in such a way that men might understand it was the life's labour of our Saint. The *Summa Theologica* is, after all, but the scientific exposition of those principles which actuate her life, and lend to her entire being its supernatural loveliness.

The vastness of the preparation must correspond to the greatness of the work to be achieved. He who would build a mighty temple must sink foundations in proportion, must cut out massive columns, and must quarry for the walls. He who would give a transcript of the mind of the Universal Church must be prepared to prosecute studies proportionate to the immensity of such an undertaking.

What are the principal instruments necessary for grasping the Church's mind? Those very studies which the Angelical had engaged in from early youth. They are principally three: the study of Revelation—of the Old Law, and of the New Covenant; the study of Tradition, that is, of the teachings of the Fathers, the Sovereign Pontiffs, and the Councils of the Church; and finally, the study of that Intellectual Science, or

Philosophy, which shows the mind how these vast subjects, with all their various groups of truths and principles, can be set up in unity, like the human organism, which is in one sense many, though in another only one.

He who could thoroughly master this threefold matter, and discover that scientific form or organic structure which displays its mutual harmony and bearing; and through a spirit of supernatural purity could see the hidden things of the spirit; and through the clearness of the intellectual eye could intue the high truths of morality and religion—such a man, if gifted with transcendent ability, with opportunity and time, would be capable of constructing a *Summa Theologica*.

It would be a life's labour, it would be a saint's work, it would require all the reverence, love, purity, and adoration man could command, to bring his spirit into harmony with such a momentous subject. He should possess a genius of the supernatural order, and live away in the world unseen.

Thus it is evident that the career of the Angelical from the first, the bias of his mind, the labours he engaged in, and the whole direction of his studies, point him out as prepared by Providence for achieving a special work for the Church of God.

The very fact of its being impossible to determine whether or no the Saint had seen his way to the end from the beginning, throws all the greater interest on his life. If he were preparing from the first, and had stretched forth consciously from his youth towards the accomplishment of his vocation, then a flood of light is cast on the character of his intelligence. If, on the contrary, he were simply led like a little child by the grace of Christ, till his life-object broke upon him, then how marvellously the guidance of an Unseen Hand directed all his ways!

It is necessary at present thus to touch upon the *Summa Theologica* in general, to look upon it as it were from afar, as one might gaze on the distant Pyramids, in order to realise it sufficiently for the purpose in hand, though without being able, or deeming it necessary, to study it in detail. There it stands, a colossal monument for all time, witnessing by its vast outline alone to the labour, energy, and genius of him who set it in its place.

The fact of the *Summa* never having been completed, far from detracting from its greatness, seems to prove it all the more. It was too enormous for any one man to begin and to accomplish. Had the Saint wholly finished it, perhaps we should find it difficult to realise its immensity. Had those vast piles — those splendid cathedrals, with their shafts, and colonnades, and arches, and solemn shade, and blazoned glass; with their massive towers, pinnacles, and spires—been run up in a lifetime, as if by contract, we should think much more lightly of them than we do. But when the life's work remains unfinished, and the hand which began it has fallen into dust, then a certain sadness presses in upon the mind, and we look on the majestic fragment with tenderness, and wonder at it, and venerate that creative brain and skilful hand which have left a token witnessing to the power of man, whilst at the same time it proclaims his absolute dependence on a Being more mighty than himself. We do not think the less of the Angelical because he did not put the last stroke to the *Summa Theologica;* nor is the monument practically injured by remaining unfinished: for the end it was intended to accomplish it abundantly suffices. Though an outer work may have been omitted, the great central fortress, the real stronghold, the *secunda secundæ*, stands out bold, distinct, and complete.

It is this work which fixes the Angelical as the great champion of the Church. It was for this that he was numbered by Pope Pius V. amongst the Doctors. And the very act of ranking him amongst them suggests a comparison to the mind. All are glorious and great, but each in his own special line: each did his particular service; each earned his own dazzling crown; each showed his valour, or his fortitude, or his political ability, or his eloquence, or his scientific intuition; each stands on the steps of the throne of the Immortal Queen, closer to her and more honourably placed than many others over whose heads circles the aureola. What was their office? How did they differ? How does the Angelical stand in their regard? What had they to do with his renown?

That the columnal Fathers and Doctors of the Church had an immense influence upon the mind and works of this great luminary of the Church is clear and unquestionable. How did he acquire so perfect and delicate an appreciation of the Church's spirit unless by coming in contact with those who were her trusty servants, who had stood by her in days of storm, and had, when the occasion demanded, poured out the red stream of their lives in her defence? Did he not hearken to their words, reverence all they said, feed his mind upon their thoughts, cherish them tenderly, and bind them in spirit to his heart as the noblest and fairest creations of Divine omnipotence? Is not the *Summa Theologica* tesselated with their gem-like sayings? and does not the Angel of the Schools, with that sweet modesty which is attached to genius, turn and shape his thoughts with their assistance? Without their steady guidance how could even he have found his way through the labyrinths and obscurities of the Sacred Scriptures? Without them what could he have known of the chequered history of the Church, of her adversaries, her combats, and her victories? Yes, because they have one and all, Athanasius, and Basil, and Chrysostom, and Jerome, and Augustine, and Ambrose, as well as Nazianzus and Pope Gregory, in their place and measure, in East and West, established, confirmed, expanded, consolidated, as well as witnessed to the undeviating doctrines of the Church; therefore is it that, in looking at the *Summa Theologica*, we can recognise a pillar from Alexandria, a capital from Constantinople, marble from Bethlehem, concrete from Hippo, bases from Cappadocia, ornaments from Milan, and foundation-stones from Rome. Had not the Angelical possessed that priceless gift of assimilating to his own plastic mind, by a certain spontaneous attraction, anything and everything which chimed in harmony with the Church's consciousness, and which illustrated her spotless life, he would never have been the bright and shining light that he is, or have exhibited in his prolific writings so preëminently that philosophic, patristic, and scientifically Catholic spirit which is displayed in his wonderful works.

CHAPTER XVI.

TRADITION AND SCRIPTURE.

THE Fathers lived in times of war and struggle, and 'bore the brunt of the conversion of the world:' the Angelical in days of peace. They were athletes of the Cross: he was the great thinker of the Church. They flourished—the larger portion of them—when the earth was still poisoned by the breath of paganism: he after the Church had planted her victorious banner on nearly all the citadels of the world. They had drunk in the civilisation of pagan Greece or Rome together with their Christianity: he had been educated from tender infancy in the midst of the very metropolis of Christian culture, and had passed his calm career amongst the purest traditions and examples of the civilisation of the Cross. They had gained experience, a rude experience some of them, of the cruelties and horrors of the old-world religion : he had tasted none of this, hidden away as he was with Christ in God under the gentle sway of perfectly-developed monastic life, finding his sweetest meditation and tranquillity in the highest empyrean of thought. And thus it was that he had time to erect a master-edifice, and, through his deep acquaintance with the technical systematic form of scholastic teaching, to plan a mighty scheme, of which the patristic labours were to furnish the materials. Living in the thirteenth century, he garnered into his mind all the advances made in theologic method during many centuries, as well as the best thoughts of the *maxima mortalium ingenia;* and through his synthetic genius welded into one splendid unity the combined teaching of the past, which he expanded, harmonised, and rendered perfect by means of exquisite Aristotelic drill, and Platonic height and width of discipline.

The columnal Fathers and the Angelical were in completest harmony: they were knit together by the monastic principle. The intellectual hinges of the Universal Church (speaking humanly) have been monastic men—that is to say, men who, through an intense cross-worship and a keen perception of the beautiful, threw up all for Christ; and through

> 'The ingrained instinct of old reverence,
> The holy habit of obediency,'

loved, laboured, suffered for Him, and died falling into His Arms.

For the one thread which pierces through all, and maintains a real communication between the Angelical and the heroes of the classic age—which creates a brotherhood between S. Thomas of the thirteenth century and the great athletes in the second and the third—which makes the 'Sun of the Church' illuminate the 'Pillar of the World,' and so reciprocally—that is to say, which renders S. Thomas and S. Anthony one in spirit and in principle, was this, that their beings were transformed into a supernatural activity, through an intense and personal love of their Redeemer.

This was the one special lesson which the Angelical drew from the wilderness and the Fathers, which came to him through S. Benedict indeed, but rather as a principle of *quies* than of exertion. In the desert athletes and those who followed them he found that principle operative, and almost military, in its chivalrous readiness to combat, and spill blood in defence of Truth. It lent to him what it exhibits in them also—breadth of view, largeness, moral freedom, stubborn courage, generosity of heart, expansion of mind, and an electric light of intellect, which bear about them a touch of the Eastern world. How could the Angelical read Anthony's life, or follow Athanasius in his exiles, or see Basil so heroically rigid in his defence of right, or hear in imagination Gregory Theologus pouring out his stream of polished eloquence, without being impressed by Truth's grace and music? How could he watch S. Chrysostom, all on fire with his love of God, and with his discriminating sympathy for men; or think of the ascetic Jerome, battling single-handed in the wilderness, or perusing his Scripture in the cave; how could he dwell in spirit with S. Ambrose, or S. Gregory the Great, or follow the career of the passionate, emotional, splendid S. Augustine, without expanding in heart and mind towards all that is best and greatest, all that is most noble and most fair, in the majestic character of God's tenderly-cherished saints?

Had he not known them so intimately, great as he was, his mind would have been comparatively cramped; his character most probably would have been less imperial in its mould, and there would have been less of that Oriental mightiness about his intellectual creations, which now reminds one of those vast monuments of other days, which still are the marvel of travellers in the East and the despair of modern engineers. The great Christ-principle is essentially creative of enormous consequences: no man has ever bent down to worship Him intensely, who has not been lifted up to carry out some master-work in himself or in another. Here then, at last, we have in their completeness the great informing principles of the character of the Angelical. The contemplative principle of *quies* at Cassino, manifesting itself in love, reverence, purity, and adoration; the principle of activity at S. James's, analytical, inquisitive, polemical, technical; and the principle of operative love through a personal friendship with the Word Incarnate, which is the life-spirit of the Solitaries of the desert, and the soul-power of the Fathers of the Church. Thus the Angelical is essentially contemplative—so he is monastic; he is essentially logical—so he is scholastic; and he is essentially large, pure, and operative, through a motive of personal friendship—and therefore he is essentially patristic. S. Benedict, S. Dominic, and S. Augustine,—contemplation, dialectics, and energising charity,—these are the three great elements which make up and explain the full character of the Angel of the Schools.

And if the influence of the Fathers on the moral build of the Angelical was great, not less remarkable was their influence upon him as a theologian. A master-mind like his would naturally seek first sources. Albertus Magnus and the teachings of the Lombard would simply lead him to the great reservoirs themselves. From his Commentary on the *Sentences*, indeed from his *Opusculum* on the Angels, to the last words he wrote of the *Summa Theologica*, his intimate acquaintance with the great Fathers and Doctors who preceded him, comes out almost in every page. If he does not mention them by name he is often merely reproducing their thoughts and establishing their principles. He appears to possess all their breadth of view and power of compassing a complicated subject; he is endowed with the genius of assimilating their theologic tone, and of drawing from them, and making part of the furniture of his own mind, those traditionary elements of knowledge which are closely connected with the

Church. He recognises their entire weight, he perceives the full bearing of their teaching, and seems to feel profoundly that depth, breadth, and stability are principally to be acquired—not so much by his own originality, as by thoroughly mastering, not merely the general tendencies, but the specialities, the genius, and the character of each separate individual. He appears, indeed, to have an intimate and personal acquaintance with each one of these classic masters of Catholic thought, and, so far as can be done by man, to have absorbed into his own system, and then to have reproduced that which was most admirable in each of them. S. Jerome and S. Chrysostom in Holy Scripture; S. Athanasius, S. Basil, and S. Gregory Theologus in dogma; S. Ambrose and S. Gregory the Great in moral disquisition; —each of these, in fact, in his own special line, has his share in the formation of the Angel of the Schools.

Then, just as Aristotle may be looked upon as representing the bloom and flower of Greek philosophy, as Dante summed up the whole knowledge of his day in the *Divina Commedia*, so S. Augustine stands as the ripe fruit of the great patristic tree, as the representative of the classic learning of East and West.

As the Angelical professed S. Augustine's Rule, so also he imbibed his spirit. S. Augustine forms the pedestal upon which stands the graceful figure of the *Summa Theologica*.

Indeed, the wealth of dogmatic and moral teaching drawn from the columnal Fathers as a body, and enshrined in the *Summa Theologica* alone, is prodigious; but perhaps the best and easiest test of the Angelical's marvellous acquaintance with their writings and their style is to be found in the *Catena Aurea* on the Gospels. If the Fathers were great in their display of self, the Angelical was no less great in his divine self-repression. Indeed his life may be said to have been a steady progress towards the Beatific Vision. As he advanced in years he also advanced in union, so that the latter portion of his career may almost be said to have been passed in heaven. Science and religion were as the steps of the ladder of his perfection; he knew that there could be little progress in love without contemplation, and that the 'Science of the Saints' is principally acquired through an intimate conjunction of the intelligence with the fount of illumination. He let the visible world go its way, and he went his: as long as he was permitted to dwell in the Spiritual Kingdom he was well content. Life was simply bearable because by means of it he was enabled to make his footing sure in his advance into the Admirable Light.

On one occasion, when he was staying at the Convent at Bologna, he manifested in a most remarkable manner the abiding temper of his mind. A Procurator had been nominated, who was a stranger to the city, and was neither personally acquainted with S. Thomas nor with the other friars of the convent. He had occasion to go shopping, and required some one to accompany him, and carry the provisions. He requested the Prior to appoint a person to fulfil that duty, and he was told to summon to his assistance the first friar that he met. Now it so happened that the very first person he saw, on descending from the Prior's cell, was the Angel of the Schools. Not dreaming who he was, the Procurator sharply told him, in the Prior's name, to take the basket and follow him briskly into the street. Without a word, the Angelical put the basket on his shoulder, and went after the Procurator, who was hurrying on in front. But, suffering as he was at the time from a weakness in his leg, the Saint found it almost impossible to keep pace with his new Superior; upon which, the Procurator turned upon him and rated him roundly for a lazy fellow, who was more burden than profit to the community, and who should show more zeal in the service of religion. This scene was witnessed by several citizens who happened to be passing at the time, and they were highly scandalised and amazed at beholding the greatest theologian of the day treated with so little courtesy, and set to do such menial service. They at once expostulated with the Procurator, and expressed their indignation that Brother Thomas of Aquino, the great luminary of the schools, should receive such scant respect. On hearing the words, 'Brother Thomas of Aquino,' the Procurator looked as if he had been stabbed. He at once threw himself on his knees before the Angelical, and with sobs and tears implored to be forgiven. The Saint said gently in reply, that he was simply carrying out the orders of obedience, and that it was he himself who should by right beg pardon, since he had not been as active as he ought to have been in keeping pace with the movements of the Procurator. To him the voice of authority was simply the Voice of Christ: it mattered nothing to a man of his intelligence what the order was, provided he knew the Source from whence it came.

It is not surprising that a man so completely absorbed in the world of supernatural perfection should day by day live more and more in heaven. He was often lifted up in ecstasy—for instance, during Mass. On one occasion this happened at Naples, in the presence of many gentlemen of the city; and for so long a time was he carried away, that, lest the Mass should be interrupted wholly, one of the friars who were present was obliged to go to him at the altar, and bring him to himself. The Saint had good reason to have recourse to the Origin of all truth and wisdom. Whenever he had a doubt about his teaching, he sought and gained light from Heaven. Thus he was enabled to explain a most difficult passage of S. Paul. On another occasion, in the course of his Exposition, he came across a most obscure sentence in Isaias. He used all the force of his thought, and all the breadth of his reading, to bring light out of the darkness: but without avail. Then he set himself to fast and pray for several days. One night, during this period of supplication, Reginald, the *socius* of the Saint, whose cell was contiguous to that of his master, heard voices speaking, and amongst them that

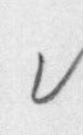

of the Angel of the Schools. He was greatly astonished at this, since he knew for certain that S. Thomas had gone to his room alone, and had closed the latch. Reginald went to the door and listened attentively; there was no mistake: he distinctly heard a voice telling S. Thomas to write, and then, as if reading from a book, the same voice dictated an exposition on that obscure passage of Isaias. Next day, Reginald threw himself at his master's feet, and implored him for the love of God to say who had been speaking to him in the night. The Saint was filled with confusion by this request; and it was only after Reginald had solemnly sworn to keep the secret as long as his master was alive, that the Angelical informed him that our Lord had heard his prayer, and sent S. Peter and S. Paul to expound to him the true meaning of the obscure portion of the prophecy.

Then he was frequently seen lifted up in the air in ecstasy, in the church of S. Dominic, in Naples. Reginald saw him thus in the church of S. Maria della Porta, in Salerno. But the most memorable occurrence was witnessed by Fra Domenico di Caserta at Naples. The Angelical was in the habit of praying in the church before the night-matins, and the friars of the convent were aware that our Lord accorded many privileges to him. Fra Domenico had a great curiosity to witness the Angelical enjoying these spiritual favours; and to this end hid himself in the church at night to watch S. Thomas whilst at prayer. The Saint, as usual, when all had retired to rest, came into the church. Fra Domenico saw him advancing, till he came opposite a certain figure of our Lord hanging on the Cross, in the chapel of S. Nicholas, when he stood still; and then, being rapt in ecstasy, was lifted two cubits in the air before the crucifix, and so remained a considerable time. Whilst the Saint was thus entranced, Fra Domenico distinctly heard Christ's voice saying from the image: 'Well hast thou written of Me, Thomas. What reward wilt thou accept for thy labour?' To which the Angelical at once replied: 'No other than Thyself, O Lord!' Something of the same kind happened at Orvieto: the Angelical had composed the Office of the Blessed Sacrament; and whilst kneeling before a figure of Christ crucified, he offered to our Lord this labour of his love; and his Master in return graciously spoke to him from the Cross, and thanked him for the service he had performed in honour of the Blessed Eucharist. A still more remarkable event took place at Paris, which shows the immense authority the Saint possessed over the Masters of the University, as well as his intimate relationship with our Lord.

A great dispute had arisen amongst the Professors of the University with respect to the position of the 'accidents' of bread in the Blessed Sacrament. Warm and angry litigation took place upon this abstruse question, and the flame of controversy was lighted up throughout the various schools of the University. But the Doctors could come to no accommodation. Finally, it was suggested to lay the whole case before the great Angelical. This idea was taken up at once; and the whole University, with entire unanimity, agreed to abide by his decision, whatever it should be,—so great was the universal trust of those fiery and imperious Doctors in the profound learning and acuteness of the Angel of the Schools. The Saint at once gave himself to prayer and fasting; and this he continued several days. Then bending all the powers of his great mind to the solution of the problem, he wrote his opinion in full, stating all the objections, and clearly laying down his replies. Having done this, he called together the Prior and brethren of the convent, and they accompanied him to the high altar of the church where the Blessed Sacrament was kept; and then he knelt in their presence before the altar, and fervently prayed our Lord to show him some sign by which he might know if he had or had not unravelled the difficulty which had been proposed to him. After thus praying some little time, the whole community heard a voice distinctly saying from the tabernacle: 'Well hast thou written, Thomas, concerning this Sacrament; and well hast thou solved the problem—that is to say, in as far as it is possible for one to do so who still is prisoner in the flesh.'

Thus did the great Angelical converse with the other world; thus did he receive divine illuminations and favours in the great work upon which he was engaged. Supernatural love and supernatural knowledge went hand in hand, and gently led him to the highest summit of perfection—flooding his mind with light, and melting into his heart the charity of the Cross. There is none of the restlessness and uncertainty of mere human talent about him; all is calm, peaceful, and secure, like the summer world when it basks at noonday in the sunshine, sleeping and yet awake, and whilst absorbing the heat and light, displaying through their very influence a thousand varied splendours of flower and fruit, of shade and tint, of sweet scent and soothing melody, of tender mountain distance and rugged broken foreground,—of all that earth can offer as a tribute to the sun.

But it is time to return to the *Catena Aurea*, and to show the Angelical's deep acquaintance with the columnal Fathers of the Church.

'By a *Catena Patrum* is meant a string or series of passages selected from the writings of various Fathers, and arranged for the elucidation of some portion of Scripture, as the Psalms or the Gospels. *Catenas* seem to have originated in the short scholia or glosses which it was customary in MSS. of the Scriptures to introduce between the lines or on the margin, perhaps in imitation of the Scholiasts on the profane authors. These, as time went on, were gradually expanded, and passages from the Homilies or Sermons of the Fathers upon the same Scripture added to them.'

The *Catena Aurea* occupies, in the Parma edition of the Saint's works, two volumes of large quarto in double columns. The first volume contains one hundred and forty-four pages, and treats on the Gospels of S. Matthew and S. Mark; the second numbers four hundred and sixty-four pages, and embraces the Gospels of SS. Luke and John.

In this striking *Catena* the Angelical makes use of the authority of over eighty authors, from S. Ignatius Martyr to the monk Euthemius. S. Augustine, S. Hilary, Origen, S. Chrysostom, and S. Gregory the Great, seem to be favourites; whilst more recent writers, such as Rabanus Maurus and Remigius, together with the *Glosses*, are continually quoted.

Take the following as a specimen of the *Catena:*

'"*And the Word was with God.*" CHRYSOSTOM: Because it is an especial attribute of God, to be eternal and without a beginning, he laid this down first; then, lest any one on hearing *in the beginning was the Word* should suppose the Word Unbegotten, he instantly guarded against this; saying, *And the Word was with God.* HILARY: From the beginning He is with God, and though independent of time, is not independent of an author. BASIL: Again he repeats this *was*, because of men blasphemously saying, that there was a time when He was not. Where then was the Word? Illimitable things are not contained in space. Where was He then? With God. For neither is the Father bounded by place, nor the Son by aught circumscribing. ORIGEN: It is worth while noting, that whereas the Word is said to come [to be made] to some, as to Osee, Isaias, Jeremias, with God it is not made, as though it were not with Him before. But the Word having been always with Him, it is said, *and the Word was with God;* for from the beginning it was not separate from the Father. CHRYSOSTOM: He has not said, was *in* God, but was *with* God; exhibiting to us that eternity which He had in accordance with His Person. THEOPHYLACT; Sabellius is overthrown by this text.

For he asserts that the Father, Son, and Holy Ghost are one Person, Who sometimes appeared as the Father, sometimes as the Son, sometimes as the Holy Ghost. But he is manifestly confounded by this text, *and the Word was with God;* for here the Evangelist declares that the Son is one Person, God the Father another.'

This *Catena Aurea* may be regarded as a sort of *tour de force*, by which the Angelical's extraordinary mastery of the Fathers of the Church is made manifest. No test could be invented which would show more strikingly the depth and accuracy of his knowledge of the classics of theology. There were no books of reference—no dictionaries and encyclopædias in the days of the Angelical. The Saint had to study the originals themselves; and he did so with advantage. Each Father's special way of viewing a dogmatic or moral truth is seized by him; whilst the very style, in the condensation of the *Catena*, is artfully preserved. And so accurately does the Saint appear to appreciate and reproduce the native cast of thought of each writer, that one would be led to believe that he had had an intimate and personal acquaintance with the mind of each one of them. It seems to have been one of his singular gifts to be able to throw himself into the intellectual position of another, whether he were an adversary or a friend, and to bring out with startling clearness the views or arguments which he adopted. There is little doubt that the Saint had thoroughly mastered the minds of the great classic writers of the Church; and that the richness of his dogmatic and moral teaching, its solidity and security, are owing to his having possessed himself of all the deepest thoughts of the deepest thinkers of Catholic antiquity. His acquaintance with their doctrine and with their lives gives a stability and steadiness to the whole character of his theology, which attracts at the same time that it subdues the mind.

Indeed so masterfully does the Angelical fasten upon the peculiar note of each columnal Father and incorporate it into his *Catena*, that any theologian who took the pains to study this golden work would be able to form a fairly just estimate, not only of the method, but also of the special characteristic of each separate writer as he falls under observation. No more striking proof than this could be advanced of the Angelical's grasp of the lives and methods of the early saints.

Added to his keen perceptive powers and his extraordinary grasp, S. Thomas was endowed with a memory equally uncommon and remarkable. The *Catena* of the Four Gospels—the smooth continued flow of patristic quotation which makes up the entire work—appears to have issued direct from the chambers of his memory. The whole was written down, so Tocco says, from previous readings. In travelling from one convent to another, the Saint had spent some portion of his time in perusing the great Church authorities. What he once had read he never again forgot. And hence he was ready at any moment, through the activity of his association of ideas, to pour out the full wealth of his capacious mind, and flood the world with light. Then, besides the *Catena Aurea*, his *Commentary* on the Lombard, his *Contra Gentiles*, his *Expositions* on the Sacred Scriptures, all testify to his wide and intimate acquaintance with the intellects of the classic Fathers of the Church; the *Catena Aurea* simply brings this out in so startling a manner as to impress it with greater vividness upon the mind. But it is only by studying the work itself, and by comparing the quotations with the originals, that the discriminating powers of the Angelical can be fully realised. Had he not possessed this deep acquaintance with S. Athanasius, S. Basil, S. Gregory Theologus, S. Chrysostom, S. Jerome, S. Ambrose, S. Augustine, and Pope Gregory, he never would have been able to have built upon so deep and immovable a basis the splendid fabric of the *Summa Theologica*. The Angelical was a scholastic, but he was a scholastic who lived in the company of 'the ancient Saints.'

CHAPTER XVII.

S. THOMAS AND HOLY SCRIPTURE.

THE second of the three great studies to which S. Thomas devoted himself, preparatory to the scientific construction of the *Summa Theologica*, was the Sacred Scriptures. His mastery of the Inspired Word was no less remarkable than his wide and accurate knowledge of the Fathers.

Those who have mastered the Angelical's Expositions on the Sacred Text can well believe that he had learnt it off by heart when imprisoned at San Giovanni. It would seem almost an impossibility for one who had not done so to have made use of it as the Saint has done in the course of his various Expositions. His extraordinary gift of seeing analogies, and perhaps his still more remarkable readiness in illuminating Scripture by means of Scripture, the exuberant richness of his applications, and the facility with which he brings texts to bear from all parts of the Sacred Volume upon the point he has in hand, from the book of Genesis to the last chapter of S. John—all this speaks of the width of his reading, the marvellous retentiveness of his memory, and of that special genius he was endowed with of being able, as it were by one intuition, to grasp and look steadily upon vast fields of thought—losing nothing in his microscopic appreciation of the detail on account of his complete comprehension of the whole. What man has ever been gifted with the combination of so vast a memory and a mind so exquisitely logical—so overwhelming in the security and the severity of its processes of reasoning, and yet so full of mystic tenderness and deep poetic feeling?

The Saint's mastery of the traditionary teaching of the Church exhibits itself in all his Commentaries on Scripture. In his treatment of the Pauline Epistles, for instance, he so draws out the words of the Apostle as to illuminate the moral and dogmatic teaching of theology, and illustrates that teaching with such a prolific richness of allusion, with so many authorities from every portion of the Sacred Text, as to throw a new light upon and to give a fresh significance to the words of the Apostle. Then his statement of objections is so lucid; his solutions are so precise and often so ingenious; there is so much matchless simplicity combined with so powerful a logic, that the reader is both overpowered and fascinated as he proceeds—overpowered by the mental force which he continually encounters, and fascinated by the beauty of illustration, by the ingenuity of analogy, and by those sudden flashes of light produced by the juxtaposition of portions of Scripture, which at first sight, to the ordinary reader, appear to have no relation whatever with one another.

Perhaps of all the Expositions of the Angelical on the Sacred Text, that on the Epistle to the Romans is the most admirable. Its depth of thought, the singular clearness in which the teachings of tradition are laid down, and the general interest of the subject-matter lend to it a special charm. In the Commentary on Job, nature and history are used in the illumination of the Inspired Word; whilst in that on the Canticle of Canticles, the Saint finds himself in his own native element, as he traces the relationship between the Soul and the Beloved, and ascends into the highest regions of mystic union with God.

Let us now briefly consider in detail the labours of the Angelical on the Sacred Text. He expounded in the schools the Gospels of S. Matthew and S. John. We have his Commentary on the Epistles of S. Paul, on Job, on a portion of the Psalms, upon the Canticle of Canticles, and upon the Prophets Isaias and Jeremias. And if this is not enough to show the Saint's wide acquaintance with the Inspired Writings, the *Summa Theologica* may be referred to, which testifies to a deep mastery of many other portions of the Ancient Law.

The Exposition on S. Matthew's Gospel was taken down from the Saint's lips by his familiar disciple, Brother Peter Andrea, who studied under him when occupying the post of *Regens Primarius* in the school of S. James's. Any one comparing the first five chapters of the Commentary on S. John with any portion of that on S. Matthew will at once perceive a difference of style. The Treatise on S. Matthew, however, possesses this interest, namely, it shows the reader how accurately the students were able to follow their professors, and how little was lost through the *viva voce* method of the schools. To hear the living voice, and then to go through the labour of writing down the words of wisdom as they flowed fresh from the lips, must have greatly tended to fix truth within the mind. The student in this day was forced out of his position of being a mere passive recipient, and was, as it were, compelled to bring his own mind actively to bear upon the matter of the lecture.

The Exposition of S. Matthew occupies two hundred and seventy-seven pages of the Parma edition. Its division follows the twenty-eight chapters in the Gospel. The Prologue of S. Jerome is given at the commencement, as an *argumentum;* and upon this the Angelical makes a short comment. The first chapter of the Gospel is then given, and this is divided into a certain number of paragraphs. For instance, the first chapter contains six, the second four, the third two, and so of the rest. Following each Gospel chapter comes the Angelical's Exposition, which is thrown into numbers corresponding to the paragraphs of the Gospel chapter. By this means the Commentary on any portion of the matter in hand can be hit upon without difficulty; for the numerals of the paragraphs in the Gospel are made to correspond with those in the Exposition.

In this Commentary the traditional dogmatic and moral teaching of the Church is brought into full relief, not only by the Angelical's method of handling the text itself, but by the weight of patristic authority which he advances in its support. Here also he manifests his singular gift of marshalling an array of Scriptural quotations in support of the point he is elucidating, and of so placing various groups of truths as to make them shed a light upon each other.

The Gospel of S. Matthew, according to S. Thomas, is principally concerned with the humanity of Christ. He divides it into three portions. The first part treats of the coming of our Lord into the world; the second, of His progress through the world; and the third, of His out-going from the world. The reader who takes the trouble to study this Exposition will at once observe how great a tendency is manifested throughout its structure towards that unity of conception which was one of the Angelical's greatest gifts.

The Exposition on S. John's Gospel is of a considerably later date. The first five chapters were written out by the Saint's own hand. The remainder was dictated by him to his disciple, Reginald of Piperno; but was finally revised, corrected, and approved of by himself. This Gospel would perhaps be one of the fairest tests of the powers of the Angelical. Its subject-matter, especially the first portion, would elicit those exceptional gifts with which he had been endowed. Here the deepest philosophy, the most abstract metaphysical speculation, would be called into play, as well as the highest theories of religion, and the cardinal principles of contemplative life.

The entire Commentary occupies three hundred and sixty-five pages. It begins with a Prologue by the Saint, which is followed by that of S. Jerome, upon which the Angelical gives an Exposition. The Gospel of S. John contains twenty-one chapters. These chapters are subdivided, and upon each subdivision or *lectio* the Exposition is made. For instance, the first chapter contains sixteen *lectiones;* the second, three; the third, six; and so on. The whole Commentary bears upon it signs of great care in the composition, and the Prologue gives evidence of the greatness of the work which the Angelical must have felt he had before him.

Besides his Expositions on the Gospels, S. Thomas wrote fourteen Commentaries on the Epistles of S. Paul, which occupy seven hundred and ninety pages of the Parma edition. The method is much the same as that adopted in the previous Expositions. The Prologue, which introduces the whole subject, is in the Angelical's best manner. Each Epistle, however, besides this general one, has a Prologue to itself. The Epistles are commented on chapter by chapter, and are divided into *lectiones*, like the Expositions on S. Matthew. The Fathers are more seldom used than in the works on the Gospels; nor are heresies so prominently discussed. The Manichæans, however, form an exception, and possibly because they represented a phase of error which was excessively active in the thirteenth century. And though the Fathers are less frequently alluded to here than elsewhere—except perhaps in the Commentary on the Galatians—they are by no means overlooked. S. Athanasius, S. Jerome, S. Gregory, S. Isidore, S. Hilary the Damascene, as well as Haymo, Rabanus, Denis, Gelasius, Seneca, and the *Gloss*, are referred to from time to time. The *Magister* and the *Philosophus* are also made use of to confirm dogmatic or philosophical positions, as the case may be.

The Commentary on the Epistle to the Romans is the most important of the number, and occupies one hundred and fifty-six pages. The Saint's treatment of Original Sin; of Faith; of the Universality of the Gospel Preaching; of the difference between the Baptism of John and that of Christ; as well as his remarks on the Negative and Affirmative Precepts of the Law; on Scandal; and on the Generosity of Christ; are well worth careful perusal.

There are very many beautiful and instructive passages in the Exposition of the First Epistle to the Corinthians, for instance, on the words 'Were you baptised in the name of Paul?' on the preaching of the Gospel—'not in wisdom of speech;' on the spiritual man being the judge of all things, yet being judged by none himself. Then in the Sixth Lesson of the Seventh Chapter the Saint shows his ability in pointing out the fallacies in popular objections. The sharpness and incisiveness of the answer, the flow of quotation, the exhaustless power of illustration, affords great gratification to the mind. There are also some very interesting points spoken of in the Eleventh Chapter, regarding, for instance, the relation of man and wife; the veiling of women in the church; heretics; transubstantiation; vision (*visio imaginaria*); and so on through the Exposition. The Second Epistle to the Corinthians offers much matter for useful teaching. The Saint's treatment of the Son as perfect image of the Father, of Satan as an angel of light, might be recommended. Then in Galatians, the explanation of the word 'anathema,' and the analysis of the method of Scripture interpretation; and in Ephesians, the full treatise of the Order of the Angels, in which the influence of the Areopagite becomes evident,—could be perused with advantage.

Perhaps the most striking of all the Expositions of the Angelical is that on the Book of Job. Here the illlustrations and quotations from the Scriptures and the Fathers are met less often than in the other Commentaries. True, S. Paul and Ecclesiasticus now and then shed a gleam across the pages; whilst at distant intervals S. Augustine, S. Ambrose, S. Gregory, as well as Denis, Boethius, and S. Isidore, Porphyry, Pliny, and Aristotle, are to be met with, either as illustrating or recommending the point under discussion.

This Treatise occupies one hundred and forty-six pages. The Prologue, as usual, is full of ingenuity. The object of the work is to prove God's Providence over the world, and its argument is, in reality, an answer to many cardinal tenets of that Eastern philosophy which had eaten its way into the Paris schools.

The subject-matter is divided according to the forty-two chapters of the book, and these are subdivided into the usual *lectiones*.

The unrivalled power of analysis possessed by the Angelical gave him entire scope for bringing out into full expression the character of blessed Job. The way in which the intellectual position of this Patriarch is described—his former prosperity, his abject misery, his vision of the future, his trust in God—exhibits great dramatic power in the commentator. Then come the groaning of his inferior nature; the maledictions which proceed from 'the lower parts of his soul;' the approach of his friends, of Eliphaz, Baldad, and Sophar, who are so occupied with their own ideas that they seem incapable of comprehending his state of mind; then his obstinate persistence in his own way of seeing things, in spite of their determination to the contrary;—all this is brought out with extraordinary vividness by the Angel of the Schools.

And no less brilliantly does he develop the main argument, in illustration of which the Exposition was principally written. Job, in his position of profound misery, still trusting in and proving the over-ruling providence of God ; and his friends, by the very method they adopt, all the more firmly clenching his conclusions ;—these different dramatic elements are so made use of in the argument as to imprint, as much upon the imagination as upon the intellect, a persuasion that, in spite of all external signs, there is an unseen Hand and an all-wise Intelligence, which are over-ruling and directing each minutest detail, as well as the general order of the world.

Since space will not permit long extracts certain passages may be referred to as singularly able, and as illustrating in a striking manner the mind of the Angelical. See, for instance, his treatment on the limits of Satan's power ; on the lawfulness of sorrow ; on the nature of visions ; on stability ; on the life of man ; on the power of human reason ; on contentions ; on the testimony of conscience ; on God's knowledge ; on tendency towards an end ; on the Resurrection—which is treated with great mastery ; on immortality ; on the prosperity of the wicked ; on astronomy ; on metals and precious stones ; birds ; asses ; reverence ; temperature ; on wisdom ; on Platonism ; on Satan ; on sleep ; on the Leviathan ; on the motion of the heavens ; and on the great Behemoth. Besides his Commentary on Job the Angelical wrote an Exposition on the first fifty Psalms. This occupies about two hundred pages. The care with which the *Prooemium* is composed shows that the author looked upon this as an important work. It consists in an ingenious, not to say profound, application of the words: 'In all his works he gave thanks to the Holy One, and to the Most High with words of glory.'

In this Exposition the Angelical enters, more perhaps than in any of his other works, into the full meaning of each word, and follows out its signification into the minutest detail. It is not at all an uncommon thing for him to devote half a column, or more, to the elucidation of a single adjective, substantive, or pronoun. He brings various portions of Scripture to bear, as in a focus, upon the elements of thought; and after having displayed them in different lights, draws out and manifests their proper meaning with a facility which is all his own. The *Gloss* is here often brought into requisition. At times a Hebrew expression gives a clue to the true signification; sometimes the force of the Greek appears to recall a thought; or S. Augustine, or S. Chrysostom, or Denis, is called in to settle, by means of his authority, texts which of themselves might be explained in different ways. Then difficulties suggested by other portions of Holy Writ are advanced—passages which seem to contradict the Psalm: these are solved, either by a principle of moral or a principle of dogma, or by the light of some telling sentence in Scripture, or by the traditionary teachings of the Fathers, or finally by that gift of intuition by means of which master-minds are enabled to cut the Gordian knot, or to unravel a tangle, with an ease which is one of the attributes of genius.

Perhaps the most valuable portion of this Exposition is that which brings out the relation of the Psalms to the Redemption of our Lord. No possible point of resemblance is omitted. Christ lives in the Psalms, and His tender loving Voice is ever and anon heard, speaking with clear articulation of His sufferings, His patience, His love, and His most merciful atonement for the sake of man. On the full treatment of so large a subject this is not the place to dwell. But the detailed method of the Saint will be seen clearly enough by citing a single example, which is selected as being interesting in itself.

For instance, take the words—

'"Truths are decayed from among the children of men." Why does he say truths in the plural? "There is no truth of God in the land." The answer is that the primeval Truth is one, and is the Divine Intellect. But as the one face of a man produces many reflections in many mirrors, and many also in one broken mirror, so many truths are produced in many souls through the influence of one Divine truth. So manifold truths appear in our soul which does not reach divine simplicity: and this is the effect of that one Truth, by which a devout soul is illuminated: and these truths diminish as the soul, through sin, recedes from God.'

The next Exposition is that on the Canticle of Canticles. It follows in the main the plan adopted in other Commentaries. But Scripture references occur here less frequently than in the Treatise on Job. The Fathers are more sparingly used. Aristotle's Ethics can be felt in many places, as fixing a basis on which is built some beautiful and stable superstructure. The ardent words of the Spouse are taken up with the same warmth in exposition by the Saint as they are poured out by the Inspired Lips. The Angelical was at home in this train of thought. His soul, ever present with his Lord, could run along the course of the glowing canticle, and, without any difficulty, keep pace with the exuberance of joy therein displayed. Continually, as if inspired himself, he takes up the rapture of Holy Writ, and pours it forth, following with a commentary thrown into rapture too, flowing with a like rapidity of love, and evidently proving that under the quiet calm exterior of the man there lived a very volcano of seraphic tenderness and charity. Then the swift comment stops, and the Saint draws out the requisites for some important office, or the ingredients of some mighty gift, stating all calmly and with measure, like a deep philosopher. Now comes the application to the words of the Canticle; next, an analysis of various expressions; then a knitting together of Scripture phrase,—the writer making his own thought flow with equal stream, text running into comment, and then losing itself, till the Angelic Doctor's mind and the inspiration of the Spirit seem to combine in one shining current of purest psalmody. Yet all this is done in order; all is subservient to a common purpose; all adds light to the guiding thought contained in the customary magic text, which here is cast in the following words: 'Let thy voice sound in my ears: for thy voice is sweet, and thy face comely.'

Two more works of the Angelical complete his Scripture preparation for his master undertaking, namely, his Expositions on the Prophecies of Isaias and Jeremias. The former occupies about one hundred and fifty pages, and is divided, according to the chapters of the prophecy, into sixty-six portions, varying greatly in length. The Scripture illustrations are in harmony with the usual method of the Saint. S. Gregory, S. Bernard, and S. Augustine are made use of; the last often, the others seldom. S. Jerome and Rabanus are touched upon, and there is one reference to Homer. The best way of giving an idea of this Exposition is to select one or two passages. For instance:

'Note, with regard to those words, "there shall come forth a rod," that the Blessed Virgin is called a rod. First, as consoling in tribulations: "But lift thou up thy rod, and stretch forth thy hand over the sea, and divide it: that the children of Israel may go through the midst of the sea on dry ground." Secondly, as fructifying: "And Moses found that the rod of Aaron for the house of Levi was budded; and that the buds swelling, it had bloomed blossoms, which, spreading the leaves, were formed into almonds." Thirdly, as satiating: "When Moses had lifted up his hand, and struck the rock twice with the rod, there came forth water in great abundance, so that the people and their cattle drank." Fourthly, as scourging: "A star shall rise out of Jacob, and a sceptre shall spring up from Israel, and shall strike the chiefs of Moab." Fifthly, as watching: "I see a rod watching.'"

The Exposition on Jeremias is an unfinished composition, the Angelical having died before he had time to complete the fifty-second chapter. In fact, the whole has more the character of an *imbozzo* than of a perfect piece. There is, indeed, the same wealth as elsewhere of Scripture illustration; and S. Ambrose, S. Jerome, S. Gregory, and the *Gloss*, are alluded to in a passing way. Take one or two examples of our Saint's method; first on various kinds of Circumcision:

'Note, that circumcision is manifold. Of the mind and of evil thoughts: "Until their uncircumcised mind be ashamed." Of the heart, from evil affections: "Circumcision is that of the heart, in spirit, not in the letter." Of the mouth, from evil speech: "I am of uncircumcised lips." Of the ears, from detraction and evil words: "Their ears are uncircumcised, and they cannot hear." Of the flesh, signifying circumcision from carnal desires: "You shall circumcise the flesh of your foreskin, that it may be for a sign of the covenant between Me and you."

Note, moreover, that the heart is washed with the water of Baptism: "I washed thee with water, and cleansed away thy blood from thee." With the tears of compunction: "Every night I will wash my bed; I will water my couch with my tears." With the wine of Divine Love: "He shall wash his robe in wine, and his garment in the blood of the grapes." With the milk of the Divine Word: "His eyes are as doves upon brooks of waters, which are washed with milk." With the ardour of correction: "If the Lord shall wash away the filth of the daughters of Sion, and shall wash away the blood of Jerusalem out of the midst thereof, by the Spirit of judgment, and by the spirit of burning." With the blood of the Lord's Passion: "They have washed their robes, and have made them white in the blood of the Lamb."'

To enter further into the Angelical's labours on the Sacred Scriptures would occupy too much space. It would fill a volume to indicate all his merits, and to show the influence upon him of the great classical Fathers of the Church. Any one sufficiently interested would speedily detect the difference between his method and theirs, by taking parallel passages of Scripture exegesis from S. Chrysostom, S. Ambrose, S. Jerome, and S. Augustine, and comparing them with the Exposition of our Saint. The schools of Antioch and Alexandria have made an equal mark upon him; he is as theological as Origen, when it answers the purposes of truth; and as practical and concrete as Chrysostom, when the literal treatment is more in keeping with his scope or with his subject-matter; whilst he surpasses all in the precision of his grasp of Faith and Morals, and in his special gift of throwing into an organic form the apparently heterogeneous elements of dogma or revelation which he meets with in the course of his exposition. S. Thomas appears incapable of touching any order of Church knowledge without at once detecting new bearings, and bringing the various portions into harmony. No man in the whole range of ecclesiastical biography knew as he did how to reduce chaos into order. The Holy Spirit seems to be painting his picture when He says:

'The wise man will seek out the wisdom of all the Ancients, and will be occupied in the Prophets. He will keep the sayings of renowned men, and will enter withal into the subtilties of parables. He will search out the hidden meaning of proverbs, and will be conversant in the secrets of parables. The Lord will fill him with the spirit of understanding, and he will pour forth the words of his wisdom in showers. The Lord shall direct his counsel, and in his secrets he shall meditate. Many shall praise his wisdom: and it shall never be forgotten. The memory of him shall not depart away, and his name shall be in request from generation to generation.'

It was thus, by the help of prayer, meditation, and the illumination of Truth, that the Angelical was enabled to penetrate into 'the subtilties of parables,' and to 'search out the hidden meaning of proverbs;' he was 'filled with the spirit of understanding,' and therefore 'his name shall be in requisition from generation to generation.' It was at the foot of the crucifix, and in the rapture of ecstasy, that his intellect was replenished with the fulness of Light.

Having seen what kind of preparation was made by our Saint, in Tradition and in Scripture, for his master-work, now we must consider the third point, and mark how Reason also, or Philosophy, was enlisted in his service for carrying out the same design.

CHAPTER XVIII.

GREEK PHILOSOPHERS.

THE mightiness of the columnal Fathers of the Church grew out of their abiding communication with the Unseen World; and they were built up into such strong and sublime moral characters through their intense personal love of a personal Saviour and Model. In proportion as they became one in will with Him, they became one in character with Him also. His divine grace, working in their beings, gradually transformed them into Christians in the highest sense of the word; into men full of love and reverence towards the Author of their salvation, filled with a spirit of genuine adoration, and spotless with a purity which alone can proceed from the free Hand of the Almighty. They understood the meaning of sin and of salvation; they knew the significance of the word 'creation,' and they believed in an eternal world to come. The mind and heart naturally turn towards them, and spontaneously adore the Power which made them what they were. They exhibit the highest types of what can be produced by Christianity, and their teaching is the genuine doctrine of the New Law. From them the Angelical drew the traditions of the Universal Church, and with the assistance of their master-minds he constructed his immortal synthesis of Catholic Theology.

But it is evident at a glance that, if the substance of the Angelical's writings be identical with the teaching of the Fathers, the form is not so. The logical precision, the brevity, the scientific formality of the Angel of the Schools, were unknown to the more emotional and rhetorical minds of the classic Doctors. If he gained so large a portion of his substance from them, whence came so great a difference in his method?

To answer this question the reader must, for a short time, leave the influences of the Christian Church, and turn to the Fathers of Greek philosophy.

To comprehend the position of the great pagan thinkers, a rapid outline must be given of the spiritual polity of the Greeks, and of the nature of their initial attempts at creating a religion.

After the fall of Adam, man, weakened in will, fell under the dominion of lust and passion. Still, the voice of his conscience was not entirely extinguished; the yearning after an object to adore was not wholly quenched in his heart. But his spiritual sight being weakened, and sometimes altogether obscured, instead of fixing itself on the unseen God of Heaven, Spiritual, Personal, One, Everlasting, was arrested by the sensible phenomena of the universe; and, with fear and trembling, he knelt down and worshipped the sun, the moon, and the stars.

Those tribes and communities which went to form what is called the Greek people introduced each its own special worship; and the fusion of the various divinities to which men offered sacrifice formed a confused medley of idolatry, rather than an intelligible system of religion.

Homer and Hesiod wrote the Bible of the Greeks. Selecting, as they thought best, the traditions and superstitions of the different races amongst which they moved, they created a system of belief, which, by means of exquisite poetry, and through the activity of wandering minstrels, was soon fixed in the mind of the entire population. Then the enthusiastic rhapsodists did their share. Dressed in bright attire, and wearing crowns of gold, they appeared in the thronging assemblies, and by means of their marvellous gift of simulating passion, and striking the 'cords of Adam' in the heart, speedily carried away with them, in the *élan* of their inspiration, the admiring multitudes who hung upon their lips. The sweet music of the voice, the touching concord of melting sounds, beauty appealing to the eye and to the ear, and lighting up the intellect, made rhapsody one of the most powerful instruments of education amongst the Greeks, one of the most telling means of popularising the theology of Homer.

The forces of nature were converted into immortal men; and the gods of the Greeks became simply the transcripts of their own passions, drawn out on a larger scale, embellished by the help of art, and thrown into epic and dramatic form by the highest masters of fascinating verse. There was not a form of lust or impiety, of thieving, perjury, imposture, and debauchery, or of any other kind of abomination, to which the Greeks could not appeal as sanctioned by the refined lewdness or gross immorality of their gods. Simply to read the history of the Hellenic priests and of their divinations, of their oracles and purifications, their sacrifices and festivals, their temples and their mysteries, is enough to make the face flush with horror. So ashamed were some poets and philosophers of these gods, that they endeavoured to give a mystic turn to the poems of Homer and of Hesiod, and to explain away the wickedness of their divinities by a system of historico-allegorical interpretations.

But the inquisitiveness of the Grecian mind was not satisfied with putting down everything to allegory. Men were anxious to trace the multiplicity of life to some primary existence; so that, whilst the people were worshipping the impure creations of their poets, the philosophers—who were to the Greeks what the Fathers are to the Christians—were feeling in gross darkness after truth. Like the rest of their pagan countrymen, they did not rise above material things. Their lives were spent in seeking and never finding; in great yearnings, accompanied by obscurity of intellect and sadness of spirit. They prove what mere philosophy, with no other help than human ingenuity, is able to effect for man.

For instance, Thales the Milesian (B.C. 600) discovered that water was the ultimate cause of all things; Anaximenes, his disciple, evolved all things out of chaos; his successor, Anaximander (B.C. 502), made air the first principle; Diogenes of Apollonia added life to air; Heraclitus the Ephesian (B.C. 500) declared that caloric was all in all; Pythagoras traced everything to the primal monad; Xenophanes of Colophon (B.C. 617) was a material pantheist; Parmenides (B.C. 500) denied the world of sense altogether, and believed simply in pure being; Empedocles of Agrigentum (B.C. 492-432) was a pantheist; Democritus of Abdera (B.C. 460), the most learned natualist before Aristotle, declared the human soul to be a fiery atom; Anaxagoras of Clazomenæ in Lydia (B.C. 500) maintained an Eternal Matter penetrated by an Eternal *Nous;* Protagoras of Abdera, the Sophist (B.C. 480-410), held the doctrine of perpetual flux; Gorgias of Leontium (B.C. 494-400), the most famous orator of his day, taught that nothing had any existence whatever.

Then Sophists took the place of the poets and the

rhapsodists. They were essentially rhetoricians, who, with a vast store of self-assurance and mother-wit, professed to prepare the young for the battle of life. They undertook to popularise philosophy; to have an answer ready made for every difficulty, and to lay down the law off-hand on every subject. Gorgias, Protagoras, Prodicus, and other such brilliant speakers—like the scholastics of the days of Abelard—travelled from city to city throughout Greece, and fascinated the eager and impressionable minds of their restless countrymen by the dash of their rhetoric, by their assumption of knowledge, and by the readiness of their resource.

Their irreverence and rationalism speedily introduced elements of unbelief. Many of them looked with contempt on the indecent mythologies and the crude theogonies which had been the favourite theme of poets. Protagoras spoke with undisguised contempt of them. Prodicus said the gods were set up by the egotism of man; Critias declared that they were the invention of the lawyers; the comic poets joined the chorus, and, with all the inconsistency of Aristophanes, turned upon the philosophers for simply doing that which they themselves were doing every day. Yet the masses of the population were desperately attached to the odious practices of their diabolical religion. Cruelty and superstition are the constant associates of sensual debauchery. Recall the frequent religious persecutions in Athens; the power of the priests over Alcibiades; the trial of Aspasia; the exile of Protagoras; the accusation directed against Æschylus; the imprisonment of Anaxagoras; or the danger in which Pericles himself stood of being branded with impiety; and the truth of this assertion becomes evident at a glance.

What a fearful state of moral and intellectual confusion must not the Greek world have been in, during the full bloom of its highest cultivation! The heavens darkened with families of disgusting gods; the earth poisoned by the impurity of their worship; philosophers doubting of all things, and, when dogmatising, teaching a code of error contradictory to the first principles of natural and moral truth. What a deep contrast between the 'Fathers' of Christian and of Greek philosophy!—between men who, on the whole, were equal in intellect and culture, but were distinguished by this one note: that the former possessed Christ, whilst the latter had no Christ at all!

In place of S. Anthony, look on Heraclitus. He was a confirmed misanthrope. He was eaten up with a devouring melancholy, and nourished supreme contempt for his fellow-man.

'He fled to the mountains, there in secret to prey on his own heart. He was a misanthrope, and misanthropy issues more from the morbid consciousness of self, than from the sorrowful opinion formed of others.'

In place of S. Athanasius, look upon Parmenides:

'Born to wealth and splendour, enjoying the esteem and envy which always follow splendour and talent, it is conjectured that his early career was that of a dissipated voluptuary.'

Diochœtes taught him to despise riches, and he devoted himself to philosophical pursuits. The result of his meditations issued in the construction of a theory which opened the door to universal doubt.

In place of S. Basil, look on Empedocles. He was of a haughty and passionate character:

'His love of distinction showed itself in priestly garments, a golden girdle, the Delphic crown, and a numerous train of attendants. He proclaimed himself to be a god whom men and women reverently adored.'

His death does not resemble that of S. Basil any more than his life. He plunged headlong into the crater of Mount Ætna.

In place of S. Gregory Theologus, look on Aristippus, the founder of the Cyrenaics. He was so enslaved to lust, which he had learnt to indulge in at Minyæ, that some say he disgusted even Socrates.

'Socrates with such men as Aristippus and Alcibiades reminds one of Dr. Johnson with the "young bloods" Topham Beauclerk and Bennet Langton: he was wise enough and tolerant enough not to allow his virtue to be scandalised by their love of pleasure. . . . From Athens he went to Ægina, where he met Laïs the world renowned courtesan, whom he accompanied to Corinth.'

In a word, Aristippus was a gay, brilliant, and prudent debauchee, who preserved his health in order to prolong his pleasure, and raised up delight into a philosophic system.

In place of S. Jerome, look upon Antisthenes:

'He was stern, and his doctrine was rigid; he was proud, and his doctrine was haughty; he was cold, and his doctrine was unsympathising and self-isolating. . . . Even whilst with Socrates he displayed his contempt of ordinary usages, and his pride in differing from other men. He used to appear in a threadbare cloak, with ostentatious poverty. Socrates saw through it all, and exclaimed, "I see your vanity, Antisthenes, peering through the holes in your cloak." . . . Antisthenes thought he could only preserve his virtue by becoming a savage. He wore no garment except a coarse cloak; allowed his beard to grow; carried a wallet and a staff; and renounced all diet but the simplest. His manners corresponded to his appearance. Stern, reproachful, and bitter in his language; careless and indecent in his gestures, . . . as he grew old, his gloomy temper became morose; he became so insupportable that all his scholars left him, except Diogenes of Sinope. . . . In his last agony, Diogenes asked him whether he needed a friend. "Will a friend release me from this pain?" he replied. Diogenes gave him a dagger, saying, "This will." "I wish to be freed from pain, not from life," was the reply.'

He was often called 'The Dog.'

In place of S. John Chrysostom, look at Diogenes. Diogenes of Sinope embraced poverty as a profession, and the contempt of his fellow-man as his end in life. His language was coarse and brutal, he lived in a tub, his only garment was a cloak.

'In public he performed all those actions which decency has condemned to privacy. Decency of every kind he studiously outraged. . . . Diogenes was so feeble in doctrine, so brutal in manner, that we doubt whether the debauchery of the first profligate in the profligate city [Athens] were more reprehensible than the debauchery of pride which disgraced the cynic. . . . One day he called out, "Approach, all men!" When some approached, he beat them back with his club, saying, "I call for men; ye are excrements." . . . Thus he lived till his ninetieth year, bitter, brutal, ostentatious, and abstemious. . . . One day his friends went to see him. On arriving at the portico under which he was wont to sleep, they found him still lying on the ground wrapped in his cloak. He seemed to sleep. They pushed aside the folds of his cloak: he was dead.'

And so, did space permit, I might draw out the characters of Socrates, Plato, and Aristotle; and they would present a very miserable picture by the side of S. Ambrose, S. Augustine, and S. Gregory the Great.

Where Christianity does not exist to maintain the balance, the moral and intellectual world ever swings restlessly between extremes. One extravagance gives birth to another. Superstition is the first-born of scepticism; and even luxury itself at length creates its contrast in the brutal asceticism of an Antisthenes or Diogenes. Zeno and Epicurus are simply examples of kicking the beam on either side.

It was, in great measure, the influence of a reaction which brought out the genius of the father of Greek philosophy. The pantheistical absurdities, the materialism and atheism, of the philosophers who preceded him, gave a powerful impetus to the faculties of Socrates. Then the ignorance and conceit of sophists, rhetoricians, and grammarians—who dealt in fine words and sonorous phrases, but had nothing solid or serious about them—disgusted an intellect like his, naturally keen, accurate, and observant.

Socrates (B.C. 469) was the son of a sculptor (Sophroniscus), and his mother was a midwife. At first he worked in his father's studio, and is said to have carved a statue of the Graces. But he soon threw down his chisel, and feeling himself divinely called, began to advocate the cause of true philosophy. His education was not conducted by the Sophists, he was too poor for that; but he was trained in the open air of Athens, in the agora, the gymnasia, and in the market-place; and in the company of poets, philosophers, and statesmen his keen and penetrating intelligence received a stimulus which it is out of the power of books to give.

But it was not an impulse in the direction of the sophistry of the rhetoricians. Socrates saw through all their hollowness, and loathed the acrobatic display of dexterity by which they imposed on the volatile Athenians, who were 'contentionis avidiores quam veritatis.' Nor was he dazzled or subdued by the philosophers. He had studied their physical, moral, and dialectical systems, and discovered that they had undertaken to treat on subjects which were beyond their depth. His feeling was rather to combat than to follow them. He perceived how their vanity and arrogance had undermined the first principles of stability, and how his impressionable countrymen were practised upon, and injured, by the extravagances and unrealities of their favourite teachers. He perceived how debauched the beautiful city had become, and that truth and honesty were little reverenced by the vain and frivolous frequenters of its agora, gymnasia, and public places.

He felt a divine call to become the apostle of truth in a world of delusion, hollowness, and rhetorical inflation. He saw clearly that the Sophists did not know what they were discoursing about, and that this species of self-deception was the ruin of all true wisdom, and a peril to the State.

He was a genius. He did not require to travel, like other philosophers, into foreign lands, to learn the just and true. His store of knowledge lay in the circumference of his own teeming brain. Unless when forced to serve in the army, he hardly once went outside the walls of Athens. He was even a stranger to the cool and classic banks of the Ilyssus. His life was spent in the free open air, amidst the crowds of the busy city. He sought men; he freely conversed with all; all loved to hear him. He was a novelty in Athens, so different from the shallow grammarian and the empty Sophist. Though of repulsive personal appearance, his intellect was so crystal clear, his reason so exquisitely accurate, his vision so swift and keen, his readiness so remarkable, his agility in throwing an opponent, in twisting him into some unbearable position, so astounding,—there was something so preternatural about these powers of his mind,—that he speedily became, amongst a city of famous men, of all the most distinguished.

The rhetoricians had been the centre of attraction. Now the charm was to witness Socrates upset these vain pretenders. They dealt in the sentimental, in phrases which were full of rhetoric, but had little point or logic. Socrates showed the world that such displays were exhibitions at once of emptiness and ignorance: that ignorance was the mother of every vice, and that the really learned man could not be vicious. He looked with contempt upon the chosen pastimes of the wrangling Athenians, and proved, by means of his matchless gift of logic, the utter inanity of those mental puzzles which seemed so greatly to fascinate the people. They never appeared happy except when in the midst of spiritual or physical conflict; the stage, the arena, the law courts, the supper-table, the rostrum, and the cock-pit,—all were made to minister to this abnormal craving, and to supply materials for an endless round of intellectual dissipation. Socrates showed what all this was worth. He, as no other, could snap their sophisms; and the 'quibble,' the 'hook,' the 'labyrinth,' and the 'snare,' and all that family of logical abortions, held out no mystery to him. He was a master of destructive as well as constructive philosophy; and his very keenness tended to lessen in the minds of the people their overweening admiration for the jugglery of sophistical contention.

Still, he appeared amongst them without boast of philosophy. He did not profess to be wise, but to be ignorant. To examine, to scrutinise, to sift the teachings of men; to weigh his own words, to get to the bottom of them, and by means of a series of drastic questions to eliminate all foreign matter, till he came to the inner core of truth,—such was the design which Socrates had in view. Thus it was that, as with the point of a pin, he touched the inflated and dithyrambic rhetoric of the pretentious Sophists, and it collapsed at once.

It is little surprising that men of great mind should have been struck and dazzled by the simplicity and directness, by the solidity and honesty, of the method of this man. His fundamental maxim was 'Know thyself.' His object was ethical; his instruments were dialectics, definition, and induction. He set on foot, and may be considered the father of, the theory of scientific knowledge. Anaxagoras, in all probability, suggested to him his high view on the objective nature of love, beauty, and truth; Zeno must have influenced him with regard to dialectics. But he it was who clipped the wings of ignorant presumption, turned men's minds from the physical world upon themselves, and encouraged a spirit of accuracy and analysis, of testing and dissecting, of the rigorous and the precise, in place of the rhetorical, the emotional, and the unreal.

It is impossible to consider the career and character of this extraordinary genius, without being affected with a sense of sadness and admiration: of admiration, on account of his earnestness, his gifts, and his hatred of sham; of sadness, on account of the blighting influences of his pagan education.

His pride came out during his memorable defence. His views on purity discover his taint in nature; the highest and noblest of pagans here witnesses sadly to Christianity. The aspirations of such men, their theories, their soaring intuitions, at times appear to be almost divine; but look on their actual lives. Theory, however beautiful and chaste, is too ethereal to counteract the emotional violence of passion; the concrete only can confront the concrete. If man's life is to be spotless, it must be through the personal power of One more mighty than himself. Here it is that the greatest pagan is inferior to the lowliest saint. Banishing the accusation that Socrates was guilty of bigamy and of corrupting the mind of youth, it is certain that he was the friend and familiar of dissolute courtesans. He was the intimate of Theodota, and he acknowledges himself that he learnt rhetoric from the beautiful and profligate Aspasia, and looked with an approving eye on the irregular courses of her life. Hence it is not so surprising that he should support the worship of gods hardly more abandoned than his tenderest friends. He offered sacrifices on their altars, and joined in the sacred rites. He protested his belief in them, and ordered an oblation to be made to one of them when he was on the point of death.

These are the words of Phædo:

'And Socrates also touched himself, and said that when the poison reached his heart he should then leave us. But now his lower belly was almost cold; when, uncovering himself (for he was covered), he said (which were his last words), "Crito, we owe a cock to Æsculapius. Discharge this debt for me, and don't neglect it."'

Such was the end of the most original, forcible, and logical thinker of pagan times. Men of high genius, when deprived of the light of revelation, with ardent longing yearn after the Unseen: like strong swimmers in a rough sea, they may battle bravely for a time, but at last their vital force becomes exhausted, and they sink back prostrated into that coarser and stifling element which belongs to the senses and the flesh.

The influence of Socrates on the Athenian mind can hardly be exaggerated. He almost emptied the school of the Sophists. His exposition of their hollowness was too thorough and too brilliant to be passed over by so emotional a people as the Greeks. There was something almost preternatural in the fascination of his conversation. Zeno, the great master of dialectic, travelled twenty miles by night, disguised as a woman, in order to attend his teaching. The wealthy Crito was his intimate friend. The beautiful Euthydemus was won over in spite of himself. Antisthenes walked four miles each day to be with Socrates. Cebes and Simmias followed him from Thebes. Isocrates and Aristippus were his disciples; Alcibiades said he would 'grow old in listening to his talk,' if he did not fly away; whilst all know the enthusiasm of Xenophon for the great master of 'philters and incantations.'

What a contrast between Socrates and many of his disciples! See them all listening to him, as he upsets a Sophist, or plays with some foolish young Athenian who imagines he has learnt the art of government and the hidden secrets of life. What a new sense for the Greek mind of that day, to find a man protesting he knew nothing, and at the same time showing himself superior to all!

See that young man hanging on the words of the philosopher; he is, in every way, a contrast to his master. Graceful and noble in appearance, his fine physique looks as if it had been developed by the trainer's skill in the gymnasium. His brow is broad and fair, his expression supremely spiritual and deeply sad; he is evidently a rare type of Greek intellectual beauty, manifested in Hellenic gracefulness of form. His whole mind seems absorbed by the thoughts suggested by his master, his eyes are riveted upon him in eager admiration. He cannot be taken by the personal beauty of Socrates, for 'in appearance he resembled a Silenus; his flattened nose, with wide and upturned nostrils, his projecting eyeballs, his thick and sensual lips, his squab figure, and unwieldy belly, were all points on which ridicule might be fastened.' But the youth does not dream of ridicule, for there is something so fascinating in his master's conversation, so bewitching in his direct and trenchant logic, so full of genius in his easy sovereignty of mind, that the very splendour of his gifts of intellect seems almost to throw a halo over his unfortunate countenance and figure. Who is this youthful admirer of Socrates? He is no other than Aristocles the Athenian, son of Aristo and Potona, now known by the name of 'Plato the divine.' This was he on whose infant lips the bees are said to have dropped their honey. Some declared his father was Apollo; others traced his parentage to Neptune; all admitted that the blood of Codrus, the patriot-king, and of Solon, the great law-giver, flowed within his veins.

He was twenty years of age when he listened first to Socrates. His education had been carefully attended to; both mind and body had been exercised, so as to become supple and strong—capable of great and sustained exertion in their respective spheres. Dionysius the grammarian, Draco and Metellus the musicians, and Aristo the trainer, were his early masters. Poetry, the lyre and the flute, wrestling, boxing and running, occupied his early years. His versatility displayed itself from the first. He seems to have excelled as a boy in poetry and in gymnastics. He is said to have entered the lists at the Isthmian games, and only began to despair of poetry after he had read the masterpiece of Homer.

Thus was his mind prepared to receive whatever impressions might be made upon it. The influence of Socrates was at the zenith. He had given an impetus to philosophy quite new amongst the Greeks. Ambition, curiosity, love of novelty, as well as desire after truth, drew the city round that grotesque-looking philosopher. The very originality of his system was in itself sufficient attraction to a people proverbially frivolous and volatile. Here was the 'wisest of men' publicly declaring the first principle of his philosophy to be that 'he knew nothing.' Plato speedily perceived that a deep and pregnant truth lay hidden from the multitude in this dictum of his master. His mind was just of that texture, of that breadth and elasticity, which would appreciate the fine irony, the inimitable analytical skill, and the thorough intellectual honesty of Socrates. Then his own natural talent for dramatic effect, his expanding imagination, and emotional nature, would find a special comfort in listening to those dialogues in which Socrates proved, with a witchery all his own, that they who professed themselves skilled in everything were either stone-blind with self-conceit, or inflated with mental vapour. Then, again, the very system itself must have stimulated so exuberant and energetic a mind as his. It opened to him, no doubt, vast fields of thought. It pointed, unlike the majority of systems which had gone before, to some steady and spiritual truths; and lifted the mind out of the flux and flow, the darkness and the obscurity of gross material things, into a higher and purer world.

Thus the great work done by Socrates for Plato was to give him a bias towards the Good and the True; and to engage his curiosity, by artistic display of dialectic, definition, and induction.

But Plato was far too universal in his tendencies to be content, as his master had been, with the voice of his own reason, and the responses elicited by its conflict with other intellects. Socrates possessed no erudition. His was simple impact and native force of mind. He had been influenced, doubtless, by independent thinkers, but he had never been to school; the vigour of his own intelligence was sufficient for itself.

Plato, on the contrary, studied with avidity the philosophical systems of other men. At an early age he had mastered the Ionic view, and the teachings of Parmenides and Zeno. It is clear from the *Phædrus* and the *Lysis*, which were written before the death of Socrates, that the doctrines of the Pythagoreans had already informed his mind. How far the theories of those monks of the pagan times influenced his philosophical career, and purified his mental vision, by encouraging him to love a mystic life, has never yet been fully realised. Of the impress of Anaxagoras, and the Eleatic school, there is abundant evidence in the *Dialogues*. Heraclitus also, with his doctrine of eternal flux, was introduced to him by Cratylus in early youth.

At the death of its founder (B.C. 399) the Socratic school broke up. It possessed no badge or bond of union. Socrates maintained no theory; he simply stimulated thought, and taught intellectual honesty.

And Plato, with his vast creative mind, with the marvellous richness of his fancy, and his power of dialectic, was destined to confer on Socrates an immortality, which he deserved indeed, but which, in all probability, would never have been his, had it not been for the genius of his disciple.

The training of Plato was not yet complete. Having learnt all that could be taught him by the greatest mind at home, he was now fit to profit by travelling abroad. He wished to have the widest education which men and things could give. In his *Laws* he clearly indicates how great a benefit he derived from seeing many famous men, and visiting many celebrated cities. He was now eight-and-twenty years of age. First, he set out for Megara. Here, under Euclid, he studied dialectic, and read greedily the writings of Zeno and Parmenides. Then he went to Cyrene, where he continued his course of geometry, most likely under the renowned Theodorus, who, when at Athens, had listened with delight to the skilful dialogues of their common master.

Next, he betook himself to Italy and Sicily, and here it was that he appears to have received his deepest mark. It was in Italy, Sicily, and Magna Græcia that the children of Pythagoras had established their *synedria* or colleges.

What could have had greater charm for a noble mind than a generous love of wisdom? And what were these colleges or monasteries but homes, in which men spent their lives in the abiding contemplation of what they looked upon as truth? There is something sadly grand in these high strivings of the nobler part of man, even in pagan darkness, after light. The special characteristic of the Pythagorean was, that he loved wisdom, not for profit, but simply for wisdom's sake. His one end in life was to make himself one with it. He abhorred, and stamped upon the idea, that science should be prostituted to gain. To facilitate their life-object, these earnest men instituted a species of monastic life. They fled the world. The Rule was most severe; its end was to exclude base and low-born minds, and to secure only such as were worthy of contemplation. Hence, the novitiate lasted five years. During this period strict silence was enjoined; those who could not stand the test were deemed unfit. They were tried by the '*dura*' and '*aspera;*' and like novices in a Benedictine house, they were practised in humiliations and self-denials. The Pythagoreans inculcated reverence, humility, a spirit of prayer and purity of thought, 'and accustomed men to associate their moral ideas with the Deity, rather than with themselves.' They practised self-examination, held the doctrine of a future state; and chastity may be looked upon as the cardinal virtue of their school. They seem also to have entertained a deeper respect for human life than the majority of pagan philosophers. They appear to have believed in a purgative and illuminative way. When they had been sufficiently purified, they were permitted to chasten their minds by the contemplation of intellectual truth. Thus they passed their days, preparing themselves by severe asceticism for the apprehension of that object which all men seek after, but few men realise.

Such a system as this was quite a novelty amongst the Greeks. They could not understand any advancement, except such as was elicited through the social intercourse of daily life. And this very fact would cause the Pythagorean system to exert all the deeper influence on Plato. He found the monastic houses in full activity in Tarentum, Crotona, and Magna Græcia. He was captivated by what he saw and heard. Archytas, who was the deepest ascetic, and the noblest representative of that conventual school, came in contact with Plato at Tarentum; and there is little doubt that the high principles of the pagan monk, his contempt of pleasure, his worshipping of wisdom, his intense love of the mystic life, must have left a lasting mark on his friend's impressionable and observant mind. Naturally sad and meditative, modest and gentle in demeanour, loving the world of thought and of spiritual entities, looking with a certain compassion, if not disgust, upon physical inquiry, mostly absorbed in the unseen, never married, loving retirement, Plato — had he been a Christian — would have been a monk, and one of the noblest Fathers of the Church. Even as it is, it is pretty certain that much of his spiritual-mindedness, many of his highest intuitions and foreshadowings of truth, are the result of his monastic bias, and of the comparative purity of his mind and heart. It is as much Plato's character as his system which offers so indescribable a fascination to noble and generous minds, and acts with a species of dynamic influence upon man's loftier nature; drawing him, even though possessing the light of Christianity, into a still tenderer love and reverence of wisdom.

From Italy Plato travelled into Egypt. He is said to have disguised himself as an olive merchant, that he might the more freely move amongst a class of men who regarded strangers with suspicion. If there was any country under the sun which would attract the attention of such a man, it certainly would be this fountain-land, it might also be called, of Grecian civilisation. Greek colonies and Greek history had already made the Athenians, if not familiar, at least conversant, with the manners and thoughts of the strange people of the East.

Had it not been for the unsettled state of those countries, Plato would have visited India and Persia also. Prudence, however, constrained him to journey homewards; and after spending some further time with his Pythagorean friends, he returned, after about ten years' absence, to teach philosophy at Athens.

With the exception of his journeys in search of wisdom, and his three fruitless visits to Sicily—which evince the immense influence which his Pythagorean friends exerted over him—Plato passed the remainder of his life in his little house and garden at the Ciramicus. It was a mile from Athens; and close upon the pleasant shady walks of that beautiful suburban spot to which his genius has given immortality. There is something sweet and pure in the thought of this great master-spirit of philosophy dedicating his whole energies to Wisdom, travelling first to find her, and then returning home, and, far from the din of the city strife, passing away his quiet days in her companionship, and in teaching others to prefer the Supremely Good and the Sovereignly True before all the vulgarities of ambition, and all the thraldroms of the senses.

Quickly did his rich fame people the shady grove. Soon did the noblest and the fairest spirits of beautiful wicked Athens flock to look on him and hear him. Unlike Socrates, Plato loved monastic solitude. He shrank from the whirl of men and the sounds of strife; and the very Athenians themselves were not displeased to quit for a time their rivalries and intrigues, to listen to the sad and graceful Plato, descanting with his thin and gentle voice on the highest happiness of man. Old and young were equally attracted. The ambitious hoped to learn something which would teach them how to rule their fellow-men. The gay young Athenian, like some summer bird, all life and plumage, would flutter around him, dazzled for the moment; the wondering youth from some far province of Asia Minor, from the wild woods of Cappadocia, or the rocky lands of Thrace, would hang spell-bound on the sage's lips, as if enthralled by some divinity, whilst the self-contained and haughty Lacedæmonian would feel himself compelled, though half unwillingly, to offer his proud testimony to the mastership of the Athenian mind. Neither the fame of Isocrates, the celebrated rhetorician, nor the tenets of Aristippus, which flattered the lowest passions of mankind, were able to cast a shade on the unapproachable popularity of the divine Academy. Men who were learning to become tyrants; future orators, governors, philosophers, and poets; men of acute intellect and restless temperament; nay, even accomplished courtesans, such as Aspasia, Lasthenea, and the profligate Axiothea, mixed with the general throng, testifying at once by their presence to the corruptions of the State, and to the hollowness of all philosophy which is simply founded on human genius and natural gifts. The whole of this picture, there is no doubt, is refined, is captivating, is sweet and soothing to the cultivated intellect of man. Nature can rise no higher. Plato manifests it at its brightest and its best. Elegance, culture, taste, delicacy, high thoughts, noble aspirations, beautiful conceptions of the mind and the imagination—all are here displayed in their most perfect grace and flower. It is a charming dream, a lovely apparition, but it lacks substance and stamina. Demosthenes, Hyperides, Aristotle, Speusippus, Xenocrates, Dion,—all these lived on the lips of 'Plato the Divine.' But what is the best of them but a specimen of weakness and impurity, compared with their master's highest theories? What is the best of them, compared with the humblest Father of the desert, but a contradiction of pride, self-love, and periodical unchastity?

Philosophy may refine the feelings and educate the taste, but it cannot control the concrete—subdue pride in the intellect and passion in the heart. And since philosophy was the highest, and certainly the purest, religion of the Greeks, Philosophy as a moral guide has proved herself to be an egregious failure.

The reader must already have been struck by the resemblance between the Angelical and the master of the Academy. Both were nobly born; both were grave from youth; both loved Wisdom with intensity of devotion; both followed her to the end. If Plato was instructed by Socrates, S. Thomas was taught by Albertus Magnus; if Plato travelled into Italy, Greece, and Egypt, S. Thomas went to Cologne, Naples, Bologna, and Rome; if, contrary to his inclination, Plato attended the court of Dionysius, S. Thomas, against his will, was Councillor to Louis, King of France. If Plato was famous for his erudition and the breadth of his research, S. Thomas was no less noted for universal knowledge. Both were naturally meek and gentle; both in their respective measure followed a monastic life; Plato, like S. Thomas, was never married; both loved solitude; both were celebrated for their self-control; both were brave; both held their audience spell-bound by their brilliant mental gifts; both passed their time in lecturing in the schools. What the Pythagoreans were to Plato, that the Benedictines were to the Angelical. Both shrank from display of self. If the Angelical is extremely objective in his method, and never mentions self, Plato only alludes to self twice in all his *Dialogues*, and that for the sake of others. Both men were ardent thinkers, deep dialecticians, keen in their power of analysis, overflowing with emotion well controlled. Both wrote on morality, politics, and religion. Had Plato been a Christian he would have been a saint; had the Angelical been a pagan he would have been another Plato.

The gulf which separated them was this: the Angelical was formed on Christ. He was sound and pure throughout. He had the workings of a personal love of his Redeemer in him; he was a model of a spotless life. His faculties were sublimated by the supernatural. What the *Dialogues* of Plato are to the *Summa Theologica*, that the character of the master of the Academy is to the character of S. Thomas of Aquino. In one there is the perfection of human beauty; in the other, the human is enlarged, elevated, purified by the Divine. In the one, we have guesses at truth, the forebodings of genius with its contradictions; in the other, the steady full-orbed revelation of Jesus Christ, in all its symmetry, concord, and scientific harmony. In one, we possess a test of how little, as well as how much, the human mind is capable of; in the other, a sample of how large a store of freedom, stability, and light the Almighty can bestow on man. The former has pleased and amused the educated few; the latter has formed the minds of succeeding generations. Plato, compared with the other Greek philosophers, is beautiful to look upon; Plato by the side of the Angelical turns to earth, and almost falls to clay. Man, though placed below, is made for heaven; his human gifts should be purified by a higher influence, and 'clothed upon' by the grace of God.

Plato died the very day on which he completed his eighty-first birthday. Some say he expired during a marriage-feast; others, in the very act of writing. Temperate in his habits, assiduous in his mental labours, he passed his life, says Cicero, 'in quietness, and purity, and elegance;' and remains to this day the most favourable specimen of what human culture and natural gifts can do, unassisted by the vigorous realities of a Christian life.

His method was eminently Socratic. He did not take for granted, like the Sophist, and build a towering system on a postulate. He was a winnower and a sifter. He grasped a question firmly, and investigated and discussed it. In keeping with the genius of the Greek people, who loved to cross-question each other in the agora, gymnasia, and bright palæstra, he threw his philosophy into the form of brilliant dialogue and dialectic. His whole tone is thoroughly in harmony with the Grecian mind. Grave and gay, flowing and figurative, now steeped in deepest thought, now bursting into play, sparkling with polished irony, at times overflowing with fancy, melody, and tenderest emotion, vivid and dramatic, cultivated and refined, so exquisite an art-work as to conceal art altogether,—the *Dialogues* of Plato, in spite of Plutarch, Cicero, and Xenophon, stand unrivalled as master-pieces of the most perfect culture of the Grecian mind.

It is true that just as the *Dialogues* cannot be thrown into order, so there is no realisation in the Platonic philosophy of any definite theory. Plato's method is mainly negative. He unravels a skein, and when he has finished, and the reader expects some grand result, he generally finds that the work is at an end. If he has not absolutely seized truth, at least he has not been deceived by falsehood; though this is by no means always the case. For instance, the *Hippias Major* is essentially dialectical, whilst the *Timæus* is a simple exposition of an important truth.

Though Plato has a strong philosophical bias, his principal aim was to liberate the mind from the trammels of ignorance, and to open before its eyes a higher, more noble, and purer range of thought. He not only looked to the beauty of abstract truth, but also to the requirements of the Greeks amongst whom he lived. The reaction created by the Sophists, the genius of Socrates, the political and moral corruption of the rulers, and the anarchical, fickle, and profligate characteristics of the people, drove the sensitive mind of Plato to seek out a method of philosophising, which should produce that steadiness, refinement, and stability, without which society quickly falls away.

Though he undoubtedly contradicts himself in his various dialogues, not in minor questions only, but even in his master-principle of the ideal world, still on the whole it must be admitted that he set in motion a principal of unity, and invented a scientific stand-point to which the world, man, and thought could be referred. The whole tendency of his mind was to live and believe in the Unseen World, and to account for what reality there was in material things by referring them to it. Considering the moral and political condition of Athens, to live in Plato's atmosphere was like raising the head out of some dank and fetid marsh, and breathing the balmy atmosphere of heaven. His system of ethics is founded on principles which never make any distinction between religion, ethics, and philosophy; all is subsumed in one ultimate Idea: for he who loves the true by that same act loves the good also, both being identified through a higher synthesis in the primeval Exemplar of all things. Love of wisdom, and the purification of body and spirit, draw man towards a participation with the Divinity.

It was the largeness and spirituality of the whole bias of Plato's mind, more than any specific doctrines, which have acted with such dynamic force upon the most powerful and cultivated intellects of every age, and which were not without their influence on the Angel of the Schools.

If he had done nothing else than teach that *man* is not the centre of existence, and the measure of the universe, Plato would have accomplished a work for which posterity would have had every reason to be grateful. But he did more than this: he is said to have—

'Penetrated through and over and beyond the superficially "god-like" of older philosophers, even to the knowledge of the "Kingly Spirit and living Creator of the world," and inserted immortality and a future retribution as the innermost core of his teaching.'

To say that he taught gross errors is simply to say that he was a pagan. Like the purest forms of pagan philosophy, his teachings bear more the character of ideal creations than of tough and potent instruments for purifying the heart of man. He displayed before the mind a new world, which, if dim and indistinct, was rich with noble thoughts and lofty principles. But neither beauty, nor culture, nor refinement, nor ἦθος, can quench the passions, or staunch the wound of man's original nature.

This fact comes out clearly in portions of Plato's theoretic teaching. For example: matter, such as he makes it, is eternal. He taught the existence of a world-soul. Whatever perceives ideas is everlasting and divine; hence all intelligence belongs to the Divine Substance. The stars are gods, and are to be worshipped by the people in preference to the demons and the genii. Plato's god was a metaphysical one, who need only be known to the governing few. He was a stranger to the Supremely Free, Sovereignly Personal, Living God of the Revealed Law. The nature of guilt was strange to him. In his ideal polity the women were to be in common, abortion was to be practised, unpromising children were to be put to death, and the odious sin of the Greeks was permitted. These are but specimens of the aberrations into which the most refined and noble intellect of antiquity was led, through the influence of education, and the imbecility of man's unassisted sense.

Plato, whilst he proves how splendid a gift human reason is, brings vividly before the mind how impotent are the highest efforts of fallen man when unsustained by the light of Revelation. How can philosophy dare to be ungrateful to religion!

And just as we saw the graceful and melancholy

Plato hanging on the lips of Socrates, so too we can now imagine another youth, with a strange mixture of reverence and pride, drinking in the flowing sentences of the 'old man eloquent,' as he, with his own mystic power, introduces his hearers to the glowing world he has created for them.

Unlike the youth who attended Socrates, the most distinguished disciple of Plato was nearly as ugly as Plato's master. He was but a boy when he first entered the Academy. He had been in Athens three years, waiting for the great philosopher's return from his Sicilian expedition. Deeply he had devoted himself, during this time of expectation, to the study of philosophy. He was preparing to profit to the full by the teachings of Plato the divine. He was a youth warmed with ambition, loving fame, courting applause; he had come to Athens to learn wisdom indeed, but also to make a name. Of small slender person, with lisping voice, a dandy in appearance, a smart, fluent, sneering talker, and yet, for Athens, half a barbarian, Aristotle looked as little like a man who was to rule the world of thought as well could be imagined. Never has vanity and conceit hidden so much hard logic, or concealed such deep sagacity. Seldom has a lover of approbation applied with such straining energy, with such dogged perseverance, to the study of universal wisdom. Plato's life and labours are full of poetry; Aristotle's are strictly prose. Plato was half a monk; Aristotle was a thorough man of the world. Aristotle was wealthy, and looked sharply after the main chance; Plato was comparatively poor, and never coveted to be rich. The latter was never married, fixing his heart on wisdom as a spouse; the former had one wife, perhaps two, possibly two at a time, and certainly a concubine as well. Though on account of his extraordinary intellectual gifts the learned have dealt tenderly with Aristotle, still there is a stain upon his character which cannot altogether be expunged. When young it is alleged that he was a spendthrift, then a military adventurer, and finally a seller of drugs. 'He has been stigmatised,' says Dr. Hampden, 'as a parasite, as gluttonous, effeminate, sordid, ungrateful, impious. Amongst his falts, too, have been mentioned a sneering cast of countenance, and an impertinent loquacity.' He is said so to have worried Plato, who was eighty years of age at the time, with his insolent logic-chopping, that the poor old man was forced to abandon his walks in the Academy, and retire out of the way into his private grounds.

How far these accusations are absolutely true it is impossible to say; that they are absolutely false it is difficult to believe. There is no doubt that Aristotle was a lover of good things, and of people in high places. His life was spent either as pedagogue at court, or teaching in the Athenian Lyceum. Though his health was delicate, his energy was unwearied, his curiosity and sagacity were almost morbid, his love of reading was an absolute passion, and his keenness of mind, especially in experiment and analysis, was supreme. He stands preëminent amongst all the ancients for the clearness of his head, the simplicity of his thought, and for his power of appreciating facts. If he was not endowed with Plato's creative gift, he knew how to verify phenomena; if he were wanting in Plato's admirable dramatic, poetic, and literary talent, he was a master in terseness of expression, in scientific method, and in his searching cross-examination of the phenomena of matter and of mind. Poetical, vague, imaginative, ideal, standing on the earth simply to look up to heaven, spurning sensible nature, embracing with a large love, without questioning, the whole world of abstract thought, and peopling it with bright and beautiful existences; in a word, synthetical beyond all comparison with other men, and intensely monastic in his companionship with wisdom—Plato was the very antithesis of the Stagyrite. Could it be that two imperial spirits met, and by consent divided the world of thought between them; or was it the natural reaction of an accurate and cautious intellect against the aërial systems of an opulent but unscientific mind? Perhaps the early influence of his father, court physician to the king of Macedon, confirmed Aristotle in his distaste for the mystic creations of the Academy? However it may be, the Academy and the Lyceum are complements of each other. Synthesis and analysis are continually wanted in philosophy, and here they are to be found. Plato's expansive intellect, and the logical exactness of the Stagyrite, represent that breadth and accuracy which are combined in their largest proportions by the Angel of the Schools.

The history of Aristotle's life is soon told. He was born at Stagyra, in the north of Greece, a town looking out over the sea on the one side, and embedded on the other in groves of oranges and lemons. His father's name was Nichomachus, physician to Amyntas II., king of Macedon, a man of considerable ability and a votary of natural science. That the Stagyrite himself had a turn for medicine is evident from some portions of his writings.

He possessed an intense craving after knowledge, and on the first opportunity he hurried off to Athens, the metropolis of philosophy and letters, to place himself under the celebrated founder of the Academy. Here he collected a valuable library, and ardently applied himself to the writings of the ancients. On Plato's return from his expedition, the Stagyrite became his disciple, and soon surpassed all his companions in his keenness, wit, and logic, in his caustic sarcasm, and in the general power of his intelligence. These great mental endowments, accompanied with an excessively ardent nature and an indefatigable love of study, soon earned for Aristotle that fame after which he so much yearned. Plato was so charmed with his new disciple that he called him 'the reader' and 'the intellect of the school,' and compared him to a young colt, so full was he of spirit and vivacity.

Aristotle remained seventeen years as a pupil and

friend of Plato; a long companionship, during which he had every opportunity of learning the methods of his master. To dwell under the eye of Plato and to breathe the pure atmosphere of the Academy must have been an education and an elevation in itself. There is little doubt that the sublime portions of the ethical teaching of the Stagyrite are drawn from a Platonic source.

Before the death of Plato Aristotle had already formed a circle of admirers, and had commenced to lecture. On Plato's death (B.C. 348), disgusted at not being appointed his successor in the Academy, he quitted Athens on a visit to his schoolfellow the eunuch Hermias, who had made himself tyrant of Atarneus in the face of the king of Persia. Here Aristotle remained three years; but on the death of his host, who was made away with by the Persians, he fled to Mitylene. He took with him Pythias, the adopted daughter of Hermias, and married her, some are kind enough to say, out of compassion for her helplessness.

From Mitylene he went to Macedon, and was appointed by Philip, whom he had known as a boy, tutor of his youthful son Alexander, who at this time was fourteen years of age. The king built a gymnasium in a shady grove, where Aristotle delivered his lectures to his royal charge. This lasted four years, when Alexander, being only eighteen years of age, was appointed Regent. Aristotle remained three years more in Macedon.

How highly Alexander prized his master is evident from this noble saying of his, that he honoured Aristotle no less than his own father, for whilst the one gave him life, the other gave him that which made life worth having. Alexander succeeded to the crown at the age of twenty; and on his setting out for Asia, Aristotle left Macedon, and after an absence of twelve years returned once more to Athens (B.C. 335).

Here he soon collected a large gathering of disciples. He taught at the Lyceum, in the most splendid gymnasium of the city. Here were the groves, avenues, and gardens, the porticos, theatres, and courts, the *stadium*, arena, and promenades, which by their magnificence lent a charm to the learning of the master, and enhanced the value of his esoteric and exoteric teaching. The morning was passed in the company of his more intimate disciples; the evening in instilling into the ears of thronging crowds, by means of more popular disquisitions, those principles of knowledge which he had been the first to throw into something like a scientific form.

Here he remained thirteen years. It was during this period that he wrote the greater portion of his voluminous works, and built up his lasting fame.

But the Athenians would not leave him alone. Alexander died (B.C. 323). His enemies took the lead at Athens. These men looked upon Aristotle, who had been the instructor of the Conqueror, with unmixed aversion. There had never been much difficulty at Athens in getting rid of a philosopher. Besides, Aristotle was a foreigner, and had been an intimate friend of two, if not three, Macedonian kings. A direct charge was made against him before the Areopagus of having paid divine honours to Hermias and Pythias. Aristotle had heard too much of the fate of Socrates to trust to the justice of a trial. He fled to Chalcis, saying to his friends that 'he did not wish to give the Athenians a second opportunity of committing a crime against philosophy.'

The Stagyrite never lifted up his head again. Intense brainwork and a weak constitution, added to the grief occasioned by the ill-usage of his enemies, brought him with sorrow to the grave. He was stripped of all his honours; even the privilege of being a citizen of Athens was taken from him. Sentence of death was pronounced against him. Some say he died of vexation because he was foiled in an experiment; others that he committed suicide by drinking aconite. However it may have been, he departed in the sixty-third year of his age (B.C. 322).

Such is the history of the great father of the Peripatetic school; as great a contrast to Plato in his life as he was in his bias in philosophy. Whilst the mind is borne towards Plato with spontaneous sympathy, there is something in the very appearance of Aristotle, in his sneering loquacity and want of reverence, in his impurity, and (if the word may be pardoned for its aptness) in his snobbishness, which, in spite of his transcendent intellectual gifts, leaves an unpleasing impression on the mind. Plato was great as a man; Aristotle was great as an intelligence. The more we know of Plato the more we love him; the more we know of Aristotle the less we love him. The more intimate our acquaintance with Plato's works, the less scientific they appear; the more we study Aristotle's, the more profoundly we are impressed with their accuracy and depth. It was the moral elevation of Plato and the spirituality of his temper which gained him so immense a sway; it was the intellectual sagacity and logical force of Aristotle which have earned for him a lasting reputation. Plato was patristic, Aristotle scholastic. The combination of the two—excluding errors and making good defects through the parallel light of Revelation—is to be found preëminently in the Angel of the Schools. His 'Angelic' bias was Platonic; his school gifts were Aristotelic. The keen intellect of the Stagyrite and the moral loftiness of Plato, corrected and purified by Christianity, and perfected by monastic life, made the Angelical the synthetic and analytic colossus that he was.

The broad difference between Plato and Aristotle lies in this, that Plato held the world of 'forms' to be the only real world, whilst Aristotle held the world of sense to be at the foundation of all knowledge. Whilst Plato, by means of reminiscence and the association of ideas, could recall before the mind the whole existing world of thought, Aristotle required a brute sensation, a phantasm, and an abstraction, in order to reach anything like a mental process. He looks upon the really existing archetypes of Plato as so much poetry or metaphor. What his master considered as possessing an objective being of its own, he taught was the result of mental action and the appreciated relations between one thing and another. Both held in common that science was of universals, but Plato's universals were of a different texture from those of Aristotle. Whilst Plato had only to open the eye of the mind and look on them, as it were, spread out ready made before him, the Stagyrite arrived at them through the activity of the thinking principle itself. Sensations give the particulars or individuals; memory can summon many individuals before the mind, and the action of the inductive process upon these results in general notions or ideas; one thing can now be predicated of many individuals.

Such was the antagonistic difference between these two philosophers. Plato treats the Stagyrite's ground-principle, the apprehensions of sense, as a deception; and the Stagyrite looks upon his master's fundamental axiom as no better than a philosophical romance. Natural science was the Stagyrite's delight; experiments on the animal creation had a special charm for him. He loved investigation. Analysis was his strongest point. He savoured more of the modern man of science than any other writer of antiquity. For an ancient he was cautious, accurate, and excessively objective. He saw the value of phenomena and facts almost as clearly as Bacon did. His philosophy found more pleasure in discussing *things* than the abstract notions which represented them; and though at times he may have forgotten, as he assuredly did forget, that creations and combinations of the mind's activity are not necessarily accurate expressions of objective truth, still he, more than any other thinker of the pagan schools, saw the marked difference between the world of notions and the tangible facts of life.

As long as Aristotle confined himself to secular philosophy, he excelled the master of the Academy; but where any religious bias is concerned Plato far surpasses him. Though Plato's theory of ideas is wrong, still it points in a more theological direction than almost any of the speculations of the Stagyrite. If the philosophy of Aristotle has been a blessing to the Church, the theologic tendency of Plato has been of no less service to her. If the Peripatetic logic, form, and nomenclature brought about a revolution in the method of theologic teaching, the soaring tendencies of Plato have scarcely been less useful in pointing out a method of grasping the *scibile* as a whole and of looking on it in its integrity. If the Angelical was indebted to Aristotle for suggestions in analysis, he was equally beholden to Plato for synthetical suggestions. It is quite possible that the conception of the *entire plan* of the *Summa Theologica* was partly the result of Platonic influence, whilst the mechanical framework in which each part is fixed manifests unmistakable signs of the Socratic and Aristotelic mind. Socrates, Plato, and Aristotle each in his measure continues still to act upon the world of thought. The intellectual honesty of the first, the creative and speculative gifts of the second, and the critical endowments of the third have left a mark which can never be expunged.

Now what is the position of the Angelical when compared with such giants as Plato and the Stagyrite?

What was their common object? Truth. In none of them are truths of the intellectual, the divine, and moral world sharply separated. Aristotle was the first to attempt such a division, but he by no means adheres to it in every case. So the *Summa Theologica* treats, without strict discrimination, of truths in the natural, the moral, and the divine order.

Did S. Thomas outshine Plato in his synthetical endowments? Compare the *Summa*, as a conception, with the *Dialogues*. Did Aristotle exceed the Angelical in his analytic gifts? Compare the *Topics* with the Saint's teaching *De Veritate*, or with his treatment on the nature and attributes of God, and it will be difficult to maintain that the Stagyrite surpassed him. How is it then that the Angelical grasps the whole form of truth, whilst the other two have simply seized fragments mixed with error? Because he who scrutinises the heavens with a glass sees further and more clearly than another equal to him in natural sight, but unassisted by an instrument; whilst the former silently contemplates the object which displays itself steadily before him, the other may be searching about for it in vain. It was in this that the Angelical had a sovereign advantage over the fathers of Grecian thought;

he was master of the Divine revelation and tradition of the Church. He firmly grasped that truth which Plato was sweeping the heavens to find, and which the Stagyrite analysed the world of sense to meet: a truth, indeed, or body of doctrine, which they in their wildest moments did not 'dream of in their philosophy,' so utterly did it escape their keenest observation.

Revelation and tradition, whilst they have to do directly with faith, morality, and the salvation of man's soul, indirectly throw a broad and steady ray upon many fundamental positions of human philosophy. They not only illuminate the heavens, but they also cast their beams upon the earth. Many truths, even of the Old Covenant revelation, were as shining light, if not guiding immediately to philosophic truth, at all events warning from philosophic error. The coming of Christ, and the giving of the New Law, multiplied the brightness. Our Lord not merely redeemed man and became his Model, but He threw the light of His humanity on deep problems of natural truth. He rescued man, not alone from hell, but from annihilation through false philosophy; He, in a way, saved the very earth itself, and defended the doctrine of substantial being. How was this accomplished? By the Word becoming *man*. Immediately Christ took flesh humanity fell under the protection of the infallible exponent of revelation. Heretics attacked the flesh, the will, the intellect, the real existence of the Christ, and the unerring authority had to define these human attributes. He lives in the Sacrament of the Altar, and is assailed again; the Voice clear and unwavering speaks once more, and such words as 'substance,' 'accidents,' 'taste,' 'space,' and 'form,' receive an illumination, and philosophy receives a help. In fact, the scheme of man's salvation is so mixed up with man and with the world, that philosophy cannot go far wrong when she does not contradict the Church's teaching. In so far forth as a man admits a revelation, to that extent he accords to S. Thomas an advantage over the philosophers of pagan times.

Bacon says that if we would grasp and understand any particular science, we should not 'stand on the level with it, but climb up, as it were, into the watch-tower of some other science,' and thus place ourselves in a position to take in all its parts. The difficulty is to find a tower. The Angelical possessed a high and mighty one—the great science of theology, built upon the infallible Word of God, and established by a Voice of faultless truth. Besides this, he had the benefit of the discoveries of his predecessors, and the multifarious experiences of the middle age. The Church and the Fathers, as well as the philosophers, had taught, preached, and explored, in their own place, the various elements of divine and human knowledge, and of these he could and did take full advantage. Plato and Aristotle were the 'hewers of wood and the drawers of water' of the Angelical. He simply made use of them. He took their truth and dropped their error. As Revelation corrects the vagaries of sense, and permits all sciences to serve her, but will suffer none to cross her path, so with the Angelical. He followed Plato and Aristotle where they did not clash with the Church, and so far forth as they were useful servants to the higher science; but he parts company with them without remorse when they swerve from the right line of supernatural revelation. He was never puzzled by them or at a loss; he saw his way clearly. He possessed a guide and an illumination which made him independent of them, whilst he enlisted all the good which they had taught into his own special service. Not that Plato, and specially the Stagyrite, failed to teach the great scholastic many things he would not otherwise have learnt. It might be said that whilst he knew a whole *cosmos* of which they were ignorant, he also possessed a *tessera veritatis* by which to test those things which they appeared to know better than himself. He may have been deceived by them in some things, as certainly he was in many matters physical, but never in those cardinal truths which are connected with God, and with the happiness, progress, and perfectibility of man.

The next point of remark is the generous freedom of the Angelical—evincing his thorough mastery of truth—in adopting not only the terms, but the views of pagan writers; and the exquisite skill by which he knows how to mend, and turn to full account, the theories and teachings of antiquity. If Plato can serve his purpose he uses Plato; where Aristotle conforms more nearly to the truth, he quotes the great 'philosopher.' In the present instance not only the terminology of S. Augustine, but the words of the Academy, are treated with marked respect, and are adopted. Is not a whole system contained in the terms *participatio, rationes, exemplaria, ideæ*, &c.?

The Angelical, through his unbiassed calmness and divine self-possession, was never warped for one moment by party feeling. He belongs to but one school, the school of Wisdom. He is not a Platonist, nor is he an Aristotelian; he could be neither, yet he is both. He was as transcendent in his power of adaptation, in knowing what to select and what to reject, in perceiving with the accuracy and readiness of instinct what harmonised with revelation and what did not, as he was in his gift of contemplation and of theological construction. He was quite as clever in choosing the materials as he was in designing and building up the house.

What are his guiding points in the article in question? The doctrine of 'creation,' of which the ancients had no proper notion, and of the nature of 'evil' and of 'matter;' then the infallible traditionary teaching of the Church concerning the Personality of the Deity, the watchfulness of Providence, the character of the Divine attributes, and the relation of the Creator to the universe. Plato and the pagans were measured by these standards, and were only permitted to assist in building up the temple when their views harmonised with the general design. If Christianity is true, what greater benefit could philosophy desire than to have its crooked ways straightened by the power of revelation? No man but an infidel would affirm that the philosophy of Aristotle and Plato is nearer truth than that of the Angelical. Where he touches their teaching he does not mar, but mend, for he was guided by a stronger and steadier light than the greatest sage amongst them. A vivid perception of the supernatural system, and a life passed in the Unseen World, gave to the Angelical a vantage-ground and a vision unknown in all antiquity.

Even in this brief article he steadily confronts the errors of Plato and Aristotle, of Algazel, Averroës, and the Arabian commentators.

The 'eternal gods' of Plato become the *exemplaria* and *rationes*, which are one in essence with the Divine Substance, and according to which things are known by God and are created.

The 'eternal matter' or *hyle* of the Academy is done away with altogether, for 'matter in itself has no being, neither is it knowable.'

The god of Aristotle, who would be 'contaminated' by knowing evil, and therefore cannot know the world, and who is a perfect *cretin*, becomes a Lord and Master who does know evil, and yet receives no stain, knowing it indirectly through His idea of good; whilst the helpless divinity who 'cannot descend to particular beings' is an omniscient Creator, who watches over His creatures by a special providence, and has a knowledge of every created thing.

Regarding the Arabians, Avicenna's eternal world is proved away; Avempace's 'separate forms' are repudiated; whilst the whole *rationale* of the *Summa* strikes straight against the method of Averroës, who prefers philosophy to the *dicta* of faith, teaches the 'eternity of matter,' denies the Providence of God, and His divine knowledge of individual existences.

This was one of the master-works of the Angelical, to remove the Greek and Arabian confusion regarding the relations of God and man, by establishing the creative act, by treating with scientific precision of the nature, attributes, and operations of the Creator, and of the conditions of human existence and human knowledge. How murky and misty are not the theology and philosophy of the most cultured of the Greeks compared with the splendid and luminous creation of the *Summa Theologica!*

CHAPTER XIX.

S. THOMAS AND REASON.

Had not the Angelical thoroughly mastered the teachings of the Stagyrite, he never could have displayed so great a command in dealing with Greek philosophy. He was profoundly convinced that no lasting work could be effected without taking complete possession of the most sagacious and scientific thinker of antiquity. He was well aware of the poisonous influences which had been brought into the Paris University through Eastern commentaries and paraphrases of the works of Aristotle. Albertus Magnus had done much, but he had not done everything. The Oriental mind, with its pantheistic tendencies, with its sceptical or rationalistic bearing, with its mystic dreamings and dangerous asceticism, could not thoroughly be confronted without striking at the very root from which its errors chiefly sprang. As long as perilous tenets were brought forward on the authority of the 'philosopher,' it was excessively difficult to meet them. No writer could be cited on the other side who was equally revered; indeed, the very name of the master of Grecian thought was almost enough to secure respect for any doctrine, independent of its intrinsic conformity to the principles of sound reason. The Angelical, with his keen intelligence, perceived at once that the authority of the Stagyrite was a power in itself—that with a certain alloy of error there was a fund of truth in his philosophy, that many of his writings had been tampered with dishonestly, and that not a few of the heresies attributed to him were in reality fathered upon him through the unfairness, misconceptions, or prejudice of Jewish or Oriental commentators. He saw distinctly that in more cases than can be mentioned, the points of difference between the Stagyrite and the tradition of the Scriptures could, without much difficulty, if treated in a conciliatory spirit, be harmonised; and that if the tendency of the commentator was to bring Greek philosophy into unison with Catholic teaching, and not to widen the breach as far as possible, then, instead of the Stagyrite being found to be an enemy to the doctrines of the Church, in many instances he would show himself their invaluable champion.

Thus in all his writings the Angelical speaks with the profoundest reverence of the 'philosopher;' whenever an opportunity offers, he explains difficult passages of his writings in a Christian sense, whilst he uncompromisingly condemns them when he finds that they directly jar with the traditionary teaching of the Church.

There is something giant in all the Angelical's undertakings. His wide, various, and accurate acquaintance with the great Latin and Greek classic fathers has been alluded to already; his incomparable mastery over the Sacred Text, and his minute and detailed knowledge of the inspired writers, must already have deeply struck the reader's mind—his preparation, in one word, in the study of tradition and Scripture, for his crowning work, could hardly have been more full or more complete. His third great study of reason, or philosophy, is in keeping in its thoroughness with his labours on the elements of theologic truth. In his prison at S. Giovanni the Saint not only read the Scriptures and the Lombard, but he also earnestly applied himself to certain writings of the Stagyrite. His vast and profound Commentary on Aristotle's principal works is but the full flower of that bud which germinated then. Perhaps, in the whole range of the writings of the Angelical, these labours on the Greek philosopher exhibit more brain power, more force of logic, more piercing vision, more indefatigable industry, and more devotedness to the one object of his life, than all the others put together. There is no mental fatigue equal to that of grasping and then expanding, of correcting and then harmonising, the metaphysical or moral teachings of a really master-intellect. Bright must have been the light of truth in the Angelic's mind, to have led him safe through the labyrinths and mazes of the Peripatetic teaching.

The Saint felt it would be useless to undertake the labour of a new Commentary, if he were obliged to content himself with the vitiated text which satisfied his less systematic predecessors. Albertus Magnus had introduced him to the full value of Aristotle's writings, but even Albert, when commenting on the *Physics*, *De Proprietatibus Elementorum*, *De Cœlo et Mundo*, and *De Meteoris*, had satisfied himself with a miserable translation of a translation—with a faulty Latin version of the Arabic, which had already been rendered from a still more faulty version of the Greek. This did not satisfy the accurate intellect of a man who was bent on achieving a work of lasting value. A good translation directly from the Greek would simplify many difficulties, would sweep away many errors, and would have a chance of reproducing the author's mind; a version was consequently made for the Angelical's special use. How keenly he appreciated the minutest variation of expression comes out again and again in his Expositions. He is never wearied of collating one rendering with another, and of comparing the ordinary text from the Hebrew with what he finds in the various *exemplaria* from the Greek. It is clearly evident that whilst writing his Commentary on the *Metaphysics*, he must have had several different Greek copies lying open on his table. What greater work could genius undertake than to grasp, purify, and Catholicise the most sagacious and masterly mind of the most gifted people of the world?

No philosophical training could have been more perfect, or more complete, than that of the Angelical. He wrote many valuable *Opuscula* on matters relating to logic, physics, and various branches of philosophy; but his master-pieces are his *Commentaria* on the principal metaphysical and physical labours of the Stagyrite. They fill four volumes of the Parma edition, occupy about two thousand four hundred pages, and in reality contain the subject-matter of the greater portion of his smaller *Opuscula* and brochures.

In these four volumes the Angel of the Schools cuts the ground from under the Eastern and Jewish commentators, and hands over Aristotle to the uses of the schools, purified of paganism, divested of Oriental colouring, Christianised from end to end, and conveying the true meaning of their author. Such was the philosophical apprenticeship which our Saint went through, of his own accord, as a preparation for writing the great *Summa*

Theologica. A brief detailed account of his principal Commentaries will not be unacceptable.

The Exposition on the *De Interpretatione*, or the *Perihermenias*, does not extend beyond a hundred pages. The text is broken up into a certain number of divisions, and each of them is expounded in turn by the Angelical. His main scope is to make the sense of the author clear by means of analysis, illustration, and development. Boethius is often quoted, whilst Andronicus, Alexander, and Porphyry are referred to, either to elucidate the meaning, to give it an authority, or as vouchers to a certain method of interpretation. The object of the treatise is to show the logical value of words and of propositions.

The same gift of seeing likenesses which the Angelical displays in his treatment of Scripture is manifested also in his Commentaries on the Stagyrite. He appears to possess quite as great a mastery over the voluminous writings of Aristotle as over the teachings of antiquity and the Sacred Text, and is continually explaining one portion of the philosopher's disquisitions by more explicit statements drawn from his various works. Even in the short *Opusculum* before us he displays a familiar acquaintance with Andronicus, Theophrastus, Ammonius, Diodorus, John the Grammarian, Algazel, and Alexander.

Throughout his Commentaries the Saint proves himself to be a steady supporter of the doctrines of the Stagyrite, in opposition to the less substantial teachings of the Academy.

Aristotle has hardly written a work of greater importance than the *Posterior Analytics,* if we regard his influence on the opinions of the middle ages. It forms one of those great fountains of learning from which Christian philosophers so freely drew, and which acted with such powerful effect upon the whole method of their philosophical speculations.

What object had the Stagyrite in view when writing this work? Nothing less than a treatise on demonstration, on the first principles of knowledge, and on that framework upon which science ought to rest. It is on this fundamental question that Aristotle parts company with Plato. Whilst the latter confuses demonstration with order in the realm of fact, the former draws a sharp line between proofs of fact and proofs of speculation. The Platonic doctrine of reminiscence melts into air when brought into contact with the theory of the Stagyrite. Aristotle shows how all demonstration implies certain principles, which are elicited from generalisations which are the product of careful observation.

The *Posterior Analytics,* with the Thomistic Commentary, consist of two books; the first divided into forty-four *lectiones,* the second into twenty. They treat upon the essence of demonstration, its conditions, kinds, and upon the most apt and useful figure into which it can be thrown; then on the various forms of ignorance, on the terms of demonstrative propositions, on the different sorts of demonstration with their relations to one another, on the relation of science to certainty, sense, and opinion, and on the fundamental principles of syllogistic reasoning.

The Commentary on *De Physico Auditu* is another important work. It occupies eight books. The first is replete with interest, dwelling on the opinions of the ancients, giving rules for method, criticising 'Being,' and entering into the theory of matter, form, and privation, accounting for the last on the principle of contraries, and showing the difference between matter and privation. The systems of Parmenides, Melissus, and Anaxagoras are refuted. In the second book the nature of physical creation is treated of, the meaning of the term is defined, and is proved to be the principle of rest and motion. The four species of causes which comprise nature are developed, and all things are shown to have their substance, form, motion, and end; whilst chance, fortune, accidental causes, and their effects, come under consideration. The third book undertakes to explain that one grand influence which runs all through the speculations of scholasticism—the theory of motion. The view of Anaxagoras is upset, the celebrated definition of motion is given, as consisting of passing from potentiality to act; whilst time, space, and infinity are treated of, as necessary to the elucidation of the Aristotelic theory. The fourth book deals with place, time, and the vacuum, according to the opinion of the ancients, and also according to the teaching of Aristotle himself. The four following books are principally occupied with disquisitions upon motion.

They dwell on its different species, on its unity and plurality, on the difference between motion and rest. Accidental, partial, and absolute motion are spoken of —phrases which are continually met with in the philosophy of the schools ; the five elements of motion are discussed; its three categories—place, quantity, and quality—are enlarged upon ; the four kinds of motion in space, proceeding from some external agency, are given ; and motion is divided into two grand divisions of natural and unnatural. The first class of motion is either in a right line, or in a circle, or mixed. Of these the circular is the perfect form, it alone is continuous, and is that of the prime-mover, who is indivisible and without magnitude. The first *lectio* of the seventh book is instructive, as evincing how carefully the Angelical deals with the opinions of learned commentators and with their various forms of mental error. He shows how Galen was deceived by an equivocation into opposing Aristotle's doctrine on motion. He states the doctrines of Avicenna and of Averroës, and displays a profound acquaintance with their writings. The third *lectio* proves that there must be a first mover, and a and a first thing moved. In the eighth book an inquiry, full of interest, is made into the *primum mobile*, th first mover and the first movement, and the Saint defends the Stagyrite against the false interpretations of his works by Averroës, which, if followed, would throw his writings into great confusion.

The Angelical did not complete his Commentary *De Cœlo et Mundo*. In point of fact this work is a continuation of the one on Physics, and has very little to do with Astronomy. What is the Angelical's general view of the order of sciences? He draws it out clearly in his *Prooemium :*

'The philosopher says, in his First Book of *Physics*, that we are said to know a thing when we are acquainted with its first causes, its first principles, and its elements; and by this he clearly shows that there is an orderly progression in sciences, advancing from first causes and principles to proximate ones; and this is according to reason, for the progress of sciences is the work of reason, whose specialty it is to reduce things into order. So in every work of reason a certain rule is observable, according to which a thing advances from one stage to another; and this is seen in the practical order, which relates to things which we make ourselves, as well as in the speculative, which has to do with what is not made by us. Progress in the practical order is fourfold. First of all, in the order of apprehension, as an architect first apprehends the form of a house, and then realises it in matter. Secondly, in order of intention, according to which he proposes to complete the whole building. Thirdly, in the order of composition, by which he first hews the stones, and then fixes them together into one wall. Fourthly, in the order of sustaining the building, according to which he lays the foundation upon which the different portions of the fabric are to stand.

A fourfold order likewise is found in speculation. First of all, according as progress is made from common things to less common, and this order, in its manner, corresponds to the first—that is, of apprehension; for universals are considered according to their absolute form, and particulars in the application of the form to matter. The second order corresponds to the order of intention, inasmuch as the whole is thought of before the parts. The third order proceeds from simple to composite, inasmuch as composites are known by simple things, and corresponds to the order of composition. The fourth order, according to which the principal parts are first considered, *e.g.* the heart and the liver before the arteries and blood, corresponds to that practical order which first lays the foundations.

And this fourfold order enters into natural science. For first those things which are common to nature are determined in the book of *Physics*, in which movable body is treated of inasmuch as it is movable. Hence it remains for other books on natural science to apply these principles to their proper subjects.

The subject of motion is magnitude and body, because nothing is moved except quantity. But three other orders must be regarded in bodies. First, inasmuch as the whole corporeal universe comes into consideration before its parts. Then, inasmuch as simple bodies are considered before mixed ones. Thirdly, inasmuch as—amongst simple bodies—the heavenly ones, by which all the rest are formed, must be taken into account first; and these three things are considered in this book, which is entitled *De Cœlo* by the Greeks.'

The work *De Cœlo et Mundo*, with its Commentary, occupies over two hundred pages, and is divided into four books: the first, twenty chapters; the second, twenty-eight; the third, twelve; and the fourth, three.

The first book treats of substance, with its three dimensions, and touches upon motion, which is either straight, or in a circle, or a compound of both. Straight motion is either up, going from a centre, or down, tending to a centre. What goes up is light, and what goes down is heavy. One of the great errors in natural science made by the ancients is here reproduced, namely, that weight and lightness are absolute qualities of bodies; not *relations*, as we know them to be, between bodies and the centre of the earth. The second book discusses, with much fulness, the contrarieties in space—right, left, and so on; like weight and lightness, these are made out to be not *relative* but positive qualities. It speaks of the perpetuity of heaven, its various parts, its figure and motions; then of the nature of the stars, their motion, sound, order, position, and figure; and, finally, of the movement, rest, and figure of the earth. The third book treats of the opinions of the ancients regarding the generation and corruption of natural things, both respecting composite and simple bodies, and reciprocal generation of the elements, which some maintained, is argued against. As in the other books, the theories of the ancients are discussed, and the teaching of Aristotle defended with great ingenuity. Parmenides, Melissus, Euclid, and the 'theological poet' Hesiod, are referred to by the Saint. The fourth book treats of the nature and differences and other qualities of gravity and levity, which are made to be both relative and absolute. But the Angelical only got as far as the end of the fourth chapter, if in reality the Commentary on the third and fourth book, attributed to him by some writers, was made by him at all.

The treatise *De Generatione et Corruptione* falls into two books. The Exposition is thrown into twenty-five and twelve chapters respectively, but since the views here treated of have, for the most part, been touched upon already, there is no call for a prolonged examination of them. The various systems of the ancients regarding alteration, augmentation, touch, action, and passion, and fusion or admixtion, are explained in the first book; in the second, the principles, number, and generation of the elements and of mixed things, together with the causes of generation and corruption, come under consideration.

The work *De Meteorologia* is in four books, and is one of the most curious of Aristotle's treatises on physical nature. Here the Angelical simply follows the philosopher, and dividing each book into a certain number of *lectiones*, he gives a brief exposition on the teaching of the Stagyrite.

The Commentary on *De Anima* in all occupies over four hundred and forty pages. The length of the *lectiones* varies, and the reference to ancient writers is not so frequent as in most of the Saint's other works. Catholic truth and the prevalent errors of the day are never forgotten, and the false teaching of the Arabian commentators is carefully exposed. It was one of the great works of the Angelical to clear Aristotle from the bad character which his writings had acquired, on account of prejudiced minds perceiving not his but their own doctrines in his writings.

For example, in the seventh *lectio* of the third book it is shown that though to understand is, as it were, to feel, still intellect and sense are altogether distinct; that intellect is incorporeal, unmixed, and impassible, and different from sense, and not a separate substance. Upon this the famous opinion started by Averroës regarding the oneness of the intellect is argued against by the Saint. He not merely proves the impossibility of understanding at all, according to the theory of Averroës, but what is perhaps still more to the purpose shows that the commentator had altogether misunderstood Aristotle, and set him in contradiction with himself.

The minor treatises on which the Angelical commented must be hastily referred to. *De Sensu et Sensato* is in one book and nineteen lessons. It treats of the five senses, of their several organs, it gives the various opinions held by the ancients upon these questions, and touches upon the generation, species, and nature of sensations in relation to each of the senses. *De Memoria et Reminiscentia* is shorter still—one book and eight lessons—and dwells on the difference and nature of memory and reminiscence, and how some have better memories than others. *De Somno et Vigilia*, one book, six lessons, speaks of sleep and waking, their nature and causes. *De Somniis*, one book, five lessons, deals with the nature and seat of dreams, in which in a particular manner the sagacity of the Stagyrite is made manifest; and, finally, *De Divinatione per Somnium*, in one book and two lessons, enlarges on the cause and issue of dreams, and on their interpretation. In commenting on these the Angelical follows his usual method, and does not do much else than elucidate the meaning of the text.

To expound the metaphysical treatises of Aristotle was a formidable undertaking. S. Thomas has given us an Exposition of twelve books, and though he has not left any writings upon them, the other two books, one of which Albert appears never to have seen, were not unknown to him.

This work occupies over four hundred pages, and each book is divided into a given number of *lectiones*. Here again is one of the rich quarries out of which the Angel of the Schools drew the materials for his fabric of Christian theology. One of the most curious and interesting portions of this commentary consists in the *Prooemium*, which contains the Angelical's independent view of the great science of *Metaphysics ;* a view indeed his own, still evidently proceeding from a mind which had been accustomed to breathe freely in an Aristotelic atmosphere.

The Commentary upon the *Ethics* of Aristotle is in ten books, and these are subdivided, according to the usual plan, into a given number of *lectiones*. These books occupy over three hundred and sixty pages. The first (Book I.) treats of the different ends of happiness, and the supreme good of the happy man, of the twofold part of the soul, and the division of virtue (p. 1-42); then (Book II.) of virtue in general and its essence; of the mean and the extremes of the relations of vice and virtue, and of the precepts by which man is drawn towards the golden mean (p. 42-68); next (Book III.) of involuntary actions, of purpose, bravery, temperance (p. 68-113); (Book IV.) of liberality, magnificence, ambition, truthfulness, shame, and other qualities (p. 113-151); (Book V.) of justice and injustice and equity (p. 151-190); (Book VI.) of speculation, deliberation, and prudence (p. 190-219). Then (Book VII.) there comes an important treatment of the degrees of virtue and vice, heroic virtue, continence and its opposites, and of pleasure and pain (p. 219-258); (Book VIII.) of friendships and many things concerning it (p. 258-293); (Book IX.) of kindness, selfishness, and self-love, and other relations of friendship (p. 293-325); and lastly (Book X.) of pleasure in its relation to ethics. The thesis of Eudoxus on pleasure, on a philosophic life, and political philosophy, is discussed (p. 325-361).

CHAPTER XX.

S. THOMAS AND FAITH.

PART I.

THERE is a picture of the Angelical in the church of S. Catherine at Pisa, painted (1340) by Traini, which vividly portrays with the pencil what I have been aiming at sketching with the pen. The Saint is in the centre; above him is represented the Almighty in a sea of light surrounded by choirs of angels; below, in the clouds, are Moses, the Evangelists, and S. Paul. From the Eternal Father lines of light strike down upon these men of God; and from them, in a threefold ray, concentrate upon the forehead of the Angelical. On either side of S. Thomas, somewhat lower down, are Plato and Aristotle, the one holding the *Timæus* open before him, the other the *Ethics*; and from each of these a beam ascends and fastens itself on the brow of the Angelical, harmonising with the Divine illumination which proceeds from the Everlasting Father. The Saint himself is seated; the Sacred Scriptures lie open before him; whilst he, calm, gentle, and majestic, points to the first words of the *Summa adversus Gentiles:* 'My mouth shall meditate truth, and my lips shall hate the impious one.' The 'impious one' is Averroës, who lies prostrate at his feet with the 'Commentary' at his side, struck by one of the flashes which shoot from the pages of the inspired writings unrolled upon the knees of the Angel of the Schools.

Here then is S. Thomas combating the aberrations of the world, and the special errors of his day, through the power of a double illumination; that which proceeds from above in the supernatural order of revelation, and that which comes from below through the light of human reason: Moses, the Evangelists, and S. Paul on the one hand; Plato and Aristotle on the other. The concentrated radiance of the supernatural and the natural orders, when brought to bear upon the intellect of a Saint like the Angelical, could not but issue in some great benefit to the Christian world. So deep a knowledge of the Fathers, so profound an acquaintance with Holy Scripture, so marvellous a mastery of human as well as divine philosophy, joined to a burning zeal for souls, resulted in a series of scientific writings which, leaving out the *Summa Theologica* altogether, would immortalise the name of any scholastic.

The character and contents of these works must be briefly indicated, in order to convey some idea of the intellectual activity and theological position of the Angel of the Schools.

Besides his formal lectures in the University the Saint was in the habit of solving the difficulties and answering the questions of any who thought fit to apply to him. The collection of these answers and solutions, which are called *Quæstiones Quodlibetales*, forms a very curious and interesting study. They are very miscellaneous in their subjects, some being profound, others quaint, a few almost absurd, according to the character of him who asked them, but they are specially instructive as evincing the general tendency of theological thought in the thirteenth century.

The 'Quæstiones' occupy one hundred and thirty pages of the Parma edition. Each 'Quodlibetum,' and of these there are twelve, contains a given set of questions, each question having under it a certain number of articles. For instance, the first 'Quodlibetum' contains ten questions, answered by twenty-two articles; the second eight, with sixteen articles; the third fourteen, with thirty articles; and so on. In all the number of articles under the twelve 'Quodlibeta' extends to one hundred and sixty, differing in length or importance according to the subject-matter. Points, for instance, which had a peculiar interest at that day are treated fully, such as questions regarding the corruption of forms; the relation of parochial work to study; the drawing of youug men into religion; the relative perfection of religious and parish priests; the reception of children to the habit who have not been practised in the precepts; the relation of precepts to counsels; the precedence of precepts or counsels; whether the angelic intellect can know individual things; whether manual labour is of precept; and many more which it would be tiring to enumerate.

As examples of quaint questions these might be mentioned: Whether an angel can pass from point to point without going through the intermediate space; whether it suffices to confess *in scriptis;* whether perjury be a greater sin than homicide; whether a monk sins mortally by eating meat; whether it is a sin to wish to be a bishop; whether the damned rejoice in the punishment of their enemies; whether this be false, 'God can sin if He wishes;' whether a crusader who is returning from the Holy Land dies a better death than one who is going thither; whether an angel can be in the convexity of the empyrean heavens; whether a person could be naturally or miraculously both a virgin and a father; whether truth be stronger than wine, a king, or a woman; and so on of the rest.

All these subjects evince the play and activity of the scholastic mind at that day, and how patiently the Angelical set himself to answer, for the sake of others, questions which he himself often thought to be frivolous or beside the point.

The *Quæstiones Disputatæ* belong to quite another order of thought. They contain the subject-matter of the Angelical's deepest Expositions. He composed them in his responsible office of teacher in the schools. After the Master had finished his 'Commentary' on the *Sentences*, he then carried the students through a more elevated course, and developed, expanded, or explained special questions of theology. This was the main occupation of S. Thomas from the time he took his Doctor's cap till he was called away to Italy. This was with him a period of great intellectual activity. He was steadily preparing and quarrying the stone for his imperial edifice; his labours on the *Quæstiones Disputatæ* bear immediately upon it, and are as direct and perfect a preparation as he could have made for the great labour of his life. The advance made by him here upon his earlier works is evident at a glance. The eye is steadier and clearer, hard knots are cut with a quicker and more incisive hand, truth is brought out as with a lens, all outlines are sharp, error is crushed, and the workman shows himself to be not merely an able man but a thorough master.

These *Quæstiones Disputatæ* occupy a large space amongst the minor writings of the Saint; they take up one thousand and ninety pages, making sixty-three questions, and over four hundred articles. The great treatise, it may be called, 'De Veritate,' which would have given a name to any theologian or philosopher, had he never written anything else, fills some four hundred and fifty pages, and was the outcome of over two years' steady labour. Twenty-nine questions, and a proportionate number of articles, are contained under that single head. None of those strange difficulties found amongst the 'Quodlibeta' are allowed to enter here. All is serious work. Some of the deepest problems of theology, some of the most abstract questions of philosophy, some of the most insidious errors of metaphysics are here discussed. Perhaps the Angelical never wrote a work which pointed more directly at the errors of his day, or sank so deeply into the well of truth. The pantheism of the Easterns, the rationalistic principles of Abelard, the various heresies which were fixed in the intellect of the thirteenth century, are combated and completely overthrown, not merely through the power of authority, but by the sharp-pointed lance of reason. The doctrines of emanation, the grotesque teachings of Spanish and Arabian philosophers, are met fairly, and are as fairly proved abortive. Any one reading the *Summa Theologica* after studying these *Quæstiones Disputatæ* will perceive that whilst he was forming the minds of his students and annihilating error, the Angelical was at the same time hewing out the great blocks and keystones for his mighty architectonic work.

These *Quæstiones Disputatæ* are thrown into certain grand divisions. The first, headed 'De Potentia,' is composed of ten questions, with a certain number of articles under each, sometimes seven, sometimes nineteen, sometimes six, according to the subject-matter. Next comes 'De Malo,' sixteen questions in all, with their various articles. Two questions succeed, each complete in itself and called a 'Quæstio Unica,' one

'De Spiritualibus Creaturis,' the other 'De Anima;' and finally there is a third, 'De Unione Verbi Incarnati.' Five more 'Quæstiones Unicæ' follow, 'De Virtutibus in Communi,' 'De Caritate,' 'De Correctione Fraterna,' 'De Spe,' and 'De Virtutibus Cardinalibus.' Lastly, there is that splendid treatise 'De Veritate,' which, as has been said, is one of the most marvellous writings of the great Angelical. It is divided into twenty-nine questions, with the usual series of articles according to the division of the object-matter. It embraces four hundred and fifty pages, the subjects are treated with the greatest care and elaboration, are developed with singular lucidity, and a thread of order runs through the whole which lends a unity to the component parts.

Under the great headings of 'Power,' 'Evil,' and 'Truth,' the Saint has treated with a depth, simplicity, and brevity all his own, some of the most difficult and most important questions of religion and philosophy. For the reader to grasp the power of S. Thomas in overthrowing error, and to acquire a notion of his driving force of mind, these questions themselves must be studied in detail. To bring out his full merit, even in this his minor work, would occupy not simply a few pages, but a moderate volume.

One of the most useful and handy of the Saint's works is his *Compendium Theologiæ*, which he dedicated to his beloved *socius* Reginald. It is a model of simplicity, lucidity, and reasoning. Most probably it was written specially for the use of missionaries who went into distant parts amidst pagans and barbarians. It is a most compendious *résumé* of Catholic doctrine, thrown into a nutshell, and yet capable of being expanded by one who knows how to elicit the fruitfulness of principle, and serviceable in every way to those having the cure of souls: it is a kind of *Summa Theologica* in its minutest form. Here, unlike in several of the *Opuscula*, the Saint does not rest so much upon authority as on reason; that is to say, he carefully confirms by intellectual arguments those positions which have been before maintained by faith.

This little work occupies eighty-five pages. The first part is subdivided into two hundred and forty-six chapters; the second has only ten; the third was never written. It was originally proposed to be in three grand divisions: the first treating of matters which could be reduced to the general heading of Faith, the second to that of Hope, and the third to that of Charity. The Angelical, however, had only time fully to complete the first portion; at his death he had not got beyond the beginning of the eleventh chapter of the second part, in which he designed to prove the possibility of obtaining the kingdom of heaven.

It stands to reason that the two hundred and forty-six chapters of this 'Compendium' cannot be very heavy ones. Their length varies; those dealing with subjects intimately affecting the errors of that day, for instance, respecting the Arabian aberrations regarding the unity of man's intellect, are drawn out at considerable length, and are argued with great care and elaboration. Then, again, all those questions which bear upon our Lord are more fully developed than any other dogmatic portions. On the whole, especially in the first part of the 'Compendium,' Scripture is but scantily made use of, whilst the Fathers are seldom referred to. Simplicity, order, brevity, and clearness of reasoning, seem principally to have been studied here, whilst the Angelical keeps within the rigid bounds of a genuine *breviloquium.* The first thirty-six articles are taken up with the consideration of God's attributes, perfections, intellect, and will. Then eight are dedicated to the Word, its relations, essence, and connection with the Father. Love is treated next. Then five chapters are spent in speaking of the Holy Spirit and His relations to the Father and the Son. Sixteen follow on the relations, distinctions, and properties of the Divinity. In harmony with his usual method, after having treated of the Divine life, the Angelical touches upon the Divine action *ad extra.* Hence comes creation in general, then in particular, and in its relation to man. Errors relating to the connection of body and soul, with regard to the light of the intellect and the generation of life, are gone into patiently; and in his analysis of them the Angelical displays the mind of a master. Next, the end of the Divine operations is spoken of. It is proved that the Divine Goodness is the last end of all, whilst the end of man's intellect is the vision of the essence of God.

Having established the true relation between God and His creatures, the Saint proceeds to consider how man either attains his last end or deflects from it. Hence, good and evil are discussed; while guilt and punishment, and the power exerted by higher natures over lower, are considered in their turn : the bearing of the heavenly bodies upon creation, and how creatures of the earth are influenced by them, are explained. The Saint demonstrates how God alone can impress the human will, and treats at length of chance, fate, providence, sin, and grace. Then the last end of man, the conditions of the resurrection, the saved and lost, the punishment of sin after death, are dwelt upon and theologically propounded; and, finally, original sin and the Incarnation are analysed, whilst 'Christ' is treated of in about forty chapters, with greater frequency of scriptural reference and of patristic authority, and with greater variety of reasoning, than is employed in any other portion of the 'Compendium.'

But a far greater work than this is the *Summa contra Gentiles.* Just as the noblest work of the Angelical is called a theological sum, so this may be justly named a *philosophical* one. Its principal practical aim at the time it was written was the enlightenment of the Moors, the Saracens, and the Jews of Spain; and also to bring into prominence those arguments from reason for the establishment of Christianity, which were beginning to be undermined by the rationalistic spirit of the age.

Had it not been for the zeal of S. Raymund of Pennafort this powerful argument in favour of the Church most probably would never have been produced. Raymund was a Spaniard, and is said to have been descended from the kings of Aragon. As a boy he gave signs of exceptional ability, and after passing through the ordinary curriculum became a public professor of theology. But having dissuaded a certain young man from entering religion, he was touched with a qualm of conscience, and throwing up his position and prospects, he became a brother of the Friars Preachers. He had scarcely ended his novitiate when he was made *socius* to the Pontifical Legate in Spain; and his reputation for learning was so high in Rome, that Pope Gregory IX. employed him in putting together the celebrated *Corpus Juris*, which has been of such great authority in the Church. He also wrote a *Summa de Casibus Conscientiæ*, in which he manifested considerable originality of genius. Of his humility, poverty, and spirit of retirement, much might be written. He shrank from several high positions, and ever embraced, as a real good, the quiet seclusion and simplicity of monastic life. In 1238 he was elected General of the Order, but it was with difficulty that he could be persuaded to retain office even for two years; and finally he resigned his post, and retired to end his days in prayer, study, and meditation in his beloved retreat. He was as famous for his miracles as for his erudition, and he is said to have raised as many as forty persons from the dead.

The one absorbing thought of his life was how he might convert the infidel to Christianity. He felt that one of the mightiest instruments for effecting his purpose would be a well-reasoned and lucid statement of Catholic doctrine. He knew that he must reach the intellect as well as touch the heart.

Who could construct a theology to satisfy these requirements? It was but natural that Raymund should cast his eyes upon the Angel of the Schools. He interceded with the General, and S. Thomas received an obedience to write a work, which is only second to the *Summa Theologica* itself in its depth of thought and its scientific conformation. He entitled it *De Veritate Catholicæ Fidei contra Gentiles*. It at once gained a high position. It was speedily translated into Greek, Hebrew, and Syriac, most probably by friars living in the Spanish colleges established by S. Raymund for the study of Oriental tongues. It was in writing this work that the Angelical manifested so great a love of holy poverty, that he made use of refuse paper, such as any other would have thrown away. He appears to have completed it between 1261 and 1264.

In this *Summa Philosophica* a decided advance is perceivable towards scientific exposition. Though it may not be compared with the *Summa Theologica* in its perfection of form, its grandeur of conception, and its multiplicity of parts, still it is a far more scientific and artistic work than either the 'Compendium' of theology or the 'Commentary' on the Lombard. The reading, study, and thought of years, the viewing difficulties in different aspects, a more intimate acquaintance with opponents' minds—all these combined insensibly carry a theologian towards the best method of manifesting truth, and suggest a system to his mind which will display it in its most engaging and most perfect shape.

The *Contra Gentiles,* whilst principally aimed at a certain class of aberration, and at establishing the opposite truths, in reality strikes at error as a whole, and builds up from the ground, that is, from principles admitted by all who possess the light of natural reason, the fundamental positions of orthodox religion. Then those other portions of the vast fabric of Christianity, though undemonstrable by mere arguments of human ingenuity, are proved to possess a higher sanction in the supernatural gift of faith. It is the beautiful completeness of the whole, the fitting of part into part, the lucid evidence, the cogent proof, the firm links of reasoning, the crushing reply, the steady building up of the Catholic Temple of Truth from the base to the summit, till it stands out majestically with its clearly-cut outline and harmony of colour, with its order, fitness, and proportion, which is as astonishing to the imagination as it is startling to the mind. It seems irresistibly to proclaim to the human reason, from the very unity of its design, that if the truths of the natural order are to be accepted, those of the supernatural cannot be denied; that if a part is to be received, the whole must be admitted; for what is so perfectly harmonious cannot have fallen together by hazard, and the mutual bearing of part upon part, of stone upon keystone, proclaims to the intelligence that the Architect was one, that what rests on the earth is intimately connected with what is lifted to the heavens, and that the supernatural revelation of Christianity is a gift, not clashing with, but elevating, perfecting, and adorning the initial revelation of the human conscience.

The work occupies four hundred pages, and is divided into four books. These may be separated into two main divisions. The two first books, and a portion of the third, appeal to the light of natural reason, and elicit their arguments from principles which would be admitted by Saracens, Jews, Mahometans, Arabs, heretics, and rationalists of all degrees. The first book dwells upon God, His being, eternity, simplicity, essence, perfection, goodness, intelligence, truth, will, life, and beatitude, forming in all one hundred and two chapters. Thus the Supreme Being, as He is in Himself, is treated of: the Lord is shown to be God. Having established the Centre of being in His position, the Angelical proceeds in the second book to manifest His relations to the works of His hands; and in this portion of the work it is that the master-heresies of the thirteenth century are riven to pieces with a power which was certainly novel in those days. Experience, reading, arguments, drawn from the 'Commentary' on the Lombard, and from some of the *Opuscula*, are thrown again into shape, united with more recent matter, and whilst forming an impregnable defence of the truths of Christianity, become a most powerful apology in their favour with the unbeliever. The Saint begins on common ground, and steadily advances, with firm step, to the full view of the Catholic Church. The third book still carries on the work which had been initiated in the second: God's divinity, providence, miracles, law, grace, are fully analysed, and brought into bold relief; and the fourth book, while putting as it were the keystone in the arch, dwells upon the supernatural truths of the Trinity, the Incarnation, the Sacraments of Grace, and Life Eternal. Thus the City of God stands out clear and bright before the eye of the mind, casting into shade the mystic and volatile dreamings of the Easterns, and shaming rationalism and irreverence itself into the homage of genuine admiration. It is such mighty constructions as these which really impress and captivate the educated mind.

Then the Angelical wrote other works of great polemical importance, touching upon certain salient errors which called for special attention at his day. Besides the rationalism and irreverence of the schools, which the Saint waged war against by the gentle majesty of his personal character, and by the great architectonic creations of his genius, there were the three rampant evils, Greek schism, Jewish obstinacy, and Eastern pantheism to be met. Against each of these the Saint directed the logic of his powerful intelligence. It is true that in reality he refutes them in his larger works, but that did not prevent him dealing with them singly, and combating in detail the fallacies by which they were supported.

Whilst Pope Urban IV. was endeavouring to negotiate a union between the Greek and Latin Churches, the Angelical was steadily writing his celebrated *Opusculum contra Errores Græcorum.*

The cardinal questions of dispute were regarding the Holy Spirit, the primacy and power of the Pope, the Sacrament of the Eucharist, and Purgatory. Both Greeks and Latins quoted tradition. Photius, in his *Mystagogia Spiritus Sancti,* endeavoured to show that the Fathers and Popes were in his favour. He said that if S. Ambrose, S. Jerome, or S. Augustine appeared to agree with the Latins, it was either because their works had been tampered with, or because they condescended to the weakness of those with whom they were in communion; or finally because, like many of the eminent Greek Fathers, such as Denis of Alexandria, Methodius of Patara, Pierius, Pamphilus, Theognostus, Irenæus, and Hippolytus, they had fallen into error; whilst with respect to the Sovereign Pontiffs, Popes Damasus, Celestine, Leo the Great, Virgilius, Agatho, Gregory the Great, Zachary, Leo III., Leo IV., Benedict III., and John VIII., were witnesses to the orthodox doctrine of the Greek Church.

Now the Angelical was employed by Pope Urban IV. to bring out before the Catholic world the true voice of tradition, and to make manifest the erroneous teaching of the Greeks. The *Opusculum* of the Saint originated in a book on the Greek question, containing arguments in favour of the Latins, which had been sent to him by the Sovereign Pontiff. In his *Prooemium* he says that he has discovered much in it which would serve the Latin cause ; and continues :

'But as it appeared to me that its effects may be lost on many because of certain statements made on the authority of the holy Fathers, which in reality seem doubtful, and which hence might generate error, and breed contention and calumny ; in order to remove all ambiguity, and that the most pure fruit of the faith may be gathered from the authorities contained in the said work, I have proposed first to explain what appears doubtful in these authorities, and then to show how the truth of the Catholic faith is taught and defended in them.'

The Saint, in fact, writes a critique upon the work, and mentions various expressions of the Fathers to which exception might be taken. His logical mind, modelled in the school of orthodoxy, and possessing a steady light, with masterly skill draws out the real meaning of the holy Doctors ; and where they appear to use terms which could be misconstrued, or which are evidently inaccurate, he casts them into their true theological position. No man who had not gone through a thoroughly sound training, and who had not been familiar with the mind and system of the Fathers, could have succeeded as our Saint has done in so delicate an operation.

Regarding the Jews, with whom there was great contention in the middle ages, the Angelical not only dwells upon the way they should be met in his *Summa Philosophica*, and fairly confronts them in the *Summa*

Theologica, but he enters into personal conflict with them, and by the clearness and power of his reasoning converted them to the faith. For instance, Paul de Burgos, one of the most famous Jewish Rabbies of the fifteenth century, abjured Judaism after studying the Angelical's exposition of the mysteries and prophecies in the old Law, and of the figurative meaning of the ceremonies, sacraments, and sacrifices of the Jewish dispensation.

The Saint met two celebrated Rabbies at the country-house of Cardinal Richard, when on his way from Rome to Naples. They had the reputation of being wealthy, learned, and stubborn men. They soon entered into controversy with S. Thomas, and descanted with great eloquence on the grandeur and antiquity of their religion, on the sanctity of their law, on the privileges of their order, and on how the Lord had solemnly sworn to be for ever the God of Abraham, Isaac, and Jacob.

The Angelical without difficulty was able to testify to the truth of the greater part of what they said, and like an able controversialist knew how to turn it to advantage. Whilst he admitted with them the canonicity and authority of the Sacred Scriptures, he maintained the necessity of conciliating God's promises with His menaces, and of interpreting each according to the true sense of Holy Writ. He proved from express texts that the Lord was to make a new alliance with His people; that the Old Testament was but a prophecy and a figure of the New, just as the New is the explanation and the complete fulfilment of the Old. He discussed the most striking passages of the Prophets—of Jacob, Daniel, and Aggeus—who foretold the character and the coming of the Messiah, and spoke with clear utterance of the place, time, and circumstances of His birth, life, actions, and death. Then, by carefully comparing what had been foretold of our Lord with the accomplishment of the prophecy, the Saint clearly demonstrated that the Christ who had already come was the promised one of Israel.

The Rabbies were excessively struck by the ability of the Christian doctor, and they were still more amazed when, after stating as forcibly as possible the strongest arguments of their cause, they found that the calm, self-possessed Angelical separated truth from error, exploded sophistry, and maintained the Christian position all the more startlingly in proportion as they plied him with difficulties against it.

The upshot of the encounter was that the Rabbies were converted; and to the surprise of the Roman people these two proud Israelites made their public recantation and received Holy Baptism in the Eternal City, and filled with the spirit of the true Gospel, began to live the lives of humble, zealous, and devoted servants of the Cross.

Of Aquino's writings as a politician this is not the place to speak; but it would be an oversight to forget his merits as a framer of holy Liturgy and as a Christian poet. His great gifts manifested themselves in the composition of the Office and Mass for the solemn feast of Corpus Christi. It is said that Pope Urban IV. gave instructions to S. Bonaventure, as well as to S. Thomas, to construct the office; and it is related that when the Angelical was arranging the Vespers for the feast, S. Bonaventure called upon him, and during conversation took up and read that beautiful antiphon for the *Magnificat*, beginning with the words, 'O Sacrum Convivium!' So overcome was he by its depth and sweetness, that he returned home and cast into the flames as useless the work which he himself had been preparing.

And indeed how could the composition of the Angelical be surpassed? What office of the Church used during the great festivals is more touching, more soul-expanding, more full of unction than that of the feast of Corpus Domini? See how the Saint culls from the sweet Psalms of David and from the ordinances of the Old Law types and figures of the New; see how his large heart and his deep affections flow, with the overwhelming force of some majestic river, into those hymns which form the household words of the sanctuary and the very language of the holy place! The 'Pange Lingua' and 'Sacris Solemnis,' so exquisitely theological, so tenderly affective, so reverently adoring, so expressive of every want and aspiration of the human heart—where are two hymns so touching, so poetical, so angelical as they? What writer has so fixed his name in every sanctuary, or has made ten thousand churches ring for hundreds of years with such an ever-repeated, never-omitted anthem of joy and praise? He who lived at the foot of the altar and drank of the dew of heaven, he whose conversation was with the Saints of God, had learnt, as no other, how to throw into human words an angel's song. He, the champion of the Blessed Sacrament, as if by heavenly inspiration, poured out his numbers in a poet's prayer. Whether it be the beautiful simplicity of the 'Tantum Ergo,' the tender and strong love of the 'O Salutaris,' or the jubilant 'Lauda Sion,' it matters not; the Angelical was master of every note of joy, adoration, and thanksgiving which could be breathed from the human soul fired with the grace of God, and knew, as no other, how to stamp the impress of his own spirit on the treasures of his genius. It was his intense energy of devotion and spotlessness of purity which made him throw into divine song the deepest feelings of humanity; for he summed up in himself all that is purest and tenderest, all that is most noble in the hearts of the redeemed.

Take a specimen of the 'Lauda Sion:'

'Lo! upon the altar lies,
Hidden deep from human eyes,
Bread of Angels from the skies,
  Made the food of mortal man:
Children's meat to dogs denied;
In old types foresignified;
In the manna Heav'n-supplied,
  Isaac and the Paschal Lamb.

Jesu! Shepherd of the Sheep!
Thou Thy flock in safety keep.
Living Bread, Thy life supply;
Strengthen us, or else we die;
Fill us with celestial grace,
Thou who feedest us below!
Source of all we have or know,
Grant that with Thy Saints above,
Sitting at the feast of love,
We may see Thee face to face.'

How full of large, free, tender adoration was the heart of the Angelical can only be fully realised by studying in its integrity the office composed by him in honour of the Blessed Sacrament.

CHAPTER XXI.

S. THOMAS AND FAITH.

Part II.

It will now naturally be asked what was the condition of the political and ecclesiastical world during the time that the Angelical was penning his treatises, delivering his lectures, and writing his poems.

By the death of our Saint's friend and patron, Urban IV., at Perugia (1264), the Church lost an able and accomplished Pope. Like many men of great energy and exceptional gifts, he had risen from the ranks to the highest dignities attainable in the Church. He started life in a tailor's shop, then received the tonsure, and having become in turn archdeacon, bishop, legate, and cardinal, was chosen Pope by eight of the nine cardinals at Viterbo on account of his high character for saintliness and wisdom.

To give a detailed account of the vigour with which he pursued the policy of Alexander IV., his predecessor, with respect to Manfred, the turbulent king of Italy, and of how he declared a crusade against him on account of his outrages on the Church and his oppression of the people, would take up too much room. Suffice it here to say that Guy, Bishop of Auxerre, and Robert, son of the Count of Flanders, overset Manfred in a pitched battle in Lombardy; but Manfred, with his noted elasticity, speedily recovered himself, and taking vengeance on his enemies, pushed his successes so far as to threaten to lay siege to Rome. Urban took refuge in Orvieto, and shortly afterwards died at Perugia. Prudence, meekness, and generosity, combined with a deep love of literature and learning, were the distinguishing characteristics of this venerable Pontiff. He governed the Church three years, one month, and four days.

Five months elapsed before a successor was chosen. The cardinals assembled at Viterbo met at length in conclave, and elected Guy Foulquois, cardinal of Santa Sabina, successor of Pope Urban IV. Guy, like his predecessor, was a Frenchman; he belonged to a noble family of Saint-Gilles, on the Rhône. He had many high qualities and a wide experience to recommend him. He had been successively a soldier, a lawyer, a secretary, a husband, a father of a family, a widower, a canon, an archdeacon, a bishop, a cardinal, and finally he was nominated Pope. He had been raised to the cardinalate by Urban IV., under the title of *Santa Sabina*, in recognition of the skilful manner in which he had fulfilled the duties of Apostolic Legate at the English Court.

Guy was absent at Boulogne-sur-Mer when the Sacred College met in conclave at Viterbo, and it was at Boulogne that he first heard the astounding intelligence that he had been canonically chosen to succeed to the tiara. It is said that the condition of Italy at this period was so insecure for prelates, on account of the violence of Manfred, that Guy was constrained in passing through Italy to dress himself as a mendicant friar; and that in this disguise he appeared at Viterbo, and implored the Sacred College upon his bended knees, with many prayers and tears, to free him from the terrible burden they wished to place upon him. But his entreaties were of no practical avail. The cardinals persisted in their choice, private feeling had to give way to public good, and Guy was with great pomp and ceremony enthroned and crowned (1265) under the title of Clement IV.

Having been forced against his will to take the responsibility of government, he was determined that his relations should not feed and flourish upon the patrimony of the Church. He wrote thus to his nephew, Peter the Fat: 'We wish neither you, nor your brother, nor any other member of the family, to come to us without our express command; for if you do, you will be disappointed in your expectations, and will be sent home again in confusion.'

But if the new Pope was severe with the members of his family, he was full of tenderness towards men who by their talents and labours had deserved well of the Holy See. His keen intelligence, which had been practised in so many varied experiences, found little difficulty in discovering where merit lay, or in hitting upon methods of rewarding it. If his first act was to calm the rising ambition of his relatives, his second may be said to have been to fix his eye upon the Angel of the Schools, whom he determined to raise to some conspicuous ecclesiastical position. If S. Thomas lost a friend in Urban, he found a warm admirer in Urban's successor. Indeed the Pope and the great theologian were by no means strangers; Clement, when a simple priest, had looked upon that quiet marvellous Dominican with wonder and delight. He had marked the extraordinary and brilliant success of his career, and had been struck by his retiring modesty, his severe simplicity, his gentleness of life, and the spotless candour of his character. It appeared to Pope Clement that such a man as this would render distinguished service to religion were he raised from the lowly estate of a simple friar and placed in an elevated position in the Church. He not only felt urged to reward S. Thomas, but also to benefit mankind.

He caused a Bull or Brief to be drawn out, conferring upon the Angel of the Schools the Archbishopric of Naples; and the revenue of the monastery of S. Peter *ad Aram*—so called from the legend that S. Peter said Mass there before entering into the Eternal City—was also made over to him, that he might not want for means to support the dignity of his position.

This formal document was in due course presented to the Saint, and when he understood its contents he was thrown into the profoundest melancholy. Neither prayers nor threats could induce him to accept the responsibility. The Bull had to be withdrawn, and S. Thomas was left in peace during the rest of his career, and allowed to prosecute that one great object to which he had dedicated his entire intellect.

He felt indeed that he was not made for the active strifes of ecclesiastical politics; he knew that his tastes and talents lay in another sphere. He was not a Basil or a Chrysostom, an Ambrose or a Gregory the Great. His vocation from the first had been in the World Unseen, and now he was about ripe for realising the one great hope for which he had lived his life. Had he consented to accept the archbishopric of Naples, in all human probability the *Summa Theologica* would never have been written.

The huge labour of preparation for this masterwork had now been accomplished. The Saint's intellect had been impregnated with the spirit and temper of the classic Fathers of theology. He was master of the Church's past, and had grasped the whole dogmatic and moral teachings of the greatest intellects which had been raised up to expand and defend her doctrine. He was familiar with the special gift of each columnal Father; he knew where each was strong, where they diverged; he could contemplate them apart and in relation; he saw them as many, and yet as one. He had written on them and quoted them, as well as read them; and by the labour of many independent works and tractates he had made their sayings as familiar to himself as household words. He had thrown off a hundred sketches, drafts, *cartoni, imbozzi,* he had practised carefully and long, before he ventured to set himself to the grand construction of his life.

The same may be said of his mastery of the Sacred Scriptures, which he knew by heart and read by the light of the most brilliant minds which have ever illuminated the *Ecclesia Docta.* He fathomed every cavern in which a single gem of traditionary truth could lie concealed, and grasped the whole *scibile* of the Catholic Christian faith.

Again, what was the secret of his intense labours upon the text of Aristotle? Why such wearisome commenting on so many of his works, on his metaphysics, politics, physics, ethics; why did the Saint think it necessary to steep his pure mind so deep and for such a length of time in that sea of pagan thought, save that he had some great end in view adequate to the intensity of the brain-work which he so freely exercised? If his study was thorough in tradition and in Scripture, no less was it so, even more it possible, in the order of human reason. He took possession of the firm framework set up by Aristotle, hammered it into shape where it was required, changed its form in places, cut out all unfitting matter—all being done carefully and tenderly—and then threw the moral and dogma of religion into it, manifesting in scientific form the connected and systematic teaching of the Church. If from the classic Fathers and from the Scriptures the Saint drew the pure waters of belief, and learnt such vastness of design, it was by the Greek philosophers that he was taught to display such breadth of reasoning, such clearness of elaboration, such minute development of detail, such unity in complexity of parts, such richness yet simplicity of thought—in one word, the highest gifts of analysis to be found in the history of human intellectual activity.

What then, once again, are the elements of power which go towards the construction of the *Summa Theologica?* First, the inspired writers, the Prophets, the Seers, the Apostles, and the Evangelists; next, the classic Fathers of the Church, such as Athanasius, Basil, Gregory Theologus, Chrysostom, Ambrose, Augustine, Gregory the Great, with the Pontiffs and the Councils; and then all that is best in Socrates, Plato, and Aristotle.

It is an inaccuracy to call the philosophy of S. Thomas the philosophy of the Stagyrite; it is Aristotelian indeed, but corrected by the light of revelation, perfected by an effluence of Platonic elevation, and with just the soupçon of the Socratic method in it to make it charming to a crystal and active mind. The *Summa Theologica* exhibits the most successful manifestation of the harmony of fullest faith with the most perfect development of reason which—in spite of all the attractions and subtleties of German schools—has as yet been elaborated by the mind of man. If the *Summa Theologica* was not laid upon the table of the Vatican Council, there was no other book found worthy to take its place.

It has been shown abundantly that no writer before the Angelical's day could have created such a synthesis. As for the scholastics who more immediately preceded the Angelical, their minds were not ripe for so great and complete a work; the fulness of time had not yet come. Very possibly, had not Albert and Alexander preceded him, S. Thomas would not have been prepared to write his master-work; just as, most probably, Newton would never have discovered the laws of gravitation had it not been for the previous labours of Galileo and of Kepler. But just as the English astronomer stands solitary in his greatness, though surrounded and succeeded by men of extraordinary eminence, so also the Angelical stands by himself alone, though Albertus Magnus was a genius, Alexander was a theologic king, and Bonaventure a seraphic doctor. Just as the *Principia* is a work unique, unreachable, so too is the *Summa Theologica* of the great Angelical. Just as Dante stands alone amongst the poets, so with S. Thomas in the schools.

The Angelical's position as a theologian becomes

evident at once by comparing the *Summa Theologica* with the classic works of the classic Fathers.

Thus the *De Civitate Dei* and the *Summa Theologica* stand like two great towers of David, representing the mightiness of the ancient and the modern world, marking out the ground, and by their very majesty showing how comparatively insignificant all other creations are which lie between them: the one standing like a massy heaven-directed citadel, strong as Rome, colossal as the East, irregular in form, and fashioned according to the growing need; the other looking more like a modern stronghold, with its crenellated walls, frowning earthworks, and gabioned parapets. All is constructed here on a scientific principle, the whole is the realisation of one grand geometrical conception, and so set up that part becomes the defence of part, battery of battery, whilst a hundred combinations of thundering artillery can be turned upon the enemy, let him show himself at what point he may. The former fortress is more picturesque, more beautiful; this is more symmetrical, more terrible in its array of strength; the one resembles some huge Roman camp, the other is more like our modern Paris, the triumph of the scientific engineer, equally capable of fascinating the mind by its exquisite construction, and of forcing gainsayers into genuine admiration by its vastness of design, its harmony of parts, and its colossal power. It forms the impregnable enceinte encircling the *Civitas Dei* on earth, whilst the works of other skilful men are but as mamelons, redans, or detached forts, formidable in themselves, serviceable in their place and measure, but of different shape and strength, and but fragments of defence compared with the firm network of adamant and iron round which they stand at various intervals to occupy and guard the ground.

Or it might, again, be looked upon as the *corps d'armée* itself which protects the Spiritual City, composed of several divisions, yet all commanded by one chief; or, as Annat calls it, a 'terribilis castrorum acies ordinata, sub cujus vexillo militant omnes Theologi.' Tradition, reason, and revelation—artillery, cavalry, and infantry—are the three arms of this mighty service, which, though different each from each, indeed because they vary, lend each to the other an overwhelming power when handled by a skilful captain, and form that *triplex funus* which possesses a proverbial strength.

First, the enemy is reconnoitred from different points by various detachments of the *corps d'armée*, one or other branch being employed according to the character of the opposing troops and the nature of the ground. Thus the chief learns the position, strength, and resources of the enemy, and prepares accordingly to launch his grand attack. So was it with the Angelical. His various Lectures and *Opuscula*, his 'Commentary' on the *Sentences*, his *Questiones Disputatæ cum Quodlibetis*, his different Tractates on the inspired writings, his *Opuscula Theologica*, his philosophical disquisitions, together with his *Contra Gentiles* and his *Expositions* on the labours of the Stagyrite, are, as it were, advancing forces, apparently disconnected with each other, yet in reality directed in combination by a master-mind, each serving a special purpose, and preparing the way for victory in a general engagement. At one time, for instance, S. Thomas marches boldly against rationalism and materialism, then he has a sharp encounter with the Saracens; now his cavalry sweeps in amongst the Averroists and the Arabians, and puts them to speedy flight; anon the three arms of the service are directed against the Greeks, who are principally defeated by the powerful artillery which thunders against their lines; then the Jews, unequal to resist a sudden onset, are cut down, taken prisoners, or made to serve in the victorious army; while as for minor raids, skirmishes, and brilliant affairs, they are too numerous to be mentioned, though most of them are recorded in vols. xvi. and xvii. of this great chieftain's operations. These more modest engagements, which would have made a lasting reputation for a smaller man, dwindle into insignificance when brought into comparison with that one decisive battle in which all the forces join, and then, by one combined movement against the enemy, achieve a masterful and crushing victory, in which all those who had been harassed one by one before are now routed in company along the entire line. That is to say, having confronted the various aberrations of the human mind in his *Exposi-*

tions and *Opuscula*, the Angelical now concentrates his divisions, and by means of his great *Summa Theologica*, which unites the perfection of them all, simultaneously attacks and defeats those enemies against whom before he had combated in detail.

Such pictures as these convey to the imagination a fair idea of the separate and combined operations of the great Angelical, of his preliminary battles, and of his general attack.

But to extricate oneself from figures, and to recur to a definition already hazarded, this *Summa Theologica* may be fairly called 'The Christian religion thrown into scientific form, and the orderly exposition of what man should be.'

For just as the material world, created by God, adumbrates, in a dark manner though it may be, the unity, beauty, and order of the Divine mind—just as it is stamped with the royal mark of supreme omnipotence and wisdom—so also, though in a much more perfect way, with the spiritual system which he has set up to manifest His glory and to secure the salvation of His creatures. This vast organic creation is called the Church of Christ, and it is vital and energises through the Spirit of God that made it. It bears His image and likeness, it is filled with the plenitude of His truth and purity, it is representative to the world of the divinity and character of Jesus Christ, 'who is head over all the Church, which is His body, and the fulness of Him, who is filled all in all.' Or, to use another expression of the same Apostle, the Church is the Bride, Christ is its Head and Saviour, who loves, nourishes, and cherishes it, 'and delivered Himself up for it, that He might sanctify it, cleansing it by the laver of water in the word of life, that He might present it to Himself a glorious Church, not having spot or wrinkle, or any such thing, but that it should be holy and without blemish.'

This glorious Bride, so cherished and nourished by our Lord, beautiful with His beauty, strong with His strength, exhibiting the highest gifts of faith, purity, and charity, manifests to the world the impress of the divine character and intelligence of Christ. The scheme of God's glorification and the salvation of man, as it exists in the mind of the Bridegroom, is reflected, as it were, in the mind of the Bride. As Christ's blessed Spirit teaches the Church, so the Church teaches the world. To grasp, in as far as man may, the mind of the Church, is in so far to grasp the mind of the Saviour Himself. The Prophets and Seers and Lawgivers of the Old Covenant, the Apostles and Evangelists and Doctors of the New, give testimony of her, as she witnesses to her Saviour. As she is formed upon Christ as her model, so man is formed by her into a likeness of Him. In the supernatural order and harmony of her hierarchy, in the imperishable stability of her faith, in the lucid development of her moral life, and in the magnificent unity and symmetry of her dogmatic teaching —which she unfolds as she advances towards the full exhibition of her glory,—we recognise her luminous intuition of the complicated method of salvation, and her scientific apprehension of the entire economy of grace. Christ has stamped her with His own image, and she in turn seals man with her own seal.

Now, as has been suggested, the Angelical spent his life in mastering the Church's intellect; and the impression left upon his mind by this familiar intercourse he reproduces, for the sake of others, in the *Summa Theologica*. And what would this reproduction naturally represent save the Christian religion imaged, not in confusion but in scientific form?

The *Summa Theologica* is more than this. As the Bride of Christ reproduces the mind of Christ, and is 'nourished and cherished' by Him, as He fashions her into a likeness of Himself, so her children are formed according to her pattern. The Church is not a mere theory, but a living and huge energy, purifying, nourishing, and saving men, as Christ purifies, nourishes, and saves her. Her work is that of transformation—of turning men out of children of wrath into heirs of heaven. For that she lives and energises, for that the grand scheme of her theology was drawn out, for that she casts the broad net to rescue man from the burning, and drag the fallen from the pit. And such being the case, would not the accurate reproduction of her mind point out the road to man's salvation? If the physician commits to writing a minute description of robust health, and of the means of its attainment, does not his theory represent the first principle of practice? Would not his scientific method lead directly to such action in the concrete as would transform a sickly man into the very type of his own ideal? So it is with the *Summa Theologica*; it is no dead theory; it is not only 'the Christian religion thrown into scientific form,' but it is also, as a necessary consequence, 'the orderly exposition of what a man should be.' Indeed, because it is the most scientific manifestation of religion, therefore it is also the most secure instrument for directing men to heaven, just as the mariner's chart in so far forth indicates with precision how the navigator is to keep the ship clear of danger and to sail steadily into port in proportion as it accurately points out the lie of the land and the depth and currents of the sea. The *Summa*, in a word, represents in perfect system those vital principles which made the Christ-loving giants of the Early Church such splendid heroes. It is the Rule of Life, as well as the Philosophy of Faith.

Hence it is a systematic exposition of the nature of the Divine Being, inasmuch as He is the Author and Finisher of all things, more especially of the rational being; or, in other words, it treats of God and man, and of the relations between them: it points out God to man, and indicates how the rational creature is to attain to eternal happiness.

Hence, naturally, it is cast into three grand divisions. The first part treats of the Godhead, His life, relations, and attributes, of creatures, and emphatically of man; the second speaks of the rational creature as tending to or from God, his last and highest end; the third of Christ, in so far as He is the way, the truth, and the life. And thus the circle is complete; the Saint sets out with the Creator, and carries the creature through the course of his pilgrimage as a redeemed sinner back to that Hand out of which he originally came. The design was never fully realised by the Angelical—he did not get beyond the ninety-ninth question of the third part.

He did not begin to set earnestly to work till after his refusal of the archbishopric of Naples. Now that he felt himself secure, as Tolomeo da Lucca tells us, he laboured with redoubled energy. But even whilst occupied on the first portion of his great undertaking his time was taken up with many other duties. He now completed his 'Commentaries' on S. Mark, S. Luke, and S. John, which he dedicated to his friend Hannibal di Molaria; and he republished his treatise on religious life in answer to another attempt of William of S. Amour. Then he was summoned to attend the general chapter at Bologna, and was appointed, at the request of the great university, to throw fresh intellectual life into the schools, and to occupy the post of professor of theology. Before taking possession of his chair he visited the tomb of S. Peter Martyr at Milan. The miracles wrought at this sepulchre before, and particularly after, the Saint's canonisation had created great excitement in the Church. On his arrival, S. Thomas found the magistrates of the city superintending the erection of a magnificent mausoleum over the relics of the Saint, and his presence amongst them was no sooner made known than he was requested to compose an epitaph descriptive of the faith, zeal, and charity of the holy athlete.

From Milan he went to Bologna, and took possession of his little cell in the convent of the order. Here he remained some weeks in retirement before commencing his lectures in the schools. His days were passed in silent meditation, and in that deep thought which seems to have been his greatest recreation, whilst the greater portions of his nights were spent at the tomb of the great S. Dominic, who lay buried in the convent church. It was at this very time that the solemn translation of the relics of that holy founder took place (1267). They were carried with public pomp from the humble sepulchre where they reposed, and were placed in a magnificent urn, chiselled with the most exquisite taste by the most celebrated artist of the day. Bartholomew of Braganza, Arnulf of Viterbo, Ægidius Gallutius, all of them bishops, and all of them Dominicans, assisted at the ceremony. In the presence of these venerable men, and amidst the press of devout and eager friars, all that was mortal of the high patriarch of religious chivalry was lifted with great gentleness and reverence out of the tomb, and after having been kissed by fervent lips, and looked upon with loving eyes, was borne away to its more glorious resting-place.

The same kind of effect was produced by the presence of S. Thomas in the schools of Bologna as had been manifested at Paris and Cologne. His fame had preceded him. The hall was crammed. Not students only, but the very citizens themselves pressed into the lecture-room to look upon and listen to the great serene Angelical, as, rapt in the contemplation of God's highest truth, he poured forth the clear-flowing stream of his simple oratory, and entranced his hearers by the lucidity, order, and profoundness of his teaching. Indeed, it is not enough to say that the citizens were attracted to him—men from distant cities, professors, students, intellectual knight-errants of every temper, were drawn to Bologna as to a centre, just as of old Socrates, Plato, or Aristotle, Roscelin, Abelard, or William of Champeaux gathered together from all quarters of the world men, it matters not of what condition, who felt the charm of genius and the fascinating attractions of syllogistical display.

Whilst the Angelical was lecturing at Bologna, penning treatises on politics, morality, and dogma, preaching, teaching, journeying from place to place on business of the order, or practising strict observance in the convent, one abiding passion occupied his mind, and that was the gradual realisation of the *Summa Theologica*, of which mention has just been made. To this all was made subordinate. To perfect and elaborate this great conception he bent all the powers and instruments of his matured and mellowed mind. A whole life of remote preparation, and two years of labour with the pen, produced the first part of the *Summa*. As some mighty sculptor, who has spent from youth up learning first the rudiments and then the last perfection of his art, through simple cultivation can strike out a figure from the rough which would make ordinary men despair—summing up as it were at one stroke of the chisel the concentrated labours of a life—so the great Angelical in the space of two short years laid the broad foundations of his lasting fame.

The Divine Being, His existence, attributes, knowledge, name, ideas, life, and will; the blessed Trinity of Persons, the Divine processions, relations, unity, and plurality; the Divine Persons, the Father and His special attributes, then the Adorable Son and ever-blessed Spirit, their relations, equality, and similitude—all presenting before the mind an overwhelming abundance of dazzling mystery and greatness incomprehensible, overawing the faculties, and by that very power witnessing to the preëminent greatness of the Creator above the creature of His hands—are some of the objects discussed in *pars prima* of the *Summa Theologica*.

Having taken the student up to heaven's gates, and pointed out to him the majesty of the Triune God, the Angelical next treats of the Almighty's creative act and power. And here it is that the Catholic theologian cut his way clear of the pantheism of the East, with its doctrine of emanation, and of that materialism which is the genuine fruit of the rationalising spirit. The unmistakable establishment of this great truth—the emphatic assertion that between the Divine nature and all things else there is an immeasurable gulf; that the creature is not the mere effluence or exuberance of the substance of the Divinity, but a creation out of nothing by His fiat; that the infinite and the finite, the eternal and the temporal, the primeval Cause and secondary agencies, are not simply different in kind, but absolutely distinct in essence as well as mode; that nothing is of itself independent, but all is preserved as all was first created by the Omnipotent, by whom everything exists, without whom everything would cease, and in whom all things live, and move, and have their being—this gulf-separation of essence and this intimate connection in the creative act, whilst establishing a cardinal dogma of religion, strikes straight out on two sides against the dreams of a philosophy which has not been set up in the light of faith: it destroys the moral disease of pantheism on the one hand, and, by proving a Divine Providence over the world, does away with fatalism on the other.

Having thus established the relative position of creature and Creator, of God, angel, and man, the Angelical speaks in detail of the angels' life, of their trial, and the fall of some amongst them; then of the next creation of God—that of the world and of man during the Scriptural week, thus bringing into prominence other important subject-matter for development. Next, man in particular, his soul, body, mind, and their various relations, are considered, whilst procreation and the different influences, spiritual and corporeal, which act upon mankind are carefully discussed.

In a word, in this first part of the *Summa* the Saint draws as it were a sketch of the *dignissima scientia*, that is, of wisdom in the highest sense, and lays out the groundwork for the realisation of that vast conception which possesses equal grandeur and simplicity in its design.

But though this portion of the great edifice of theology may justly be considered as fundamental in its relation to the *prima secundæ* and the *secunda secundæ* and the *tertia pars*, still it would be a mistake to imagine that there is anything about it unfinished, or wanting in logical accuracy or precision of sequence, or in the concatenation and development of its members. The network of systematic integrity, with its lines and joints and unities, with its exquisite bearing of part on part, with its reciprocal illuminations, with its combined methods of support, with the multiplicity of its elaborated detail, and with the marvellous synthetical oneness of its complete design, appeals as much to the reason and the imagination as does the majestic simplicity of the original conception.

It is to be regretted that, from the very nature of the case, assertion must here to a great extent take the place of proof. But if the reader would, for example, select at hazard one point out of this *prima pars* as a sample of the rest, he would speedily convince himself of the justice of the criticism: the *Summa Theologica* is as organic as the human frame itself, and its elements are compacted together with as much nicety and harmony.

Quitting the form for a moment, and reverting to the subject-matter, which represents the whole store of learning of the past, it may be said that the intimate acquaintance which the Angelical manifests here with Scripture and the Fathers, the breadth and accuracy of his knowledge, have something about them of the preternatural at least. There is nothing of the sharpness and flippancy of the schools, no random brilliant Abelardine fencing, none of the dangerous originality of Roscelin, none of the extravagant philosophy of William of Champeaux, and none of the difficult mysticism of Richard of S. Victor's. Mere human talent counts for little, inventive genius is not rated high, self and simple ingenuity are altogether sunk, the tone and temper of the noisy self-asserting university, with its rationalistic tendency and irreverent spirit, with all its fallacies and smartness, are here thrown into their proper light, not by any direct attack, but by a method far more powerful than that: by erecting a vast monument of organised truth, composed of the teaching of the massive-minded classic Fathers, of the words of Holy Writ confirmed by high authority, and of the purest of philosophies serving as handmaid gracefully and willingly to the more majestic truths of the supernatural order. The appearance of the *Summa Theologica* in the midst of the crudities of the schools was as if the Basilica of S.

Peter's were brought into juxtaposition with the Zions and Ebenezers of our more modern days.

For instance, in the first part of the *Summa* Scripture and the Fathers advance in support of reason, as drawn from the corrected teaching of the Arabians and Greeks. The royal Psalmist, S. John the Divine, and the Apostle of the Gentiles; then S. Augustine, S. Jerome, S. Hilary, the Areopagite, and Boëthius, each speaks authoritatively on his own strong point, and adds the weight of his own prestige to the well-digested teachings of the great Angelical. Then, from time to time, S. John of Damascus bears his witness, S. Gregory the Great confirms some weighty truth, S. Ambrose falls in with his high morality, whilst the pure philosophy of S. Anselm is not lost sight of amidst so many other glorious names. The Creed of S. Athanasius, the *Glossa Ordinaria*, and the Œcumenical Councils of the Church add their venerable testimony to the general teaching; so that the *Summa* seems to be as it were one glorious song, in which the voices of the greatest heroes of antiquity, the purest and the best, chime in with the solemn chaunting of Prophets and Apostles, who, full of the strength and sweetness of the Spirit of God Himself, seem, like the alternate Seraphim around the Throne, to proclaim the love, beauty, strength, and mercy of the great Omnipotent, and the nature, character, and the high destiny of man.

And whilst the Angelical was thus working out the great scheme of salvation in the solitude of conventual life, or in presence of eager and earnest students, bitterness and strife were ravaging the world outside. A rapid sketch of the relation of the Empire and the Holy See must here find place, before proceeding to the consideration of the second portion of the *Summa*.

So long as the spirit of Frederick Barbarossa or Frederick II. animated the ruling spirits of the world, there was little chance of peace in Church or State. As was the case in the days of Gregory IX., the Pope and the Empire were still in violent antagonism; and Clement IV., in the main, was doing his best to carry out the policy of Urban and Alexander. The Sovereign Pontiffs had had enough of the Hohenstaufens. Bold, ambitious, and imperious, implacable as enemies and false as friends, they had done little else than overset religion, inflame discord, spill blood, and harass the Papal States. The Popes at last made up their minds to use all their efforts to prevent any member of that family coming into power, either in Germany or in the South.

At the death of Frederick II., Innocent IV. emphatically declared that the Holy See would never consent to any one of his family being invested with the crown. Naples and Capua, and many other cities, sided with the Pope; and when the ambassadors of Conrad, son of Frederick, and of Manfred, Frederick's natural son, made advances to these Italian cities, they were informed that the Italians had grown weary of interdicts and excommunication; and that if their masters desired to be received, they must present themselves with the blessing and investiture of the Sovereign Pontiff.

But there was far from being unanimity in respect of Pope Innocent IV. The restless and ambitious children of Frederick succeeded in ingratiating themselves with the Germans and Venetians, and were so powerfully supported by these, that for a course of years they were enabled to worry the Popes, and keep the greater part of Italy in continual fermentation. For instance, in 1251, Conrad entered Italy with a powerful army, and forthwith advanced against the Counts of Sora and Aquino, who had declared themselves in favour of the Pope. Doubtless it was excessively mortifying to these princes that the Aquinos should not only have turned against them, but moreover should have preferred the policy of the Holy See to the traditions of the past, and have had the courage to maintain the Pope in opposition to the interests of their own relations. Whilst bravely resisting the pressure of numbers, the Count of Aquino was overpowered, and Conrad advanced through Puglia with his victorious force, anticipating, no doubt, an easy conquest, when he was struck down by death at the early age of seven-and-twenty, leaving Conradin, his son, a little child of two years old, the heir to all his troubles.

But if Conrad had died, Manfred, a man of great vigour, and well versed in the arts of diplomacy and war, was still alive. He forthwith declared himself tutor of little Conradin, and in spite of the menaces of the Pope, and an actual threat of war, he carried everything before him. Pope Alexander, however, was not easily dismayed. He cited Manfred to appear before him; and as he took no notice of the summons, the Pontiff at once declared the crown of Sicily vacant; and according to the usage of those days sent the Bishop of Bologna, James Bonocambio, to London, to present it to Edmund, second son of the English king. The kingdom so graciously offered was as graciously accepted; and in the midst of a splendid assembly of the great ones of the land the Apostolic envoy placed a ring on the finger of the youthful Edmund, as the symbol of his acceptance of the crown. But all this pomp turned out to be merely an idle ceremony. The English monarch was too much harassed at home to be able to carry out ambitious projects in foreign parts in favour of his children. Manfred in the mean time was vigorously pushing his successes. He speedily possessed himself of the whole of Sicily, of the Principality of Trent, of Puglia, and of the Terra di Lavoro, and made the world conscious of his achievements by having himself crowned with great solemnity at Palermo in the autumn of 1258. This act, it might be called of bravado, added greatly to his prestige, and very shortly Sienna, Pisa, the larger part of Tuscany, and the Marches of Ancona, besides many other portions of the Papal States, declared themselves subject to his authority.

Perceiving the critical position of affairs, Urban IV., who had succeeded Alexander, resolved to act with rigour against this disturber of the general peace. In the presence of a great multitude the Pope cited Manfred to appear before him, and caused the citation to be fixed against the doors of the church at Orvieto (1262), but Manfred made as light of this citation as he had before of the Papal censures. Urban then turned his eyes to France. He sent the Cardinal of S. Cecilia to wait upon S. Louis, who had just returned from his crusade, and to offer the crown of Sicily to his brother Charles, Count of Provence and Anjou. The king at once perceived in what a difficult position the Pope was placed. He urged his brother to accept the offer, and with the agreement of Church and State a tax was levied upon the clergy to defray the expenses of the undertaking. But Pope Urban did not live to witness the issue of the enterprise upon which he had set his heart. However, Clement IV., who succeeded him, carried out his policy with the earnestness of a man who knew how great an interest was at stake. He published two Bulls: in one he annulled the gift made by his predecessor to Edmund (1265); in the other he conferred the kingdom of Sicily on Charles, Count of Anjou.

Prince Charles did not lose time. Having celebrated Easter with King Louis, he hurried to Marseilles, embarked with a thousand knights, arrived at Ostia, and then without delay proceeded to Rome. He was received with acclamation by the Romans as the liberator of the Church, and the defender of the liberties of the people. The Pope, who was still at Perugia, sent four Cardinals to wait on him, and he was invested, amidst great ceremony and display, in the Lateran Basilica with the sovereignity of Sicily (1265).

Charles was not long in setting to work to consolidate his position. The armies of Manfred and of the new king came into collision at Beneventum. The battle was long, obstinate, and bloody, but at length the French obtained an advantage; then Manfred himself was slain, and finally his whole army was routed and cut to pieces. This was a severe blow to the Ghibelines, and of immense benefit to the Pope.

But if Conrad had fallen in battle fighting for the Sicilian kingdom, and if Manfred had met a similar fate, there was still one more of that fierce and thirsty race remaining—the young Conradin, who had now attained his fifteenth year. Upon hearing of the death of Manfred he at once had himself proclaimed emperor; and urged on by the Germans, and by a party which was always to be found in Italy, he gave himself out as king of Sicily. The Pope threatened those who dared to offer him encouragement and assistance with censure and interdict, and forbade the young Prince either to assume the title or to take possession of the crown. But Conradin cared about as much as those who had preceded him for the thunders of the spiritual power. He established his ministers in Tuscany and in the Italian kingdom; he himself invaded Italy, took Verona, advanced on Pavia, and having marched through Lombardy and Tuscany, entered Rome, where he was received with marks of extraordinary honour by the unprincipled and fickle inhabitants, as well as by Henry of Castile, who, in betraying Charles of Anjou, branded himself with the threefold infamy of being a traitor to his relation, his benefactor, and his king.

So far fortune seemed to favour Conradin in an extraordinary degree. He did not remain long in Rome. He marched out into Puglia with a large force, composed of Germans, Italians, and Saracens. Charles went forth to meet him, and Conradin prepared a second time to hazard the fortune of a battle. The armies came to collision near Tagliacozzo. Conradin's host, which was under the command of several princes, after a sanguinary engagement suffered total defeat. The Pretender, Henry of Castile, the Duke of Austria, and many men of high distinction, were made prisoners of war. Henry, at the intercession of the Abbot of Cassino, was set at liberty; but Conradin and the Duke of Austria were both beheaded (1268). Such was the end of the fierce and warlike family of Suabia, such was the beginning of the mastership of the house of Anjou over the Sicilian kingdom. The Popes at length found peace, and the Aquinos at last found safety.

Clement IV. did not live long to enjoy the victory of Tagliacozzo. The Church was deprived of a great [illegible]e, and Thomas of Aquin lost a great admirer and [illegible]d, when death carried him away. Those who were [illegible]ainted with this Pontiff's daily life, those who knew [illegible]is rigid fasts, his hard bed, his hair shirt, and his mighty self-cotrol—who were aware how charitable, prudent, and learned a man he was—were conscious that a pillar of the Church, in his demise, had been removed. Few men have possessed so profound a knowledge of law, or have been so gifted with sweetness, tenderness, and zeal. He was buried amongst the Dominicans at Viterbo (1268), and upon his tomb reclines the graceful figure of S. Hedwige, whom, in his lifetime, he had catalogued amongst the Saints.

During all this period the great Angelical was living in his own ideal world, not so as to be useless to mankind, but so as to effect a work which, in its very first appearance, created a most unusual sensation. No sooner was the *prima pars* of the *Summa* published than the authorities of the various schools of Italy and France perceived it to be a book of priceless value. Many were the petitions made to the Saint to lecture, many the earnest efforts to secure his services in universities and schools. But his obligations at Bologna retained him at his post. So high a prestige did his new work lend to the Dominicans, that simply on account of the reputation of S. Thomas many new foundations were commenced, and the power and the position of the Friars were greatly strengthened. For example, Archbishop Matthew della Porta, who had been the Saint's disciple, purely out of veneration for his master founded the Convent of S. Maria della Porta at Salerno; whilst the Abbot of Monte Cassino, at the Angelical's own request, and with the unanimous consent of a synod of the clergy, established another house at San Germano.

During the interregnum which ensued between the death of Pope Clement and the election of a successor, S. Thomas went for a time to Paris. He had already spent three years lecturing in Bologna. During this period he had been actively employed on the second part of the *Summa Theologica*.

He appears to have been called to France for several reasons. In the first place, a general Chapter of the Order was about to be held in Paris (1269), at which many nice points of theology were to be discussed; then John of Vercelli was particularly anxious to receive the Saint's advice; whilst some affirm that he was summoned as Definitor of the Roman province, and was intrusted with a delicate mission to the King of France in connection with the condition of the Church and of the clergy.

The king, who at this time was about to set out on his second crusade, received the Angelical with exceptional marks of reverence and affection. Any one who has studied, ever so superficially, the character of that tender-hearted, just, and gentle monarch, so full of genuine heroism, so bright a picture of high chivalry and of the *cuor gentil*, will at once perceive how close a bond there must have been between him and the Angelical. Who, in history, has ever read of so priestly a prince, and of so princely a Dominican? Naturally of lofty mind, nurtured from his tenderest infancy by a mother who was a Saint, formed on the highest model, his one striving was to promote his people's greatest good, to maintain truth, to foster justice, and to avenge wrong.

> 'Indeed he seems to me
> Scarce other than my own ideal knight,
> "Who reverenced his conscience as his king;
> Whose glory was redressing human wrong;
> Who spoke no slander—no, nor listened to it."'

There is no question that the bloom of such a character as his was brought to its full perfection through the influence of such men as S. Bonaventure and S. Thomas. Both king and priest were chosen souls and governing spirits, each in his own special sphere; S. Louis in the active, ruling a kingdom; S. Thomas in the contemplative, dealing with high theories of philosophy.

Besides fulfilling certain important duties, the Angelical now took up his old position as professor at S. James's; and during two years dazzled the students and the lively Parisian citizens by the depth and maturity of his mind, which now combined the highest gifts of ripe and educated genius with the mellow experience of many years.

The subject-matter of his lectures appears to have had a twofold scope: that of preparing and clarifying principles and reasonings towards the completion of the *Summa Theologica*, and that of striking with vigorous boldness at the prominent errors of the day. The calm majesty of that great intellect gathered up the follies and aberrations of human pride, and then before the most keen-sighted audience in the world brilliantly displayed their inconsequence, and still more brilliantly (because it was more difficult) drew out a plan of Christian truth, solid, united, compact, which thoroughly satisfied the reason by the severity of its process, and pleased the imagination by the harmony and oneness of its parts.

First, there was the still-threatening heresy of Averroës, which acted with a strange fascination on the mediæval mind. Against this the Angelical brought forth his questions on the human soul: he showed its true nature and position, he manifested its relations to the lower world of sense and to the superior world of spirit, and by the unanswerable cogency of his logic, and the clearness of his exposition, aimed a mortal blow at a deadly system of philosophy. Then he launched out straight at that insidious foe of all soaring minds, pantheism, in his questions on the power of God. The relations of creature and Creator are here determined: God's power is studied in His external acts, and creatures are proved to be the effects of His almighty power, not parts of, or emanations from, Himself. Then the Saint discussed a subject bearing on the union of the Word with the created substance,—as the point of contact between the Infinite and the finite,—and thus a species of Manichæism, which had considerable hold on many minds, was combated and overthrown; and finally, he handled important questions regarding vice and virtue, dwelling upon the true notion of evil, showing forth the weighty responsibility which lies on every rational creature, and displaying the reach of those duties which are incumbent on men as members of society.

The Angelical's work was by no means simply theoretical. He drew out theory to serve for practice, and this becomes evident on reading the theological decisions which were formally promulgated by Bishop Stephen Tempier. This accomplished prelate assembled a body of divines in 1270 to discuss the various philosophical and theological errors of the day, and to suggest some means of stemming the rationalism and irreverence of the schools. The work of this learned meeting was summed up in a document of great importance, in which the principal false maxims and theses which had infested the University were drawn out in order and condemned. Now these maxims and theses are the very same against which S. Thomas had been combating with all his energy for many years, not only at Bologna, but at St. James's; and there is little doubt that the stringent measures taken by the Bishop Tempier were in great part owing to the skill with which the great Angelical had displayed in their true light the insidious bearings of those poisonous propositions.

Having fulfilled his duties at S. James's, the Saint gave up his chair to his friend Br. Romanus and betook himself to Bologna, where he was to bring out the second part of the *Summa Theologica.*

After two years of labour, the *prima secundæ* and the *secunda secundæ* appeared, that is to say, the second grand division of the *Summa,* which is subdivided, one half being called the *first of the second,* and the other the *second of the second.*

This grand division forms the main body of that mighty superstructure which the Angelical erected on the foundations he had laid two years before; and just as the second part is founded logically in the first, so the second portion of the second part is grounded in the first portion, which occupies four hundred and sixty pages. God and His divine works were treated of in the fundamental part of the *Summa;* now, man, the image of God, whose end is the contemplation of the Divine Essence in the world to come, becomes the subject of a most searching analysis.

Here, be it remarked, the three great elements which go to the construction of the *Summa* can be easily seen as they help in the building up of the Angelical's synthesis of theology,—Aristotle's *Ethics* representing Reason, S. Augustine standing for Tradition, and the words of our Lord Himself speaking with luminous distinctness declaring the infallible teachings of the Scriptures. Whilst the pagan moral does not point beyond earth, S. Thomas points up to heaven. His spirit was too great to be satisfied with happiness that fails; he began to gaze upon the bright speck in the distance till it grew before his eyes and enlarged its disk, and unfolded before his contemplation into the effulgence of supernatural vision, imperfect here, yet never to be quenched, but rather to be perfected when Christ's Face shall be unveiled, and His glory shall appear.

This second part of the *Summa* appeared in two large volumes, the first containing one hundred and fourteen questions, including six hundred and nineteen articles; the second nine hundred and seventeen articles, and one hundred and eighty-nine questions.

On the appearance of the master portion of this work the General Chapter of the Dominicans, which was sitting at Florence, was besieged by applications from various universities, imploring the Fathers to send the Angelical to teach in their several schools. Bologna, fearing to lose him, did all in its power to persuade the Chapter to allow him to remain; Paris, for the third time, forwarded its warm petition; Rome intreated that the greatest of theologians should be permitted to give *éclat* to the most Christian city of the world; whilst beautiful Naples, which years ago had been dazzled and charmed by his brilliancy and virtue as a youth, and which had not forgotten his early history, more fervently than all the rest prayed the Fathers in Chapter assembled to allow Brother Thomas to return to the university of which he had been so bright an ornament, to pour out his matured knowledge as a finished theologian. Charles, King of Sicily, joined in this supplication; and it was finally decided that the wishes so earnestly expressed by so admirable a Prince should prevail over all the rest.

The Saint, therefore, left Bologna for Naples, and passed some little time in the old convent of S. Sabina, where he renewed the recollection of his youthful years, when, hurrying away from maternal influence at Naples, he had found peace in the palace-convent of Hyacinth and Ceslas, and comfort in the simple church where S. Dominic had loved so much to pray. Here, where his little cell still may be seen, he commenced the third part of the *Summa*, and wrote his Commentary on Boëthius.

In due course he set out for Naples, and *en route* visited his old friend, Cardinal Richard, at whose country-house he had converted two Jewish Rabbies some years before. Here he fell ill, but he speedily recovered; then his *socius*, Reginald, was attacked by a violent and dangerous fever. The Angelical applied a relic of S. Agnes to the invalid, a relic which he carried about his person in admiration of the spotlessness of the Saint, and Reginald was instantly and wholly cured. An adequate idea of the enthusiasm of the entire population when St. Thomas entered Naples cannot be conveyed by mere description. It was, historians say, a genuine ovation. It recalls to mind the reception of S. Athanasius in Alexandria. The whole city turned out to meet the man of God. The highway was one sea of human heads, which flowed steadily in one direction, when, touching upon the simple *cortège* of the Angelical, and surrounding him, and almost swallowing him up, it gradually flowed back towards the city. Frantic were the shouts of joy amongst the people, wildly and enthusiastically they bore their prize along towards the great convent of S. Dominic; triumphant was the entry. His genius and gentleness captivated serious and learned men; the orator saw in him one possessed, if not of powers of display, of marvellous powers of persuasion; religious men in looking on him beheld the champion of their order, and a pattern to be copied only at a distance; theologians saw him, and felt that he was beyond the range of envy; kings and nobles recognised under the rough tunic of the friar the bluest and purest blood of Italy; whilst the poorest of the poor, and the unlettered simpleton, in casting their eyes upon the great Angelical, remembered how he had abandoned all earth could offer, and all that pride of place could give, to serve God, like them, in the midst of poverty and in company of the poor.

To the Angelical himself it must have been a strange sensation to feel himself borne along in the surging frantic crowd, if he was not altogether unconscious of their jubilant applause—to find himself the idol of that hour, if he was not still serenely living in the sunlight of the upper world. Anyhow, he speedily set himself once more to his accustomed work, lecturing, preaching, contemplating, corresponding, and penning the remainder of the *Summa Theologica*. Here he was in his old city once again, which he had known so well in early boyhood; where, as an infant, he was taken to the baths; where the bright light had shone around his brow; where our Lady chose him for her own; and where he first learnt to love S. Dominic, and to exercise his extraordinary powers of logic and of memory. Here he was comparatively within easy distance of Rocca Sicca, San Giovanni, Loreto, Belcastro, and Cassino—of his old haunts where he had spent so many pleasant days. It almost seemed as if a pilgrim had come home again after a long absence in an alien land—home again to labour a little more, to rest, and then to die.

During the year and a half he was at Naples he composed several important works. He finished his Commentary on the first fifty Psalms, and did all he was destined to do to the *Summa Theologica*. He wrote ninety questions, including five hundred and forty-nine articles of the third part; and though he did not absolutely complete his great scheme, he had, in reality, finished it in the main, after he had treated of the Incarnation, and had drawn out a scientific exposition of the knowledge, grace, and perfections of Christ, of the mysteries of His life, and of His merits and His passion.

This third part then dwells on three great subjects—the Incarnation of the Son of God, the Sacraments of the New Law, and the General Judgment—thus completing the circle of salvation; beginning with God as man's Maker, and ending with Him as his Judge. And although the Angelical did not get beyond the Treatise on Penance, still this third part was made up of extracts from his other works. The treatise on our Lord falls into two main portions, one dwelling on His Person, the other on His life and works.

First, S. Thomas speaks of the hypostatic union in itself, of the person assuming human nature, of the nature assumed, of the parts of human nature, and of the order of its assumption; next of the accompanying gifts, of the grace of Christ as man and as Head of the Church; of His knowledge in general, of the knowledge possessed by His soul, of infused and experimental knowledge, and of the power of the soul of Christ; then of the defects which He assumed as to His body and as to His soul; then again of the results of the union as they affect Christ Himself, as to His being, His will, His operation; as they regard the Eternal Father in respect of subjection, prayer, priesthood, adoption, predestination; and finally as they influence us in respect of adoration, and of the Lord's mediatorial office in regard of His creatures. His work on earth, His passion, and His glorification fall under four heads: His coming into the world, His progress through the world, His going out of it, and His exaltation, which begin with the twenty-seventh and end with the fifty-ninth question.

And in this we have an outline of the great moral instrument for forming men into Christians. Here we see the influence of the Solitaries, whose companionship was with Christ, of the Fathers who lived to Him alone, and of the great founders of Monastic Orders, whose one end and aim was to reproduce His likeness upon the earth. Here we perceive the influence of S. Anthony and his courageous abandonment in the desert; of S. Athanasius and his indomitable battling in the cause of the Word Incarnate in the world; of S. Basil and S. Gregory Theologus in their abiding adoration of His Image; of S. Chrysostom, whose life was lived away in defending His revelation; of S. Jerome and S. Augustine, who, out of love of Him, quelled the giant rebellion of their natures; and of S. Ambrose and S. Gregory the Great, who, in moulding their intellects and hearts on His model, were enabled in turn to fashion the civil order of society according to the methods of the Cross. The Christ-principle which animated them was paramount in the will and reason of Thomas of Aquino. If his one real striving was to conform himself to the image of the Saviour, his one solitary ambition was to construct a scheme or instrument for forming men after the same pattern; for elevating, purifying, and widening their natures; and for filling them with the force and generosity, with the purity and charity of the Crucified. All that is mighty in intellect, and all that is sovereign in will, by the action of this organism, can be turned towards the noblest end in imperishable endurance. The rulers of the Church here can see the nature of true force of character, true justice, true benignity, and breadth of view; here they are taught that noble art which combines giant strength with divine gentleness, whilst they learn how to exhibit the uprightness of a judge with the tender consideration of a father. Here the theologian or philosopher can instruct himself in the hidden mysteries of true development of mind, of expansion and accuracy, of grasp and steadiness, in the intuitions of faith, and in the deductions of the reason; here man's brain, if he will but open it, may be flooded with light, and invigorated by an element which is next door to a revelation; here, in a word, is exhibited a complicated yet sublimely simple moral machine, constructed by the illuminated genius of a Saint, for widening all the faculties, ennobling the character, and fashioning the intellect of man upon the highest principles of Christianity.

If the impression of the wax is exquisite, equally perfect must be the die sunk into the steel; that is to say, the theory of the *Summa Theologica* must exactly correspond with its impress on the soul in the order of active life. And as each delicate line, and spiral whorl, and gentle curve which goes to form the whole design is brought into existence by the very act of stamping out every preëxisting form, so is it with the *Summa* of S. Thomas. The perfect Christian theory is the annihilation of all other schemes which do not harmonise with it, be they founded on philosophy, politics, or religion; and the perfect Christian man, by the very act of being what he is, becomes an active foe and sworn antagonist to every principle in the order of action and ideas which crosses the imprint of Christ's image on the heart. Thus the *Summa Theologica* is not only a colossal challenge to the unbelieving world, but it is a mighty instrument for creating patristic men, and turning out matchless champions of the Cross. It simply embodies the principles which animated the soul of S. Anthony in the desert, and of S. Athanasius, S. Basil, and S. Gregory in the world.

And though his own great specialty was contemplation, though he shrank away from active life, S. Thomas was not moved one hair's breadth in the just balance of his mind. His perfect type of highest perfection is not exclusive contemplation after all. The outcome of his *Summa Theologica*, the noblest and the best which that huge moral instrument would aim at turning out, points straight at those great specimen-men who have been spoken of before, those who, anointed with the unction of the Episcopate, possess the plenitude of the priesthood, and cherish in the centre of the heart, from the very nature of their calling, that self-immolating heroism which is the life-spring of noble deeds. It is not the pure contemplative, nor is it the man of pure action, who represents the pattern Christian of the Angelical: but it is he who, from the very overflow of his contemplating spirit, pours out upon others the riches of his piety and the fulness of knowledge; who, if he has not actually renounced all created things, is prepared to do so in his heart, and to trample on them out of love of God and man; who, *ex abundantia dilectionis divinæ*, in the wideness of his charity, embraces all mankind, and, as it were, possesses, through the nobility of nature and of grace, those highest gifts of sacrifice, charity, and tenderness, which others generally acquire through the pressure of rule and the yoke of self-restraint. Whilst the religious, under vow, is striving towards perfection, the bishop holds a position which implies that he is already perfect: he is the head and crown of the moral order, the king and pattern of every perfection of mind and heart: his depth of contemplation only renders his actions more divine; and his actions, from their very purity, stimulate his intelligence in the practices of contemplation,—they are, with him, the steps by which he mounts up into the kingdom, and enters the threshold of the Holy Court.

What, then, is the practical object of the *Summa Theologica?* Is it not to furnish us with the moral framework upon which are fashioned the greatest and best of men? Does not the culminating point just mentioned usher, as it were, into our very presence those great classic Fathers, whose lives so largely influenced S. Thomas? Does not the Angelical seem to say, 'Here is the instrument by which men made of clay, through the grace of God, can be transformed into lights of the world and salt of the earth'? Let the full force of the *Summa Theologica* be brought to bear upon a soul of noble original nature and high intellectual gifts, only let the plastic mind and tender heart be moulded and stamped by such a die as this, and the result in the contemplative order may be a S. Thomas, a S. Anthony, or a S. Jerome; in the active, a S. Chrysostom, a S. Augustine, or a S. Gregory the Great.

The supreme in intellect and the supreme in will here find their place.

If the Episcopal estate represents the Angelical's highest pattern, the monastic represents the next in eminence. The monk is but striving after that sublime perfection which the bishop already has attained. His instruments are potent ones,—forces which give his spirit freedom: poverty, that is, trampling on perishing clay, that he may be free to embrace eternal light; chastity, that is, abandonment of earthly ties, that his only bond may be in heaven; and obedience, that, under the mighty will of God, he may shake off the despicable slavery of self: and all this under a solemn irrevocable vow, that human weakness may not prevaricate and look back upon the flames in which all its fetters have been consumed. Such as these were the men of the *Collationes Patrum*, of whom the Angelical loved to read. Here we see S. Anthony, S. Pachomius, and S. Arsenius, S. Benedict, S. Dominic, and S. Francis of Assisi.

Such, then, are the two great classes of pattern men: such are the instruments which the Angelical saw clearly were wanting to the world. The *Summa* was his moral machine for making salt and light—for turning out detached men, men of incorrupt life, of illuminated and widened charity. He wished to bring the Fathers back. Rationalism, which is simply the sharp edge of one side of the human mind, would, by degrees, break up like frost before the sun, when brought in contact with them; irreverence could hardly be irreverent in the august presence of men so truly great; whilst heresy and schism would find opponents filled with the light of knowledge and the flame of love. Could S. Athanasius, S. Basil, S. Augustine, S. Jerome, and S. Gregory the Great be multiplied on earth, there would indeed be many a fierce battle, but there would also be many a crushing victory.

But it will be asked, Does the Angelical expect all men to be bishops and monastic men? Assuredly not. He would be the first to say that all are not called to be, and, from the nature of the case, cannot be patterns for the world. Models and patterns are few in every order. They are made for the rest to look upon, and, in their place and measure, to imitate. The theologian and the contemplative will find his type in the Angelical; the statesman in S. Athanasius, S. Ambrose, and S. Gregory the Great; the orator in S. John Chrysostom; the recluse in S. Anthony; the poet in S. Gregory Theologus; the champion of liberty and freedom in S. Basil; the controversialist in S. Augustine; whilst the monastic state itself holds out to view true principles of progress, stability and freedom, of government, self-restraint, and self-forgetfulness, in the very construction and mechanism of religious life. What the bishop and the monk carry out *ad literam,* that the rest should aim at in spirit and at a distance.

The world is not reformed, the civil order is not conquered, by great ideas alone, nor simply by courageous and gifted men: it can be subdued by these in combination only. Society has lost her standards, her pattern heroes ; the high theory of Christian life is fading out of the mind of men. A thousand discordant voices cry, a thousand hideous forms are lifted before the eyes ; and the world becomes confused in the midst of the delirium of rampant pride and passion, of hideous democracy, and the fury of the half-educated masses. Set up, before it is too late, the chaste, the pure, the tender Saints of God, the tramplers upon wealth, the lovers of the poor, the champions of true freedom, true beneficence, which forgets self in the very act of giving, which stamps upon pride in its very effort after good, and never feels itself to be so rich as when it is pouring itself out for the benefit of others. Pull the pagan patterns down : set up the heroes of the Cross ; educate men, not on the morality of the Stagyrite, but on that of the Angelical. Let the *Summa Theologica* take the place of the Ethics of the infidel, and let the Kings of Christianity be set before the angry eyes of the ever-growing populations of the world, to tame them into subjection by the meekness and giant power of their lives, to show them that a system of religion and world-government still remains, which, whilst it teaches princes to be poor and humble, renders them so supremely great, that the wayfaring man has but to see them to acknowledge that their sovereignty is half justified by the intrinsic royalty of their characters and hearts.

The masses of the people have a certain instinct

within them, which, though it does not see truth, is ever restlessly seeking after it; and they will, without remorse, break down polities and institutions until they find it. The day must come when the standards shall be set up; whether that day will dawn after a sea of blood and tears has purified the land, or whether the horrors now casting their shadows at our feet will be averted by thrusting truth boldly before the world, a prophet only could determine. The day has passed for mere material politicians. *Divine* patterns alone can work a cure. If there is an instrument for forming them, it is the *Summa Theologica*; if they ever exist at all, they will be to their own age what S. Athanasius, S. Basil, S. Chrysostom, S. Augustine, and S. Gregory the Great were to days gone by. They will be as lights and beacons, proclaiming, not so much in blatant words, but rather in their private and public lives, those principles which speak to the hearts of restless multitudes, and preach the divine teachings of the Crucified. In their coming pagan philosophy, materialism in religion, dogmatic 'science,' and the coarse cunning of the demagogue, as well as the refined inanity of those who are too weak to be very wicked, will be lighted up by the flames of truth. Men filled with the Spirit seem doubly transfigured in the presence of men of clay. Men formed upon the *Summa*—which itself is compacted of Tradition, Reason, and Scripture—would, by their very presence, were they placed before the eye of the world, command a veneration and secure a respect which is elicited neither by power nor position, and which the diplomacy of statesmen is too crafty to attain. Purity, Truth, Justice, and Gentleness, springing from an intellect and heart moulded on Christ-principles, alone could stem the torrent, and cast a light into the darkness of our day.

It was the Christ-principle of the Benedictine Pope, S. Gregory the Great, and of S. Augustine, the Benedictine Monk, which converted England to freedom, to order, and to faith, in days gone by; it is their principle, and their principle only, though it may be under modified conditions, that will introduce into our threatening chaos, into our increasing darkness, into our growing peril from the people, such elements of reverence and liberty, of progress and obedience, of enlightened science and unswerving faith, as alone are able to secure to a mighty nation that cohesive force, that expansive elasticity, and that graduated order of development which constitute the difference between a national *cadaver* and a body politic animated from end to end by the healthiest energies of a spontaneous and yet well-regulated life.

CHAPTER XXII.

DEATH OF S. THOMAS.

Having given a brief outline of the subject-matter and method of the works of S. Thomas, we must now turn our eyes on the Saint himself, the beauty, sanctity, and loveliness of whose life shone forth even more gloriously at its setting than it did in its noon-day splendour. As he approached the end of his great labours on the *Summa*, his spirit, which had from his boyhood been living in the World Unseen, became more and more absorbed by heavenly things. His trances and ecstasies became more frequent, his converse with the other world more preternatural, his visions and his gift of prophecy, his absorption, and his knowledge of men's thoughts, more astonishing. The Hand of God seems to have been placed upon him with stronger pressure, and that bright transfiguration, which is perfected in Heaven through the Beatific Vision, appears almost to have been begun on earth. As the fruit in the sunlight day by day ripens, growing in fulness, and deepening in colour, till at length it is ready to drop golden from the bough, so the great Angelical seems to have advanced steadily and gradually to his spiritual perfection, till, mature for Heaven, he was gathered by a Divine Hand, and garnered into the Everlasting Home.

Indeed, he not only dwelt in the Unseen World, but he absolutely conversed with its inhabitants; so that what was hidden from the gaze of ordinary mortals became visible to him,—what we see was, as it were, withdrawn from him; what is veiled from our senses was miraculously opened before his eyes.

For instance, at Paris, his sister who had died

appeared to him in vision, said she was in purgatory, and implored Masses for her soul; the Angelical requested his students to say Mass, and pray for her. Shortly after, she appeared to him in Rome, and said she was in glory. He asked her about himself. She said: 'Thou standest well, brother, and wilt join us speedily: but a greater glory is prepared for thee than for us. Preserve, however, what thou hast.' He asked after Landulf. She said he was in the penal fire. Again, whilst praying, according to his custom, in the church at Naples, B. Romanus, whom he had left in Paris as master of theology, stood before him. S. Thomas approached his friend, and said: 'Welcome here! When did you arrive?' 'I have passed from this life,' replied the figure, 'and am permitted to appear on your account.' Overcome by the apparition for a moment, then collecting himself, the Angelical said: 'In the name of God, then, I adjure you to answer me these questions: How do I stand? and are my works pleasing to God?' 'Thou art in a good state, and thy works do please God,' was the reply. Then 'What about yourself?' inquired the Angelical. 'I am now in eternal life,' answered Romanus, 'but I have been in purgatory.' 'Tell me,' continued S. Thomas, 'the answer to the question which we have so frequently discussed, whether the habits which are acquired in this life remain to us in Heaven?' 'Brother Thomas,' replied Romanus, 'I see God, and do not ask me more.' 'How do you see God?' rejoined the Saint; 'do you see Him immediately, or by means of some similitude?' The other answered: 'As we have heard, so have we seen, in the city of the Lord of Hosts!' and then instantly vanished. So habitual had the ecstatic life become to the Angelical, that at last he could scarcely fix his mind in contemplation without being carried away in rapture, without being lifted off the ground entranced. At length he was so absorbed in divine things, that even the *Summa* itself failed to interest him. He finally ceased writing, after a marvellous rapture which seized him, and shook his whole frame, whilst celebrating Mass in the Chapel of S. Nicholas, at Naples. After this Mass, contrary to his invariable custom, he did not sit down to his desk, nor would he consent to dictate anything; and though engaged on the tractate concerning 'Penance' in the Third Part of the *Summa*, he put away his pen, and became wholly lost in contemplation. Even Reginald, who knew him so intimately, could not account for this. He said, with amazement, to his master: 'My Father, why hast thou cast on one side so great a work, which thou didst begin for the glory of God and the illumination of the world?' All he replied was, '*Non possum*' —'*I cannot* write any more.' Reginald, fearing lest over-work had affected his master's brain, was continually imploring him to continue writing, but the Saint ever made the same reply: 'I cannot, Reginald, for everything I have written appears to me as simply rubbish.' From this time forth S. Thomas may be said to have lived, not on earth, but in Heaven. Shortly after his great ecstasy he visited his sister, the Countess of San-severino, whom he tenderly loved. Even on the journey he was perfectly carried away, and it was with difficulty that his *socius* could get him to the Castle gates. His sister, seeing him approach, hurried out to meet him; but he, being so absorbed, scarcely noticed her. She turned terrified to Reginald, and exclaimed: 'How is this that Brother Thomas is altogether tranced, and will scarcely speak a word to me?' Reginald replied: 'Ever since the feast of S. Nicholas he has been like this, and from that day forth he has not written a word.' Then he began again with great earnestness to beg the Angelical to say why he refused to write, and how he had become thus beside himself. Being pressed with such importunity, S. Thomas at length exclaimed to Reginald: 'I adjure thee, by the Omnipotent and Living God, by the holy vows and by the charity which binds thee now, not to reveal during my lifetime what I am about to say!' And then he added: 'All I have written appears to me as so much rubbish, compared with what I have seen and what has been revealed to me!'

Meanwhile, after three years' vacancy following the death of Pope Clement IV., Theobald, Archdeacon of Liége, was chosen Pope, and took the title of Gregory X. This Pontiff dedicated himself to carrying out two special objects—the union of the Latin and Greek Churches, and the recovery of the Holy Land from the hand of the infidel. He it was who made Tomaso d'Agni di Lentino Archbishop of Cosenza, and then

Patriarch of Jerusalem ; and he it was who, being aware of the Angelical's deep acquaintance with the vexed points of Greek and Latin theology, issued a special Bull commanding his attendance at the II. Council of Lyons, and requesting him to bring with him the famous Tractate he had written in the days of Pope Urban IV., against the errors of the Greeks.

In obedience to the voice of authority, the Angelical set out for Lyons towards the end of January 1274, with his inseparable *socius*, Reginald. His health was feeble, and his mind was still fixed on the visions of another world. They travelled by way of Campagna, and called at the Castle of Maienza, in the diocese of Terracina, where Frances, wife of Hannibal Ceccano, niece of the Angelical, resided. Here the Saint, weak and faint, reposed a while, but did not rally. He wholly lost his appetite, though the fish he seemed to fancy, to the amazement of all, was miraculously provided. After a while he felt himself a little stronger. The report of his being in the neighbourhood spread with rapidity. It reached a Benedictine abbey which was about six miles distant from the Castle. The monks remembering, no doubt, the close connection of S. Thomas with S. Benedict, how his family had lived under the shadow of the Holy Rule, how his uncle had been an Abbot, and his sister a Benedictine Nun, and how he himself had been grounded by the monks in the first principles of holocaustic sacrifice, invited him to Fossa Nuova, where the silence was seldom broken save by the matin call to prayer, or by the voices of the monks pleading in the choir. The Saint gladly accepted the invitation, saying: 'If the Lord means to take me away, it were better that I should die in a religious house than in the midst of seculars.' So he quitted the Castle of Maienza, and protected by the monks, who had come to escort him, he rode in the midst of them towards the distant monastery. See him as he gets from off his horse, and is led by the Fathers into the monastic church; see him kneeling there in silent adoration as they all assemble and surround him, so broken, yet so angelical, pouring forth his heart to God before the altar! He rises; they follow him; the Abbot conducts him through the church into the silent cloister. Then the whole past seems to break in upon him like a burst of overpowering sunlight; the calm and quiet abbey, the meditative corridor, the gentle Benedictine monks: he seems as if he were at Cassino once again, amidst the glorious visions of his boyish days—amidst the tender friendships of his early youth, close on the bones of ancient kings, near the solemn tomb of Blessed Benedict, in the hallowed home of great traditions, and at the very shrine of all that is fair and noble in monastic life. He seemed completely overcome by the memories of the past, and, turning to the monks who surrounded him, exclaimed: '*This* is the place where I shall find repose!' and then ecstatically to Reginald, in presence of them all: 'Hæc est requies mea in sæculum sæculi, hic habitabo quoniam elegi eam'—'This is my rest for ever and ever; here will I dwell, for I have chosen it!'

The fever which had seized upon him, instead of diminishing, was increasing in its force. He was conducted to the Abbot's cell, which, out of respect for so great a Saint, and so profound a genius, had been vacated by the Prelate purposely for him. Here, during the whole of his illness, which lasted about a month, the community watched over him with all the tenderness and reverence of sons towards a father. The Benedictines would suffer no one to wait upon him but themselves: all servants were excluded; even the wood to make his fire was cut down in the forest by the hands of the brethren, and borne on their willing shoulders to his hearth. They were overjoyed to receive him into their home, and to minister to him of their choicest and their best. He, on his part, full of calmness and peace, patient as a child, gentle as charity itself, knew he was amongst his own; and yearning continually after his release—fixed in the thought of the Eternal Rest of God—was ever repeating over these words of S. Augustine: 'So long as in me there is aught which is not wholly Thine, O God, suffering and sorrow will be my lot; but when I shall be Thine alone, then shall I be filled with Thee, and wholly set at liberty!'

It was the Christ-principle which filled his entire being, and bore him up out of this visible scene into those expanding realms of light, from which light comes into the mind of man. Knowing how faith and science had illuminated the man of God, especially with respect to the union of the soul with its Beloved, the monks, notwithstanding his feeble condition, could not refrain from asking him to expound to them the Canticle of Canticles, which has wholly to do with the mystic marriage of the soul with Christ. Ever since his great vision the Saint had put aside his pen. All his learning, in the brightness of the light which shone upon him at that hour, appeared to him as a faded flower in the mid-day sun. Still, the monks implored him, reminding him how Blessed Bernard had done the like. The Angelical looked at them with unutterable gentleness, and said: 'Get me Bernard's spirit, and I will do your bidding.' Finally, he gave way to them, and surrounding the bed on which he lay, they heard from the lips of the dying theologian how there is no strength, or peace, or light, for man in earth or heaven, without the charity of Christ and the merits of His Cross.

Growing still weaker, the man of God became conscious that his hour was drawing very nigh. He sent for Reginald, his *socius*, and with deep contrition and many sighs, made a review of his entire life, which, in reality, was simply a manifestation of the abiding and angelic purity of his heart and spirit. Having done this, he then begged the brethren to bring him the Body of our Lord—that Lord Who, from infancy up, had been the mainstay of his life and the one desire of his large and tender heart. The Abbot, accompanied by his community, proceeded to the chamber of the dying man, solemnly bearing the Blessed Sacrament. The door was gently opened, the monks one by one went in, and speedily surrounded the bed and filled the cell: then, with slow and silent step, the Abbot came, bearing the bright ciborium containing the Nourishment of Eternal Life. Immediately the great Angelical perceived his Master's presence, with the help of the brethren he rose from his pallet, and, kneeling upon the floor, adored his King and Saviour; and whilst shedding many tears, amidst the sobs of the monks, who could not control their emotion, he made his act of Faith in the real presence of his Lord. When he had made an end, and the Abbot was on the point of administering the Saving Host to him, he exclaimed, in the hearing of all the monks: 'I receive Thee, the price of my soul's redemption, for love of Whom I have studied, I have watched, and I have laboured! Thee have I preached, Thee have I taught, against Thee never have I breathed a word, neither am I wedded to my own opinion. If I have held aught which is untrue regarding this Blessed Sacrament, I subject it to the judgment of the Holy Roman Church, in whose obedience I now pass out of life.' Then, as the Abbot lifted up the Spotless Element to administer to him, with a sweet torrent of tears and with mighty devotion the glorious man uttered his favourite ejaculation: 'Thou, O Christ, art the King of Glory; Thou art the Everlasting Son of the Father!' and received gently upon his tongue the

Angelic Bread which came to him from Heaven. And, as he was approaching close upon his change, the Abbot with the brethren still watched about his bed; and those senses, which had served their Master with such generous loyalty, were one by one anointed, with the Sacred Unction, by loving Benedictine hands at his request, whilst he, quite conscious of what was going on, answered 'Amen' to the prayers of the minister of God. See them, then, for the last time, bending over him. See the Prince of Theologians, passing out of life, or rather advancing through his labours into rest, to realise away from the twilight of earth the one dream of his soul—to see the King in His Glory, and the Blessed adoring before the Everlasting Throne! There he lies, the great Angelical, calm and self-contained, as if reclining in the mighty Hand of God—'expectans beatam spem et adventum Domini,' looking forward to the blessed hope and coming of his Lord!

The brethren, meanwhile, with untold tenderness and reverence follow his countenance with their lustrous eyes, and watch life gradually ebbing away, till, at last, that moment comes which it is not given to any man to know, when the spirit secretly flies swiftly away out of the world of time and sense.

He was taken from exile on the early morning of the 7th of March, in the year 1274, in the prime of manly life, being scarcely eight-and-forty years of age.

It is but natural, it is but beautiful, that he, who in early boyhood had been stamped with the signet of

S. Benedict, should return to S. Benedict to die. He had gone forth to his work and to his labour in the morning, and he returned home to his brethren in the evening-tide.

THE END.

were caught up, and repeated, and circulated amongst the lower orders; they were popularised by self-made idiots, court buffoons, and wandering poets; and were improved upon, and embellished, by all the idlers and gossipers about the town. Rutebœuf, the crowned court poet of Louis IX., who was as spiteful as a monkey, and about as mischievous, was never wearied of pouring out his splenetic and scoffing humour upon the Order of S. Dominic. He declared that the Dominicans taught peace, and spoke of unity and of faith with their tongue; but, from the practice of their lives, he found that to talk was one thing, and to act was quite another. 'I refer to the Jacobites' (Dominicans), he says, 'who preach to us that it is sinful to be angry, and sinful to be envious, whilst they themselves carry on war for a chair in the University; they must, they *will* obtain it. . . . . When the Jacobites first came on the earth, they dwelt with mother Humility; they were then simple and pure of heart, and troubled themselves little with what did not belong to God. Now, it is no longer so; envy and haughtiness have entered into them, and all uprightness has departed from amongst them.' This scoffer, by his very scoffing at the religious bodies, gives testimony to their power and influence. 'The Jacobites are persons of such weight,' he says, 'that they can do everything in Paris, and in Rome. They are kings, they are apostles; their riches are so great, that they pass all calculation. Woe to him who does not make them his executors, for he is certain to lose his soul! . . . How fortunate that such folks are our instructors! No one dare tell them the truth; for to do so would be to set one's life in jeopardy.' Is it to be wondered at, when such a tone as this pervaded the poets and troubadours, and those who afforded amusement to the people, that deep-rooted prejudice should have been created against the friars?

The jealousy and passion of the masters, scholars, and auditor s of the secular schools added to the general disturbance. These men went about amongst the Parisians, doing all they could to prevent them giving alms to the Mendicants, so as to reduce the enemy by starvation. Besides this, not content with moral force, the secular party occasionally used physical violence against the friars; so much so, that, at one time, the Dominicans had not the courage to leave their convent of S. James's to seek from the faithful the food necessary for their support. To this harsh treatment was added a determined resistance to the teaching of the friars. The masters and scholars of the rival schools would not permit young men to attend the lectures of the Dominicans, nor allow the young Dominicans to be present at secular disputations and defensions. To such a state of misery had the friars been reduced, that the Pope had several times to interfere; and no better notion of the despotism, brutality, and cruelty of the University doctors could be gained, than by reading the Bulls issued in defence of the Mendicants by Pope Alexander. The Pope always speaks with great rever-

A SELECTION FROM BURNS & OATES' PUBLICATIONS

28 ORCHARD STREET
LONDON
W.

Telegrams:
Burns Oates London

Telephone:
2706 Mayfair

ANCIENT CATHOLIC HOMES OF SCOTLAND.

By Dom ODO BLUNDELL, O.S.B. With an Introduction by the Hon. Mrs. MAXWELL SCOTT, of Abbotsford. Crown 8vo, cloth, extra gilt, 3s. 6d. net (postage 4d.).

THIS work, which in copiously illustrated, deals with the history of some of the old Scotch Houses, which were the centres of Catholicity during the three hundred years between 1550 and 1850. The author gives an insight into the sufferings undergone by those who remained true to the old faith, and shows their devoted adhesion to the House of Stuart, which involved them in the risings of 1715 and 1745.

The progress of Catholicity is also traced from the days when Mass was celebrated in secret, with scouts watching the approaches, to the happier times which have seen the restoration of much which was ruthlessly swept away in the sixteenth century. Each of the ten chapters affords pleasant reading, the more serious narrative being enlivened by anecdotes, which yet help to impress their own lesson on the mind. This is also the case with the forty illustrations, which are partly in the text and partly separate. Every effort has been made to secure the best workmanship, and also to keep the price within the most moderate limits.

SISTER MARY OF THE DIVINE HEART.

DROSTE ZU VISCHERING, Religious of the Good Shepherd, 1863-1899. By the Abbé LOUIS CHASLE. Translated from the French by a Member of the Order. New and revised edition. With Illustrations. 6s.

THIS is one of the most attractive and most important spiritual biographies published for many years.—*Irish Monthly*.

THE FATHERS OF THE DESERT.

Translated from the German of the Countess Hahn-Hahn by EMILY F. BOWDEN. With a Chapter on the Spiritual Life of the First Six Centuries. By JOHN BERNARD DALGAIRNS, Priest of the Oratory. A New Edition. With a Reproduction of the Picture of St. Simon Stylites on his column, by FRANK BRANGWYN, A.R.A. In two volumes. Crown 8vo, cloth, 8s.

A SPIRITUAL RETREAT. By Father H. REGINALD BUCKLER, O.P. Author of "The Perfection of Man by Charity," &c. Crown 8vo, cloth, 3s. 6d. net (postage 4d.).

"A SPIRITUAL RETREAT" is a distinct gain in the line of Catholic manuals of solid and attractive piety. . . . In plan, in matter and in style it takes high place in the class of retreat manuals. It may also be used very profitably as a book of spiritual reading.—*Universe.*

MADAME ROSE LUMMIS. By DELIA GLEESON. 2s. 6d. net (postage 3d.).

FIFTY years ago, in the Northern American States, the name of Madame Rose Lummis was one to conjure with. Born of a high and wealthy family, she decided to devote her life to the poor, and in the telling of her life story Delia Gleeson relates a tale of wonderful pathos and bravery. Madame Lummis's story reads like a romance, but one that breathes tenderness and piety in every page. Her life story should be one of the most treasured possessions on the bookshelves of lovers of pure, interesting, and well-written literature.—*Irish Independent.*

WATERS THAT GO SOFTLY: or, Thoughts for time of Retreat. By JOSEPH RICKABY, S.J. Crown 8vo, cloth 2s. 6d.

THIS is a remarkable book by a remarkable man, and is, all things considered, the best half-crown's worth of spiritual reading we have met with in a search of many years.—*Catholic Times.*

LIST OF APPROVED CHURCH MUSIC FOR THE ARCHDIOCESE OF WESTMINSTER. Published by Authority. Price 2s. 6d. net (postage 2d.).

CONTENTS: Masses. Incidental Mass Music. Requiem Music. Vespers. Compline. Benediction. Music for Occasional Offices. For Holy Week. Solemn Te Deum. Sequences. Offertories and Motets. Solemn Reception of a Bishop. Miscellaneous.

JESUS OF NAZARETH. The Story of His Life Told to Children. By Mother MARY LOYOLA, of the Bar Convent, York. Edited by Father THURSTON, S.J. Large crown 8vo, with 24 full-page Illustrations, 5s. net (postage 4d.).

MY heart was delighted on reading the proof sheets of *Jesus of Nazareth*, by Mother Mary Loyola. The book is eminently practical, simple, unctuous and interesting. It will make a powerful impression on the minds of the children. In fact, no one can read it without loving God more, and therefore becoming better. Parents, teachers, and instructors will find Mother Loyola's works very useful in the difficult task of forming the minds of children to a life of virtue. We should be glad to see a copy of *Jesus of Nazareth* in every household in the land. We wish it God-speed in going out on its great mission.—*Cardinal Gibbons.*

MEMOIR OF FATHER DIGNAM, S.J. Revised with Preface by Father EDWARD IGNATIUS PURBRICK, S.J. New and Cheaper Edition, 5s. net (postage 4d.).

A DAILY THOUGHT. From the Writings of Father Dignam. New edition, 32mo, leather, gilt edges, 2s.

FATHER GALLWEY. A Sketch, with some Early Letters. By PERCY FITZGERALD, M.A., F.S.A. 2s. net (postage 3d.).

A MODERN PILGRIM'S PROGRESS. With an Introduction on the Prevailing Unrest by Father SEBASTIAN BOWDEN, of the Oratory. Second Edition. 6s.

THE FLOWER OF THE MIND. A Choice among the Best Poems made by ALICE MEYNELL. Printed on antique paper by Messrs. T. and A. Constable. With a Cover Design by L. HOUSMAN. 4s. 6d. net.

A BEAUTIFUL volume, rendered still more beautiful by all the delights of clear type on excellent paper.—*Westminster Gazette.*

THOUGHTS AND FANCIES. Verses on the Madonna, Sonnets and Sacred Thoughts. By the Rev. F. C. KOLBE, D.D. 2s. 6d. net (postage 3d.).

THERE is about all a sincerity of thought, and a kind of chaste serenity of expression which is often extremely pleasing.—*Times.*

A SELECTION FROM THE VERSES OF JOHN B. TABB. 2s. 6d. net (postage 3d.).

THIS selection from the poems of Father Tabb proves conclusively that he is the greatest living master of epigram in verse.—*Daily Chronicle.*

THE GARDEN OF ROSES OF OUR LADY. The Excellences of the Rosary and the Best Method of Reciting it. By Father MESCHLER, S.J. Demy 16mo., 2s. 6d.

A NICE little devotional book treating from the spiritual point of view of the excellences of the Rosary. The author works in very practical instructions on prayer and meditation.—*Tablet.*

FREE WILL AND FOUR ENGLISH PHILOSOPHERS: Hobbes, Locke, Hume and Mill. By Father JOSEPH RICKABY, S.J. 3s. 6d. net (postage 3d.).

THE LITTLE OFFICE OF OUR LADY. A Treatise, Theoretical, Practical, and Exegetical. By ETHELRED TAUNTON, Priest of the Diocese of Westminster. Demy 8vo, strongly bound, leather back, 10s. net.

THIS work is a guide to the Spiritual Life based upon the Liturgical Prayer of the Church. Its spirit is large, wide, and essentially Catholic. It will be useful to those just beginning the Spiritual Life as well as for those who, for many years, have consecrated themselves to God's service, for it contains in one volume the gist of the greatest, holiest, and most learned writers.

SPIRITUAL CONFERENCES OF ST. FRANCIS DE SALES. Translated into English from the new and authentic Edition of the Saint's Works, with several Additions and Supplementary Notes, under the supervision of ABBOT GASQUET, O.S.B., and the late Dom BENEDICT MACKEY, O.S.B. 6s.

DECREES OF THE VATICAN COUNCIL. Edited, with an Introduction, by the Rev. VINCENT McNABB, O.P. Demy 8vo, 2s.

"I AM THE WAY." A Treatise for Followers of Christ. Translated by the Hon. A. WILMOT, M.L.C., from a French edition of *L'Esprit du Christianisme, ou la Conformité du Chrétien avec Jésus-Christ*, by Father NEPVEU, S.J. With a Preface by the ARCHBISHOP OF WESTMINSTER. 2s. 6d. net (postage 3d.).

THE CHURCH AND KINDNESS TO ANIMALS.

1. Condemnation of Bull-Fights; 2. Animals in the Lives and Legends of Saints; 3. A Cloud of Modern Witnesses. Crown 8vo, Illustrated, 2s. 6d. net (postage 3d.).

THIS work, which has received the blessing of Pius X., contains delightful reproductions of Old Master Pictures of Animals and Saints.

SAINT BENEDICT JOSEPH LABRE

(Votary of Holy Poverty and Pilgrim). By C. L. WHITE. With Portrait and other Illustrations. 2s. 6d.

THIS charming little book will help its readers to understand the spirit of one who, though in the world, was not of the world, and whose life was deeply hidden with Christ in God.—*Catholic Weekly.*

THE APOCALYPSE, THE ANTI-CHRIST, AND THE END.

By J. J. ELAR. 5s.

The whole book deserves study by those who reverence Holy Scripture.—*Tablet.*

A sober, thoughtful, ably-written treatise, which will, we feel sure, be prized by Biblical students.—*Catholic Times.*

THE RELIGION OF OUR FORE-FATHERS.

By the Rev. VINCENT HORNYOLD, S.J. 214 pages. In wrapper, 6d. (postage 2d.); cloth, 1s. 3d. (postage 3d.); or in Seven Parts at 2d. each (postage ½d.).

Part VIII., "The Church in England, Past and Present," and Part IX., "Catholic Orders and Anglican Orders," are published separately in pamphlet form only (post free 2½d. each), and are not contained in the volume.

FAITH AND FOLLY. By the Right Rev. Mgr. JOHN S. VAUGHAN. New and Revised Edition. 5s. net (postage 4d.).

JUST the very book for meeting the new combination of hostile attack upon revealed religion. We deliberately recommend it as the most *readable* book of the kind we have ever met.—*Catholic Times*.

THE HOLY CATHOLIC CHURCH: Her Faith, Works, Triumphs. By a CONVERT. 3s. 6d.

IT has been a pleasure to read this handy guide to the truth concerning the Kingdom of God on earth. The work shows clear signs of originality in its arrangement and of diligent inquiry after unhackneyed materials. Its aim is not to make a man a Christian, but to show him what Scripture and the Church mean by being one.—*Tablet*.

MANUAL OF SCRIPTURE HISTORY. By the Very Rev. Dr. RICHARDS. New and Improved Edition. 415 pp., with Maps, etc. 2s. 6d. net (postage 4d.).

BEING a complete analysis of the historical books of the Old Testament. Adopted as a text book in our colleges and training schools.

ST. JOHN BAPTIST DE ROSSI. Translated from the Italian by Lady HERBERT. With the renowned Introduction on Ecclesiastical Training and the Sacerdotal Life by Cardinal VAUGHAN. With a Portrait of the Saint. A New Edition. 8vo. 5s. net.

ST. CATHERINE DE' RICCI: Her Life, her Letters, her Community. By F. M. CAPES. Introduced by a Treatise on the Mystical Life by Father BERTRAND WILBERFORCE, O.P. With a Portrait of the Saint, a Facsimile Letter, and other Illustrations. 7s. 6d. net.

PERIODICALS.

THE DUBLIN REVIEW. Edited by Mr. WILFRID WARD. Published Quarterly. Single copy, 5s. 6d. net. Advanced Yearly Subscription, £1 1s., post free.

CHURCH MUSIC. Issued By-Monthly. With Musical Supplements in every copy. Annual Subscription, 6s. 6d. per annum, post free. Single numbers, 1s. 3d. net each.

THE NEW YORK REVIEW. A Journal of Ancient Faith and Modern Thought. Issued every two months. Terms, 12s. 6d. a year. Single Copies, 2s. 6d. net.

Messrs. BURNS & OATES *receive Subscriptions to any of the Reviews, Magazines, or Weekly Papers published in the United Kingdom or America. Subscriptions may commence at any time, but cannot be received for less than six months; or in the case of those published abroad, twelve months. A Selected List sent on request.*

CATHOLIC STANDARD LIBRARY.

PRICE 12s. EACH VOLUME.

EDMUND CAMPION. By RICHARD SIMPSON.

THE GREAT COMMENTARY ON THE GOSPELS. By CORNELIUS à LAPIDE. Eight Volumes.

COMMENTARY ON THE HOLY GOSPEL OF ST. MATTHEW. By JOHN MALDONATUS, S.J. Two Volumes.

EXPOSITION ON ST. PAUL'S EPISTLES. By BERNARDINE à PICONIO. Three Volumes.

THE HISTORY AND FATE OF SACRILEGE. By Sir HENRY SPELMAN, Kt.

EDWARD VI. AND THE BOOK OF COMMON PRAYER. Its Origin, illustrated by hitherto unpublished documents. With Facsimile pages of MS. by ABBOT GASQUET, D.D., O.S.B., and EDMUND BISHOP.

THE WORKS OF ST. BERNARD. Translated into English from the Edition of Dom Joannes Mabillon. Vols. I. and II. containing the Letters of St. Bernard; Vol. III., Sermons and Letters.

HISTORICAL PORTRAITS OF THE TUDOR DYNASTY AND THE REFORMATION PERIOD. By S. HUBERT BURKE. Four Volumes.

Bibles and Prayer Books.

HOLY BIBLE. *Octavo Edition* (9 by 6 inches). Cloth, red edges, 5s.; and in a great variety of leather bindings, at 8s., 10s., 15s., 18s., 30s., and 35s. each.

Pocket Edition (size $5\frac{1}{4}$ by $3\frac{1}{4}$ inches). Embossed cloth, red edges, 2s. 6d.; and in leather bindings at 4s. 6d., 6s. 6d., and 7s. 6d.

NEW TESTAMENT. *New Large Type Edition.* With annotations, references, and an historical and chronological index. Crown 8vo (size $7\frac{1}{2}$ by 5 inches). 500 pp. Cloth, 2s.; and in leather bindings at 4s. 6d. and 8s. 6d.

Pocket Edition. Limp cloth, 6d. net (postage 2d.). leather bindings, 1s., 1s. 6d., 3s. and 4s. 6d.

MANUAL OF PRAYERS FOR CONGREGATIONAL USE. With Epistles and Gospels. Pocket Edition, 6d. net, or with Enlarged Appendix, 1s. to 7s. 6d.

THE CHILD'S MASS BOOK. By Hon. Mrs. Kavanagh. Popular Edition. Cloth, 6d. Revised Edition, with Sixteen Coloured Illustrations. Cloth, gilt, 1s.; leather, 2s. 6d.

GARDEN OF THE SOUL. Five Editions. 6d. to 10s. 6d.

KEY OF HEAVEN. Three Editions. 6d. to 5s.

THE PATH TO HEAVEN. The Cheapest and Most Complete Book of Devotions for public or private use ever issued. Upwards of 1,000 pages (size, $5\frac{5}{8}$ by $3\frac{5}{8}$ inches). Cloth, 2s.; best cloth, red edges, 2s. 6d.; roan, grained, 3s.; smooth grain roan, gilt edges, 4s.; French Morocco, full gilt, with clasp, 4s. 6d.; Persian calf, 4s. 6d.; Rutland, limp, 6s.; calf or Morocco bindings, 7s. 6d.; German calf or Morocco, soft cushioned, 8s. 6d. each.

MANUAL OF CATHOLIC PIETY. Three Editions. 6d. to 5s.